# Community
## versus
# Commodity

SUNY Series, The New Inequalities

A. Gary Dworkin, Editor

# Community
# versus
# Commodity

## Tenants and the American City

## Stella M. Čapek
## John I. Gilderbloom

State University of New York Press

Published by
State University of New York Press, Albany

For information, address State University of New York
Press, State University Plaza, Albany, N.Y., 12246

Production by M. R. Mulholland
Marketing by Fran Keneston

**Library of Congress Cataloging-in-Publication Data**

Čapek, Stella M., 1953–
    Community versus commodity : tenants and the American city /
Stella M. Čapek, John I. Gilderbloom.
        p.    cm. — (SUNY series, the new inequalities)
    Includes bibliographical references and indexes.
    ISBN 0-7914-0841-8 (CH : alk. paper). — ISBN 0-7914-0842-6 (PB :
alk. paper)
        1. Rent control—United States. 2. Social movements—United
States. 3. Urban policy—United States. 4. Santa Monica (Calif.)
—Politics and government. 5. Houston (Tex.)—Politics and
government. I. Gilderbloom, John Ingram. II. Title. III. Series:
SUNY series in the new inequalities.
    HD7288.82.C36   1992
    307.3'3616'0973—dc20                                      90-24906
                                                                CIP

10   9   8   7   6   5   4   3   2   1

*For Hans and Max,*
*and for people everywhere who work to construct*
*humane, livable, and democratic environments.*

# Contents

# Abbreviations

| | |
|---|---|
| ACTION | A Committee to Insure Owners' Needs |
| APV | Allen Parkway Village |
| ASMC | All Santa Monica Coalition |
| CC | Citizens' Congress |
| CCSM | Community Corporation of Santa Monica |
| CDBG | Community Development Block Grant |
| CED | Campaign for Economic Democracy |
| CHAIN | California Housing Action and Information Network |
| CHOSM | Concerned Homeowners of Santa Monica |
| CIPA | Commercial and Industrial Properties Association |
| CPI | Consumer Price Index |
| HEDC | Houston Economic Development Council |
| HUD | U.S. Dept. of Housing & Urban Development |
| NJTO | New Jersey Tenants Organization |
| NSM | New Social Movement |
| NTU | National Tenants' Union |
| OPCO | Ocean Park Community Organization |
| OPEN | Ocean Park Electoral Network |
| PN | Planners Network |
| PNA | Pico Neighborhood Association |
| PSI | Public Service Initiatives |
| SCLF | Southern California Legal Foundation |
| SDC | Systems Development Corporation |
| SMCFR | Santa Monica Committee for Fair Rents |
| SMFHA | Santa Monica Fair Housing Alliance |
| SMI | Social Movement Industry |
| SMO | Social Movement Organization |
| SMRR | Santa Monicans for Renters' Rights |
| SMS | Social Movement Sector |
| TMO | The Metropolitan Organization |
| TOP | Tenant Organizing Project |

# Foreword

I doubt that any middle-sized American city in the past decade has received as much combined media and scholarly attention as my hometown of Santa Monica, California. Perhaps, this was a kind of "man bites dog" phenomenon: In the age of Reagan, at least one city appeared to buck the conservative political winds by electing a left/liberal, reform-minded government led by 1960s activists. Publications as ideologically divergent as the *Wall Street Journal* and the *Village Voice* sent correspondents to chronicle this political happening. The most widely watched news program in America, *60 Minutes,* aired a sequence on Santa Monica entitled, "Left City." Numerous foreign journalists and foreign visitors found a side trip to Santa Monica to be suddenly necessary. At least two college senior theses, one M.A. thesis, and one Ph.D. thesis were written on the Santa Monica experience during the 1980s. Urban scholars devoted chapters of books to Santa Monica, and a political scientist at the University of Southern California wrote an entire book on the city's new political movement.

Unfortunately, most of what has been written to date is colored by the ideological predilections of the various authors and publications or is simply badly flawed as serious social science research. This study by Stella M. Čapek and John I. Gilderbloom goes a long way toward remedying this situation. Their well-researched and thorough study is a model of a community political inquiry. They successfully describe and analyze the development of progressive politics in Santa Monica and objectively consider the effects of this political mobilization on the public policies of the city.

Increasingly in the United States, politics appears to many to be a game of ego and money played by upper-middle-class professionals and dominated by special interests who ultimately decide the shape and content of "the public interest." In most instances, this is not an inaccurate description. However, in Santa Monica and in a handful of other political jurisdictions in the 1980s, groups of political activists who had come of age in the extra-party movements of the 1960s and 1970s—the anitwar movement, the feminist movement, the consumer movement, the environmental movement, the civil rights movement, and the community organizing movement—moved into the electoral arena, most successfully at the local and state levels. The motivation underlying their efforts was a democratic impulse: the desire to increase the participation of "average" people in the formal political processes of the society—and there was also a vision of community life that guided their actions: of a society where everyone, not just the white upper class, could enjoy safe, friendly, well-planned, decent neighborhoods with good schools, affordable housing, well-kept parks, and lively shopping areas.

In looking critically yet objectively at such political efforts as that in Santa Monica, it is important to try to assess the extent that political actors have been successful at achieving these twin goals of citizen empowerment and community revitalization. Using the tools of social science and not riding a particular ideological or theoretical horse, Čapek and Gilderbloom have produced the most thorough and honest assessment of the Santa Monica political experience to date. It will be the standard by which any subsequent studies will be judged.

As someone who was actively involved in Santa Monica politics for much of the decade—I managed the winning campaign in 1981 that brought the progressive majority to power in city hall; I served as a member of the city planning commission from 1981 to 1986; and I was "first husband" from 1981 to 1983, when my wife, Ruth Goldway, served as the city's mayor (in addition, many of my students from the M.A. program at the UCLA Graduate School of Architecture and Urban Planning were hired as professionals to work for the city)—I am proud of what we accomplished in improving the daily lives of the citizens of the city, as well as ways in which our programs and policies served as models or inspirations for other urban governments across the United States.

Santa Monica is widely recognized as one of the most pleasant, interesting, and decent places to live in California—and in large part, our governmental policies helped to make it so. Because of rent regulation, laws against speculation, assistance for tenant ownership, and provision of moderate-cost housing by the city-sponsored Community Housing Corporation, housing is more affordable for low-and middle-income people and for seniors than it would otherwise have been. The Santa Monica oceanfront and its historic pier have been renovated and redesigned, and animated by free summer concerts, new shops, and recreational facilities. The downtown pedestrian mall on Third Street has become a lively center of day and nighttime theatergoing, shopping, dining, and walking. A designated visitor-serving hotel district provides the city with new revenue from the hotel bed tax and brings in customers for the city's shops and restaurants. City commissions promote the arts, develop new senior programs and social service centers, and study the status of women. City council meetings are broadcast on public radio and on the cable television access channel. Large-scale developers are required to include in their projects day-care centers or other amenities, or pay into the city's affordable housing fund. Design requirements for new buildings include mandatory street-level pedestrian-serving uses, such as shops or outdoor restaurants. The city-owned bus system provides safe and efficient transit for those without cars, especially seniors, young people, and minorities. A city-sponsored farmers' market on a closed-off downtown street every week allows citizens and downtown office workers the chance to buy fresh fruits and vegetables direct from producers—an almost pure free-market exchange.

These programs (and others as well) were the outcome of democratic political mobilization in the city, followed by the conscious development and implementation of a vision of urban life converted into law and policy. The point is a simple but too often forgotten one: In a democratic society, political action can make a difference in people's lives. In the case of Santa Monica, the difference is visible to the eye: You can see it in the form of the built environment and in the daily life of the city as people go to work, to school, to shop, and to play.

Of course, I am not arguing that Santa Monica is an urban utopia. Except for the most exclusive suburbs and resorts, few cities in the United States can escape the consequences of the decade of Reagan's neglect of urban policy and promotion of greed. In Santa Monica, thousands of homeless line up each week for their free meals distributed on the front lawn of city hall. Mentally ill people live in boxes and harass citizens as they go to the post office, video store, or gas station. At most supermarkets, out-of-work men offer to wash shoppers' car windows for small change. Minority students still lead the dropout list at the local high school, and the schools do not have enough money to educate well. These are consequences of the failure of national policy, not problems that can be solved by any urban political jurisdiction acting alone.

Those of us who spent almost ten years of our lives in local politics in Santa Monica are rightfully proud of what we achieved in a conservative era. We would like all citizens to live in a city such as Santa Monica, where the government genuinely cares about improving the quality of life, but we know that for this to happen will require progressive political change at the national level.

—Derek Shearer

# Acknowledgments

Both authors made equal contributions in the research, writing, and production of this book. The order of the authors' names was picked randomly. As this project has evolved through its various phases, there are many people and institutions to whom we owe special thanks. Although it is not possible to name all of them here, we would like to begin by thanking the following:

Research for this book has been continuously collected since 1975. Our book was greatly aided by the numerous research grants and consulting jobs awarded to us. Our earlier research efforts provided important background information that was useful in putting together the final draft of our book. The Foundation for National Progress—Housing Information Center, located in San Francisco and coordinated by John Gilderbloom, received grants from Shalan Foundation, the Seed Fund, the Sunflower Foundation, W. H. Ferry, Stanley Sheinbaum, Mary Ann Mott, Murray Gilderbloom, and Katherine Tremaine to conduct research on rent control and tenant organizations. Government consulting work also aided our research efforts, and we appreciate the consulting work of the California State Department of Housing and Community Development; the city of Orange, New Jersey; Seabrook, Texas; the City of Houston Department of Planning and Development; Harris County, Texas, Community Development; and the Houston Metropolitan Transportation Authority. Finally, we received important financial assistance from various universities around the country including: the University of Houston Department of Sociology, the University of Houston Center for Public Policy, the University of Houston Office of Sponsored Programs Research Initiation Grants, the University of California Department of Sociology, the University of Texas at Austin Department of Sociology, the University of Louisville Urban and Public Affairs Ph.D. program and School of Urban Policy, and the Hendrix College Travel Grants Committee. The Urban Research Institute at the University of Louisville provided office space for the final rewrite of this book.

Special thanks to the Social Science Research Council Committee for Public Policy Research on Contemporary Hispanic Issues, which provided John Gilderbloom and Nestor Rodriguez (1990) a generous grant to study rental housing conditions facing disadvantaged households nationally, with a special case study of Santa Monica and Houston. This research produced a specific monograph, "Hispanic Rental Housing Needs in the United States: Problems and Prospects," by John Gilderbloom and Nestor Rodriguez (1990), that provides a detailed discussion of the housing crisis facing minorities and proposes policy programs that can be enacted at the local, state, and national levels. Our thanks to Nestor Rodriguez for being supportive and cooperative in our reanalysis of the data set developed from the original research endeavor and for providing us the use of his computer and advice on word processing.

Ethnographic data for the case study on Santa Monica are selectively drawn from Stella Čapek's dissertation research ("Urban Progressive Movements: The Case of Santa Monica," University of Texas at Austin, 1985). Additional interviews and data gatherings were done by John Gilderbloom between 1978 and 1981 and 1988 and 1990. We have done our best to honor requests for anonymity by certain individuals who do not want to be publicly associated with a particular statement.

We would like to express deep appreciation to all who gave time for in-depth interviews in Santa Monica. Thanks to Derek Shearer, director of the Public Policy Program at Occidental College in Los Angeles, for his insights and documentation on the progressive movement, and to Pierre Clavel for sharing his files of news clippings on Santa Monica. Dale Eunson very generously shared her transcripts of interviews with Santa Monica activists, which gave us a richer understanding of the historical development of the progressive movement as well as its intersection with individual biographies. We deeply appreciate her spirit of sharing. Others who gave us access to their personal collections of movement clippings, documents, and memorabilia include Michael Tarbet, Denny Zane, Wayne Bauer, Dora Ashford, Irene Wolt, and Moe Stavnezer. Allan Heskin provided us with his original survey of tenants in Los Angeles and Santa Monica. Nancy Desser provided telephones and five large boxes of newspaper clippings (*Evening Outlook* and *Los Angeles Times*) on the Santa Monica tenants' movement as well as rent control campaign literature used by both tenants and landlords in Santa Monica. A thousand thanks for their generosity. One drawback to using these files was the occasional inability—after an exhaustive effort—to get a complete reference (i.e. page number or precise date); on the other hand, these materials were of such historical importance that we chose to include them.

We wish to thank also those who provided housing, transportation, and support for this project in Santa Monica and elsewhere: Tom Donovan, John and Edith Shure, Patricia Hoffman and Gene Oppenheim, Julia Curry, Hans Baer, Richard Habib, Marta Lopez, Victor Becerra, Susan Walton, Derek Shearer, and Nancy Desser.

Portions of this book were given various public readings, and we benefited greatly from these suggestions, criticisms, and direction. Students from John Gilderbloom's graduate seminar in Urban Sociology (Fall 1987) at the University of Houston had to "endure" the first draft of this book. We especially appreciated the criticisms made by Kathy Murphy, Ellen Slaten,

Tina Mougouris, Robert McKenzie, and Scott Lyskawa. In addition, students in Gilderbloom's graduate seminar in the Sociology of Urban Planning and Design (Spring 1988) at the University of Houston read a second draft and gave us valuable suggestions for making this book stronger and more readable. Another version was read by students in Gilderbloom's graduate class in Urban Social Structure (Fall 1988 and Spring 1990) at the University of Louisville. A revised version of Chapter 4 was originally presented at the International Conference on Urban Minorities in France, Great Britain, United States, and West Germany in Nancy, France, in June 1988. Chapter 5 was presented at the Association of Collegiate Schools of Planning in Austin, Texas on November 2, 1990. We appreciate the comments and support of Robert Fisher and Sophie Body Genderot. Portions of Chapter 6 were read at the annual meeting of the American Society of Public Administrators on April 11, 1990, in Los Angeles. We also received valuable criticisms from the referees who examined the original book prospectus in 1986: Ralph Turner, Richard Flacks, and Peter Dreier. Additional assistance was given by a number of referees from SUNY who examined a completed draft in 1988. Janet Chafetz and Joe Feagin gave us valuable feedback on our theoretical orientation. These suggestions pushed us to make significant revisions on the book.

Editing and computer assistance were provided by numerous individuals. Hank Savitch, Chester Hartman, Pat Bailey, Tina Mougouris, Ellen Slaten, Carrie Donald, Patricia Gilderbloom, Jackie Hagen, and Susan Erwin gave us valuable editorial suggestions. We especially appreciated Bert Useem's willingness to read and critique several versions of Chapters 1 and 7. Special thanks to Daniel Sanders and Dave Collins for their careful editing of the notes and references. David Romero and Jin Jin He helped conduct the computer data analysis on the mainframe computer at the University of Houston. Jon Lorence was a helpful troubleshooter.

We wish also to thank Lois Patton, editor in chief at SUNY Press, for her encouragement and patience with a project that took us longer than we anticipated. The extra time permitted us to refine our analysis and to get additional input from colleagues and students. Gary Dworkin helped us get the book contract with SUNY. We would like to thank Megeen R. Mulholland and Fran Keneston at SUNY who were helpful in the completion of the book. We would also like to thank Diane Bonner, who was the copy editor, and Karen Shapiro who was the cover designer.

We are also busy producing a companion videocassette of *Community versus Commodity* that will include lectures by urban progressives and activists. Please write to John Gilderbloom, School of Urban Policy, University of Louisville, Louisville, Kentucky 40292, for further details.

We realize that the reality of any social movement is complex and that its "story" is often contested. Sociological fieldwork on Santa Monica has sensitized us, we hope, to the range of perspectives held about the tenants' movement and has made us aware of the many groups that had a part in it. We are aware that we have been able to present only a part of the much larger story and to thank only a fraction of the people who made this book possible. On the other hand, by preserving parts of the story, such as the role of senior citizens and various generations in the progressive movement, and by correcting research biases that we feel have appeared in some past analyses of Santa Monica, we hope that our contribution is unique and reflective of the complexity of urban social movements.

Finally, thanks to Joe Feagin and Richard Appelbaum (our respective mentors) for encouraging us to write *Community versus Commodity*. We hope it will match their high standards of scholarship and contribute to the revitalization of urban sociology in the United States. Any mistakes or omissions are the sole responsibility of the authors.

*—Stella M. Čapek*
*John I. Gilderbloom*

I

# Tenants
# and Urban Social
# Movement Theory

1

# Introduction and Overview

Tenants as social actors and protest movements based on housing constitute a largely unwritten chapter in the study of urban social movements in the United States. This is true despite a growing body of literature on social movements and recent efforts to analyze and to document the importance of housing struggles in the nation's history (Heskin, 1983; Lawson, 1986; Dreier, 1982, 1984). Historically, significant organizing has taken place around issues of tenants' rights. Tenants have mobilized defensively during the depression and during times of wartime scarcity, and with increasing sophistication and consciousness on broader social policy issues in recent decades, they have constructed organizations to further their aims (Lawson, 1986). The most recent wave of activism has come in response to a nationwide rental housing crisis during the 1970s and 1980s, when tenants formed hundreds of locally based tenants' unions, as well as statewide organizations (Atlas and Dreier, 1980a, 1980b; Dreier, Gilderbloom, and Appelbaum, 1980).

Despite a broad repertoire of collective action, rent control was frequently the outcome of these actions. As a direct result of tenant organizing, roughly two hundred cities and counties in the United States currently have some form of rent regulation. Most of these cities enacted controls in the early 1970s, including over one hundred municipalities in New Jersey as well as cities and counties in Massachusetts, New York, Virginia, Maryland, Alaska, Connecticut, and California. Over half of all rental units in California, New York, Massachusetts, and New Jersey are presently rent-controlled. Altogether it is estimated that approximately 10 percent of the nation's rental housing stock falls under some type of rent control (Baar, 1983).

Although controversial, the nationwide presence of rent control in a society resistant to the regulation of private property signals the possibility of a broad social movement where, to borrow the words of Joseph Gusfield, "something new is happening in a wide variety of places and arenas" (Gusfield, 1981:322; also Marwell and Oliver, 1984).[1] In view of this, it is surprising that little empirical research has been methodically conducted into the behavior of tenants, and their role as a social group remains to be conceptualized. A small number of theorists have devoted serious scholarship to the subject of tenants and tenants' movements (Atlas and Dreier, 1980b; Castells, 1983; Dreier, 1982, 1984; Gilderbloom, 1981b, 1988; Gilderbloom and Appelbaum, 1988; Heskin, 1983; Lawson 1983, 1986; Lipsky, 1970; Rosentraub and Warren, 1986), but sociological research remains scanty. This permits economists, for example, to offer a simple supply and demand theory (Johnson, 1982) to explain tenants' movements.

The thinness of the research agenda on the subject of tenants is a problem characteristic of scholarship in the United States (Dreier, 1982). By contrast, European theorists have made housing a central concern of inquiry in urban/social movements sociology (Saunders, 1981:232). Led by neo-Weberians such as Rex and Moore (1967) and Pahl (1975) and by neo-Marxists Castells (1983) and Harloe (1977), housing analysis tends to be dominated by sociologists (Gilderbloom and Appelbaum, 1988). According to Pahl (1975:206), housing and other related urban problems "are too big to leave to traffic engineers, economists and what have you." On the other hand, a review of sociological journals in the United States reveals that housing is rarely a major concern. Where it is discussed, tenants receive a disproportionately small share of attention (Foley, 1980).

The research gap in U.S. sociology has not gone unnoticed. As president of the American Sociological Association in 1947, Louis Wirth (1947:142) declared that housing policy was an important area of sociological inquiry:

As sociologists we have the skills and the insights, the systematic framework and the background by virtue of our scientific training to view the problem in the perspective of a systematic science.

Wirth was joined by Robert Merton (1948) in designating the institution of housing as sociologically significant not only as a site for observing social change but as a field in which solutions to social problems could be sought. Merton (1948:166) believed that sociologists could play a special role in analyzing this area of social experience traditionally resistant—due to emotional feelings and vested interests surrounding private property—to scientific analysis. Merton also recognized that this could be a professionally "hazardous reconnaissance in a sociological no-man's land," where one would be subjected to cross fire from those vested interests (Goering and Modibo, 1988).[2]

For these and other reasons, sociologists in the United States have been slow to take up the challenge and have in particular slighted rental housing and tenants as a social group. As late as 1982, Peter Dreier lamented the fact that since the founding of American sociology tenants have been ignored. According to Dreier (1982:179), sociology in the United States has treated tenants as virtually nonexistent, with little known about them as agents of social change:

> ...in many ways tenants and homeowners are socially distinct categories. It is surprising, therefore, that within sociology tenants are almost invisible as a group. Indeed this neglect has a long history...[and] is reflected in the leading textbooks in urban sociology and urban politics.

Dreier argues for more sociological research on this subject. Similar suggestions have come from Duncan (1981:251), who maintains that, given the existing state of our knowledge, "Our understanding of the effects of housing reform on social relations and political consciousness is left notably deficient." A review of the sociological literature reveals that tenants are relatively unexamined social actors, with very little known about the views that they have of themselves or about the kind of social impact that they can have on others and on the society as a whole.[3]

Tenants are unexamined not only as social actors but also as *urban* social actors. A salient feature of tenants' movements is their urban character (Castells, 1983). While living conditions in rural areas have frequently been miserable, historically the public perception of housing as a social problem has emerged in urban areas. Urban theorist Peter Saunders (1979:17) places housing struggles at the heart of the study of urban social change:

> Housing is the most significant element of consumption in the urban system. Most of the struggles which occur outside the factory gate are related directly to questions of housing...such conflicts often occur between political groups expressing tenure divisions (tenants' associations, residents' associations and so on). The problem of how to analyze the political significance of tenure divisions is thus fundamental.

The significance of housing movements for the study of social change suggests yet another point: Tenants must be understood as urban social actors *linked to particular conceptions of space.* The importance of the dimension of space or territoriality for tenants' movements is striking since they lay their claims according to a reinterpretation of spatial justice. The movements are played out in the boundaries of community, neighborhood, and an urban culture that includes the built environment. This is not true of all social movements, although the rising visibility of community-based as opposed to class-based movements has been noted in the urban literature (Fisher and Kling, 1989). While tenants' movements may draw on the same culture and share "nuts-and-bolts" strategies with other movements, the spatial dimension remains crucial to their analysis (Castells, 1983; Marwell and Oliver, 1984; Harvey,

1985; Gottdiener, 1985).[4] The project of bringing tenants and tenants' movements into the mainstream of sociological analysis suggests to us, then, the need to seek an intersection between urban sociology—including the important analyses of the social control of space—and the collective behavior/social movements tradition.[5]

## Our Approach

### Rent Control as a Social Movement Goal

We have made the deliberate choice to focus our analysis on tenants' movements that have rent control as their outcome. We do this in part as a response to the actual prominence of rent control as an organizing strategy. Rent control is probably the most popular—if controversial—program advocated by tenant organizers in the United States (Atlas, 1982; Atlas and Dreier, 1980a, 1980b; Harvey, 1981; O'Connor, 1981; Lowe and Blumberg, 1981; Heskin, 1981a, 1981b, 1981c; Gilderbloom, 1981a, 1981b). Almost every tenants' group has rent control on its agenda. Its popularity rests on its provision of a concrete demand with immediate and tangible results. Of the many actions that tenants could take, rent control generates the greatest amount of tenant involvement. Frequently other actions do not create the support necessary for successful outcomes of protest activities. Rent strikes or squatting involves a high degree of personal risk—arrest, loss of possessions, legal costs, fines, and perhaps even imprisonment.[6] On the other hand, campaigns to lower interest rates or to increase housing subsidies are "too remote in their targets, too long term in their potential results, too indirect and diffuse in their impact and, at least in the United States today, too little" (Marcuse, 1981a:87). Rent control, therefore, is unique as a low-risk strategy with immediate impacts on rent. From the perspective of sociological research, the fact that millions of U.S. renters in various cities are covered by rent control provides us with an opportunity for measurement, comparison, and generalization.

We also focus on rent control for the sake of analytical clarity. As Gusfield (1981) and others have pointed out, social movements are highly complex creations due to the "nested" and intertwined nature of their elements. They operate at a number of different levels, and not all participants share the same goals and motivations (Melucci, 1981; Kriesi, 1988). We purposely focus on the involvement of tenants in rent-control struggles as a subset of broader issues relating to housing and to the practice of democracy in a culture imbued with the values of private property for profit. At the same time, the "collective campaign" for rent control as a unit of analysis permits us to specify, observe, and evaluate a particular social change goal (Marwell and Oliver, 1984:12) while facilitating comparison between different communities.

Data and Methods

To fill the research gap on tenants as social actors, our book offers a case study of the tenants' movement in the 1980s, using a variety of research methods. To capture its many dimensions, we employ both quantitative and qualitative techniques. While merging these is a challenge, we have derived inspiration from the important work of Manuel Castells, who in *The City and the Grassroots* (1983) integrated the two approaches. Although many sociological methods textbooks argue for a range of methods, such integration is rarely achieved in practice (Babbie, 1988:99). By incorporating a variety of sources ranging from census data to interview and case study material, we seek to capture the movement's richness and complexity, examining not only direct actions but also their constructed cultural meaning. Our data are unique in providing a wide ranging empirical examination of the renters' movement in the United States.

Our empirical data base consists of cross-sectional ecological data, detailed interviews with tenants, and a qualitative case study of why and how one city with an active tenants' movement chose to enact rent control. Our national data set consists of 161 rent-controlled and non-rent-controlled cities in the United States. This allows us to examine the political, social, economic, and ecological characteristics of rent-controlled and non-rent-controlled cities. In addition, we are able to explore the role of structural strain, effects of previous social movements, and class character with respect to rent-controlled and noncontrolled cities.

An additional data set consists of interviews with tenants in a rent-controlled city (Santa Monica, California) and with tenants in a noncontrolled city (Houston, Texas). This data set is based on a detailed questionnaire focused on why renters support or oppose rent control. It includes such variables as political orientation, relative deprivation, class consciousness, willingness to act, perception of system blame or inefficacy, and landlord/tenant conflict. As "ideal types," or polar contrasts, of the regulated versus the "free enterprise" city (Feagin, 1988), Santa Monica and Houston serve as important illustrative examples for a study of social movements. While Santa Monica experienced one of the most significant urban social movements in the 1970s and 1980s, Houston has been devoid of any significant social movements since the 1950s. By examining data from a city with a tenants' social movement (Santa Monica) and a city without such a movement (Houston), we can probe the broader implications of such movements for urban policy.

We also include a detailed, qualitative case study of Santa Monica. Our case study is based on over one hundred open-ended interviews that we conducted with key actors including landlords, tenant leaders, grass-roots activists, elected officials, developers, and homeowners. It also includes participant observation and the use of primary and secondary materials. Moreover, although we are academics, our knowledge of the movement is not purely scholarly. Both of us strive to integrate the professional objectivity required by our disciplines with engaged social action. One of us (Gilderbloom) was involved in the Santa Monica tenants' movement from its inception by providing information about rent control to grass-roots activists, by supporting progressive politics and working on campaigns, and by serving as an expert witness on the subject of rent control. The other (Čapek) entered the scene later (1984 and 1985) and conducted field research in Santa Monica regarding the tenants' movement.[7] Together we had access, not only to the "frontstage" presentation of the movement, but also to backstage areas—private letters, memos, confidential documents and group discussions of goals and tactics. Our presentation is strengthened by interviews with the movement's opposition.[8] Since rent control is a politically controversial subject on the right and on the left (Angotti, 1977; Devine, 1986), we perceive our work as a contribution to a balanced analysis of the subject.

Significance of the Santa Monica Case Study

Santa Monica, California, is an oceanfront city of approximately ninety thousand residents and is adjacent to Los Angeles. Tenant organizing efforts there in the late 1970s and early 1980s led to the passage of one of the strictest rent-control laws in the nation and propelled a majority of politically progressive candidates into public office. Throughout our book, we make use of Pierre Clavel's (1982) definition of "progressive" as representing a commitment to the redistribution of wealth and power and participation in a nonelite direction. Because of its challenge to unregulated "free market" policies and the growth ethic, Santa Monica has attracted a good deal of analytical attention (Bellah et al., 1985; Boggs, 1983, 1986; Čapek, 1985; Cockburn and Ridgeway, 1981; Clavel, 1986; Daykin, 1987; Feagin and Parker, 1990; Fulton, 1985; Heskin, 1983, 1984; Kann, 1983, 1986; Kasindorf, 1982; Kuttner, 1982; Mankin, 1981; Moberg, 1983a, 1983b; Shearer 1982a, 1982b, 1982c, 1984a, 1984b, 1984c; Walton, 1984a; Zeitlin, 1981). From a social movements perspective, Santa Monica is noteworthy because its progressive urban program was the outcome of diligent social organizing at the community level when skyrocketing rents threatened the city's affordable housing supply, particularly for elderly and low-income tenants. It gives us the opportunity to explore the genesis and development of a social movement, including the role of resources, leadership, technology, and ideology in the framing of public issues. In electing a progressive majority to a city council that was committed to the democratization of urban decision-making, redistributive economic policies, a "human-scale" environment, and local control of resources, Santa Monica quickly became a national symbol of the heated debate over the place of regulation in the United States. Taking up the cause of those most vulnerable to displacement, the progressive movement also helped to construct a new social definition of "fairness" by asking that tenants be considered as legitimate members of the community and that private property rights be treated from the perspective of "community" rather than "commodity." We consider this issue significant enough to take from it the title of our book. For many progressive activists, rent control was but a small part of a more far-reaching commitment to the "empowerment" of nonelite groups in the community and in a broader capitalist culture.

While this case provides intrinsically interesting data for the study of urban social movements, we have an additional reason for highlighting it in our book. Although we respect his general analyses of left politics and practice in the United States, we were dismayed by Mark Kann's work, *Middle Class Radicalism in Santa Monica* (1986), which inaccurately portrays the causes and consequences of the tenants' movement. From reading Kann's account, one comes away with the impression that what occurred in Santa Monica was orchestrated by Perrier-drinking yuppies whose goals were not genuinely progressive. We hope to show that this is a gross distortion of what actually occurred. With his emphasis on "middle class radicalism," Kann glosses over important historical details, including the role of senior citizens and nonaffluent tenant activists. By contrast, we feel that Santa Monica represents a progressive ideal for other U.S. cities to examine, a place that successfully tries to address many of the urban ills found elsewhere. Actively trying to combat rather than accommodate such problems as pollution, homelessness, traffic congestion, sprawling development, housing shortages, and nonaccessible public space, Santa Monica has generated innovative urban programs.

Previous evaluations of Santa Monica's progressive government have often failed to document these accomplishments. Santa Monica's strong rent control, for example, might result in tenant savings of over $1.1 billion between 1987 and 1997 and the creation of 6,000 affordable units—a substantial income redistribution between landlords and tenants. Without controls, average rents could climb as high as $1,123 a month, but with strong regulation, rents will be almost half that much in 1997. Development agreements with builders of office parks have resulted in "give backs" to the community such as the creation of roughly 500 affordable housing units, public parks, day-care centers, homeless shelters, a tough affirmative action commitment, and close to $250,000 donated for a citywide arts program. There has been significant city funding of progressive neighborhood activist organizations and urban planning that attempts to emulate the "human-scale," mixed-use vision of such urbanologists as Jane Jacobs (1961) and Lewis Mumford (1961). Finally, progressives have made Santa Monica the most accessible city in the country for the disabled. Every street has a sidewalk with curb cuts, and all buses have lifts. Compared to other cities, Santa Monica is extraordinary in its attempts to significantly improve and empower the lives of its renters, elderly, disabled, and homeless persons.

While most social scientists have documented that U.S. cities are governed by a "growth machine," Santa Monica is one of the few to be governed by a "rainbow coalition" of tenants, seniors, disabled, gays, minorities, and environmentalists opposed to an unlimited growth ethic (Logan and Molotch, 1987). Santa Monica thus provides an example of the possibilities as well as the limitations of what one city can do to meet the needs of the disadvantaged in a capitalist culture that often makes such people invisible. It also illustrates the political and economic gains that tenants can win by organizing themselves as a collective force.

## Houston: The Antithesis of Regulation

If Santa Monica represents the "ideal type" of progressive government, then, for comparative purposes, Houston provides the antithesis of this model: the free enterprise city. Houston is the largest U.S. city that is without zoning, a comprehensive master plan, or effective neighborhood organizations. The lack of planning and neighborhood organizations has resulted in Houston having a cheap and tawdry aesthetic, a severe housing and hunger problem, rampant crime, traffic gridlock, poor parks, and public space that is largely inaccessible to the disabled. Houston's downtown of monumental glass-and-steel buildings reaching as high as 70 stories is cold and largely absent of people on the sidewalks; the downtown is a textbook example of William H. Whyte's (1988) critique of new American cities failing to provide "human spaces" for people to interact with each other. Instead, the towering buildings make people feel small, helpless, and unimportant. Many of the poor live in neighborhoods that are comparable to the "shanty towns" of Central American barrios: no paved roads, sewage, or water. Overcrowded, rat-infested housing is not uncommon. For disabled persons, the city has become an invisible jail where 70 percent of the streets are without sidewalks with curb cuts. In addition, buses are without wheelchair lifts, and many buildings are not accessible. Over half of Houston's renters are currently paying unaffordable rents according to government standards. Houston is a city ruled by wealthy elites and ignores the essential needs of poor, minority, and disabled persons.

Why are these cities so different? Although a variety of factors contributes to the distinctiveness of Houston and Santa Monica, part of the explanation rests in political culture. Specifically, we will examine the role and location of a "sixties" protest culture in facilitating or suppressing political change in cities across the United States. Whalen and Flacks (1989:291) have noted that the "extent and impact of left activism in American communities in the aftermath of the sixties remains to be systematically documented." Furthermore, they claim that:

> It seems safe to conclude that the activism crystallized in the sixties New Left has been carried forward two decades. . . . In literally hundreds of American towns and neighborhoods and work settings, such continuing activism has fostered increased grass roots participation, more equitable policies and practices, and more protection for individual rights and community interests against the depredations of economic and political power (1989:258).

Although Whalen and Flacks argue that sixties activism was a generational phenomenon that rippled across America regardless of location, we will argue that it was most broadly felt along the Washington, D.C., to Boston corridor and in California, where demonstrations against the war in Vietnam were most intense. It is in these areas that most rent-control laws have been passed. Sixties culture was both place specific and generational in terms of its overall impact and its ability to provide ongoing social movement resources.

Goals for Our Project

Although propositions about the tenants' revolt in the United States have not been investigated empirically with reliable research and statistical procedures, social movement theories provide certain plausible explanations for the rise of the tenants' movement. Like other social movements, tenants' movements face the problem of mobilizing and creating resources among a relatively powerless population, activating supporting "publics," solving organizational and motivation problems, warding off "countermovement" initiatives, and articulating goals that are both viable in practice and draw on sanctioned cultural traditions for legitimation.

In the first part of our book, we will systematically review and investigate the explanatory power of social movements theory as it addresses questions of organizational tactics (Zald and McCarthy, 1973, 1977) as well as ideology and personal transformation (Turner, 1983; Klandermans, 1984; Zurcher and Snow, 1981; Melucci, 1985; Snow et al., 1986). We will also draw on urban theory as it bears on tenants' movements (Castells, 1983; Gottdiener, 1985). Since the existing sociological literature often deals only marginally or selectively with tenants' movements per se, and since little dialogue exists between the different explanatory traditions—such as the ecological, neo-Marxist, and neo-Weberian schools of urban sociology—one of our major goals will be to bridge these traditions and to arrive at useful formulations that permit empirical testing and contribute to both urban and social movements theory. We also hope to show that objective scholarship of a high standard can be combined with a commitment to progressive values.

To follow through the life cycle of the movement and to probe the social change question further, we will also examine the consequences of the tenants' movement in the second part of our book. An analysis of one of the more immediate goals of rent control as a social movement to redistribute wealth from landlord to tenant demonstrates the types of gains that renters can achieve through collective action as well as certain structural limitations to urban reform movements that challenge private property relations. The Santa Monica case permits us to explore the extent to which housing issues can act as a springboard toward other social change goals. By using our data on Houston, we also provide a contrasting case where social movements have been virtually invisible and have not had a significant impact on urban policy.

Finally, we are interested in broader repercussions of the movement that affect the terms of cultural debates over the meaning of private property and its relation to the practice of democracy (Gusfield, 1981). Has the tenants' movement been part of a "cultural drift" toward a gradual redefinition of human rights, as people reflect on the fact of its occurrence (Blumer, 1939:256)? Have leaders or rank-and-file participants made their way into other organizations, to surface in a related cause (Evans, 1979; Chafetz and Dworkin, 1986; Rollins, 1986)? Have they helped symbolically to stock the public memory (Castells, 1983:72) or to nurture "submerged networks" that create future possibilities for social change action (Melucci, 1985:800; Kriesi, 1988)? Historically, tenants have been disorganized and have been a relatively ineffective force in affecting the general conditions under which they live (Heskin, 1981a, 1981b; Marcuse, 1981a; Dreier and Atlas, 1980). What happens when tenants become organized?

The order of our chapters is as follows. In Chapter 2, we provide an overview of social movements theories relating to urban tenants' movements. We extract relevant theoretical suggestions that we can empirically test in the following chapters using the qualitative data of our case study and quantitative data on Santa Monica and Houston. In Chapters 3 and 4, we provide a detailed case study of the progressive tenants' movement in Santa Monica throughout its mobilization phase, drawing on the theories presented in Chapter 2 and evaluating their relevance. We follow this with the contrasting scenarios of accomplishments of an urban progressive movement in Santa Monica (Chapter 5) and the consequences of the lack of such a movement in Houston (Chapter 6). Finally, we conclude with an overview (Chapter 7) that examines the relevance of our findings for urban social movements theory and suggests some progressive directions for the future.

In a time of pessimism, this book offers hope for progressive social change in the capitalist city. Urban sociologists have painted the typical American city as simply a profitable commodity run by and for elites. Consequently, the interests of community are generally seen as losing out to "downtown" elites. Cities do not necessarily have to be turned into commodities; the forces of community can win. A "rainbow coalition" can remake the city to serve the interests of environmentalists, disabled, elderly, poor, gay, and others.[9] The success of such a coalition depends on the political savvy of the leadership in terms of framing issues, choosing spokespersons, undertaking research, building coalitions, utilizing computer technology, and accessing resources. In remaking the city, this new coalition is united by a consensus that the city should meet the needs of everyone, not just the few.

We hope this book will inspire individuals to organize additional grass-roots coalitions throughout the country and to create a public agenda for progressive democratic reform of cities. As we move toward the year 2000, more and more cities will move away from the free enterprise approach and embrace the progressive managerialist form of running a municipality. While Santa Monica is far from perfect and has been attacked from both left and right political perspectives, it could provide a model of progressive municipal reform and "new urban populism" that sparks the necessary vision for cities to seize upon across the nation. According to Derek Shearer (1989:293):

> The new urban populism is based on a vision of the city as a place where people should be given priority over buildings, cars and businesses—and a place where citizens have basic rights as residents of the city whether or not they own property.

With environmental and slow-growth movements gaining ground nationwide, Santa Monica represents the future and Houston the past in terms of governing cities. Community or commodity? This question raised by the tenants' movement has common grounds with other movements for social change and poses a powerful challenge to existing definitions of the "good city" and social relations in a capitalist culture.

# 2

# Tenants and Social Theory

## The Social Experience of Tenants

All theories of social movements take up the question of broad social practices and conditions that facilitate or hinder the emergence of collective behavior. To understand tenants as social actors, our first task is to identify their position in relation to political, economic, and cultural institutions. As Peter Dreier (1982) has noted—and as each housing census of the United States reaffirms—there are systematic and sociologically significant differences between the lives of tenants and other groups in the society. Despite a range of income and life-style characteristics, in the United States renters are disproportionately likely to be of low-income, minority, elderly, and nonunion status, as well as members of households headed by single women (Dreier, 1982). Their housing is typically older and in poorer condition than that of homeowners, although tenants pay a greater proportion of their income for such housing.

The rental housing crisis is one of the most serious domestic problems facing the nation. A recent national poll indicated that next to AIDS housing is the second most important problem facing the United States (Gilderbloom and Appelbaum, 1988). The proportion of tenants' income going into rent has steadily risen in recent years, so that today half of the nation's renters make housing payments that are considered unaffordable by conventional government standards (Gilderbloom and Appelbaum, 1988). From 1973 to 1983, the percentage of income going into rent increased from one fourth to almost one third for the average U.S. renter. Today, one fifth of all renters pay at least one half of their income into rent. Black, Hispanic, disabled, and female-headed households face even greater problems in terms of paying rent (Gilderbloom and Rodriguez, 1990). High rents contribute to overcrowding, disruption of social networks, family stress, and even social unrest. One key indicator of the extent of the current housing crisis is homelessness, whose victims number around one million (Gilderbloom and Appelbaum, 1988). And these conditions are expected to get worse in the 1990s.

The structural position of tenants in terms of income and demographic characteristics is thus significantly different from homeowners. The National Opinion Research Center 1985 survey of U.S. citizens allows us to break down respondents by tenant and homeowner status. The differences between these two groups can be dramatic (Table 2-1). In terms of income, tenants are disproportionately poor compared to homeowners. Almost two fifths of the nation's tenants can be classified as poor. In addition, tenants tend to be younger, have lower occupational prestige, live in multifamily structures, are unmarried, and live in integrated neighborhoods.

In *Tenants and the American Dream* (1983), Allan Heskin argues that the status of a tenant in the United States is that of a second-class citizen. There are many dimensions to this status. At the broadest level, the position of tenants is vitally influenced by a cultural value system that glorifies property ownership as a symbol of accomplishment, especially the "American dream" of owning a house (Adams, 1984; Halle, 1984). Moreover, the concept of homeownership is underlined by its crucial linkage to other patterns of consumption, such as those relating to automobiles and durable goods (Jackson, 1985). Despite the difficulties of achieving homeownership, the tenant population in the United States is considerably smaller than it is in many other countries; thus, tenants are "the unpropertied in a society where property is central" (Heskin, 1983:xi). The intense identification with private property ownership as a measure of character and as a component of freedom has been characterized as a "civil religion" (Bellah, cited in Dreier, 1982) in the United States, causing tenants to be perceived as "an out-group who are unsettled and unsettling" (Agnew, 1981:467). This is reflected in everyday cultural practices such as the unfavorable portrayal of tenants in the media and in literature (Dreier, 1982; Heskin, 1983). Seen as more tenuously attached to the central value system, their power in the society is measurably different from that of homeowners and landlords, and their self-image has tended to reflect this relationship.

Second-class citizenship is underscored by legal and governmental practices that take place on an everyday basis. The political economy within which tenants are situated is organized around a tax structure that vastly favors homeownership. In the United States, homeowners can deduct mortgage interest and local property taxes from what they owe in federal taxes, a privilege that increases with income. They pay no capital gains tax if their money is reinvested into a new home within two years. Landlords have traditionally possessed the additional benefit of depreciation write-offs as well as numerous other incentives for turning over property quickly and engaging in speculative purchases. Tenants bear the brunt of these "gifts" to other social groups, paying a larger percentage of their income for housing that is documentably worse than that of homeowners. As Barnes (1981:16) points out, their rent pays not only for "profit for banks, insurance companies, real estate agents," but also for a

## TABLE 2-1

The Impact of Housing Status on Political, Economic, Social, and Demographic Factors*

|  | Tenants | Homeowners |
|---|---|---|
| Income: | | |
| Low Income ($1,000 to $9,999) | 38% | 15% |
| Moderate Income ($10,000 to $24,999) | 41 | 31 |
| High Income ($25,000 to $99,000) | 22 | 55 |
| Political Party: | | |
| Democratic | 52 | 49 |
| Republican | 37 | 43 |
| Independent | 11 | 8 |
| Children: | | |
| None | 40 | 21 |
| 1 or more | 60 | 79 |
| Age: | | |
| 18 to 30 | 42 | 16 |
| 31 to 49 | 33 | 36 |
| 50 to 99 | 26 | 49 |
| Occupational Prestige: | | |
| Low | 28 | 17 |
| Medium | 64 | 68 |
| High | 9 | 15 |
| Housing Structure: | | |
| Single-Family Structure | 22 | 84 |
| Non-single-family structure | 78 | 16 |
| Presidential Choice: | | |
| Reagan | 57 | 64 |
| Mondale | 43 | 36 |
| Education Completed: | | |
| Grades 1 to 12 | 59 | 61 |
| Grades 13 to 18 | 41 | 39 |
| Any Opposite Race in Neighborhood? | | |
| Yes | 66 | 41 |
| No | 34 | 59 |
| Race: | | |
| White | 81 | 91 |
| Nonwhite | 19 | 8 |
| Sex: | | |
| Male | 44 | 46 |
| Female | 56 | 54 |
| Marital: | | |
| Married | 37 | 68 |
| Nonmarried | 63 | 32 |

* Numbers may not add up to 100 due to rounding

Source for raw data: NORC 1985

parade of present and past landlords who have sold and engaged in refinancing. In 1990, the federal government provided homeowners with a $47 billion subsidy in the form of mortgage and tax write-offs as well as protection against capital gains taxes (Čapek and Gilderbloom, 1990).

The disproportionate financial burden carried by tenants has been matched by an inferior legal status in the United States, where laws have regularly favored the landlord's right to make profits over the tenant's right to decent shelter. Indeed, some analysts have seen feudal remnants in the relationship between landlord and tenant (Heskin, 1983). In the state of Arkansas, nonpayment of rent is still a criminal offense, while tenants are advised by the office of the attorney general that they have virtually no rights in the state (Čapek, 1989). Where tenant protections have been instituted, there has often been a considerable reluctance to enforce them (Lipsky, 1970), and tenants frequently play no active role in the process (Morrissy, 1987:8).

A recent analysis of tenants' associations in the United States reminds us that formal solutions to tenant-landlord problems have been local in nature, thus resulting in "fifty different environments" in which tenants' organizations must function (Rosentraub and Warren, 1986). This allocation of responsibility to state and local governments is a significant feature of the political economy of the United States and vitally influences the possibilities for the emergence of tenants' movements. On one hand, it tends to prevent a unified solution to renter problems and the emergence of a national movement. On the other, as in the case of Santa Monica, tenants' organizations that become strong locally may be able to "capture" their governments and to set important precedents for other localities through model legislation and organization (Clavel, 1986; Shearer, 1984b).

The social experience of tenants is further shaped by the fact that both formally and informally renters' living space is not treated in the same manner as is that of other groups. Numerous theorists have pointed out that the need for a home does not stop with the need for shelter (Fried, 1973; Cox, 1981; Castells, 1983). The need is also an expressive one (Saunders, 1984; Dreier, 1982), for a secure bounded space in which one is free to "be oneself" and to keep at a distance the capriciousness and intrusions of the outside world (Suttles, 1972). However, the right to such a space is unevenly distributed. If one accepts Lyman and Scott's (1967:238) definition of "home territories" as those "areas where the regular participants have a relative freedom of behavior and a sense of intimacy and control over the area," tenants' dwellings are not, because of the vulnerable and often transient status of tenants themsleves, home territories. The rent may go up, the building may be converted, repairs may no longer be made, or the tenant may be evicted. All of these possibilities are usually out of the control of tenants, with the result that, unlike the homeowner, the tenant's need for a dignified space does not materialize.[1]

Until recently, tenants in the United States have been unable to appeal to a basic set of shelter-related rights that are equated with human rights.[2] Instead, the law has counted the "risks" to be all on the side of landlords or investors, while those of tenants have been ignored. An apartment becomes less than a home even though it is paid for dearly and with far less state assistance than that given to the homeowner. The problem is compounded by the fact that real estate is popularly seen as a "cash cow" to be milked; while not all landlords are guilty of this, all too many enter the business without having considered their responsibility to tenants. When profit, rather than a two-way relationship of responsibility, governs landlords' thinking about rental property investments, a frequent outcome is "blaming the victim," or resenting the tenant for asking for repairs or maintenance. For this reason, tenants have historically feared to claim their rights to decent shelter, fearing eviction or retaliation.

It is of vast importance that it is not only housing space that tenants occupy in a fragile and tentative way. This relationship has traditionally extended to civic and political space. Historically, tenants have been outside the political process, especially in terms of participating in electoral politics. U.S. history is filled with such examples. When the first settlers came to America, those who did not own property were not permitted to vote or to seek elected office (Heskin, 1981b:95). Tenants did not have the right to vote in federal elections until 1860 (Martin, 1976). Even after tenants became eligible to cast a ballot, landlords in certain parts of the East were able to control large blocs of tenant votes (Flanigan and Zingale, 1979:12). Today, tenants are still barred from voting in certain property bond, tax, and special district elections (Heskin, 1981b, 1981c).

In a study done by the U.S. Census Bureau (1979), homeowners voted twice as often as renters. In the November 1978 election, only 46 percent of the eligible voters turned out. Of those who turned out, 59 percent of the homeowners voted, compared to only 28 percent of the renters. According to the U.S. Census study (1979:1), of all the variables related to voting (age, income, region, sex, and race), housing status "appeared to have the strongest relationship with voting." Interviews conducted by the Census Bureau (1979:84) found that the most prominent reason given by renters—39 percent of them—for why they did not vote was because they were "not interested, they did not care."

Although political citizenship no longer depends as directly as it once did on landownership, the inferior status of tenants persists through both formal and informal norms. Public areas technically open to all citizens are defined in practice by those who ordinarily use them (Lyman and Scott, 1967). In the United States, private property ownership has consistently been a ticket to political participation, and this relationship continues even after formal property requirements have been abolished. City councils have typically been dominated by owners and investors (Molotch, 1976; Logan and Molotch, 1987; Domhoff, 1978; Nader, 1973), while tenants have been viewed as transients and noncitizens in their own communities. Thus, through a mixture of their own views of themselves and definitions imposed upon them by others (Čapek, 1985), tenants have not traditionally seen public forums as their "home territories."

This is a microcosm of a more general problem attaching to the practice of democracy in the United States, where numerous citizens have the legal right to participate, but civic space is colonized for years by other groups to such an extent that nonparticipators take their second-class status for granted (Gaventa, 1980). In recent years, theorists Sara Evans and Harry Boyte (1982, 1986) have given attention to this problem, documenting how disadvantaged groups construct "free social spaces" in order to produce more direct democracy. The ambiguity between formal/legal and informal definitions of "civic space" in a democracy may spark a challenge by the excluded group, which may design ways to test this space (Lyman and Scott, 1967; Castells, 1983). As we will note below, tenants' movements are a prime example of such strategies.

To conclude, one can document a clear and specific set of characteristics and grievances attached to tenants as a social group. It is evident that they range far beyond economic inequalities and into what Judith Rollins (1985:6) has called "interpersonal rituals that somehow reinforced the desire for accepting the systematic inequality of entire categories of people." Any effort to explain housing movements must consider the interlocking dimensions of this experience, which is played out against a backdrop of human rights set within a private property culture. We return now to our original question: What causes tenants' movements, and how may we theoretically understand their emergence?

## Sociological Explanations of Tenants' Movements

Housing movements organized by tenants, like all social movements, invite systematic explanation. As Smelser (1963:1) notes in his classic work on collective behavior, social movements

> ...occur with regularity. They cluster in time; they cluster in certain cultural areas; they occur with greater frequency among certain social groupings....This skewing in time and in social space invites explanation: Why do collective episodes occur where they do, when they do, and in the ways they do?

In this section, we examine in sequence some of the major explanations for tenants' movements advanced by social theorists from a number of traditions. A body of literature has emerged that bears both directly and indirectly on tenants' movements. Although some of the explanations offered overlap or address tenants' movements only indirectly, for the purposes of exposition we will divide them into several major categories.

First, we will look at the power/conflict school, which is rooted in Marxist and Weberian paradigms and argues that housing status can play a significant role in the formation of class consciousness and political behavior. Next, we will address the conventional sociological theories of social movements that have developed out of the collective behavior tradition, giving special attention to the resource mobilization model (Gamson, 1975; McCarthy and Zald, 1973, 1977; Oberschall, 1973; Tilly, 1978). We will consider the critiques addressed toward this model by those working in social-psychological and symbolic interactionist frameworks (Ferree and Miller, 1985; Klandermans, 1984; Snow et al., 1980; Turner, 1983; Gusfield, 1981); in the European "new social movements" school (Klandermans, 1986; Kriesi, 1988; Melucci, 1980); and in a tradition of ideological "framing" (Turner, 1969; Snow et al., 1986). Finally, we will examine some recent perspectives on the social control of urban space, considering their implications for tenants' movements (Castells, 1983; Cox, 1981; Gottdiener, 1985). We will conclude by extracting some theoretically interesting suggestions relating to tenants' movements in the United States, which we will proceed to investigate empirically in subsequent chapters.

## Power and Conflict: Marxist and Weberian Views of Tenants

History has shown that social strains such as severe shortages in low-income housing can eventually lead to "violent confrontations between citizens and authorities, and even revolutions, when societies and their governments failed to provide adequate housing" (Rosentraub and Warren, 1986). This is persuasively demonstrated in Roger Friedland's (1982:162) comprehensive study of black urban riots during the 1960s, which left 100,000 arrested, 10,000 injured, and 300 dead. Conducting a regression analysis to discover determinants of aggregate riot severity in U.S. cities, Friedland found that—all else being equal—the amount of urban renewal and the lack of low-rent housing relative to demand were positively correlated with riot severity. He concluded that "local public policies played an important role in conditioning the city's level of black political violence."

In recent decades, strains on the housing market in the United States have been growing. Between 1949 and 1974, urban renewal demolished 500,000 low-income housing units; only 100,000 units were replaced, and most of these were for middle-income people rather than for the poor (Shipnuck, Keating, and Morgan, 1974). Even traditionally conservative observers anticipate "a major housing calamity," as one of the rental housing industry's most prominent spokesmen put it (Preston Butch, co-chair of the National Multi-Housing Council, as quoted in Betz, 1981). Moreover, this has been an international phenomenon. During the late 1970s and early 1980s in West Germany, Holland, Switzerland, and England, riots broke out over the lack of affordable and decent housing (Hall, 1981:15–16; Glen and Shearer, 1980).

One school of thought that has explicitly addressed tenant movements has been the Marxist tradition, beginning with theorist Friedrich Engels. Engels was one of the first social theorists to write about the movement for decent and affordable housing within a political economy perspective. Even though he wrote about housing struggles over one hundred years ago, his analysis is still lauded as insightful and important by contemporary theorists (Angotti, 1977). In *The Housing Question,* Engels (1955:19) called the housing crisis "one of the innumerable, smaller, secondary evils, which result from present day capitalist mode of production." While sympathetic to the plight of renters, he generally frowned on housing rights movements as a distraction from the "primary struggle" of the proletariat seizing power and transforming the state from a capitalist economy to a socialist system. Only under socialism, he argued, would the "housing problem" be resolved. Struggles demanding more affordable housing by *themselves* were seen as futile attempts to change historically prescribed circumstances under which people live.

Engels's opposition to the movement for workers seeking more affordable housing was both economic and political. He opposed programs that allowed tenants to purchase homes, even if these meant a substantial reduction in the amount of wages going into shelter (1955:18, 48). He argued that the net gain tenants received by owning their houses was negated by a corresponding reduction in wages, calling this the "iron laws of the doctrine of the national economy" (1955:48). Citing Germany, Engels (1955:14) wrote that its ability to produce goods with "extraordinary cheapness" was due to inexpensive worker-owned housing, which allowed capitalists to pay the workers "infamously low wages":

> The workers are compelled to accept any piece wages offered them, otherwise they would get nothing at all and they could not live from the production of their agriculture alone, and.... it is just this agriculture and landownership which chains them to the spot and prevents them from looking around for other employment. It is this circumstance more than any other which keeps the wages and the living conditions of the German workers also in other industrial fields below the level of the West European countries.

Engels opposed homeownership opportunities for tenants not only on economic grounds; he also criticized them as poor political strategy. Housing struggles, he argued, do not materially contribute to the building of class consciousness that would be necessary to challenge the capitalist system. In fact, movements for better housing could result in a more conservative work force. This is because the housing crisis hurt not only the proletariat but also the "petty bourgeoisie." As a result, when tenants organize for better housing, the class consciousness of workers becomes blurred; workers may organize *with* the petty bourgeoisie, rather than against it, viewing it as a class that shares a similar exploitation (Engels, 1955:70–80). Engels argued: How are workers to see themselves as a distinct class, if other classes—petty bourgeoisie—share the same socially defined problem? While some contemporary theorists see cross-class alliances as powerful challenges to entrenched elites, Engels considered them a mistaken strategy.

From the point of view of "class consciousness," housing struggles contained some other pitfalls. Engels (1955:48) argued that "The worker who owns a little house to the value of a thousand talers is, true enough, *no longer a proletarian....*" Homeownership makes it more difficult for workers to be organized to resist exploitation by capitalists since they are less mobile than their counterpart workers/tenants. Worker/tenants are more apt to resist exploitation by moving to a place with higher wages. Worker/homeowners, on the other hand, are forced to remain in the area with low wages because of debt payments owed. Property ownership could also have a conservatizing effect on the workers because they become a part of the system of capitalist private property relations with a stake in its continuance.[3] Engels (1955:96) concluded that worker/homeownership "is reactionary, and that the reintroduction of the individual ownership of his dwelling by each individual would be a step backward." The contradictory nature of the worker/homeowner meant that his class allegiance fell with neither the worker nor the capitalist class. Far from being confined to Engels's time, this argument, grounded in the Marxist tradition, has resurfaced as a bone of contention for modern-day tenant organizers and academic theorists.

Theorists working in the tradition of sociologist Max Weber have upheld the claim that homeowners are politically more conservative than are tenants (Saunders, 1978; Rex and Moore, 1967; Kingston et al., 1984; Kemeny, 1980). Weberian sociologists have proposed the concept of "housing classes" (Rex and Moore, 1967) to capture this dimension of social stratification. According to Weber (1947:181), classes are distinct groups of individuals who share similar life chances, possess approximately the same kinds of consumer goods, have relatively the same income-making potential, and are located within the context of commodity and labor markets. According to Saunders (1979:68), Weber's discussion of classes is rooted in the sphere of economic activity as opposed to the relations of production, as analyzed by Marx.[4] From this definition, Rex (1968:215) was able to divide the working class into seven distinct groups including—among others—small landlords, homeowners, and renters. Along the lines of Engels, the Weberians argue that as a result of housing classes political conflict within the working class is heightened and a common class consciousness becomes fragmented (Rex and Moore, 1967; Saunders, 1979; Kingston et al., 1984). The implications for organizational unity and a shared class consciousness among tenants are thus the same as those outlined by Engels, suggesting pessimism about the effectiveness or viability of tenants' movements for social change.

A final important point regarding tenants' movements concerns the role of the state in capitalist societies. Engels argued the futility of appealing to the state for improved housing conditions. Engels (1955:67–80) claimed that, since the government is dominated by capitalists, it is foolish to believe that it would ever take action opposed to the interests of capital:

> It is perfectly clear that the state as it exists today is neither able nor willing to do anything to remedy the housing calamity. The state is nothing but the organized collective power of the *possessing classes, the landowners and the capitalists,* as against the exploited classes, the peasants and the workers (our emphasis).

This view by Engels, that the state works primarily in the interest of capitalists, has been elaborated and critiqued in recent works of political sociology (Domhoff, 1978; Esping-Andersen, Friedland, and Wright, 1976; O'Connor, 1973; Offe, 1985; Poulantzas, 1968). Domhoff (1978) has shown that, both on the local and national levels, interests connected to capital generally dominate the operation of government institutions. James O'Connor (1973) has argued that the state operates not only to maintain existing economic relations under capitalism, but also involves itself directly in the accumulation process. Through an "accumulation" function, the state maintains and creates conditions profitable to capitalist activity, while through a "legitimation" function it acts to squelch disharmony among the working class by providing a better standard of living for them. Esping-Andersen, Friedland, and Wright (1976) argue that the parameters of the state are not static, but are in a process of continual change resulting from class struggle. The state will give concessions to the working class in relation to its political cohesiveness. Under capitalism, the working-class standard of living can be affected by a particular political party in power (Stephens, 1986; Carnoy and Shearer, 1980). In making concessions to the working class, it is sometimes necessary to sacrifice the short-term interests of a particular faction of capital for the long-term interests of capital as a whole. The state therefore becomes an object of class struggle, rather than simply a tool of capital, and thus social policy is the outcome of the clash between capital and labor (O'Connor, 1981).

A theoretical literature exists regarding the more specific problem of state intervention in landlord-tenant relations. Harvey (1975) argues that the state cannot afford to have a policy that causes a sharp decline in the construction, maintenance, or tax base of its rental property. The foremost concern of municipalities is to maintain and enhance the value of property so that an adequate tax base can be maintained to support government functions and services. Harvey (1975) asserts that cities must maintain the value of the already existing built environment. If policies are adopted that undermine the growth and value of the built environment, then the viability of the financial superstructure as well as the state could be undercut. Various researchers have documented that the state has traditionally operated to accommodate the needs of the real estate industry by funneling billions of dollars into subsidized rehabilitation programs, affordable mortgage programs, attractive capital gains structures, and generous accelerated depreciation allowances in order to encourage more housing construction and rehabilitation (Sawers and Wachtel, 1975:502-3; Starr and Esping-Andersen, 1979:15; Feagin, 1983). As a result, most government housing programs are designed to benefit the interests of bankers, builders and landlords (Sawers and Wachtel, 1975). According to Starr and Esping-Andersen (1979:15):

The role of government has been to repair or boost the workings of the private market not to challenge it. The government's underlying assumption as to why a housing crisis exists is because of supply and demand factors. The solution as seen by the state is to create a profitable investment climate so that supply will be increased.

Endemic to all capitalist cities, according to Marxist theorists, are slums, shortages of affordable housing, crime, unequal access, and a host of other significant problems. While Weberians would not deny that these problems exist in most cities, they would acknowledge that some metropolitan places have successfully combated such problems. Housing is a case in point. The degree of unaffordable housing varies widely across cities. The average price of a three-bedroom, two-bath home is approximately $261,000 in San Francisco, while in Peoria the price is $47,000 (Dreier and Stevens, 1990:6-7). In San Francisco, a household needs a yearly income of $99,000 to buy the average-priced home, while in Peoria, only $17,317. For rental housing, the proportion of tenants' income going into rent will drop sharply in Santa Monica—under a grass-roots managerial style of government—while in Houston—under a free enterprise approach—rents are rising sharply. Moreover, the "housing crisis" is not an inherent problem in every Western industrial country. Sweden contrasts sharply with the United States by virtually guaranteeing every citizen a decent and affordable home, which, combined with funding of social programs and aggressive planning, has also eradicated homelessness and slums (Gilderbloom and Appelbaum, 1988). On the other hand, housing problems in Eastern bloc cities are just as bad—if not worse—than their capitalist counterparts.

While mode of production is a key explanatory variable, Weberian analysis places a major emphasis on the social and political organization of the city for explaining such things as the housing problem. For Weberians, the question becomes, "Why do variations among cities exist?" Gatekeepers and managers play a fundamental role in allocating essential resources that are spatially located. Their behavior, along with opposition groups, becomes the focus of a Weberian urban analysis. Pahl (1975) provides a Weberian perspective that argues that the central concern of urban sociology is to develop an understanding of the social and spatial constraints on scarce basic necessities such as housing, health care, and transportation. The urban sociologist should attempt to understand how and why access to these fundamental needs varies among urban areas since "access to such resources is systematically structured in a local context" (Pahl, 1975:203). In terms of housing, urban sociologists should focus on the key actors who manage the urban housing system (owners of property) and on the recipients of their housing (tenants—"those who must rent") (Pahl, 1975:244-6). Thus, the actions of bankers, landlords, public officials and tenant organizations are central in the location, access, and price of an essential resource such as rental housing.

These various theoretical arguments have important implications for tenants' movements, their likelihood of success, and the appropriateness of particular goals such as pressuring the state. Progressive movements that incorporate rent-control and housing rights strategies, for example, are only justifiable if the state is viewed as vulnerable to pressure and responsive to popular social movements. Although they disagree regarding how permeable the state is to opposition groups, the above-mentioned views suggest that tenants will only be effective if they organize themselves based on a realistic knowledge of the biases in the system.

## Tenants: Political Behavior and Tenant Consciousness

The widespread belief in the conservatizing impact of homeownership has had a strong influence on both national housing policy and progressive movements for social change. The view that housing ownership leads to conservative social and political behavior is widely held by contemporary theorists on both the left and right of the academic and political spectrum (Kemeny, 1977, 1980; Saunders, 1978; Ball, 1976; Harvey, 1976; Castells,

1977; Sternlieb, 1966). The belief that homeownership will cause individuals to rethink their politics and move to the right has become conventional wisdom. According to Herbert Hoover (1923) who later became President of the United States:

> Maintaining a high percentage of individual home-owners is one of the searching tests that now challenge the people of the United States. The present large proportion of families that own their homes is both the foundation of a sound economic and social system and a guarantee that our society will continue to develop rationally as changing conditions demand.

Housing analyst George Sternlieb (1966) echoes these words when he states that "homeownership is what glues people to the system."

Leaders in the housing rights movement and progressive elected officials in the United States have declined to place homeownership on the political agenda, citing fears that their constituents' political sentiments will shift to the right.[5] As a result, the modern housing movement channels its energies into winning greater "tenant" rights and better public housing. While some important gains have been made in this direction, this approach ignores the fact that most renters do not want to be tenants, but dream of someday becoming homeowners (Morris, Winter, and Sward, 1984; Heskin, 1983; Hohm, 1984). The political right, on the other hand, has traditionally pushed for greater homeownership opportunities, hoping this will translate into greater political gains for their political parties. This is an attempt to appeal politically to the desires of the working class and to build a more unified conservative base.

A growing body of empirical literature investigates this connection between housing status and political behavior. Research has shown that homeowners are more likely than are tenants to be involved in community political activities (Alford and Scoble, 1968; Steinberger, 1981), to be more neighborly (Fisher, 1982), to be members of church and community organizations (Homenuck, 1973), to make greater claims on government services (Guterbock, 1980); to be less residentially mobile (Cox, 1982), and to be more aware of local affairs (Sykes, 1951). However, Kingston et al. (1984:132) note that "their [homeowners'] substantive orientations are not directly considered" in terms of a political ideology. For example, contrary to conventional wisdom, support for the tax revolt cannot be distinguished by housing tenure in a majority of the studies conducted (Lowry and Sigelman, 1981). Moreover, national survey data show that support for tax-slashing initiatives does not substantively vary by housing status (Lowry and Sigelman, 1981).

Survey research conducted on voting patterns in England between 1964 and 1979 finds that housing tenure is a key determinant for voting behavior (Kelley, McAllister, and Mughan, 1984). The authors (Kelley et al., 1984:16) declare that the impact of homeownership on support for national political parties in England is both "dramatic" and "substantial." On the local level, Kevin Cox (1982) has found that neighborhood activism in the United States varies according to whether an individual is an owner or a renter. Research by Terry Blum and Paul Kingston (1984:159) has found that homeownership plays a role in measuring attitudinal support for the status quo, participation in voluntary organizations, and informal interaction with neighbors. Although only a negligible impact on political attitudes was found, this issue was pursued more fully by Kingston, McAllister, and Mughan's study (1984) using a different data set. They found that housing status had no measurable effect on party identification, ideological views, or socioeconomic policy. They did find, however, that homeowners tended to vote more in presidential elections and that these votes were for Republicans.

As noted above, both Marxists and Weberians claim that important political differences exist between renters and homeowners within the working class. Why are homeowners more active in local politics than are tenants? The traditional explanation rests on the concern for home as investment. A major inference drawn from this finding is that local political participation is conservative in orientation, signaling an attempt to preserve and enhance positive neighborhood externalities and, concurrently, to reduce or abolish negative neighborhood externalities (Harvey, 1973: 57-60, 1978; Agnew, 1978). This argument implies that local political activity is a proxy for homeowners, developers, landlords, and commercial enterprises hoping to increase their property values. These interests tend to lean toward the conservative side. Tenants, on the other hand, lack any investment stake to involve them in local political affairs.

Kevin Cox (1982:107) rejects this strictly "economist" explanation by testing the argument empirically in a detailed survey of four hundred Columbus, Ohio, owners and renters. He compares those homeowners who bought their house *primarily so they could sell it for profit in the future* versus those homeowners who indicated this was not a primary consideration in their decision to buy. Cox finds that the presence or absence of this economic concern has virtually no effect on neighborhood political involvement. He points out that a more realistic approach for homeowners with a strong investment orientation is simply to move rather than lobby city hall (or fight, as the case may be) (see also Orbell and Uno, 1972; Williams, 1971; Wingo, 1973). Cox finds that homeowners facing strong "transaction cost barriers to relocation" are the ones most likely to be active on the local political front over "mobile" homeowners. Homeowners are also, as a group, less mobile than are tenants, causing the former to be more active politically.

Despite the consistently important theme of class consciousness that surfaces among Marxist and Weberian scholars, little empirical research has been conducted, using sophisticated statistical techniques, to assess the overall impact of homeownership on political attitudes (Kingston et al., 1984:133). Most of the research has focused on political *behavior* rather than on political attitudes. Work in this area has been limited because of the lack of a suitable data set. National survey data sets are deficient either because they do not determine the housing status of the respondent or, in cases where they do (such as the University of Michigan survey put out by the Institute for Social Policy Research), because the questions do not adequately measure progressive belief structures, ignoring such things as an individual's political ideology, trade union consciousness, local political participation, and attitudes toward distribution of wealth.[6] As previously noted, some work has been done to measure the impact of housing tenure on political participation (voting, neighborhood organization, etc.) but it has failed to look at progressive political beliefs.

A major exception is the work of Allan Heskin (1983), who specifically explores "tenant consciousness" and its relationship to social movements, and John Gilderbloom's forthcoming work on housing status and progressive political beliefs. As we noted above, there is a paucity of research on the impact of housing status on political attitudes. Gilderbloom (forthcoming) bases his conclusions on a regression analysis of various factors measuring political opinions on two data sets. In one study of a midwestern industrial city, he finds that politically active homeowners do not hold a conservative ideology in regard to environmentalism, political ideology, distribution of wealth, or trade union consciousness. Pursuing these questions further using the National Opinion Research Center 1984 survey, Gilderbloom developed eight dependent variables through factor analysis. He finds that housing status had no measurable impact on seven of the dependent variables measuring equal rights for women, spending on city problems, domestic spending, support for socialist countries, sexual tolerance, civil liberties, and support for President Reagan (Table 2-2). His results are consistent, however, with previous work showing homeownership status as positively correlated with local political participation (Cox, 1982; Blum and Kingston, 1984). Gilderbloom's findings indicate that homeowners are more likely to vote, but when this variable is run as an independent variable in the regression analysis, no correlation is found with the other seven dependent variables. Given these results, the traditional theoretical proposition of the relationship between homeownership and a conservative political ideology needs to be reexamined.

## TABLE 2-2

### The Impact of Housing Status on Political Beliefs

| | Factors | | | | | | | |
|---|---|---|---|---|---|---|---|---|
| | 1 | 2 | 3 | 4 | 5 | 6 | 7 | 8 |
| Religiosity | -.12** | -.04 | .02* | .01 | .37** | -.17** | .05 | .18** |
| Household Income 1985 | .08* | .05 | .02 | .02 | .07* | .08* | .10** | .10** |
| City Size | -.03 | .05 | .01 | .00 | -.09** | -.07** | .02 | .02 |
| Region (South = 1, Other = 0) | -.09** | -.01 | -.03* | .07* | -.04 | -.06* | .06** | -.05 |
| Political Party | -.16** | .25** | .05** | -.09** | -.02 | .00 | .58** | -.03 |
| Gender | -.05 | .05 | .01 | -.11** | .00 | .00 | .05* | -.06* |
| Number of Children | .02 | .03 | .01 | .04 | -.06* | .01 | .03 | -.00 |
| Religion | -.02 | -.02 | .01 | .00 | -.13** | -.06* | .03 | -.04 |
| Race | .03 | -.17** | .01 | .17** | -.06* | .07* | .16** | -.00 |
| City Size at age 16 | .01 | -.13** | -.02* | -.00 | .02 | .07* | .02 | .03 |
| Occupational Prestige | .10** | .03 | .01 | -.04 | .06* | .07* | -.00 | .03 |
| Age | -.17** | .14** | .07** | .04 | -.13** | -.16** | -.08* | .22** |
| Marriage Status | -.02 | -.03 | -.01 | -.00 | -.10** | .01 | .00 | .04 |
| Housing Status (1 = homeowner) | -.03 | .05 | .02 | .06 | -.04 | -.01 | -.00 | .08* |
| Education | .17** | -.01 | .93** | -.10** | .14** | .28** | -.13** | .18** |
| R Square | .18 | .11 | .89 | .08 | .35 | .31 | .44 | .17 |
| F | 16.80 | 8.60 | 582.6 | 6.61 | 43.5 | 35.6 | 62.5 | 17.1 |

Significance Levels:

\* .05

\*\* .01

Factor 1: Women's Rights; Factor 2: Spending on City Problems; Factor 3: Domestic Spending; Factor 4: Support for Socialist Countries; Factor 5: Sexual Tolerance; Factor 6: Civil Liberties; Factor 7: Support for Reagan; Factor 8: Voted in 1984

In the most exhaustive study to date examining why tenants support rent control, Heskin (1983) conducted a survey of tenant attitudes shortly after Santa Monica passed its rent-control law in 1979. He attempted to study the proposition offered by Manuel Castells (1977) that urban social movements result in a greater political class consciousness. Following Gramsci (1971), Heskin (1983:xiii–xiv) argued that tenant consciousness develops through political action on housing issues. In a movement for even the mildest kind of government-imposed rent restrictions comes a rise in "tenant consciousness." According to Heskin (1983), efforts for better housing reveal that capitalism by itself cannot solve the housing problem and that government is needed to intervene directly in the housing market. The market cannot provide affordable housing for the poor because of the high capital cost of new housing, speculation, high interest rates, and landlord cartels (Marcuse, 1981b; O'Connor, 1979; Achtenberg and Stone, 1977; Dreier, Gilderbloom, and Appelbaum, 1980). Demands for government intervention range from mild forms of limits on allowable rent increases to more extreme measures such as producing on a massive scale non-market forms of housing—limited equity housing or "human-scale" public housing (Hartman and Stone, 1980).

Heskin (1981c) proposes that tenant consciousness develops when the following conditions are met: (1) tenants view themselves as a group sharing similar problems; (2) they have a common understanding of the causes of their problems; and (3) they have a collective political purpose which responds effectively to these problems (Heskin, 1981c:1; Atlas and Dreier, 1981:34). Heskin (1981c:1) argues that tenants with high consciousness tend to view the market as incapable of supplying decent and affordable housing; tenants feel that government must regulate the housing market either by limiting rent increases or by developing more public housing, and they feel that they must become politically organized and active in politics. The tenant who takes the above view contrasts sharply to what Heskin (1981c) characterizes as the tenant who is "a landlord lover." These are tenants who take the side of landlords on all housing issues, oppose any form of rent control, view supply and demand as the cause for rising rents, feel landlords have the right to raise rents by any amount, and oppose any kind of political actions against the landlord. Following Max Weber, Heskin argues that class distinctions appear to exist among tenants. The success of the tenants' efforts to pass progressive legislation depends largely on the degree of tenant consciousness shared by fellow renters.

To test this theory empirically, Heskin (1983) asked the University of California to conduct over 700 interviews with Santa Monica residents and 1,400 interviews with residents in non-rent-controlled Los Angeles County. His data were unable to support Castells's contention that social movements are an independent source in the creation of radical political consciousness. Heskin (1983:158) found that "a worsening rental housing situation and landlord-tenant conflict in one form or another are necessary first elements in the emergence of a tenant movement." In addition, Heskin (1983:95–119) argued that certain demographic characteristics mold tenant consciousness. Individuals who were English-speaking, female, young, and low income expressed the most radical beliefs concerning landlord/tenant relations.

Tenant organizers argue that movements in support of rent control can lead to a broad-based cross-class tenant coalition (Lawson, 1983; Čapek, 1985) that includes the middle class as well as seniors, blue-collar workers, and minorities (Jacob, 1979; Leight et al., 1980; Kirschman, 1980). These are the same divisions that have traditionally hampered low- and moderate-income persons from having political clout. The uniting of working and nonworking people in the struggle for better housing is particularly significant since conservative politicians have historically used the nonworking poor as a scapegoat for the working person's problems (O'Connor, 1981:54–55). Atlas (1982) has argued that better housing conditions are accomplished through collective actions, not individual feats.

*Theoretical Implications for Tenants' Movements*

Marxian and Weberian analyses of housing issues raise a number of interesting theoretical questions from the point of view of tenants' movements. Is urban reform really co-optation in disguise, as Engels argued? Can oppositional progressive movements "capture" the state and alter the life chances of urban residents, or does the state inevitably reproduce existing inequalities and power relationships? What impact does housing status have on political beliefs? Do urban social movements result in a higher "class consciousness"? Under what circumstances can tenants be radicalized to act in a collective manner? What happens when cities are run by progressives instead of a "growth machine"? What role do inequitable conditions play in the building of an urban social movement? The conditions and the politics of cities have changed radically since the time of Weber and Marx. To what extent do their analyses capture the present reality of urban social movements and housing problems? The answers to these questions have important implications for organizing strategies for the 1990s and for the analysis of urban social movements. We will explore them through our case study and our quantitative analysis.

Resource Mobilization

Arising out of the collective behavior tradition (Blumer, 1951), social movements theory has undergone major shifts in focus in the course of its development. In recent years, research has moved away from an emphasis on irrational actors (Cantril, 1941), deprivation theories (Gurr, 1970), and a strain-oriented paradigm (Smelser, 1963) toward an examination of rational motives, successful organizational strategies, and structural opportunities for mobilization (Traugott, 1978; McCarthy and Zald, 1973; Tilly, 1978; Gamson, 1975; Oberschall, 1973). On the heels of the social movements of the 1960s, Zald and Ash (1966) and McCarthy and Zald (1973, 1977) first outlined a historical trend toward the professionalization of social movements in the United States, grounded in such things as the "bureaucratization of social discontent" (McCarthy and Zald, 1973:3), the development of government policies and private funding patterns, the possibility for full-time careers in social movement organizations, and discretionary time available among relatively affluent and well-educated social actors. This represents a clear shift away from the "consciousness" issues we discussed in the previous section.

The resource mobilization model was conceived as a deliberate departure from the "hearts and minds" interpretation of social movements (Leites and Wolf, 1970). Its most provocative thesis is the claim that social movements are shaped by mobilization opportunities rather than by the pressure of insupportable grievances (Tilly, 1978). Instead of seeking an explanation for individual participation in social movements, resource mobilization theorists borrow from organizational and economic models to focus on the professionalized social movement organization (SMO) as the theoretically significant unit of analysis (Selznick, 1948; Olson, 1968; Marwell and Oliver, 1984). This vision not only places the SMO at the center of the social movements landscape, but also locates social movement sectors (SMSs) and social movement industries (SMIs), which exhibit the competition and product diversification characteristic of a marketplace model (McCarthy and Zald, 1977; Zald and McCarthy, 1980).

At the same time, analytical attention shifts away from mass participation and toward a core of movement organizers, often dependent on funding resources of elites. As professionalization increases, broad membership participation is neither elicited nor sought for the emergence of successful social movements; indeed, grievances may be "defined, created and manipulated" by social movement entrepreneurs and organizations (McCarthy and Zald, 1977:1215). Hence, social movements come to be conceptualized through "entrepreneurial mobilization" (Jenkins, 1983) and measured through the "occurrence of associations" (Gusfield, 1981:322).

Because the units of analysis in the resource mobilization model are social organizations, special attention has been devoted to organizational boundaries and how these affect the tactical choices of social movement organizations. McCarthy and Zald (1977) have drawn attention to the distinction between "beneficiaries," or those who directly benefit from a particular goal or action, and "adherents" of a movement, or those who desire a particular goal.

Following earlier priorities of Smelser (1963) and Turner (1969), resource mobilization theorists have highlighted the role of "bystanders," "conscience constituents," and third parties (Harrington, 1968; Lipsky, 1970) who lend crucial assistance to initially powerless groups. Michael Lipsky (1970), for example, concluded in his analysis of tenant protest activities in New York City that the main task for tenant organizations was the activation of third parties—including middle-class society women—who could speak for them and lend symbolic legitimacy to the movement.

The relationships of movement organizations among themselves and to the "multi-organizational field" in which they are immersed have been a focus of interest for resource mobilization theorists (Curtis and Zurcher, 1971; Zurcher and Snow, 1981), as has been the manipulation of the environment by SMOs (Jenkins, 1983; McCarthy and Zald, 1977; Zald and McCarthy, 1980). A historical dimension is captured through the analysis of the dynamic interplay of movement and countermovement over time (Gale, 1986; Mottl, 1980; Zald and Useem, 1987), and through attention given to processes of growth, decay, and institutionalization in social movements (Zald and Ash, 1966). Particularly important are long-term historical shifts that create mobilization opportunities, such as previous "cadre" experience in other social movements (Jenkins, 1983:531) or the use of organizations that are already in place (Oberschall, 1973; Tilly, 1978). All of these factors affect the availability of group resources and are seen as conditioning mobilization opportunities more consistently than do grievances.[7]

### Theoretical Implications for Tenants' Movements

The resource mobilization framework is neither unitary (Perrow, 1979; Jenkins, 1983) nor free of contradictions (Zurcher and Snow, 1981), but it has been enormously influential. Moreover, a cursory glance at the model reveals propositions that are helpful in the empirical analysis of tenants' movements. It suggests, first and foremost, that the tenants' movements that surfaced in the United States in the 1970s and 1980s should be understood in the context of broad structural changes in the social movements "sector" that have strongly shaped leadership and funding opportunities (Garner and Zald, 1986). The historical expansion and contraction in this sector—which includes outside funding and the role of the state—restrict and facilitate mobilization possibilities (Jenkins, 1983; Freeman, 1983; Perlman, 1979).

Second, resource mobilization theory directs attention to the presence of an educated cadre that has experienced similar or prior movements in the same general movements sector. Experience gained in the antiwar movement or the civil rights movement thus becomes "translatable" to other movements. This brings into focus the need to examine the role that different generations of activists play in the construction and transformation of social movements (Braungart, 1984; McAdam, 1989; Ross, 1983). Can particular "generational units" (Mannheim, cited in Flacks, 1971:51) be identified as primary actors in the emergence of a tenants' movement? The generation of the 1960s, for example, or at least an important subgroup within it, has continued to exercise a strong impact on movements of the 1980s (Flacks, 1988; Gitlin, 1989; Whalen and Flacks, 1989). What place do generations have in tenants' movements? According to Cloward and Piven (1986:x–xi), the movements of the sixties generated a particular kind of experience that had lasting consequences, even though the movements themselves came to an end:

> The movements of the sixties established a community organizing tradition in the United States. Although there had always been neighborhood organizing, which Saul Alinsky had developed into a kind of credo, in the context of the 1960s, organizing acquired a meaning that went beyond the essentially localistic, neighborhood-based focus of past efforts. It came to be thought of as a way of empowering the most subjugated people in the United States to transform society itself.

They also note that:

> A good many of the activists who had worked to organize the poor in the 1960s turned in the 1970s to organizing middle- and working-class constituencies, and turned also away from "direct action" to concentrate on lobbying and education strategies compatible with their new constituencies.

A resource mobilization perspective compels us to ask, therefore, whether the emergence of the tenants' revolt in the 1970s and 1980s stemmed from mass resistance to housing grievances or rather from the presence of effective "movement entrepreneurs," a supportive climate provided by the state, and prior organizational experience. Did the historical and nationwide sharing of experiences from different social movements (civil rights, antiwar), including the "demonstration effect" that diffuses successful scenarios to other locations (Jenkins, 1983), make tenant mobilization possible in the late 1970s?

Critiques of Resource Mobilization: Social Psychology and Interactionism

Critiques of the resource mobilization perspective have come from a number of directions. A major criticism addresses the lack of attention to the social-psychological and interactional elements in social movements (Ferree and Miller, 1985; Zurcher and Snow, 1981; Klandermans, 1984). In a review of social movements literature, Craig Jenkins (1983) identified this as one of the primary future research directions that needs to be developed by resource mobilization theorists to balance their organizational and institutional emphasis. Since the resource mobilization perspective arose in response to theories that assumed an excessively simple correspondence between psychological variables—such as authoritarianism, powerlessness, relative deprivation—and collective action (Zurcher and Snow, 1981:450), it is no surprise that it has cast its nets in a different direction.[8] However, by neglecting cognitive and interactional processes highlighted by social psychology, some crucial questions remain unanswered.

Primary among these is the question of how social structure can become collectively redefined as something that may be acted on (Smelser, 1963; Zurcher and Snow, 1981). As Marwell and Oliver (1984) have noted, most people choose to continue to behave according to the rules rather than to change the social structure around them. How do they come to define it as subject to change through their actions? Social psychologists argue that the response to this question must bring together attitudinal and interactional variables. Not only do ideas and definitions of the situation change, but this frequently occurs in emergent fashion as social interaction takes place. In order to understand social movements, therefore, it is necessary to ask: "What are the structures of support, the resources, and the experiences that generate the capacity and the inspiration to challenge 'the way things are' and imagine a different world?" (Evans and Boyte, 1986:2). Moreover, how are these resources activated interactionally?

Resource mobilization theorists have de-emphasized social psychology— and ideology—because they find evidence of extremely diverse motivations coexisting in the same movement (Tilly, 1978). They have therefore looked to institutional opportunities as a better explanation for the emergence of movements. Recent efforts to resurrect a psychology of social movements acknowledge the complexity and heterogeneity of movement participation, but do not see this as negating the usefulness of social-psychological approaches (Klandermans, 1984; Klandermans and Oegema, 1987; Ferree and Miller, 1985; Zurcher and Snow, 1981). Instead, they seek explanatory power in microsociological features such as social networks, face-to-face interactions, and recruitment strategies (Snow et al., 1980; McAdam, 1986). While personal frustration is not dismissed as a variable, social interaction and "perceived efficacy" (Opp, 1985; Klandermans, 1984) are conceptualized as important intervening variables that add a more rational cast to the model.

It is this "micromobilization" approach (Zurcher and Snow, 1981, Gamson et al., 1982) that provides the analytical tools for understanding the place of ideas and emergent cognitive definitions of the situation in producing social change. It shares with resource mobilization theory an interest in identifying preexisting infrastructures that promote movement activity (Oberschall, 1973; Freeman, 1983), including "socialization" into prior movements, customary "repertoires" of behavior (Tilly, 1978; Klandermans, 1984; Barnes and Kaase, 1979), and leadership and organizational skills that diffuse ideologies through direct social contact (Rogers, 1983; Klandermans and Oegema, 1987). Unlike the resource mobilization approach, however, the interactional model attempts to capture the process as it occurs, highlighting the social learning of roles and the creation of new resources unavailable to isolated individuals.

Attentiveness to the interactional context leads away from an overemphasis on assumptions of economic rationality and self-interest and toward social solidarity considerations and nonmaterial incentives that cancel the "free-rider problem"—individuals who do not participate in movements for a "public good," because they will benefit from the efforts of others (Fireman and Gamson, 1979; Oliver, 1984, Carden, 1978; Kanter, 1972; Opp, 1985). A body of research has provided evidence that group action can heighten a sense of efficacy that promotes further active involvement. Protesters are shown to benefit from a "personal environment" that includes protest norms, expectations of significant others, and private sanctions; the so-called soft (nonmaterial) incentives that encourage participation and mitigate the impact of external social controls (Opp, 1985). A critique by Snow et al. (1986:466) points out, however, that although current research recognizes the significance of social interaction, the models used still tend to neglect process itself, such as how "certain lines of action come to be defined as more or less risky, morally imperative in spite of associated risks, or instrumentally pointless." Such critiques suggest the need to understand collective protest as a social learning process (Eder, 1985), where learning takes place "along dimensions other than the strategic" (Cohen, 1985:685). This does not negate the usefulness of the resource mobilization frame, but rather supplements it; as Ferree and Miller (1985:55) have noted, it is indispensable to recognize that "participation is a critical aspect of the process of establishing control over resources."[9]

Critiques of Resource Mobilization:
The New Social Movements School and New Populism

A European counterpoint to resource mobilization theory has emerged in recent years (Klandermans, 1986; Klandermans and Tarrow, 1988; Kriesi 1988). Commonly designated as the "new social movements" (NSM) school, it is macrostructural and cultural in its orientation rather than focused on social movement organizations. Like resource mobilization theory, it represents various constellations of theoretical and empirical work (Touraine, 1971, 1985; Melucci, 1980, 1985; Habermas, 1975), but contains some common underlying themes and propositions. NSM theory makes the assumption that social movements arise in response to macrostructural changes that are linked to the emergence of a post-industrial, information-based society (Touraine, 1985; Habermas, 1975; Inglehart, 1977), where domination is no longer expressed primarily through relations in the workplace. In such a society, it is argued, groups do not simply struggle over economic resources along class lines, as orthodox Marxist theory suggests, but over the production of culture and the symbolic realm of information. Struggles are broadly diffused and are played out beyond the workplace in the "life space" of neighborhood, housing, and the natural environment. These arenas, once considered solely part of the private domain of individuals and their families, have increasingly become the focus of new organizing efforts by social movement participants. The new social movements organize around issues such as the natural and built environment, planetary survival, physical and psychic health, the control of information, and gender relations (Klandermans, 1986). Typical examples include the ecology movement, the women's movement, student movements, the peace movement, and urban citizens' initiatives (Offe, 1985).

As Klandermans (1986) has noted, several theoretical strands in the NSM school bridge Marxist and non-Marxist traditions of social thought. The inexorable dynamics of the capitalist system are seen as creating a situation conducive to struggle; at the same time, the central importance assigned to workplace struggles by Marxists is bypassed. Habermas, for example, has argued that there is in postindustrial capitalist societies an increasing "economic and administrative colonization of life space" (Habermas, cited in Klandermans, 1986:22). Both the state and the capitalist economy make historically new incursions into what has hitherto been considered the realm of private life; hence, the need for symbolic resistance and a kind of "reappropriation" of power over the invaded realms. Resistance to domination is thus broadly defined and cuts across many spheres.

Although NSM theorists disagree over details of interpretation, there is agreement among them that the recent movements are "new" with respect to the constituencies they mobilize and the values they express. The actors are considered new because many of them are recruited from a relatively affluent and well-educated middle class; indeed, rather than following class lines, new social movements cut across class identities, giving rise to many single-issue and temporary alliances. Actors surface periodically out of "submerged networks" on specific issues:

> The normal situation of today's "movement" is a network of small
> groups submerged in everyday life which require a personal involvement

in experiencing and practicing cultural innovation. They emerge only on specific issues, as for instance the big mobilizations for peace, for abortion, against nuclear policy, etc. The submerged network, although composed of separate small groups, is a system of exchange (persons and information circulate along the network); some agencies, such as local free radios, bookshops, magazines provide a certain unity (Melucci, 1985:800).

This form of interaction opens the possibility for new coalitions and forms of solidarity that may coexist with more traditional identities (Melucci, 1985). No longer sited exclusively in the workplace, the "contested terrain" broadens and in turn affects—and is affected by—social movements.

The values at the core of new social movements are also seen as more broadly holistic than those expressed in past movements, and have been characterized by some NSM theorists as "postmaterialistic" (Inglehart, 1977; Touraine, 1971). These movement theorists express a new type of hermeneutic self-understanding and reflexive questioning of one's place in society—and in the universe—that is different from the consciousness of past social actors, particularly "Old and New Lefts" (Cohen, 1985). Just as the public quest for certain types of human rights is historically new (MacIntyre, 1984), so certain types of self-understandings were not sought by prior movement activists. Touraine (1985) claims that the issue is "self-production," or having symbolic control over defining, not only one's life space, but also the production of one's identity. Melucci (1985:807) similarly suggests that

. . . what is at stake in contemporary movements, and particularly in peace mobilizations, is the production of the human species, at the individual and collective level: the possibility for men, as individuals and as species, to control not only their "products" and their "making," culturally and socially (and more and more biologically). What is at stake is the production of human existence and its quality.

Critics of this perspective point out that this is not necessarily new and that the politics of class and the politics of culture are not mutually exclusive or distinctive categories. David Plotke (1990:81), for example, argues that

. . . "new social movement discourse" overstates the novelty of the movements it analyzes, selectively depicts their aims as cultural, and exaggerates their separation from conventional political life in this country.

In addition, Plotke and others object to a Western European framework being applied wholesale to a U.S. political context.

Nevertheless, NSM theories have received attention because they fill a gap left open by the dominant resource mobilization perspective. We noted above that resource mobilization has tended to ignore the process of value construction, activation, and transformation through collective action. NSM theorists situate their work quite specifically in response to this perceived problem:

> The notion of resource mobilization has been used to transform the study of social movements into a study of strategies as if actors were defined by their goals and not by the social relationships—especially power relationships—in which they are involved (Touraine, 1985:769).

Melucci (1985:793) suggests that social movements need to be understood as collective, negotiated social relationships, as dynamic "action systems" rather than as empirical phenomena. In this way, the vital concern for organizational resources already found in resource mobilization theory can be supplemented with a study of meaning and social interaction.

A final point about new social movements is that they frequently use "repertoires" that bypass the institutionalized political sphere (Melucci, 1985). This does not mean that they are apolitical. They are political in the sense that they make seemingly private questions (housing, sexuality) amenable to public discussion.[10] At the same time, they retain their independence from institutional politics, using nonconventional tactics:

> A new political space is designed beyond the traditional distinction between state and "civil society": an intermediate public space, whose function is not to institutionalize the movements nor to transform them into parties, but to make society hear their messages and translate these messages into political decision making, while movements maintain their autonomy (Melucci, 1985:815).

Since the goal need not be the seizing of power in a political sense, the new social movements have a certain kind of freedom: They "cannot survive without the mediation of political actors, but cannot be reduced to them" (Melucci, 1981:190). Likewise, it has been suggested that they should not be judged in terms of political accomplishments alone, but rather in terms of their effect on the diffusion of values in civil society. Their function is as much "prophetic" as it is political (Melucci, 1985:797), and much of their work is done in the sphere of civil society and everyday life.

Although NSM research has been mostly conducted by European scholars, there are strong parallels between their theoretical emphasis on civil society and the work of American scholars Evans and Boyte (1986), who have proposed the concept of "free spaces" as a breeding ground for social movements. Free spaces are defined as interactional settings—such as churches or bars—grounded in local communities and traditions, where people meet face-to-face to discuss problems and to practice direct democracy in some form. Free spaces are "interstitial" spaces between private and institutional structures, as yet uncolonized by invasive economic or political authorities. As such, they provide a potential challenge to existing relationships of domination by permitting nonelites to define themselves in their own terms. At certain times, under certain conditions, "free spaces" can become "insurgency spaces," creating a basis for progressive populism (Boyte et al., 1986). A search for the conditions under which this takes place links Evans and Boyte's work to general social movements theory.

Like NSM theorists, Evans and Boyte (1986:viii) challenge not only resource mobilization theory, but also Marxist class analysis:

> The idea of free spaces, and the lived realities behind the idea, highlight limitations in the very language and terms of much of social science. Democratic values, human dignity, or the themes of citizenship and a vision of the common good are not reducible to the "resource mobilization" approach of most contemporary social movement theory, nor the charts and graphs used by Marxists to define the "class location" or "objective determinants of oppression" of various social groupings, nor the voting behavior profiles of which modern political science is enamored.

A dialogue between the Evans-Boyte approach (characterized in U.S. journals as the "new populism") and their Marxist critics has invigorated the discussion of social movements (Boyte and Riessman, 1986; Boyte et al., 1986). New populists do not naively assume that democratic interaction will always emerge from the free spaces they describe; there is evidence, after all, of reactionary and defensive populism alongside democratic populism. There is also evidence that community integration has no consistent impact on social activism (Opp, 1988; Useem, 1980; Useem and Kimball, 1989). However, unlike orthodox Marxists—and in the tradition of historian E. P. Thompson (1966)—they emphasize the transformative potential of community and tradition:

> Community institutions reproducing the bonds of historical memory and culture also serve as the arenas where people can distinguish themselves from elite definitions of who they are, can gain the skills and mutual regard necessary to act as a force for change. From the outside, values and rituals of community life and folkways are all too easily seen in static and monochromatic terms, dismissed as "opiates" (Evans and Boyte, 1982:56).

Hanspeter Kriesi (1988:389) argues that in this new populists depart from NSM theorists, who presuppose "the demise of precisely those traditional institutions and the liberation of people from traditional ties and identities."

It is significant that free spaces are conceptualized as spaces for interaction and rehearsal of roles, where social learning and emergence of new elements take place. This makes transformation possible, even in a traditional context. In such spaces, successful challenging repertoires are constructed and rehearsed; as McAdam (1986:69) has noted, "Playing at being an 'activist' is a prerequisite to becoming one." The focus of this research becomes, then, meaning and social identity as they are processually created in a group context.

## Theoretical Implications for Tenants' Movements

The theoretical stance found in the work of Evans and Boyte and among the NSM theorists dovetails with the social-psychological and interactionist critiques of resource mobilization theory, cited above. For our project, the implications are methodological as well as theoretical. They suggest that the "truth" of social movements is methodologically captured "in the concreteness of particular stories" (Evans and Boyte, 1986:20), which reveal a new set of resources in the making (Ferree and Miller, 1985). Not only do NSM theory and new populism suggest the need to explore cross-class alliances, but they also suggest the need for a process- and symbolically-oriented approach rather than the more static, organizationally-oriented approach that they identify with resource mobilization theory. Ethnography as a research tool is particularly compatible with this understanding (Orum, 1990:4–6).

Moreover, as urban social movements located in the private sphere, housing rights and tenants' movements are clearly amenable to analysis as "new social movements." New social movements place heavy emphasis on the control of the symbolic realm of information and culture, which, according to Melucci, Touraine, and others, is increasingly contested in postindustrial societies. What is disputed includes the right to define basic categories of experience such as time and space (Habermas, 1975; Harvey, 1985) as well as the right publicly to name the situation and one's opponent in a social struggle (Touraine, 1985; Melucci, 1985). Housing movements should provide a rich ground for theoretical exploration in this regard. The suggestions of the above-mentioned theories underline to us the importance of studying the process by means of which tenants have struggled for the right to name themselves and their situation and for the right to redefine private property and urban space in the context of the practice of democracy. This compels us to seek out symbolic dimensions of the tenants' movement that range considerably beyond pure economic survival and accomplishments confined to the political arena.

Critiques of Resource Mobilization: Ideology and Symbolic "Framing"

Some further light is shed on these processes by theories emphasizing the social construction of ideology and symbolic framing, particularly their intragroup and intergroup dimensions. Framing refers to activities that seek to direct the process of social interpretation of actions and ideas in a particular direction. In contrast to the resource mobilization model, where "ideas are not the central stuff" of social movements (Marwell and Oliver, 1984:6), and where ideologies are viewed as an "optional tool" for analysis (Freeman, 1983:3), a number of sociologists have long insisted on the significance of "definitions of the situation" in the development of social movements (Thomas and Thomas, 1928; Blumer, 1951; Smelser, 1963; Turner, 1983; Gusfield, 1981; Gamson et al., 1982; Snow et al., 1986). In his groundbreaking *Theory of Collective Behavior,* Smelser (1963) recognized that social movements require the growth and spread of a generalized belief that provides a "common culture" for movement participants; this permits actors to redefine an ambiguous situation as one that is problematic and can be acted on collectively (Smelser, 1963:82). It is not objective conditions that are most important, but rather how they are collectively interpreted. How do social actors interpret and attribute meaning to their world and to their own place in it? What are the processes by means of which they read sense into their own actions as well as those of others? In the case of social movements, how do individuals come to have the kind of understanding of themselves and of their surrounding social structure that permits its transformation (Moore, 1978; Gamson et al., 1982)? This area of experience has been generally ignored by resource mobilization theory, although not, as we noted above, by new social movement theorists.

If one assumes that "meanings are attached to events as an aspect of intergroup process" (Turner, 1969:829), then it becomes particularly important to note how a situation is defined as just or unjust, and how the naming of responsible agents is accomplished. As feminist theorists and others have increasingly recognized, the act of naming a situation contains an inherent power dimension (Rose, 1986). It is typically a social endeavor, as different groups struggle to appropriate the right to name a given situation (Schur, 1980).

In the United States, the tradition of sociologists such as Herbert Blumer and Ralph Turner has offered insight into questions of "naming" and "framing" issues and identities. Over time, a number of theorists have made it their project to identify strategically effective symbolic social movement tasks, including the crucial issue of the social construction of fairness. Turner and Killian (1972) discussed the construction of a public around a given issue, emphasizing how specific tactics give a social movement the label of "respectable" or "revolutionary." In a classic article, Ralph Turner (1969) endeavored to identify the circumstances necessary for a "bystander" public to perceive social action as legitimate protest activity. In doing so, he laid out the elements of a folk concept of "just" protest activity that the public uses to "test for credibility." Gamson et al. (1982) have investigated how perceptions of fairness are linked to the social construction of an "injustice frame," a process that involves not only a bystander public, but movement participants themselves. Scott and Lyman (1968) have enumerated strategies associated with the honoring or dishonoring of narrative accounts of various social groups, while Coser (1969) has discussed how language and perceptions are manipulated to produce the visibility or invisibility of particular social groups and problems.

These analyses emphasize that the adoption of a selective vocabulary, images, and frames for interpretation (Gamson, Fireman, and Rytina, 1982; Mills, 1940; Snow et al., 1986) has a crucial impact on the mobilization and success of social movements. Hence, the symbolic "presentation of self" of social movements has become the object of analytical and empirical research (Scott and Lyman, 1968). Unlike resource mobilization theory, this symbolically oriented perspective tends toward an emphasis on cognitive, processual, and emergent elements of social movements, with a special interest in the appropriate mixture of ideas that produces a particular kind of social action (Turner and Killian, 1972; Zygmunt, 1972).

Snow et al. (1986) have contributed to the systematic study of ideas and symbols as they relate to various movement outcomes and to both participants and observers. Their work draws on a social construction of reality perspective (Schutz, 1962; Berger and Luckmann, 1966) and on an expansion of Erving Goffman's (1974) frame analysis work to suggest that the manipulation of interpretative frames, or the use of "frame alignment" processes, plays a fundamental role in explaining the ongoing and dynamic character of social movement participation. Snow et al. identify four processes—"frame bridging," "frame amplification," "frame extension," and "frame transformation"—that they correlate with particular "micromobilization" tasks such as computer outreach or conversion. Moreover, they identify specific hazards for social movements associated with each frame alignment process, such as an oversaturated direct-mail market or the risk of "clouding" a frame by overextending it. Drawing on Tarrow (1983), Snow et al. (1986:477) also suggest that different types of frame alignment may be associated with cycles of protest, with some movements supplying "master frames that provide ideational and interpretive anchoring for subsequent movements later on in the cycle." In response to gaps that they perceive in resource mobilization theory, they conclude that the analysis of "framing" tasks is critical to the understanding of social movements:

The ways in which SMOs manage and control these frame vulnerabilities, as well as interpretative resources in general, thus seem as crucial to the temporal viability and success of an SMO as the acquisition and deployment of more tangible resources, which to date have received the lion's share of attention by research informed by the resource mobilization frame (Snow et al., 1986:478).

Finally, a limitation of the resource mobilization perspective—and frequently that of its critics as well—is its focus on "movement entrepreneurs" and top-down strategies rather than on grass-roots reformulations that blend traditional ideas with new insights to produce new cognitive schemes. A salutary departure from this set of priorities has been the work of theorist George Rudé, who, while acknowledging the crucial role of leaders, makes efforts to displace some theoretical attention back toward the daily sense-making activities of the "masses." Rudé (1980:9) notes that prevailing ideologies are "often 'contradictory' and confused and compounded of folklore, myth and day-to-day experience" (Rudé, 1980:9). They therefore require a special kind of analysis:

> ...as I have come to realize, the study of motives—even when some attention is paid to such elusive concepts as N. J. Smelser's "generalized beliefs"—is an unsatisfactory one in itself, as it tends to present the problem in a piecemeal fashion and fails to do justice to the full range of ideas or beliefs that underlie social and political action, whether of old-style rulers, "rising" bourgeois or of "inferior" social groups (Rudé, 1980:7).

Following Gramsci, Rudé suggests that ideology consists of an inherent "mother's milk" component that is based on tradition and direct experience. It also consists of a stock of ideas and beliefs that are "derived" or borrowed from others, and are learned through group interaction. These two realms blend together with "a set of circumstances and experience that determine the nature of the final mixture" (Rudé, 1980:35). Rudé's work presents a balance between a mass-based and an elite-based approach to social movements.

Recent efforts to study community mobilizations have recognized the need to give analytical attention to how ordinary people make sense of their world at the grass-roots level. As Celene Krauss has noted, "...citizen struggles suggest that we need to treat as important the ways in which people experience and wrestle with crisis in bits and pieces, in the moments of daily life" (Krauss, 1983:50). This is a departure from Neil Smelser's (1963) tendency to assume that collective behavior depends on a kind of simplified, irrational and quasi-magical type of thinking that facilitates action; on the contrary, grass-roots-oriented theorists observe that the process that ordinary people use to redefine issues is often highly rational, but is a challenge to powerful groups that have a monopoly over the definition of what is and is not rational in a particular society (Portes, 1971; Gaventa, 1980). The latter argument implies that social movements help to construct—or sometimes recapture—a kind of "common sense" that is cognitively rational, but that has been silenced by existing power alignments.

## Theoretical Implications for Tenants' Movements

Insights of the theorists cited in the previous section draw our attention to the framing of issues in the tenants' movement. Popular conceptions of tenants and their rights offer a fascinating glimpse of an ideology in transition, permitting a view of American values as they are transformed and activated, often by extension from existing rights (Evans and Boyte, 1986). The emerging debate in the United States over whether or not housing should be a right or a privilege can be comprehended in light of a debate over fairness and even "common sense," as different social groups exert their influence and contest the right to some of the most cherished terms in the language.

The theoretical tradition emphasizing the central role of symbols and ideology suggests that it is at least as important to study interpretation as it is to study technical and organizational resources collected by social movement organizations. Hence, in the case of tenants' movements, the social construction of fairness and the winning of the right to name their situation would appear critical to their success. How do tenants achieve the goal of making other groups, including landlords and city governments, accountable to them? Scott and Lyman (1968) suggest that, under conditions of "cultural distance and hierarchy," subordinates are not offered any accounts at all. Therefore, as we noted above, a tenants' struggle is not only over allocation of material resources, but over the cultural rules by means of which narrative accounts are constructed and different social groups become accountable to each other.

More broadly, the contributions of Snow et al. (1986), Turner (1969, 1983), Rudé (1980), and others suggest the need to approach social movements as interactional phenomena that generate and alter personal and social meanings. The dimension of personal transformation is especially salient in a representative democracy, where people are activated to participate only selectively and sporadically. It is particularly significant for tenants, who are frequently defined—even by themselves—as outsiders to their communities (Čapek, 1985). As Ralph Turner (1983:6) has put it, "Altered ways of viewing both the self and larger systems of social relationships are often more important products of social movements than any specific organization or political accomplishment." Recent assessments of a variety of grass-roots movements have provided support for this position (Fisher, 1984; 1987; Castells, 1983; Delgado, 1986), which is also upheld by NSM theorists. A focus on consciousness and symbolic identity furthermore suggests the need to explore tenant consciousness at the grass-roots level, as well as the symbolic manipulations of "frames" by movement "entrepreneurs" and leaders. Finally, the work of Snow et al. (1986) provides a useful framework for the systematic identification of types of framing activities employed by various social groups involved in tenants' and progressive urban movements.

Production of Urban Space

We close our discussion of theories bearing on tenants' movements with a brief review of a perspective that emphasizes the social production of urban space (Gottdiener, 1985). In doing so, we return to our claim in Chapter 1 that one of the distinguishing features of tenants' movements—and of housing movements in general—is their spatial component. Housing rights are played out in a disputed social space—most often urban—which suggests a specific geography of such movements. Marwell and Oliver (1984:14) have called for a recognition of the values of territorial or "ecological" units in the analysis of social movements, while Lyman and Scott (1967) have drawn analytical attention to the neglected dimension of "territoriality" and use of space in social behavior. How this spatial component should be conceptualized is, however, the subject of much theoretical debate. The debate, in turn, has strong implications for the interpretation of housing rights movements, rent-control strategies, and progressive urban agendas.

Human ecologists in the United States have long given attention to large-scale, aggregate census variables in their analyses of urban areas, including population size and location (Berry and Kasarda, 1977). One approach to a geography of social movements is to examine correlations between urban social movements and structurally descriptive variables such as size, region, and density of social relations. This view is consistent with "strain" theories, including that of Marx, who wrote in the *Communist Manifesto* that worsening conditions in the urban workplace would facilitate greater class consciousness and eventually a revolutionary movement capable of overthrowing capitalism (see also Fainstein and Fainstein, 1974). There is some evidence for such strain theories; as we noted above, Friedland (1982) finds that racial riots in the United States in the 1960s occurred only in cities with a high percentage of blacks, poor housing opportunities, and high rates of unemployment (see also Piven and Cloward, 1971).

Critics of the "abject conditions," or strain model, point out that such correlations do not have sufficient explanatory power in the study of urban social movements; instead, urban theorists such as Mark Gottdiener (1985) highlight the significance of human agency and social movement organization as an intervening variable. This is consistent with the general "resource mobilization" view of movements advocated by McCarthy and Zald (1973, 1977). Neo-Marxist urbanists also criticize human ecologists for ignoring the significant role of the state, and of power relationships in general, in shaping social space and the fate of particular communities (Castells, 1983; Jaret, 1983). While we touched on some of these theories in our earlier section on Marxist and Weberian conceptualizations of housing movements, here we emphasize the spatial dimension in particular.

Mark Gottdiener (1985:214) calls attention to how power relationships "translate" uneven development into spatial patterns, causing certain communities to exist at the expense of others:

> Such communities are mere enclaves existing in what Lefebvre calls privileged space—a space made possible by the balance of power relations in society, which requires the subjugation elsewhere of the working class...revolutionary transformation requires the extension of new sociospatial relations to the unprivileged spaces...(Gottdiener, 1985:285).

These spatial patterns then provide the potential basis for social movements that challenge the existing power structure. Although the "unprivileged spaces" are often politically passive—or what Herbert Gans (1982) termed "placid villages"—they can, under certain circumstances, become the objects of successful social movement organizing (Castells, 1983), or "insurgency spaces" (Evans and Boyte, 1982).

Neo-Marxist urbanists point out that in order to be profitable capital must remain in motion and investments must be incessantly turned over in search of new outlets in order to generate "almost infinite exchange value possibilities" (Gottdiener, 1985:188; Harvey, 1973). This logically requires the constant "commodification" of space and an emphasis on economic exchange value over use value (Cox, 1981:431). To render it profitable, living space must be broken up, leveled, or "pulverized" into abstract space (Harvey, 1985; Tabb and Sawers, 1978; Friedmann, 1981; Bluestone and Harrison, 1982). In the process, "community" is transformed into "commodity," and life space is transformed into space that is for sale to the highest bidder. Because this type of investment is always attractive, a fixed urban landscape is impossible; the built environment freezes capital, and thus must be constantly reconstructed into a consumption artifact (Harvey, 1985).

Gottdiener (1985) has charged that neo-Marxist political economists reduce the phenomenon of social space, which is also cultural and political, to economic dimensions alone. A truly radical practice, he argues, must concern itself with seizing space and promoting a transformation to community self-management. He gives credit to environmentalists for establishing a successful and radical tradition of "transformational interventions in space" (Gottdiener, 1985:155). Such efforts challenge the cultural ideology of growth that fuels the transformation of community landscapes and is supported by a range of groups, including portions of the working class and labor unions. Indeed, according to Gottdiener (1985:222):

> The clash between growth and no-growth represents a basic cleavage in society involving economic, political and ideological practices, and remains unrecognized by most analysts of urban development. It is as fundamental to the production of space as the struggle between capital and labor.

Thus, the growth ideology is viewed as a crucial point of intersection between various shifting interests participating in the negotiation of power over the definition of social space. The "capitalist class" is not viewed as monolithic and all-powerful, nor is the working class necessarily uniformly opposed to it on issues of growth. Increasingly, housing is recognized as holding a pivotal position in this debate (Gottdiener, 1985; Protash and Baldassare, 1983; Pickvance, 1985).

### Theoretical Implications for Tenants' Movements

An emphasis on the dynamics of urban space calls attention to the social processes operating there and to the power of different social groups to define that space. Low- and moderate-income populations, and tenants in particular, find themselves trapped by this process. Tenants find themselves locked in a contest for shelter rights as they make an effort to reclaim community space for their own use as "life space" rather than as "abstract urban space" that is for sale to the highest bidder (Cox, 1981; Bluestone and Harrison, 1982). In contemporary urban politics, no question is more significant than the following: To what degree should urban places be "commodity"? to what degree "community"? Because of their need to claim living space in areas controlled economically by others, tenants' movements represent a crucial effort to work out the answer to this question.

The implications of the social construction of space perspective extend beyond tenants' movements to urban social movements in general. Significant tensions are created as urban space is contested (Castells, 1983). Some of these arise strictly out of a consumer perspective; as Cox (1981) has noted, if consumers take their consumption seriously, they will begin to oppose growth and development as it infringes on their property values. Developers, on the other hand, build projects that interfere with each other's profitability. These tensions are not played out strictly along class lines, but cut across them, forming new alliances that are increasingly common in urban politics. This line of argument is consonant with that of NSM theorists and Boyte et al. (1986), cited above. Growth issues are therefore open to constant negotiation among the groups that bear the burdens of growth (Gottdiener, 1985:227). These shifting networks and cross-class alliances offer new possibilities for the study of urban social movements, including those focused on tenants' rights.

## Conclusion

In this chapter, we have offered an overview of sociological theories that have a bearing on tenants' movements. We examined, in sequence, Marxist and Weberian theories about tenant "consciousness," the resource mobilization perspective, social-psychological and interactional critiques of resource mobilization, new social movements and new populism theory, symbolic framing approaches, and, finally, a social production of space perspective.

Each theory offers suggestions or propositions regarding the emergence of tenants' social movements. Ecological as well as structuralist Marxist theories suggest that structural variables such as size, demographic characteristics, or high rents give rise to social movements. The arguments of Engels support the thesis that home ownership will influence political behavior in a conservative direction and that urban social movements cannot achieve genuinely progressive goals. Some neo-Marxist as well as Weberian theorists call attention to specific social alignments and circumstances that may hinder or facilitate urban social movements, suggesting a more optimistic view of tenants' movements and social change. To these theorists, the implications of tenant "consciousness" and urban social movements are more circumstantial than deterministic. The social production of space approach suggests that social movements in urban settings emerge in response to a symbolic contest (driven by economic power alignments) over the definition of space as "community" versus "commodity." Resource mobilization theory suggests that social movements arise not in response to structural conditions or grievances, but rather through mobilization opportunities offered by particular organizations and linked to material resources, leadership skills, generational experiences, and strategic repertoires. Social-psychological and interactional approaches emphasize cognitive definitions of the situation as they arise in a group context, linking movements to changes in collective definitions of the situation. New social movements theory connects the emergence of social movements to broad structural changes inherent in postindustrial societies, among which is the desire of individuals and groups symbolically to control the "self-production" of their identity. New populism theory looks to the emergence of challenging repertoires out of traditional settings that function as "free spaces" where democratic interaction can take place. "Framing" approaches connect the emergence of social movements to particular interpretive and micromobilization tasks that social movement organizations engage in to gain adherents.

Each theory not only makes suggestions about social movements, but also implies a different method and point of focus for capturing the reality of movements—the organization, the social interactional processes, the construction of ideologies and symbolic attribution.

In the next two chapters, we will examine the usefulness of these theoretical implications empirically, using data on tenants' movements in the United States. We will offer a case study of a strong tenants' movement in the city of Santa Monica that draws on the theoretical interpretations offered in this chapter. We will then contrast the case of Santa Monica with evidence from Houston, and we will try to understand where tenants' movements have been successful more generally. We will conclude by drawing out implications of our findings for urban settings and urban social movements theory.

# II

# A Case Study
# of a Tenant Movement:
# Santa Monica

# 3

# A Case Study
# of Santa Monica's
# Progressive Movement

Santa Monica provides rich material for a case study at the intersection of urban social history and movements for social change in a capitalist society. Twice it became a national symbol of the debate over free enterprise versus regulation—first in 1979, when tenants won a strict rent-control law, and again in 1981, when progressive tenant-supported candidates were elected to a majority in city hall. Adding to the drama was the fact that the progressive grass-roots organization, Santa Monicans for Renters' Rights (SMRR), swept city hall after being vastly outspent by its well-funded opposition. Just as progressive groups nationwide cheered the efforts of SMRR, so national real estate industry groups poured money into the city to defeat rent control and its representatives. SMRR's opponents labeled the city "The People's Republic of Santa Monica."

Santa Monica offers an excellent opportunity to study the ongoing dynamics of social movements. It provides an avenue for grounding and examining in detail social movement theories as they apply to a tenants' movement observed over time. It also offers an opportunity to generalize about urban social movements as we contrast the Santa Monica scenario with that of Houston. Moreover, it permits insights into the culture within which social movements succeed or fail. A culture shaped by the values of private enterprise interlocking with the values of democracy presents fundamental tensions. How are the rights of property owners to be balanced against those who do not own property? Are landlords entitled to reasonable or unlimited profits? The issue of regulation has always been volatile in the United States, and has the power to summon up an enormous repertoire of contested cultural symbols. Social movements maneuver among these symbols and in some cases help to construct them. As a case study, Santa Monica is a microcosm of the national debate over the appropriate combination of democracy and free enterprise. The experience of tenants as a social group is particularly significant for this debate; as non-property owners in a property owners' world, and therefore "second-class citizens," they are a kind of test case for the moral and political belief system in the United States.

In Chapter 2, we noted that Sara Evans and Harry Boyte (1986) suggested that the *process* of social transformation is best captured through concrete, particular stories as they evolve over time. In this chapter, we follow their reasoning by allowing some of the key actors related to the tenants' movement to tell their stories. We preface this by looking at some of the sources of structural strain in Santa Monica prior to the tenants' movement, in particular at the tension between the definition of the city as "community" and the city as "commodity." Apart from capturing the story of the movement, we include a discussion of two important themes relating to progressive movements: the tension between "people power" and technology, and the role of particular political generations in shaping movement strategies. We supplement our qualitative methodology by presenting the results of our quantitative analysis of variables that play a role in the support of rent control. In doing so, we place the Santa Monica scenario in a broader, national context and use triangulation to explore the consistency of our findings (Babbie, 1988:99).

## Santa Monica: Community or Commodity?

A quick glance at Santa Monica's history reveals that, like most cities in the United States, Santa Monica was first a business proposition, or commodity, and only subsequently a community. We found that the community versus commodity theme surfaced frequently as a focal point of tension between social groups in Santa Monica. Should the city be defined as space for rooted community life, or should it be defined as abstract investment space (Appelbaum, 1978; Appelbaum et al., 1976; Dreier et al., 1980; Logan and Molotch, 1987; Feagin, 1983, 1988)? When, in the late 1970s and early 1980s, a fledgling social movement in Santa Monica began to challenge the growth-oriented "commodity" model in the interests of "community," this represented a revival of old tensions rather than a historical break with the past (Čapek, 1985).

Although its settlement dates considerably further back, Santa Monica found its way into U.S. urban history in 1875, when two entrepreneurs, Senator John P. Jones and Colonel Robert S. Baker, laid out plots of land for public auction. Baker, an Easterner, purchased the 38,409-acre Rancho San Vicente y Santa Monica from Don Jose de Carmen Sepulveda and other members of the Sepulveda family in 1872. This purchase fits a broader social pattern operating in southern California in the 1870s, as ranch property under Mexican family ownership was purchased by speculators who turned enormous profits by subdividing the land. As Ricardo Romo (1983) has noted, droughts and floods, high taxation of cattle, and a falling demand for cattle after the height of the 1848 gold rush led to hardships that facilitated the cheap purchase of the land from its owners. Likewise, the selling of land as prospective harbor property was a common money-making strategy in the 1885–87 regional real estate boom (Romo, 1983:28).

While both Jones and Baker acquired their wealth through their connections with the mining industry, Jones was also a railway entrepreneur whose vision was to construct a transcontinental railway that would terminate at the projected major port of Santa Monica (Crump, 1962:43). One of the earliest battles for Santa Monica's identity concerned whether or not it would become the principal port for Los Angeles over the rival city of San Pedro. Railway interests controlled most of the seaside land at Santa Monica, and in the political battle that ensued over federal funding for the port, Santa Monica lost the contest (Crump, 1962:32).

The episode thematically foreshadowed future battles over Santa Monica's identity and unmistakably demonstrated two things: the extent to which the town itself figured as an investment commodity and the significance of the role of outside forces in determining its fate (Čapek, 1985). Commitment by successive administrations to boosterism and an urban growth model involved the city in the boom-and-bust cycle typical of capitalism (Feagin, 1983). Residents who were concerned to make a community out of Santa Monica were fully aware of their vulnerability; when, in the 1880s, Southern Pacific Railways abandoned the city wharf as unsafe and put an end to maritime commerce there, many residents blamed the railroad companies directly for the ensuing depression (Storrs, 1974:11). A century later, the tenants' movement revived the terms of the same debate: Should a city be foremost a community or a commodity?

While Santa Monica is a unique, and in many ways a privileged, community, its urban history shares important elements with other cities around the United States. Like all cities, its features have been shaped by powerful social actors committed to a particular set of interests and definitions of what a city should be. Until 1981, these actors were almost invariably drawn from the business, banking, and real estate communities. While they did not always agree with each other, and while political alignments and administrative arrangements periodically shifted, there was relative consensus around one belief: that growth would provide the best strategy for developing the city of Santa Monica. Much of the city's present fate—including the progressive social movement that developed there—is connected to its past history as it was shaped by the urban growth model.

The urban growth model is supported by the ideology that growth is best for cities. Growth is associated with a free-market model that argues for a trickle-down theory of wealth. It suggests that the surest path to wealth and prosperity for all is a business climate unfettered by regulation. Critics of the growth model, on the other hand, have pointed to new social problems spawned by a nonregulatory climate: segregation by race and income, uneven development resulting from profit-oriented investment decisions, and an increasing burden of social costs such as traffic and pollution, higher housing costs, and increased crime (Appelbaum, 1978). Commitment to the growth model has been critical to the development of Santa Monica.

As was the case in many other U.S. cities, Santa Monica's early history was closely linked to railroads. The city became increasingly accessible as a popular resort town when, in 1896, an interurban trolley system known as the "Big Red Cars" connected it to other areas in the Los Angeles region and expanded the volume of business in the city (Crump, 1962). Railroad investments also had implications for the growth of a minority community in the city. The interurban railroads recruited Mexican laborers for construction work, many of whom stayed in the area:

> In Santa Monica, a community promoted as a resort paradise, a labor camp at the outskirts of the town kept the rail line operating from that location to downtown....As the communities around the labor camps grew, small oases of Mexican residents became surrounded by suburban residents of a different class and nationality (Romo, 1983:69).

Hence, stratification by income and neighborhood began early in the city's history, leading to symbolically separate communities side by side.

A consistent pattern was the targeting of low-income communities for speculative development. Because they were not politically or economically powerful, they were more "placid" targets for such activities (Gans, 1982). Snapshot views of city politics in various eras consistently reveal this process. In 1929, developers made incursions into a moderate-income beachfront community by supporting a city ordinance vastly increasing zoning for apartment construction. They sought to replace the typical and inexpensive wooden beachfront bungalows with higher density apartments to serve seasonal tourists rather than local residents. In the 1960s, elderly residents of the Ocean Park neighborhood were displaced to make way for an urban renewal project. At the same time, a freeway was built through the heart of the minority Pico neighborhood, scattering its largely black residents by destroying affordable housing (see below). In all cases, residents of the lower-income neighborhoods lacked de facto representation in city government. More affluent homeowner neighborhoods staved off zoning that would have raised density or altered the "single-family home" definition of their neighborhoods. It appeared that the right to call one's living place a community rather than a commodity was a politically and economically stratified right, differentially available according to neighborhood (Čapek, 1985). Although at the time they occurred without much visible protest, the Ocean Park and Pico neighborhood episodes later provided powerful evidence in support of the tenant movement's case for social justice in the community for low- and moderate-income residents.

In the intervening decades between the depression and the 1980s, Santa Monica evolved from a popular resort and retirement town to a bedroom community linked directly to downtown Los Angeles. During World War II, it hosted the home plant for Douglas Aircraft, which at its peak employed forty thousand defense workers; this and related industries not only provided jobs, but also contributed to greater pressures on land use, which left the city with a legacy of housing problems. Concerted efforts were made to rezone the city for even higher-density dwellings, with particular emphasis on the construction of apartments. A series of political and economic decisions made by a succession of city councils eventually had the effect of creating an almost 80 percent tenant population by the late 1970s. Although the city experienced changes from a commissioner to a city manager form of government, the commitment to the urban growth model remained constant. During the 1960s and 1970s, ten- to fifteen-story apartments and condominiums began to be built along the shore. Santa Monica was well on its way to becoming the Miami Beach of the California coast. The potentially negative effects of the patterns this encouraged were neither evident nor subject to public debate.

### City Spaces as Free Spaces: Ocean Park and Pico Neighborhoods

We noted above that public reaction to the city's urban renewal efforts in the Ocean Park and Pico neighborhoods eventually fed into a culture of opposition to the "free-market" policies of the city. In fact, as the tenants' movement began to emerge in the later 1970s, these neighborhoods themselves helped to create a new kind of spatial politics in the city that permanently altered its political complexion. Both evolved institutions that began to function as classic examples of "free spaces" (Evans and Boyte, 1986). We begin, therefore, by taking a careful look at their social histories.

Like other major cities in the United States, Santa Monica was affected by the Federal Housing Act of 1949, which laid the foundation for "urban renewal" (Friedland, 1982; Hartman, 1984; Hartman et al., 1981). In Santa Monica, a community redevelopment agency selected the beachfront neighborhood called Ocean Park as the target area for demolition and redevelopment. Ocean Park consisted of former summer homes crowded onto narrow lots that were inexpensive for retirement. Its population was a stable and lively community largely made up of elderly Jewish residents. The neighborhood served as a haven for low- and moderate-income groups and tended to be politically bypassed. The business community that shaped the city's policy, however, felt that this area was "ramshackle" and blighted, a poor investment for the city compared to its potential for generating revenue. The fact that it was an oceanfront location served to increase its economic value. Never was the community versus commodity argument more clearly stated. Significantly, none of the individuals deciding Ocean Park's fate actually lived in this neighborhood.

In 1962, approximately 1,400 residential units were cleared on 25 acres. Redevelopment led to the displacement of over 1,501 residents, a significant number for a city of Santa Monica's size. Among them were many who had a long personal and business history in the community.[1] The city's goal was to build high-density housing and commercial structures to increase the economic value of this area. Although assistance was promised to those displaced, as in many other cities the new housing was not affordable for most of them (Hartman 1984; Gans 1982). To compound the bitterness felt by many senior citizens, much of the land lay vacant for fifteen years, and the redevelopment project was still problematic for the city in the 1980s.

A parallel development affected low- and moderate-income black residents of Santa Monica's Pico neighborhood. This neighborhood was similarly defined by city hall as "blighted" and, in this case, as an appropriate site for a proposed freeway to connect Santa Monica directly to downtown Los Angeles. When, in 1965, the Santa Monica Freeway was constructed through the heart of the neighborhood, many families and social networks were broken up. As in Ocean Park, the people displaced had a long history in the city; 40 percent had owned their homes for more than seventeen years (*Santa Monica Seascape,* July/August 1983). As Vivian Linder, a black resident and Pico neighborhood community activist, recalled:

> The freeway was built through the Pico neighborhood, and it broke up so many families. We had a mayor then who had a very poor opinion of those who couldn't afford high rents. . . . With the freeway, people in the Pico neighborhood were not really aware of what the end results would be. Being poor, they had no sources to go to but their clergymen, and they allowed this to just happen. The ministers tried to tell the people, "Don't sell your homes." But when you're poor, things have a way of controlling you instead of you controlling them."[2]

Again, the Pico neighborhood itself had little say in the decisions made about its future in Santa Monica's city hall.

The construction of the freeway led to massive changes in the makeup of Santa Monica—many of them unanticipated. Among the most important was the influx of a new tenant population following a surge in mass-produced apartments. Not only did tenants begin to outnumber homeowners, but the political profile of the city changed (Shearer, 1982a). The traditional Republican constituency of the community gave way to a Democratic base, although the latter was primarily activated in national rather than in local elections. These demographic changes helped to provide a reservoir of support for the rent-control movement in 1978.

The Ocean Park community remained a politically contested neighborhood. Among the white, middle-class tenants who were attracted to Santa Monica—even as substantial numbers of minorities and elderly were being displaced—were students, many with a history of social and political activism in the civil rights, antiwar, and feminist movements, among others. Many were searching both for affordable housing and, equally importantly, for a place to build and participate in a community (Shearer, 1982c). Ocean Park in particular was attractive due to its diversity, its affordability, and its general ambience. Unlike Los Angeles, with its smog and its anonymity, Ocean Park provided a beachfront neighborhood with strong social networks that included an activist church and an alternative community newspaper (see below). It was a prime setting for the emergence of a culture of opposition to city growth policies.

Stirrings of opposition surfaced in the early 1970s. Having witnessed the displacement of the elderly and having felt a general threat to the mixed-income community, some younger Ocean Park activists such as Ruth Galanter and Ernie Powell began to organize around the issue of housing. Through the agency of a Coastal Commission, created in 1972, they made a successful appeal for replacement housing in the redevelopment project. Although the help came too late for some, it was the first significant battle over affordable housing in Santa Monica. As Roger Genser, an Ocean Park resident and activist recalled, "In the sixties this redevelopment project just leveled the entire area. It would have kept going had it not been for community involvement."[3] For many, this was the genesis of a movement that bore its most exciting fruit between 1979 and 1982.

Several other developments in the early and mid-1970s were crucial to the future progressive movement. Opposition to city policies surfaced as rapid growth began to have effects detrimental to the quality of life. A growing regional environmental movement supported these concerns and provided pressure for liberalization of the real estate dominated city council and for zoning to curb developers. A classic incident in the city's history pitted commodity against community by mobilizing a cross-class, nonpartisan opposition. In 1973, City Manager Perry Scott proposed that the historic

Santa Monica Pier be demolished. The complete project would have included the construction of a causeway out to a luxury island to be built in Santa Monica Bay. Led by activists such as Dora Ashford of Ocean Park, residents of various political and socioeconomic backgrounds protested by creating a "Save the Pier" organization.[4] As a surprising volume of protest surfaced, it became clear that not only Ocean Park activists, but much of the city's population cherished the pier as a symbolic community landmark. The pier was saved, and the city council was shown to be increasingly out of step with its constituents.

In Ocean Park, battles took place over voter redistricting in 1974 and over the construction of a new mall, Santa Monica Place, in 1976. The mall was favored by the city council as a "downtown revitalization" project several blocks from the beach. It was opposed by Ocean Park activists because it was environmentally unsound (a glassed-in air-conditioned mall one block from the beach made little sense to environmentalists) and because it would cause inflated real estate prices and drive out current moderate-income residents. A lawsuit over the displacement issue was filed by two women, Lynda Vitale and Sharon Gilpin. As activist Ernie Powell recalled:

> By the mid-seventies a fundamental analysis was reached that there was a systemic problem at city hall based on the city being run for years by developers, real estate interests, and homeowner interests north of Montana [Avenue]. . . . We went on to fight the shopping center. We sued the city. We thought it was a rip-off because it was being subsidized and it would cause traffic and environmental problems.[5]

In the meantime, two other significant events galvanized the activist community in Ocean Park. In 1976, former antiwar activist Tom Hayden, then married to Jane Fonda and residing in Santa Monica, ran as a candidate in the Democratic primary against California Senate incumbent John Tunney on a platform of economic democracy (Carnoy and Shearer, 1980). He lost, but left in place a highly sophisticated campaign organization that became the Campaign for Economic Democracy (CED). The CED functioned as a statewide network of grass-roots organizations that took on local issues such as the environment, rights for farmworkers, voter registration, and, eventually, housing rights (see below). It also provided training for progressive candidates running for office and for activists working on ballot initiatives. From its headquarters in Santa Monica, it served as a focal point for activism, and eventually, its resources would feed into the tenants' movement.

The other noteworthy event occurred in 1977, when local consumer activist Ruth Yannatta—later Ruth Yannatta Goldway, progressive mayor of Santa Monica from 1981 to 1983—ran for the California Assembly. Many activists acquired their mobilizing and campaigning skills while walking precincts and organizing for this election. Although Yannatta did not win, the race energized the progressive community. Among other things, the Yannatta campaign sponsored speakers' forums to educate the community about progressive policies in other cities, including the first public discussion of rent control and tenants' rights. Examples included Derek Shearer on economic democracy; Ed Kirshner on cooperative housing; Paul Soglin, progressive mayor of Madison, Wisconsin; Ken Cockrel, socialist black activist on the Detroit city council; and John Gilderbloom leading the first public discussion of rent control.

The Ocean Park neighborhood served as a focal point for these activities. Its newspaper, the *Ocean Park Perspective,* played a vital role in bringing attention to such issues as gender, housing rights, the environment, community art, the liabilities of unrestrained growth, and consumer rights. The *Perspective* counterbalanced the conservative presence of Santa Monica's "hometown" paper, the *Evening Outlook,* where such issues were not discussed. The Reverend Jim Conn's Church in Ocean Park provided yet another "free space" where a counterculture could flourish (Conn was later elected to the city council as a progressive SMRR candidate and eventually became mayor); the Methodist Church supplied a base of operations where ideas were freely discussed, where community organizing was encouraged, and where the Ocean Park community could resist elite definitions of who they were and instead could formulate their own identity. As it emerged, this identity was strongly tied to the "community" rather than to the "commodity" definition of neighborhood space in Santa Monica.

In the dismembered Pico neighborhood, there was, likewise, opposition to the commodity model foisted on residents by city hall. One of the most vital free spaces was created within the church structure. Although the Pico Neighborhood Association (PNA) was not founded until 1980, efforts to organize the community began in 1978, when Pastor Ellis Casson of the First African Methodist Episcopal Church called a community meeting for those who were concerned about neighborhood problems. Organizing people by residential blocks, Casson helped to mobilize the community around the issues they identified as important. It was Casson who first discovered that the Pico neighborhood was receiving less than 2 percent of the money to which it was entitled through Community Development Block Grant (CDBG) funds. The money was being spent on pet projects elsewhere in the city, such as the construction of features related to the Santa Monica mall, a growth project favored by the city council. (In Chapter 6, we take note of similar misallocations of money in Houston.) Casson's organizing began to make the city accountable to the Pico neighborhood for the first time in its history.

Thus, the two neighborhoods—Ocean Park and Pico—that had been most damaged by the "commodity" model of urban space played a major role in reinstituting arguments for "community" and provided not only "free spaces" but also "insurgency spaces" (Evans and Boyte, 1986) where residents could organize around a set of problems as they themselves defined them. The neighborhoods also supported each other; when the PNA was founded in 1980, it was assisted by the Ocean Park Community Organization (OPCO), which had been in existence for one year. The OPCO model, patterned on the block-by-block organizing style first advocated by Saul Alinsky, was in turn used to organize PNA. Thus, both neighborhoods played a pivotal role in constructing a new "story" of the city that included its less-advantaged residents. Beginning with the later 1970s, tenants would become the most prominent representatives of this category. When they connected their own social history to the experience of these two neighborhoods, a new set of resources was created that provided a support structure for the emerging tenants' movement and that began dramatically to reshape not only political alliances but also the folklore of the city and its overall self-definition as an urban space.

### Responses to the Housing Crisis in Santa Monica (1970–78): Structural Strain

Neil Smelser (1963) has drawn attention to the role of "structural conduciveness" and structural strain as prerequisite to the emergence of collective action. Strains in Santa Monica prior to the tenants' movement are easily documented. As we noted above, city policy toward revitalization and development led to the displacement of the most vulnerable segments of the population and to the attraction of a more affluent category of tenants to fill the structures created by the apartment boom. In the mid-1970s, some additional factors caused affordable housing to disappear nationwide (Gilderbloom and Appelbaum, 1988). In his study of Santa Monica, Allan Heskin (1983:40) substantiated the steep decline in the new construction of multifamily housing units, a vacancy rate dipping below 5 percent, rents increasing faster than the consumer price index (CPI), and "an extraordinary increase in building turnover and speculation," tenfold between 1972 and 1977. Foreign and absentee ownership of apartments rose together with turnover of properties, leading to a dramatic increase in the "velocity" at which investment capital moved through the city (Bluestone and Harrison, 1982; Gilderbloom and Appelbaum, 1988).

Each turnover resulted in higher rents for tenants, for whom there were no safeguards. As a small landlord and supporter of Santa Monicans for Renters' Rights remarked, many of the purchases were made at such inflated prices that by all normal standards they should have been considered "wild" investments and not been eligible for loans. He recalled, however, that when asked about this policy a bank official responded: "If we don't do it, the other bank will."[6] Under these conditions, ordinary restraints were eliminated.

The destruction of affordable housing was both indirect and direct. Not only were rents going up, but apartment construction virtually stopped, replaced by a focus on luxury housing such as the construction of, or conversion to, condominiums. A 1978 Southern California Association of Governments study found that in 1977 in Santa Monica 8,641 out of 46,000 households spent more than 25 percent of their incomes for housing. Of these households, 42.6 percent were elderly or disabled. Over 6,000 housing units were judged as needing rehabilitation or replacement, a majority being rental units. Moreover, a comparative study of local conditions found that between 1970 and 1978 landlords in Santa Monica were increasing their rents more than twice as fast as landlords elsewhere in southern California (Shulman, 1980). Looking back at the situation after the passage of rent control, Santa Monica's Housing Element (1984) found the following:

1. In 1978 and 1979, a total of 1,294 housing units were demolished, a 592 percent increase from the prior two years (the total number of rental housing units in Santa Monica was 34,194 out of 46,418 total housing units in 1980).
2. In 1978 and 1979, over 500 rental housing units were converted to condominiums.
3. In the private sector, expensive condominiums and single-family homes accounted for 85 percent of the new units developed between 1978 and mid-1981.
4. Median rent rose by 125 percent from 1970 to 1980, while median home values rose by 656 percent. This was combined with high interest rates.
5. In 1979, the federal government gave funds for over 17,000 assisted housing units to the Los Angeles Area HUD Office. In 1981, this was cut to 7,900 units, while in 1982, no funds at all were allocated for this purpose.

In 1980, the median household income for Santa Monica was $16,604, lower than the countywide average of $17,551. According to the Santa Monica rent board, this was due to the large percentage of households that were elderly and on fixed incomes (Neighborhood Support Center, 1989). While the real estate industry stubbornly maintained that there was no housing crisis except "in the eye of the beholder," a variety of sources converged to indicate extraordinary structural pressures on the affordable housing market.

The political decisions made during the mid to late 1970s in Santa Monica demonstrated a firm commitment to the free-market model for solving urban problems, housing in particular. Tenants during this period faced a situation in which the city council—openly allied with the real estate industry—was essentially unsympathetic to renters and few legal protections for them existed. The composition of the council, and its economic and symbolic refusal to enact any controls on private property, dramatically raised the level of "structural conduciveness" for a rent-control movement. As the housing market "heated up," the sense of crisis spread.

An initial grass-roots effort to obtain rent control in June 1978 was unsuccessful (we discuss these events in greater detail below). A group of senior citizens gathered signatures to put rent control on the ballot, but it lost locally, while Proposition 13—a statewide tax-cutting measure that was presented as a boon to tenants—won. Howard Jarvis himself, author of Proposition 13, presented tax cuts as the road to lower rents. The small margin of defeat for rent control did encourage tenant activists, however, and the housing crisis became an increasingly mainstream political issue in Santa Monica. Ballot Proposition N, a 1978 effort by the city to use Community Development Block Grant funds to rehabilitate and build affordable housing units, drew support from groups as diverse as the Santa Monica Chamber of Commerce, the Santa Monica Fair Housing Alliance (SMFHA), and the Gray Panthers. As Proposition 13 went into effect and the promised benefits to tenants did not materialize, increasing numbers of people became disaffected with landlords and the real estate industry and questioned the effectiveness of a free-market approach. The city council, however, sought solutions only within a nonregulatory framework and explicitly rejected rent controls.

An interesting problem in the study of social movements is the ability of dominant groups to ignore challenges by outgroups for long periods of time; when the crucial event occurs that finally draws their attention, it is often too late. Santa Monica's city council appears to have slept through a series of such alarms. Not only did Santa Monica's city council hold an unwavering belief in free-market principles, but it was confident that tenants would not vote in significant numbers. The *Evening Outlook* quoted councilmember Seymour Cohen, himself a realtor and landlord, as saying that the council's inaction was a "calculated risk" based on faith in the ability of the free market to alleviate any housing problems.[7] The dominant vote on the city council consistently took this direction. Franco Erspamer, who chaired a committee opposing the 1978 rent-control initiative, responded to the second rent-control effort by saying that its proponents were "like the guy who keeps knocking his head against the wall" (*Evening Outlook,* October 20, 1978). Consistently, the attitude was displayed that tenants could not organize themselves and win.

Proposed solutions to the housing crisis were accordingly mild and ineffective. A braking and neutralizing tendency among some of the city councilmembers prevented the implementation of any meaningful regulatory action. As Frank Hotchkiss, a liberal member of the planning board, recalled:

> In '78, in June, the rent-control initiative failed. The year before I was very concerned at the flood of conversions. Although they make sense—it is a dream in the U.S. to own your own home—I believed they should be paced. I helped to redraft the ordinances to protect the consumer. I was a hero to a lot of the SMRR people. In the fall of '78, a motion was made by Pieter [Van den Steenhoven], Chris [Reed], and Nat Trives for a moderate rent-control proposal. It failed by one vote, John Bambrick's.[8]

In retrospect, all sides recognize that a moderate rent-control measure would have quieted burgeoning tenant activism (Gilderbloom, 1981b). Seen in this light, few moments seem more significant to Santa Monica's future history than Mayor John Bambrick's decision to cast the deciding vote against it. Lest there be any doubt as to who shaped city policy, Bambrick was later quoted as saying, ''I let three friends directly involved in the real estate business talk me out of it.'' He also acknowledged that had he voted differently, ''They would have called me a Marxist'' (*Los Angeles Times,* April 2, 1981).

Given these constraints, the city council—taking a cue from Governor Edmund G. Brown, Jr.—suggested a thirty days' ''jawboning'' effort aimed at convincing landlords to voluntarily give rebates. It also sponsored voluntary mediation. Neither effort had any significant impact on the housing crisis. While this demonstrated concern on the part of some city officials, at the same time it reaffirmed the importance of the progressives' subsequent insistence on electoral politics: One vote in either direction could change a city's policy for years to come. Relying on sheer goodwill of elected officials was clearly ineffective under the circumstances.

One more feeble effort was made in January 1979, when the city council voted in favor of a once-a-year limit on rent increases. However, the amount of the increase was unregulated, leading tenants to scoff at the measure. It was at this time that councilmember Seymour Cohen made his memorable remark to tenants: ''Some people wisely invested in property and I don't condemn them for their actions. Some of you are too lazy to go out and do the same thing'' (*Evening Outlook,* January 24, 1979). His statement captured the essence of the cultural definition of tenants, long customary in the United States, as less responsible, second-class citizens (see Chapter 2). One of the important tasks of the social movement would be to shift the collective definition of tenants away from this image.

As tenant activism grew in intensity, moderate members of the city council continued to be overruled by conservatives. None of this built confidence in the city council's impartiality as a governing body in an atmosphere of crisis. Torn between providing a favorable climate for private business and holding on to legitimacy supplied by voter approval, the council continued to lose credibility. The last straw for the city was a "demolition derby" that took place in March 1979, during which landlords leveled approximately 500 dwelling units in a stampede to beat the threat of regulation (see below) before the second rent-control election. This act boomeranged against landlords as public sympathy for them waned. Citizen outrage spilled beyond the ranks of tenants and flowed into the general community. Dissatisfaction with Proposition 13, the nonresponsiveness of the city council, the ongoing housing crisis, and the entry onto the scene of an expertly organized set of pro-tenant coalition actors led to a dramatic turnaround in the next city election in June 1979, when rent control became a fact of life in Santa Monica. Below, we will explore details of this social movement.

## Building the Movement

"You either have money, or you organize and struggle."—a senior activist[9]

"We have it down to a science."—Dennis Zane (*Los Angeles Times*, August 9, 1979)

The story of rent control begins outside of Santa Monica itself. Cary Lowe, who was to become one of California's foremost tenant activists in the late 1970s, was at a turning point in his career in 1976. He recalls that

By coincidence, Tom Hayden had just finished his unsuccessful campaign for U.S. Senate. Hayden and his main policy adviser wanted to rework the campaign apparatus into an ongoing organization and to set up a technical support entity. It so happened that there was a "shell" entity, the California Public Policy Center, which had been incorporated a few years before by Derek Shearer, but was not used significantly except to put on conferences. Hayden was able to take over a ready-made entity with nonprofit status.[10]

Lowe helped to set up the California Public Policy Center in a downtown Los Angeles office and began to work at creating a link to California progressive activists. He recalls that at the time there was no statewide tenants' organization in California, merely loose, occasional activity. But 1976 was in many ways to be a significant year for tenants.

Despite the absence of a statewide movement, there were certain "hot spots" of tenant activism in California. Among these was Berkeley, a highly politicized university town with a legacy of radical and progressive organizing that included the passage of rent control in 1972. In response to landlord challenges, a legal decision (*Birkenfeld vs. City of Berkeley*) handed down in 1976 found Berkeley's rent-control law confiscatory and therefore unconstitutional. Nevertheless, the state supreme court did not find the *concept* of rent control unconstitutional. The court found that, if local communities could work out a nonconfiscatory formula, rent control was a viable option. Landlords rightly saw this as a door left open to tenant activism. The *Birkenfeld* decision was one of the first enabling actions that made the Santa Monica movement possible at a future date.

Spurred on by this legal decision, landlords moved quickly at the statewide level to head off the organizing potential of the rent-control issue. In the summer of 1976, one of their organizations, the California Housing Council (affiliated with the National Housing Council, now the National Multi-family Housing Council) sponsored a legislative effort directed at preempting local rent control. Lowe recalls that there was some irony in this: "It's funny, they were way ahead of tenants, the revolt didn't exist." In fact, the major tenant mobilization and organizational solidification came as tenants took their cue from the landlords' statewide offensive. In a reversal of the usual sequence, the landlords' "countermovement" called into being the "movement" to which it believed it was responding, providing a classic illustration of the self-fulfilling prophecy (Merton, 1968).

The landlord mobilization set off a chain of events in the summer of 1976 that occurred in quick succession. As Lowe remembers,

> It [the landlord anti-rent-control effort] started to become controversial when the State Department of Housing got wind of it. They hired John Gilderbloom, at that time a graduate student at UC Santa Barbara, to do an analysis of rent control. In retrospect it was done in record time, and it became the *key* technical document for tenants. Tenant groups began to get involved, galvanized. I got involved as the L.A. coordinator of that effort around July, August, 1976. . . .Eventually, we were successful, and Jerry Brown vetoed the bill at eight minutes to midnight. *If that bill had become law, none of this would have happened.* The landlords were brilliant, but it really makes you aware of human foibles in history. So an opportunity was left in existence. . . . Then everybody "breathed a collective sigh of relief"—"Wow, did we just nearly get killed! We can't let it happen again."[11]

With the anti-rent-control bill defeated, activists decided to organize the California Housing Action and Information Network (CHAIN), the first statewide tenants' organization. A meeting was called by John Gilderbloom at the home of Myron Moskovitz, a well-known lawyer and tenant activist. According to Lowe:

> We agreed to have a founding convention in L.A. in January 1977 to try to pull together a statewide organization. We got a big meeting room at the People's College of Law. It was quite astonishing. We had about a thousand during the course of the day, nearly half from outside of L.A. One guy came down from northern California, seven hundred miles, hitchhiked. All were involved with tenants' groups from all over. . . . So we had the convention. It was semichaotic, but we all agreed to have an organization and put together a board. I had a base, the Policy Center, and some money. I was asked to be the statewide coordinator, and I also was a staff person. The next month was the CED founding convention in Santa Barbara. There were a lot of the same people. For the next two years, CED and CHAIN thrived. We got money, hired organizers, we had twelve paid organizers, we were able to get VISTA slots, foundation grants. You couldn't do it *now,* the money, the organizers. It was truly a confluence of people and opportunity in 1977.[12]

The above-mentioned account provides evidence that events in Santa Monica were linked to a broader nationwide and historical process that provided "chains of opportunity" as well as stumbling blocks for the local movement (Wilson and Orum, 1976). Not only were many community activists carrying a personal history of involvements in other movements (see below), but at certain points, critical decisions were made elsewhere that enabled, rather than prevented, a future rent-control movement in Santa Monica. Lowe's recollection, corroborated by other activists, reveals the emergence out of somewhat haphazard beginnings of a systematic collection of resources such as organization, networks, material arrangements, and technical skills. It is important to note the national climate of support for local organizing that existed during the Carter administration (Perlman, 1979; Delgado, 1986; Piven and Cloward, 1979), including funded resources through VISTA, Legal Services, and the Community Services Administration, among others (Dreier, 1982:191). In California, some overlap between the CED and CHAIN organizations contributed to a resource base.

Skills of tenant organizers included learning how to produce a big public impression on a small budget. As Cary Lowe recalled:

> It was phenomenal because tenant groups were not nearly as together as people thought they were. When you do that kind of work you learn— like guerrilla warfare, you create an illusion of numbers. It doesn't take

much to create a presence, say, a press conference of three. There was a lot of smoke and mirrors.[13]

Lowe qualified this, however, by noting that this was not so much the case in Santa Monica, where there was a more solid organizational base, including CED, labor, and seniors' groups. The rent-control cause was also aided by other cost-cutting factors such as government phone lines and mailing lists. This facilitated the creation of a network at little cost to the participants, who were not wealthy individuals and had far less money at their disposal than organized real estate groups.

Initially, Santa Monica was not linked to these statewide activities and came later to the rent-control issue than had a number of other cities. In the early 1970s, it struggled with its own private problems, which included displacement of the elderly. The crucial link to statewide and national efforts was made when Syd Rose, a Santa Monica housing commissioner, read about Cary Lowe and the CHAIN organization in the newspaper. Struck by the similarity between tenants' problems in Santa Monica and those experienced statewide, Rose telephoned Lowe, who recalled:

In 1977, I was approached by Syd Rose—and this was the real genesis of the Santa Monica rent-control movement—Syd Rose was a retired labor arbitrator, a homeowner, a humanitarian. He had lived in New York and knew rent control in the East. He saw my name in the paper and called me out of the blue. I didn't know him. My only interest in Santa Monica was that it was the headquarters of the Hayden campaign, and CED was now functioning. . . so this guy Syd Rose calls me up, tells me he wants to do something. We met at a Legal Aid office in downtown L.A. He said, "I know you're involved with a tenants' organization. Santa Monica would be a good place to do some work." I agreed.[14]

The contact between Syd Rose and CHAIN provided the possibility for linking a range of resources already developed at a statewide level to Santa Monica, nourishing a progressive network. The fit was a good one; it was a conscious strategy of CHAIN to encourage local organizing, and its help was welcome among tenants in Santa Monica, many of whom were not accustomed to working with housing issues.

Here, the story shifts to Santa Monica itself.

## The First Rent-Control Campaign

From an organizational perspective, to tell the story of the progressive tenants' movement in Santa Monica is to document how a range of groups in the city came together to construct one credible organization, Santa Monicans for Renters' Rights. In view of their later unity, it is remarkable to note how ignorant they were of each other's work in the early days of the movement. The manner in which younger activists chose to join with senior citizens had important implications for the organizational resources of the movement. The groups were distinct generationally and in terms of goals, techniques, and experience (see below). Interest in rent control as a concept initially was not high. When John Gilderbloom was invited by the progressives to give the first public forum about rent control in the basement of the Church in Ocean Park, he was one of only four people present (two were senior citizens who later became involved in the tenants' movement and the last was Ruth Yannatta Goldway, who would later be elected mayor by the progressives). Thus, the bringing together of the groups and the rent-control issue is a social fact that remains to be explained.

Syd Rose and the Seniors

One of the most crucial and yet elusive figures on the scene was Syd Rose, the man who led a group of activist senior citizens in a successful attempt to get rent control placed on the ballot in 1978. Serving as Santa Monica housing commissioner from 1976 to 1980, Rose was a controversial figure. Gruff and autocratic, he was at the same time tenacious and utterly dedicated to the rent-control issue. As suddenly as he appeared on the scene in 1977, he vanished from it in late 1978 during the second, electorally successful, rent-control campaign.

Through the recollections of early movement activists, Syd Rose—who died in 1983—emerges as somewhat a loner, enjoying a love-hate relationship with the people who worked with him. Yet all agree that if the credit must go to one person for "starting something big" in Santa Monica, it must go to Rose:

> He was the sort of man that one would not soon forget. He was single-minded, and he was a cantankerous old fuddy-dud sometimes, but he began something that, when everyone else didn't begin it, or backed out of it, he stuck to it, and now a lot of people are taking credit.[15]

In his capacity as a housing commissioner in 1976, Rose began to learn about the high rents and the housing crisis in Santa Monica, which particularly threatened senior citizens. He quickly encountered the city's foot-dragging on this issue and committed himself to creating a public forum for it:

> He then created his own commission and began to hold public hearings. He took testimony from person after person. He was a labor arbitrator.

He was used to dealing with people in a civilized way, but on this issue he found that he couldn't deal with anybody else on the other side in a civilized way. They had no reason to.[16]

As a result of the city council's unwillingness to become involved in housing regulation, Rose turned to other sources. According to Cary Lowe of CHAIN:

He started talking mainly to seniors and some labor groups. I talked to the Santa Monica CED, which had no previous background with this issue, but conceptually agreed with it. Some others were pulled in too. Our first meeting at Syd Rose's house was the first coming together of a potential coalition of interest groups. We were awkward and uncertain, but motivated.[17]

A crucial contact was made with Robert Myers, a staff attorney at Legal Aid in Venice (later city attorney of Santa Monica under the progressive administration). It was Myers who authored the rent-control charter amendment in 1978 at the request of Syd Rose and a group of senior citizens organized by Rose. This group—a large percentage of whom were women—took the name Santa Monica Committee for Fair Rents (SMCFR). Through their efforts, they collected enough signatures to put the rent-control issue on the ballot in 1978. Senior tenant activists David and Dorothy Merken reminisced about these early days of the movement:

The tenants were afraid, and it so happened that Syd Rose was around. He was mixed up in labor and housing. He got people together and decided to write up something. We had meetings in the garage; we didn't want it to be known, because we felt it would stir up the landlords and speculators and he would have trouble. There were about fifteen of us at most. A few of us were on the board, and each would speak to other groups, hand out brochures at markets. When we said there would be a meeting at Santa Monica High School it was *packed*. We collected money, signed up people for membership.[18]

Although the later involvement by younger groups tended to overshadow the fact, senior citizens played a key role in beginning the rent-control movement in Santa Monica. As younger activist Cheryl Rhoden—later a SMRR city councilmember—noted, ''Here it's not an issue just of their participation; they *started* the whole thing; they were the backbone.''[19] Those who participated were far from the stereotype of the frail, elderly person; the movement's folklore was enriched by stories about individuals such as Ida Singer, a hard-working volunteer in her nineties who refused to budge from an office while the building's landlord made illegal alterations and tore down walls around her. Despite the spirited organizing by senior citizens, however, many younger activists in Santa Monica were ignorant of their activities.

### The Santa Monica Fair Housing Alliance and the CED

Moe Stavnezer, one of the younger activists involved in the early phase of the tenants' movement and at that time a CED member, recalled that his acquaintances were vaguely aware that the seniors were doing something relating to rent control, but the groups did not know each other at the time. The only group that had organizationally joined with the senior citizens was the Save the Pier group in 1973 (see above). Since then, younger and older activists had pursued separate routes. Now, suddenly, there were hints of a major senior campaign:

> Sometime around the beginning of 1977 all the other activists in the world in Santa Monica were rallying behind Ruth Yannatta's Assembly campaign. . . . Rumors filtered out about the rent-control thing. To give you some idea, the first I ever heard of it—Jim Conn [Ocean Park minister and future SMRR city councilmember] went over to talk to Syd and couldn't get along with him at all. The same thing happened with Ruth. No one paid a lot of attention. The whole liberal group, the young ones and some of the old ones, worked on Ruth's campaign, with the exception of a small group of seniors. One or two younger people attended their meetings, but we didn't know them yet. We didn't really, until after the election.[20]

There was curiosity, but some hesitation about joining the seniors. As Stavnezer wryly admitted, "Because of who was involved, we weren't familiar with the activists. So—[he laughs] how could it be worth anything? We hesitated."

On the other hand, when "things were really slow and people were really dejected" in the aftermath of the Yannatta campaign, a number of committed progressives actively began to search for grass-roots organizing issues.[21] Many of them belonged to the local CED organization, which was committed to ongoing mobilizing efforts. Among them was Parke Skelton, a tenant activist who was to play a key role in orchestrating and running the rent-control campaigns in Santa Monica. Skelton recalls that the significance of the housing issue was accidentally discovered during the Yannatta campaign:

> During the campaign, doing a lot of precinct walking and work in Santa Monica, we definitely found that the hot issue was housing cost and rent control. We knew that there were groups of senior citizens in Santa

Monica that were going to be involved in drafting an initiative. At that time we really didn't know any of them and we didn't know Bob Myers, who was drafting the initiative with Syd Rose, but it sounded like a good idea to us and like something we wanted to get involved in.[22]

Not only was housing a hot issue, but it had other virtues from the point of view of symbolically mobilizing a constituency. As Dennis Zane—CED member and future SMRR city councilmember and mayor—pointed out, although rent control is a ''pocketbook'' issue to many, it has ideological content and is therefore cohesion-creating in ways that other issues are not. By pointing up shared injustices, it counterbalanced the individualistic bias in U.S. culture. In 1978 and 1979, it served as an avenue for bringing together abstract urban problems and a social movement geared toward housing. To progressive activists, therefore, rent control was not merely an economic issue; it was also an ideological issue related to notions of justice and fair play. Parke Skelton remembered that:

There was a real consensus in the [CED] chapter that some type of political work in Santa Monica would be good, although virtually none of the CED people lived in Santa Monica. There were maybe thirty-five or forty people active in the chapter in some way or another, and I think only six of them lived in Santa Monica. Denny and I were heading up the political work, and both of us lived in Venice.[23]

While this does not imply that younger activists did not have serious problems as tenants—they did, and many of them were first politicized by their personal experiences with landlords—housing was one of many ''justice'' issues that they were willing to take up. There was a consciously rational and calculating element in the choice of Santa Monica as a viable target for social change. According to Skelton, Santa Monica was chosen

Because it was a definable political entity that had a potential progressive voting pattern in municipal elections if turnout was increased. And there was a real overriding issue there, and some people were starting to work on the issue.[24]

These accounts reveal the importance of the Campaign for Economic Democracy as a local force in the future tenants' movement. As we noted above, a significant number of younger activists had become involved in Santa Monica community issues and electoral politics through participation in Tom Hayden's Senate campaign and subsequently in CED, the abiding legacy of the campaign. Although headquartered in Santa Monica, CED was a statewide, but local issues-oriented organization. Its stated goal was to "build an organization that has many layers of participation that works around bread-and-butter issues" and to "build a social movement in the state" (*Los Angeles Times,* September 7, 1979). This was to have important resource implications for the emerging progressive movement. A CED member, reflecting in 1984 on CED's evolving role in local progressive politics, noted:

> This is where Hayden's state headquarters was based. A lot of people that came out of that campaign originally became the Westside [CED] chapter. People got into electoral politics in a hard way. Because of the electoral history, Ruth's [Yannatta] and Tom's campaigns, it wasn't purposely calculated, just certain people took the initiative. Some people gained expertise that a lot of chapters don't have. And we're in an area where it's winnable. CED ended up being the most vital group [in the progressive coalition] because its people are a little more free to put in full time on the campaign. As a result of all that, almost all of the paid staff positions on the campaign are from the chapter.[25]

For many reasons, then, CED activists were "biographically available" for social change actions (McAdam, 1986:70). Despite its later crucial role in the tenants' movement, however, it is important to note that the CED organization was not officially involved in supporting the first rent-control campaign in 1978. This is a critical issue because many conservative opponents of the tenants' movement in Santa Monica later claimed that the entire movement was a façade that concealed a power grab by Tom Hayden and CED. Documentary evidence reveals quite the opposite—CED was reluctant to become involved in housing issues. CED's initial reticence can be explained by a number of factors. Its operating philosophy at that time—particularly after the intense outpouring of energy into the losing Hayden and Yannatta campaigns—was to enter only into contests that seemed "winnable." Also, rent control had just been defeated in Berkeley, and its future as a strategy was unclear. Finally, CED was focusing on a statewide push for solar energy use (the SolarCal campaign). Despite CED's major role later in the movement, its early abdication left it, in the opinion of some observers, with "egg on their face."[26]

Some individual members of CED, on the other hand, were far ahead of others in recognizing Santa Monica's potential as a model target community with an electorate whose majority was, to use William Gamson's (1975) term, a "privileged group" with a strong interest in rent control. The 80 percent tenant constituency would prove to be one of the most important resources for the rent-control movement (see below). When they could not find an outlet their activism within CED, individuals acting on their own initiative became key players in the tenants' movement. Following the loss of the Yannatta campaign, and generally unaware of the seniors, a number of such individuals, including Parke Skelton and Dennis Zane, looked for viable community issues to work on.

The conflicting agendas of individual CED members and the organization as a whole led to some stress. As Skelton recalled:

After the Yannatta for Assembly campaign, Denny [Dennis Zane] and I formed the Housing Committee in the Westside CED chapter. We started meeting with Syd and tried to figure out how we could get involved in the campaign, what kind of work we could do. He was real happy to have some younger people with more energy, maybe, interested in getting involved, but he was very, very cautious about CED being involved in it in any way, shape, or form. There were months of debates that went back and forth between Syd and within the Committee for Fair Rents [SMCFR], which was Syd's group. And inside of CED about whether we wanted to get involved when they clearly didn't want CED participation in it except in a kind of under the table kind of fashion.... They were more conservative and understood—rightly—that CED involvement would subject the campaign to a form of red-baiting.[27]

Moe Stavnezer similarly recalled:

At the time, there was a very activist committee in CED, the Housing Committee. We debated a long time over housing. Denny Zane and I became the official representatives from CED—we half volunteered and half were chosen to attend Syd's meetings. He ran the meetings with an iron fist, insisted on doing everything his way. He was terribly suspicious of us and rejected sharing power. At the end of the summer, we recommended that we join and participate in the rent campaign. This led to a really bad split in CED. The chapter voted after the end of the summer to support rent control, but we couldn't get them to *do* anything. We had a showdown meeting, and I felt, and some others felt, that people from the L.A. headquarters, at the behest of Hayden, came to the meeting and voted not to support rent control. Their pitch was for redistricting, despite the fact that it had lost and no one else cared about it. Steam had really built up by then; they [the seniors] were out with petitions; it was a movement.[28]

Younger activists had at least two main objections to Syd Rose's group. The first was their judgment that Rose did not know how to put together effectively a campaign organization. Second, he had an authoritarian style and was not willing to share power or to have any democratic input. Some of the younger activists felt frustrated, having a different vision of how to build an organization.[29] At the same time, CED could not be prevailed on to support overtly and to contribute resources to rent control. In response, about eight or nine key activists came together in Cheryl Rhoden's Ocean Park living room to form the Santa Monica Fair Housing Alliance toward the end of 1977:

> Probably to a person the Housing Committee left [CED], but we didn't know what to do, because we didn't want to be part of Syd's group. First informally, then formally, a group met together and formed the Santa Monica Fair Housing Alliance. Eventually, we persuaded Syd to let us use his garage—complete with chemical toilet—as our headquarters for the campaign. It was not an easy relationship. We were doing the work, but it was always tenuous. There were screaming arguments. Thank God he worked a lot![30]

Organizationally, the younger activists were able to attach themselves to a set of resources that sprang up "while they weren't looking." For those who were frustrated with CED's unwillingness to become involved in a rent-control campaign, and with Syd Rose's autocratic tendencies, SMFHA was a viable organizational solution. SMFHA worked with, but not under, Syd Rose. In a move to lend credibility to the organization, consumer activist Ruth Yannatta was asked to chair SMFHA. According to recollections of participants, meetings were ebullient and well attended at this time, with about half of the volunteer force coming from the Ocean Park community.[31]

The new organization also permitted younger activists to "rationalize"—in sociologist Max Weber's sense of rendering more calculable—the campaign by using calculated strategies newly learned in recent progressive campaigns. Younger activists felt themselves to be more organizationally astute than the seniors:

> Most of the older people were not so organizationally interested. A couple of the old Lefties were. But the rest just worked a hundred hours a day. And they did; they busted their asses every single day for a long time. We were doing the organization work, and they were doing everything else. They were the people out there collecting the signatures day after day, doing all the "grunt" work that needed to be done on the campaign. We were answering telephones and doing organization kinds of work, but we weren't out there like they were; we weren't mobilizing younger people like they were mobilizing older people. We did outreach, but the seniors did most of the work.[32]

A symbiotic relationship existed between individual CED members and SMFHA during the first rent-control campaign. According to Dennis Zane, SMFHA coordinated the work, while "CED did a lot of precinct walking." A May 1978 newsletter for the West Los Angeles CED chapter in the first campaign clarifies the relationship:

> CED supports Prop P [the ballot designation for the first rent-control initiative] because we believe it is high time that the concept of democracy be applied to housing, a necessary and basic condition of our lives. This is a prime example of what we mean by "economic democracy."... Although CED as a chapter is not directly organizing the rent-control campaign, we urgently encourage all members and supporters to join us in working with the Santa Monica Fair Housing Alliance...to produce a "yes" vote for Prop P on June 6th.

A typical example of division of labor might include a SMFHA meeting where decisions would be made, with CED then helping to carry out the work, such as the 4 A.M. leafletting of neighborhoods that became an institution for activists. This cooperation between organizations, and in some cases joint membership, greatly expanded the potential for outreach in the campaign.

As the June 1978 elections approached, SMFHA began to grow as new members joined and attended meetings. It gradually began to replace the Committee for Fair Rents as a center of gravity for the movement. As an SMFHA activist recalled, "We attempted to mesh our stuff with Syd, but it was rare that we could convince Syd to do something other than what he had already decided." While there was not competition between the groups, they retained a separate identity; both somewhat ad hoc organizations, one was centralized and relatively unsophisticated, the other democratically structured with a better grasp of mobilization techniques.

Although laying an important foundation for future organizing in the city, all of this nevertheless came to naught electorally when, on June 6, the electorate chose Proposition 13 over Proposition P, the rent-control initiative. A traditional "market" solution was sought to the housing crisis. Fifty-six percent of the vote was against the rent-control option. The rent-control activists stood defeated, but optimistic that rent control was winnable.

Uneven Resources

The 1978 rent-control campaign was the first experience of the expense of electoral politics for many of Santa Monica's younger activists. They were able to raise $15,000, while their opposition, composed heavily of landlords and real estate interests, raised approximately $200,000. Braun Campaigns, the professional political consulting firm hired by opponents of rent control, flooded the city with campaign literature that connected rent control with slums, abandonment, curtailed construction, higher taxes, bureaucracy, and an invasion of privacy. As one mailing put it, "In many cases rent control appears to be the most efficient technique presently known to destroy a city—except bombing." Another claimed:

> We don't want to see decent apartment buildings turned into abandoned shells. We don't want to see senior citizens forced to live in substandard housing without decent plumbing or heating. We don't want to see our city turned into a slum.

The chair of Santa Monica's Housing Commission claimed that speculators and rent gougers would not suffer under controls since they were already well organized enough to manipulate the system. Thus, the "little guy" would suffer most.

Perhaps most importantly, rent control was posed against the "free market" alternative of Proposition 13, a tax-saving measure for property owners. Landlords worked hard to frame this as a "trickle down" gain for tenants. In an apartment industry magazine, landlords gave themselves the following advice:

> LANDLORDS: SEND THIS LETTER ON PROPOSITION 13 TO YOUR TENANTS AND PUT YOUR MONEY WHERE YOUR MOUTH IS!!! The biggest hesitation tenants have in voting for Proposition 13, perhaps justifiably, is their suspicion that cutting property taxes won't really lower their rent, that landlords will hoard all the newfound profit for themselves. You can allay that suspicion and win many votes for Proposition 13 by retyping this letter on your own stationery—substituting correct tax figures for your own building—and passing out copies to each of your tenants, as I did to the 370+ units which I operate. . . . we apartment owners are just too small a minority to swing the vote. But we can exercise powerful leverage by getting our tenants to vote with us. . . . Sure we'll have to live up to it and actually cut rents (think of the news that will make)! But it isn't costing you a cent of profit and in the long run we'll be money ahead. . . . (*Apartment Age,* May 1978).

SMFHA literature, by contrast, pointed to abuses suffered by tenants in the city as a result of nonregulation. It backed up its support of rent control by citing the California Department of Housing studies conducted by Gilderbloom (1976, 1978), which found that "moderate" rent controls had no negative impact on quality and quantity of housing stock in over one hundred American cities. SMFHA also emphasized the "big real estate money" funding their opposition and the threat to nonaffluent residents (see below). There was, however, no equality either in material resources or sophistication between the two sides in this initial campaign. Contrasted against its future technical proficiency, the early days of the pro-rent control movement were humble. As Parke Skelton recalled:

> Denny [Zane] and I really didn't know what we were doing. We had no idea how to run a campaign like that. We raised very little money. . . . We had no get-out-the-vote program except that Denny painted some signs. We all went over to Denny's house and painted these signs that said, "Vote Today". . . . and we went and stood out on the street that Tuesday morning with these signs. . . . and we weren't ready at all for what happened. We just got blitzed out of the water—we'd never really seen a major direct mail campaign! They spent two hundred and fifty thousand dollars or something like that. This stuff started coming out in the mail, and we had never seen stuff like that.[33]

Dennis Zane, too, recalled in a newspaper interview that " . . . we spent $1,000 for an opening rally. You don't *spend* $1,000 at an opening rally, you *raise* $1,000 at an opening rally."

Much was learned from such early mistakes. Experience with running a local campaign as well as an acquaintance with the approach and technology of the opposition led to a rational reassessment of the situation by SMFHA activists. By the second campaign, their expanded organization and their tactics were unbeatable.

### The Second Rent-Control Campaign

#### The Tide Turns

While tenant activists were disappointed with the defeat, the voting margin encouraged them to see rent control as a winnable issue. The summer following the Proposition 13 election was a troubled one for landlord-tenant relations. Events moved ahead almost in spite of the organized activists.[34] Proposition 13 had been presented as a boon to tenants, either in the form of rebates or an understanding that rents would not be raised. When rents continued to rise despite tax relief to landlords, the general public as well as tenants took an extremely negative view of landlords. Riding on a spontaneous wave of indignation, SMFHA helped to channel these sentiments, organizing them and bringing them into public view. Tenant organizers active at the time recall in wonder how they were besieged by tenants voluntarily requesting to be organized. Parke Skelton, who organized over sixty buildings in Santa Monica, recalled sometimes attending five tenant union meetings in one evening in addition to his other work.[35]

Bitterness over Proposition 13 was not confined to Santa Monica, but was found in many communities around the state. CHAIN, having mobilized a constituency, provided a broader protest environment for the activism in Santa Monica. It fanned the flames by creating a strong public presence. Demonstrations of tenant anger became media events. Cary Lowe of CHAIN recalled:

> The true watershed came with Prop 13, *which had big tenant support.* The disenchantment led to a spontaneous wave of tenant activism. We were positioned perfectly to take advantage of this. We had an organization now, a statewide network. We raised hell! Sit-ins, demonstrations, press conferences—it was instant news. Every media outlet was calling me every day wanting to know what would happen. As this built up momentum, by January 1979 Santa Monica had put the second rent-control initiative on the ballot.[36]

In the meanwhile, important organizational changes occurred among the rent-control activists. First, Syd Rose began to remove himself from the scene. With this, the movement entered a new phase of its life cycle. As one activist recalled:

> After the campaign, Syd simply vanished for a mixture of political and personal reasons. During the first part of the summer we did things that Syd was not particularly interested in—rallies, demonstrations, we packed the city council. There was a bill in the assembly to pass on Proposition 13 profits to tenants, and we drafted a local version and presented it to the city council. None of this was Syd's forte. The first campaign spawned an organization that in fact didn't need Syd Rose.[37]

The movement at this point provided a classic illustration of sociological "emergence"; begun by a few individuals, it was now greater than the sum of its parts. It had also itself become a resource. Organizations already in place, such as CED, attempted to attach their energies to it and to shape it. As Dennis Zane put it, Syd Rose's role as a "unifier and initiator was no longer needed. The movement had a life of its own."

Opponents of rent control had a less benign view of Rose's disappearance. While evaluating Syd Rose as a well-motivated and good-hearted man, some felt that he was used politically. A member of the Santa Monica Board of Realtors recalled:

Syd Rose was a leader, a focal point. But Ruth Yannatta brought in busloads of people to demonstrate in front of our apartments when we raised the rent. The CED was actively looking for a constituency and were willing to bus people in to one of our buildings. They brought in eloquent organizers and speakers for the purpose of helping Syd Rose. He had good intentions; he felt that gougers should be checked. But his proposal was written by [Robert] Myers, pushed by CED. After the election they dismissed him, like a dummy. They wanted power, not to check the rents.[38]

As Syd Rose withdrew, the Committee for Fair Rents gradually disintegrated. A number of the seniors then joined SMFHA, which in the future coalition became known as a group dominated by seniors.

The summer of 1978 was a milestone in the development of the tenants' movement and progressive politics in Santa Monica. First, the increasingly sophisticated CED organization at last decided to commit its resources to supporting the local rent-control campaign. A number of its local activists in the relatively independent Westside chapter, such as Dennis Zane and Parke Skelton, worked hard to bring this about. As we noted above, this was ironic in view of the fact that opponents of Santa Monicans for Renters' Rights later characterized the tenants' movement as a creature of Tom Hayden. Far from dictating the agenda, his support came late and after much persuasion. However, by the summer of 1978, the voting margins from the previous election and the freeing up of statewide CED resources made rent control in Santa Monica a more convincing proposition for the organization. As one CED activist recalled, "The situation was different now—we had organizational experience; we knew how to turn out votes; we had contacts with computer people." CED's historic decision to support a second rent control campaign changed the face of the movement.

The other milestone came in the early fall of 1978, when the Santa Monicans for Renters' Rights' coalition was formed—an organization that still has clout at the polls over a decade later and that produced a lasting change in the social and political life of the city.

Constructing the SMRR Coalition

Analysts of social movements have remarked that making use of preexisting infrastructures and relationships lowers the cost of mobilization (Tilly, 1978; Oberschall, 1973). Coming from an underfinanced "outsider's" position, Santa Monicans for Renters' Rights had to become particularly adept at resource conservation for the sake of survival. In 1981, Dennis Zane would remark that "organizing the campaign was largely a matter of playing on the groups that were already there'' (*Evening Outlook,* September 30, 1981). The groups existed, but they had never been mobilized to form a powerful electoral base prior to SMRR's efforts. Constructing the initial coalition in 1978 was a masterful bit of political play quite beyond what the city was accustomed to.

The Santa Monica Fair Housing Alliance had gained in numbers and experience in the last campaign. However, among rent-control activists, the idea of building a broad electoral coalition gained currency in the latter half of 1978. This was seen as a wise strategy because the 1979 municipal election included not only rent control, but also three city council seats. This raised the stakes and encouraged rent-control activists to seek active support from existing organizations in order to broaden their electoral base.

Already in place was CED with its electioneering skills and trained canvassers. The involvement of CED did more than any other single organization to make the movement's strategy more calculable. Because its young activists were full-time organizers and strategists, they could plan offensive as well as defensive tactics, carefully weighing the alternatives. CED could therefore harness the passion of spontaneous events while keeping an overall goal—such as economic democracy—in mind. On the other hand, the participation of CED carried a liability with it: The perception of a conscious plan being carried out by these political "outsiders" greatly unnerved local elites and considerably raised the level of hostility in the community.[39]

Given the organizational nature of coalitions, linking the disparate elements into a workable whole would prove to be a major task. As Ferree and Miller (1985) have observed, when a group tries to link up with another that has resources already in place, it often tries to get its problem placed on that group's agenda. Rent-control activists became particularly interested in taking this approach to the local Democratic Club in Santa Monica. If it could be recruited, the Democratic Club would be at once the most moderate of the political organizations in the SMRR coalition and the most legitimate in terms of the established politics of the city. While it displayed some progressive interests, it was less radical than CED and SMFHA, and generationally older with a different kind of political experience. The legitimacy of the Democratic Club was a valuable resource because it could offer a "respectable identity" (Turner and Killian, 1972) to the SMRR coalition. Furthermore, it had established resources that could be contributed to the progressive effort.

The immediate political challenge was to persuade the Democratic Club to join the coalition. It was hesitant about doing so. Its recalcitrance could be explained by its clear realization that it would "inherit" the traditional enemies mobilized to oppose the younger activists. It knew, for example, that the CED connection would open the door to red-baiting, something that a number of older members had experienced in the McCarthy era and had no desire to relive. However, the rent-control issue was one that fit the club's political agenda. Dennis Zane recounts that after being introduced to the club by some members interested in rent control he was able to persuade the leadership—which at that time included William Jennings, a later defector from SMRR—to join the coalition.[40] In this manner, an existing friendly organization was transformed from "consensus" to "action" mobilization (Klandermans, 1984). The Democratic Club lent valuable resources, but remained the most cautious group in the coalition. As Moe Stavnezer recalled:

> There were lots of discussions that required mediation. Especially with the Democratic Club. Always they needed more accountability, time, caution. Jennings was president; he was very responsible for the Democratic Club becoming involved with rent control. He led that club into being part of the rent-control movement. He played a very positive role; he was a tireless campaigner—he went to buildings, rallies; he was everywhere. He only became equivocal on the city council. He was a turncoat. He didn't communicate. . . but then there was always a problem about communicating in SMRR. . . .[41]

The caution of the Democratic Club proved to be well founded. When it did join the SMRR coalition, it was singled out for criticism with special zeal by the business community. The same negative treatment was later given to other "respectable" community figures who joined SMRR, including Presbyterian minister Al Smith, who was harassed and almost driven out of his church in 1983 for running on a SMRR city council ticket.[42] By joining SMRR, the Democratic Club opened itself up to factionalism and to "takeover" attempts. After a landlord group attempted unsuccessfully to take it over, a splinter group calling itself the New Deal Democratic Club broke off and supported an anti-rent-control platform in 1983. A number of civic groups in Santa Monica experienced similar splits, which increased the feeling of bitterness in the city.[43]

The original SMRR coalition included SMFHA, CED, the Democratic Club, and a tenants' union.[44] The credit for the design and the integration of the coalition organization is generally given to Dennis Zane. Working closely with Zane were other tenant activists such as Cheryl Rhoden and Parke Skelton. Individual personalities were important resources in the Santa Monica movement, from the leaders and politicians with a nationwide network (see below) to the local grass-roots organizers such as Rhoden and Zane. Zane defined his role strongly at the time as a builder of relations between people through trust and "an infinite number of meetings." He recalled:

> When SMRR first developed, I was on the executive board of every organization. I was the link. There were meetings every night, and I

gained the trust of all the regular players. Also the CED chapter trusted me; I dragged them into Santa Monica politics practically by myself. And by then the SolarCal campaign was over, and the statewide organization was willing to put in money. It was a challenge, but I had gained credibility.[45]

Zane was thus not only a hard worker and an innovative strategist, but he was highly conscious of the need to build up the social interactional, face-to-face component of a social movement that leads to a sense of trust and community.

    Such resources are not uniformly available to all movements, nor even to the same movement at different times. Looking back in 1984 from the vantage point of an elected official, Zane noted the change in the movement:

Before I was elected and the first year after I was elected, I spent all my energy being the glue between the SMRR organizations. I've had to let that go. There is nobody now that has all these elements together—thinking that it's important enough, the time and willingness to do it, and the ability to relate to the coalition in a congenial manner and able to overlook differences and motivate themselves and others around common objectives.[46]

    In 1979, however, the coalition was freshly organized and morale was high. Structurally, each group had two representatives to the SMRR Steering Committee, and each group had veto power, which encouraged a dynamic of consensus-based decision-making. As Rosabeth Moss Kanter (1972) has affirmed, shared value systems play an important role in holding together groups that try to create alternative subcultures. In Santa Monica, many of the activists adhered to this decentralist progressive value system. Cheryl Rhoden recalled that, while it could slow down the process, it was also a valuable organizational safeguard:

The operating principle was consensus on major decisions. I think that played a big part in our keeping together. What typically happens in political organizations when groups come together, as opposed to individuals, is that there are territorial imperatives, the old pissing-on-the-perimeter syndrome. People are fearful that some others want to go faster. With consensus, everyone can feel safe, and if they really want something, they can really push for it, but they have to persuade everyone else. It's safer, and it requires more dialogue.[47]

Dialogue, in turn, requires constant work at "reducing the knowledge differential," something indispensable for democratically oriented social movements (Rothschild-Whitt, 1979). While the consensus orientation later contained pitfalls for the SMRR coalition, in its early days it functioned to energize and safeguard it.

Mobilizing Strategies

SMRR was formed in September 1978. It opened an office and began to circulate petitions for a new rent-control amendment, which was a legally tighter and also more publicly "supportable" version of the amendment voted on in June (see below). Seniors, who had gravitated to the SMFHA when the SMCFR disintegrated, retained a prominent role in these efforts despite the growing role of younger activists in CED. Indeed, according to the latter, seniors contributed irreplaceable resources. Their participation was viewed by the larger community as "legitimate" because they were perceived as victims rather than as subversives. Even more importantly, they worked hard and assumed tasks that some younger activists disdained. As CED member Hank Barnard put it:

They didn't mind doing the grunt work that had to be done. They had very little ego investment, unlike some professional in his thirties—you tell him to go photocopy something and he feels degraded. They simply knew it had to be done, and did it. And they get a lot of sincere thanks. I've learned a lot from them, and I hope I'm like that when I get older.[48]

The role of the seniors thus contributed to an effective of division of labor in the campaign.

The proposed rent-control amendment received enough signatures by the end of 1978 to be placed on the municipal ballot for April 1979, as Proposition A. SMRR also selected two individuals, Ruth Yannatta Goldway and William Jennings, to run for seats on the city council. They were felt to have credibility and name recognition, while their campaign could be linked to support for rent control. Although three slots were open, SMRR decided against fielding candidates for all three, feeling that this would lessen their chances of winning.[49]

One activist recalled the seeds of some future problems in the process of choosing candidates:

The leadership did the power brokering and chose people to run who weren't involved in the first campaign. Ruth Yannatta and Bill Jennings were chosen because they looked good. We didn't feel it was wrong because we wanted to win. We didn't ourselves know city politics; we needed them. We won the election, although it was just two seats, still a voting minority. The conflicts were not so visible then. We still needed a strong, broad grass-roots movement, and many were included. The power brokers pulled together the Democratic Club, CED, and SMFHA. But they were building a base among the top leadership.[50]

These problems with "participatory democracy" were, however, temporarily overshadowed by pragmatic considerations of winning, although they would turn up regularly over the course of SMRR's existence.

In the 1979 rent-control election, the opposition again mustered rhetoric about the destructive impact of rent control, combined this time with more emphasis on the "anti-American" nature of it (see Chapter 4). The official entrance of CED into the campaign unleashed a great deal of Tom Hayden- and Jane Fonda-baiting, precisely as the Democratic Club had anticipated. Former mayor Clo Hoover, a staunch opponent of rent control, wrote in the newsletter published by the Santa Monica Taxpayers and Residents Committee:

There is one central issue in the April 10th election and it isn't rent control. The issue is whether Tom Hayden and his ambitious political machine are going to be allowed to take control of our community.[51]

However, this rhetoric did not play well to the community. In the wake of Proposition 13 and an ongoing housing crisis, supporters of the free market model were less sure of themselves. Landlords, in the meanwhile, did nothing to endear themselves to tenants. The *Los Angeles Times* reported in March 1979 that in less than a year tentative approval had been given to 3,000 condominium conversion permits in Santa Monica, as compared to 70 in 1977. Not all were used since some were requested in anticipation of regulation. However, this did not make for good public relations. This was followed by an event that achieved almost mythical status in the city's history: Shortly before the April rent-control election, landlords leveled 500 housing units in a rebellion against possible regulation. Termed by the newspapers as the landlords' "last hurrah" and a "demolition derby," this action left parts of the city "looking like a war zone" and sealed the fate of landlords in the next election. This event drew the attention of Ralph Nader, who supported the rent-control initiative and remarked that "Nobody wins in this demolition derby except absentee landlords who wax fat at everyone else's expense" (*Los Angeles Times*, April 10, 1979). Most importantly, the incident produced votes among "bystanders" who, although they were not direct beneficiaries, became willing to support tenants and provided the 20 percent swing vote needed to win rent control. These developments underscored the important role of "conscience constituents" in social change as argued by McCarthy and Zald (1973), Lipsky (1970), and others.

All of these events contributed to a heightened sense of drama and intensity in the second rent-control campaign; riding a wave of public outrage that it helped to strengthen and legitimate, the movement also consolidated its technical know-how and constructed a strong coalition organization. It was abetted by the city council's mishandling of the housing crisis (see above), during which it drew a dangerous symbolic line between itself and the tenant majority in the city. At the same time, landlords were particularly maladroit in their public "presentation of self." Such actions brought widespread support for tenants' rights and the SMRR coalition. This time, when the dust settled, the city awoke to find itself with a rent-control law and two progressive candidates on the city council. As Cary Lowe summed up the winning campaign:

Santa Monica won a very solid victory in April 1979. They by then had good resources, Hayden approved, and I was still head of CHAIN. It was a nice confluence of resources and thinking. By then Syd Rose was long gone. SMRR was a pretty effective vehicle, although already then the arguments were going on over whether it should be a coalition or a membership organization. There were different arguments. It became more evident that there was a flaw—the lack of a tenant membership organization.[52]

## From Rent Control to Community Control

### Broadening the Coalition

Splashed across the front page of the *Evening Outlook* on April 11, 1979, the banner headline read: "Rent Control Approved in SM." A wildly cheering crowd, diverse in age and race and packed shoulder to shoulder, provided a symbolic cross section of the movement. Winning rent control in Santa Monica was a euphoric moment for progressives in general and for tenant activists in particular. In their eyes, the "little guy" had won against big odds.

There was, however, no rest from politics in the city. In June, a SMRR-supported slate took all five elected seats on the newly created rent control board. Then began a tense and confrontational period in the city, as landlords confronted the rent board, shouting, waving American flags, and booing through the pledge of allegiance. Rent board members and rent-control technical experts—lawyers and social scientists—needed a police escort, and a number received death threats. One meeting over allowable rent increases broke up into a melee when John Gilderbloom, called in as an expert witness on rent control, recommended that rents be increased by only half of the consumer price index (Gilderbloom and Jacob, 1981). The day after rent control was passed, a landlord group immediately filed a challenge to the law. We discuss these issues as well as features of the rent-control law in greater depth in Chapter 5.

Despite all of this, victories continued for the SMRR coalition. In November 1979, SMRR defeated a landlord-sponsored initiative (Proposition Q) that threatened to weaken the rent-control law by instituting ''vacancy decontrol'' and increases in rent tied to the cost of living. At this time, Cheryl Rhoden, a third SMRR candidate, was elected to a vacant position on the city council, strengthening SMRR's position. In 1980, landlords hit back with a statewide initiative, Proposition 10, which was designed to preempt local rent controls throughout California. Tenant groups united to defeat it despite being vastly outspent by landlord groups. Activists in Santa Monica consistently achieved victories in all of these campaigns, which came in rapid succession and which left them with a sense of both euphoria and combat fatigue. Parke Skelton, for example, managed the statewide campaign against Proposition 10, using the equal-time rule to gain television spots that countered the landlord campaign and provided access to the media for the largely low- and moderate-income tenants:

> They [landlords] started off with a series of ads that really played directly into our hands. They got these tenants on the air that said, ''I'm a tenant and my rent is too high. I'm going to vote for Prop 10 because Prop 10 means fair rents and reasonable controls.'' That was their slogan. Then they went on to talk about how radical rent control destroyed housing and fair rent control would stop gouging. . . . So, we immediately countered with a TV spot with Jack Lemmon in it which immediately made it a lot more credible than anything they could put together. . . . We started it off looking like one of their spots. We got an actor standing in front of an apartment door that said ''10'' on it. There was a little tree and birds chirping in the background. Then he said, ''My rent's too high; I'm voting yes on Proposition 10 because we need reasonable rents and fair controls.'' By that time everyone had seen the spot about twenty times. Then the director yells, ''Cut, cut, cut.'' The director runs on stage and the makeup people run on stage and start powdering them up, saying ''not convincing enough, let's take another cut.'' And the camera is cutting away and revealing that they are on a Hollywood sound stage and revealing that this is a false front. Someone is standing there holding the tree. The camera keeps moving into the background and Jack Lemmon is standing in the foreground, kind of shaking his head with a very sad look. He's holding a clapboard that says Prop 10 on it. He says, ''We've all seen commercials like that. But do you know who's behind it?'' Then he turns the clapboard around and it says Big Landlords

and Real Estate Speculators and he goes on to denounce it as a fraud. We figured that if someone would just see our spot once, every time they saw the other side's spot they would immediately remember Jack Lemmon telling them that and they would say, "Aha, I remember, there's something wrong about this one."[53]

The landlords were forced to cancel their television spot because this strategy was so effective.

Despite tenant victories, and despite impressive gains that SMRR received through its minority voting position on the city council—including a fair housing law banning "adults only" apartment buildings, consumer protection measures, and funding for rent-control administration (Shearer, 1982a)—progressives realized that a city council still dominated by traditional business elites would not be likely to safeguard the rent-control law. Still others saw the rent-control issue as an electoral pathway that could lead to the implementation of a broader progressive vision for the city.

Encouraged by the vast reservoir of support they had discovered through the rent-control issue, activists belonging to a broad range of the progressive spectrum singled out the upcoming 1981 city council race as one in which they would try to win a progressive majority. As in 1979, the key to this was seen as broadening the electoral coalition. This time, a solid base was already in place as a result of SMRR's identification with rent control. However, some outreach was needed to solidify this base and to move beyond the single issue of rent control.

In electoral terms, the single most crucial decision was to run SMRR candidates as a slate for city council. With the name identification that SMRR had built up during the rent-control campaign, it was possible to run progressive candidates by merging them with the rent-control issue. The name "Santa Monicans for Renters' Rights" had already become a priceless resource in the city. Most observers agreed in retrospect that, if the four SMRR candidates had run separately, they would have had little chance of winning.[54] The use of a slate and its social composition was new in Santa Monica politics. The four candidates chosen included Dennis Zane, math teacher and CED organizer; Ken Edwards, a probation officer with a sociology degree who was active in Democratic politics; Jim Conn, longtime organizer and minister in the Ocean Park neighborhood; and Dolores Press, a clerical worker for the Retail Clerks' Union. SMRR was able to emphasize that its candidates were free of compromising links to those interests that were pushing for excessive development and driving out lower-income residents.

Progressive labor groups were an important new element in the coalition. Their participation yielded endorsements for SMRR candidates as well as the provision of free phone lines for mobilizing voters, a valuable contribution of infrastructure that nonelite groups frequently lack access to. Outreach was done locally, regionally, and even nationally. According to progressive activist and city planner Derek Shearer (1982c:13):

> SMRR candidates received the endorsement of the L.A. County Federation of Labor and many local unions, as well as support from many leading Democratic party leaders in Southern California, even many who had mixed feelings about rent control as a strong party program. In addition to the direct mail and door-to-door fund-raising, SMRR organized fund-raising events featuring Ralph Nader, former Arkansas governor Bill Clinton...and television star Ed Asner. In particular, the Nader event was both a fund-raising operation and an effort to link the local battle in Santa Monica to similar progressive efforts around the country.

Nader had already made a name for himself locally by speaking out in favor of the 1979 rent-control initiative. Through Shearer, local events in Santa Monica were regularly connected to a broader progressive network (see below).

At this time, a fourth group, the Ocean Park Electoral Network (OPEN), was brought into SMRR. As we noted above, the Ocean Park neighborhood played a major role in the Santa Monica rent-control movement, first through fighting displacements of the elderly, then through the efforts of younger activists to promote community control and affordability for tenants in this mixed-income area. In 1978, Jim Conn, minister at the Methodist Church in Ocean Park, sought a grant to organize the community, using information about crime-reduction tactics that had been adopted in the neighborhood. By December of that year, Ocean Park had a community group, the Ocean Park Community Organization, whose first issue was fighting gentrification. OPCO's funding, however, prohibited it from explicitly political work, including supporting rent-control candidates. As a result, an offshoot group was formed, the Ocean Park Electoral Network.

OPEN was formed for two reasons. The first was to pursue electoral work. The second, however, gives a clue to a shadow falling over the movement already—internal problems over democracy. OPEN—as one activist pointedly remarked—stood for "openness in government and in the *movement*."[55] It raised the issue that, as a progressive organization, the coalition needed to listen to the community more and to work democratically at incorporating it. According to participants in OPEN, the organization convinced the SMRR coalition to incorporate into its platform the funding of neighborhood organizations and the promotion of openness in city government through the institution of citizen task forces.[56]

While the tensions in the movement were far from resolved, as a result of the push for democracy, the 1981 process of choosing candidates was "wide open, a clean process," with broad participation in the candidates' public interviewing.[57] In addition, the coalition's elements came together and wrote up a document expressing progressive goals for the city on which they could generally agree. Known as the "Principles of Unity," the document worked its way upward through a debating process within each group. The process effected a healthy renewal of energy and social bonds among the groups in the coalition, and they experienced a high degree of mobilization and volunteer activity.

On the other hand, SMRR ceded quite a bit of control to campaign manager Derek Shearer, who was viewed as a brilliant strategist, and accepted less direct democracy in this area for the sake of winning the campaign. Shearer encouraged the SMRR coalition to run an "up front," progressive campaign, clearly distinguishing between itself and its opponents (*L.A. Weekly,* November 13–19, 1981). This included not only support for rent control and curbing development, but preemption of the crime issue, which was providing a focal point for conservative organizing. By encouraging the organization of neighborhood anticrime programs and the provision of better locks, SMRR won the endorsement of Santa Monica's chief of police, James Keane. Other issues centered on quality of life and included environmental protection, recycling, and neighborhood preservation (Shearer, 1982a). Through its innovative stands on community issues, the SMRR coalition also forced its opposition into a reactive stance and a negative campaign. At the same time, it worked to keep the rent-control issue prominently in sight. It further benefited from some circumstantial events, including a judge's pronouncement that the rent-control law in Santa Monica was "confiscatory." This legal threat to the law helped to galvanize voters who supported SMRR.

Demonstrations and "direct-action" tactics continued to be part of the movement's repertoire. Ruth Yannatta Goldway, for example, organized a demonstration in front of the First Federal Bank when it was discovered that a group calling itself Good Government (chaired by William Mortensen, chairman and president of the bank) was providing money to the Citizens' Congress, a landlord-dominated group formed to oppose SMRR. As Mortensen recalled:

Ruth Yannatta Goldway was a very effective media person. Just before she became mayor she had a demonstration on Fourth Street. I got a call that she was going to demonstrate against our company because I'd given money to the anti-rent-control people. I'd given money to people running for the city council, and it was personal, not corporate. She claimed that a group that we had formed to educate the city was using political money, that it was illegal, and that I should go to jail. She had ABC, NBC, and CBS covering it.[58]

With a blend of democratic participation and technical expertise such as computerized direct mailing (see below), SMRR's mobilizing powers were extraordinary. When election returns came in, SMRR overturned historic voting patterns in the city. The entire progressive slate was elected, 57 percent to 43 percent. Age, income, and geographical location in the city had important effects on the election. SMRR victories in 35 out of 54 precincts relied primarily on middle- and low-income voters of mixed racial and ethnic backgrounds, under age forty and over sixty (*Evening Outlook,* September 30, 1981). The Citizens' Congress (an anti-SMRR organization), on the other hand, carried 14 precincts and relied principally on middle-aged voters of middle to upper income. The poorest neighborhoods gave their allegiance to both tickets. In addition, SMRR received the support of 25 percent of homeowners, who provided a crucial swing vote. Conversely, the Citizens' Congress got votes from 30 percent of tenants. This breakdown of the voting population indicates that Mark Kann (1986) was wrong in his contention that the renters' rights movement was middle class and not related to the interests of poor and working-class people.

The SMRR victory was a culmination of years of effort on the part of activists to build a community movement. Many could scarcely believe that they had won, and now controlled city government. As one of them recalled with a mixture of awe, irreverence, and glee:

The first two years were incredibly exciting. It was like changing history. Everyone had higher hopes. Many had taken it on the chin by the old minority government. There was so much satisfaction in beating the shit out of them! And it was great, the feelings, the friendships and craziness that went on during it, and after.[59]

Winning a majority on the city council activated some new elements in the always multileveled movement. As Cheryl Rhoden recalled:

Rent control was focused on with a kind of tunnel vision. The whole possibility of the movement and victory opened up new vistas of laughing children on streets, livable neighborhoods—especially with everyone feeling so controlled by housing markets.[60]

A vision of community was activated that was much broader than the single focus on rent control. While some levels of the activist network had this vision all along, to others it was a new, exciting possibility that had never been realizable before. This began a new phase of the movement, where tenants' issues merged into a wider range of progressive issues. We will consider this phase in more detail in Chapter 5.

## People Power versus Technology: Implications for the Movement

In the '79 election, there was a SMRR Steering Committee involved. Everything was volunteer and committee work. Now it's all done by professionals. People need to feel more involved, enchanted. The problem is that as we have become tactically more efficient, we have lost our humanity. —a CED activist[61]

Some people think that the tenant organizing done in 1977 and '78 led to the victory, and I'm not sure that's the case at all. A lot of tenant unions organized around a specific issue, then collapsed. If you're very lucky, one or two of those people would become an activist. The others played no role. —Parke Skelton[62]

The two quotes above express contrasting inside views of the tenants' movement and encapsulate a fundamental debate among progressives in Santa Monica and elsewhere in the nation. Jenkins and Eckert (1986:813) have observed that the impact of professionalization on an entire social movement is a neglected research topic. Here, we examine some evidence from the Santa Monica movement. A theme that emerged with increasing insistence since the 1979 rent-control campaign was the growing technical sophistication of the SMRR campaign organization. While this sophistication—such as computerized voting lists and direct-mail targeting—brought electoral victories to the movement, some activists grew concerned that technical skills might replace the "people power" that originally gave life to the movement. Just how should the two be balanced, they asked themselves, in a movement committed not only to tenants, but to the encouragement of progressive community-building?

The movement in Santa Monica fits into a broader trend prevailing in U.S. social movements, a trend exemplified by a reliance on what John McCarthy (1983) has labeled "thin infrastructures." Responding to the restructuring of electoral politics around computer technology, McCarthy conceptualized a difference between "thick" social infrastructures, which depend on face-to-face mobilization, and technologically created "thin" infrastructures, which are basically informational—names and addresses, demographic characteristics, and so forth. The former require social interaction for mobilization and have in the past been an important aspect of campaign work. The latter provide structural information about the social location of particular individuals. They make it possible to aggregate individuals who have never come together socially, but whose structural location is seen as conducive to movement participation. The mobilization task for a social movement organization is to identify these "reservoirs" of support, to connect to them through computer technology, and to give the people in question an extra push toward an active expression of their beliefs, whether this is monetary contributions, votes, or some other form of action (McCarthy, 1983; Snow et al., 1986). A logical consequence of this emphasis is a shift away from social interaction and personal transformation and toward the identification and mobilization of existing supporters. It is possible, under these circumstances, to produce the anomaly of a powerful social organization *without social interaction*. In effect, this can take the "social" out of social movements.

McCarthy and Zald (1973, 1977) have suggested that many professionalized movements in the United States no longer depend on direct adherents or social interaction between leaders and grass-roots constituents. Although not all theorists agree with them (Jenkins and Eckert, 1986), if they are correct then they present a dilemma for progressives. Progressive beliefs imply social change through direct democratic participation. Election formulas and mobilization based on thin infrastructure are often one-way, nondemocratic ways of relating. Yet without an electoral victory, putting a progressive agenda broadly into practice is usually impossible. Since SMRR's higher echelon actors tended, as political pragmatists, to have a "resource mobilization" perspective on the movement (see below), computer technology was favored as an efficient resource. The challenge for the movement—as for other movements in the United States—is to find the appropriate balance between transformative social interaction and technology.

The Benefits of Technology

It has been hotly debated whether SMRR's string of victories was due to technology or to organizing people. Parke Skelton, whose skills were developed during the Santa Monica campaigns that began with the Yannatta race, insists that it was the former. For example, a feature of Santa Monica politics that is often pointed to with interest is SMRR's ability to win electoral victories even though it was outspent many times over by its opposition. This is often presented as an instance of "people power" triumphing over technology. Skelton, however, found the technology decisive:

> In 1979, we spent about $45,000, which was miniscule compared to the opposition, but it made the difference between getting the message out to voters and not reaching them.[63]

Accordingly, a number of Santa Monica's key activists shifted their energies toward discovering the optimum electoral formula and a professional campaign model that would structurally guarantee successful voting patterns. Skelton himself had strong feelings on this subject:

> Some people disparage the electoral part of what was done in Santa Monica. Organizing tenants is important, but you don't win elections by organizing tenants. You can't; you get smashed. Politics on the Westside and in L.A. county is unlike politics in a lot of the country. Quantitatively, the amount of money spent in Santa Monica and the technology used are really outrageous, and you have to be able to compete in that arena, or you lose every time. You need to know things like direct mail, targeting, and phone banking. It's not magic or anything, but you have to be conversant with the skills to win.[64]

The 1979 Proposition A rent control campaign was the first in which rent-control activists focused on direct mailings. As Skelton recalled, "In 1978 we got smashed. We didn't do a single piece of direct mail. We were doing these stupid fliers and handing them out in front of Lucky's." Moe Stavnezer agreed: "They looked like a kid had done them." In an effort to improve their outreach, SMRR put Skelton in charge of the mail campaign for the 1979 election while others—Dennis Zane in particular—worked on fund-raising from the expanding electoral base. Campaign manager Derek Shearer's strategy was to simplify and personalize the electoral message, attaching human faces to the statistics (Shearer, 1982c). For example, one of SMRR's most effective (and controversial) pieces depicted an elderly man dying of cancer who had been evicted from his apartment and who gave SMRR permission to use his photograph and his story. The caption read: "My last act as a Santa Monican will be to vote for rent control." Seniors were prominently depicted on other fliers, offering personal testimony about their plight as tenants. SMRR combined this strategy with one that offered more objective information, such as mailing out a full text of the proposed rent-control amendment.[65]

The pragmatic implications of the shift to direct mail were clear. Looking back over the evolution of SMRR strategies since 1979, Thom Poffenberger— SMRR campaign manager in 1983 and 1984—asserted:

> Targeting is the coming thing. We keep track of everything we learn about people for the next election, and put it into our computers. We fine-tune those techniques year after year. This year, for example, we want to identify the type of building.[66]

Not only does this conserve resources—the same literature is not sent to renters and to homeowners—but a carefully tailored message can often have a deeper impact on the receiver than a generic one. SMRR's "computer wizards" became convinced that in a competitive arena such as the Westside, where Santa Monica was located, any group not having access to these techniques was at a disadvantage.

An additional twist is that under these circumstances "people power" and how to achieve it become a marketable commodity to be traded with other groups and other cities. According to McCarthy and Zald's (1973, 1977) conceptualization, social movement entrepreneurs are people with a good instinct for the politics of resource acquisition. As campaign manager in 1981, Shearer expressed himself as the classic entrepreneur:

> ...a core of about 20 learned all of the technology, which is really neutral, learned how to do electoral campaigning at the local level. We got very good at it. What we learned were skills that other people and candidates pay tens of thousands of dollars for. So I've got people I can send to explain to people—just the way the Republicans did over these last few years (Cockburn and Ridgeway, 1981).

The novelty of this was, of course, that it was *not* the Republicans who were offering advice, but rather their less-well-heeled opponents. With both sides activated in Santa Monica, however, a serious and largely unanticipated consequence was that the technological and financial stakes rose with each campaign.

These stakes helped to shape the movement/countermovement dynamics in the city (Mottl, 1980; Zald and Useem, 1987). The initial anti-rent-control campaigns were run by a professional political consulting firm, Braun Campaigns, and relied on outside polling firms for outreach. Beginning in 1983, a public relations firm called Marathon Communications—which achieved a reputation for defeating a number of "left" campaigns in California—was hired by SMRR's opposition. Marathon played a role in the 1983 election that saw the defeat of progressive mayor Ruth Yannatta Goldway. By targeting an identified population, in this case angry homeowners who had become alienated from SMRR over a zoning issue, it boosted voter turnout enough to defeat the SMRR slate for all three open seats for the city council, leaving SMRR with a voting majority of only one (see Chapter 5). As in a number of other California cities, the activation of absentee ballots—a conservative element in the community—proved crucial. This came as a blow to the by now technologically sophisticated SMRR campaign organization. Low tenant turnout was explained by some as a response to a lack of perceived threat to rent control. A more haunting explanation offered by others was, however, that the spark of participation was missing.

The Benefits of "People Power"

In contrast to those who laud movement technology, others have attributed SMRR victories to organizing and to a great deal of footwork and face-to-face contact (Zeitlin, 1981). In comparing Santa Monica with other progressive cities, observer David Moberg (1983b:2) noted:

> ...although they [SMRR] employed the best affordable contemporary campaign tactics in their media efforts (and there are a number of leftists now with expertise in advertising and running campaigns), door-to-door work by candidates and their grassroots army—or platoons—were the key.

Another source concluded that SMRR's election success was fueled by its ability to "become very good at ground-level electioneering, widely thought obsolete in the era of TV and computerized mailing" (Mankin, 1981:24). Although committed to computer technology, SMRR campaign manager Thom Poffenberger pointed out that:

> The opposition outspends us dramatically—they have to pay so much more to consultants, and they don't get nearly so much for their money. They outmail us too. *But they have never beaten us in the field,* which is a tribute to our movement.[67]

To walk precincts and to have "encounters" were perceived by progressives as important, not only for the sake of outreach and persuasion, but also for developing the social solidarity that people derive from acting together in groups. The election leafleting that was done in conjunction with CED in the wee hours of the morning was just such a social mechanism. According to their own testimony, progressive grass-roots activists knew that people in social change organizations are often sustained by evidence that their contributions make a difference. The 1979 rent-control campaign relied on considerable "people power." Tenant demonstrations were organized by SMFHA, CED organized extensive neighborhood canvassing, and a number of key activists arranged their lives around participation in the movement. For example, a CED member recalled dropping out of school and spending "the whole month of March [1979] in the little upstairs room of the Church in Ocean Park, working with seniors."[68] This degree of commitment was not unusual, particularly in the core group that came together in SMFHA and CED. SMRR was eventually able to muster approximately three thousand contributors from the community and approximately one thousand volunteers.

By 1983, two years after progressives won city hall in Santa Monica, a significant number of testimonies by those who had distanced themselves from the movement revealed that energies waned precisely because the chance to participate was seen as diminished or artificial. As a result, even though precinct walking was being done, the "spark" was missing from the campaign. As one activist—representative of the views of many others—put it:

> A lot of us who never would have been able to participate *have*, even without money. The reason for it is that Ruth and Derek, and Jane and Tom, were able to draw lots of money in. As they [SMRR] got more sophisticated in electoral techniques and in running the city, the stage at which a lot of people were brought in was over. They didn't need the people, except to vote, and their computers helped with that. I kept saying at CED meetings that we need the people. But they didn't want to teach or lead; it was more technical than that. They had maximized their utility—minimum resources for maximum results. Those resources were technical. Anyone else brought in was a nuisance.[69]

SMRR campaign managers acknowledged the problems of running a democratic campaign:

> The electoral system in this country doesn't lend itself to maintaining an organization, but rather patronage. Maybe we should never have raised expectations. In the beginning, we had participation because there was no other way to do it. It raised expectations. How do you make it democratic? That isn't what gets you the votes.[70]

Being involved in a highly competitive electoral arena encouraged SMRR campaign managers to think in a cost-effective manner and to evaluate the "rate of return" on thin infrastructures as opposed to democratic participation. They favored the former because they believed it rendered elections more calculable. As progressives, however, they knew the dangers of this emphasis—it could put a damper on social activism. Consequently, they tried to balance the social dimension of people power against technology, even though in their view the rate of return on democratic participation was lower. Thom Poffenberger noted:

> We need a mass meeting to vent everything. In terms of the electorate, they need to get things in the mail in the last three weeks. SMRR doesn't have to do anything until that point. But the problem is, if you do that, you lose many of the activists. You must balance the two.

He concluded:

> Speaking as a cynic, you have a meeting, and there's a turnout. It *feels* better, but it still doesn't get the work done. I'm probably too cynical; I try to temper it. But we've tried all those things before. I don't want to get off the track. Last time we gave the neighborhoods specific responsibilities. We saw no concrete results, although it took tremendous time and effort. What works in this town is for people to clearly know what SMRR is supporting. You provide a litany of things supported and reinforce it over and over, especially since the opposition tries to be as confusing as possible. The phone bank during Prop X [a 1984 ballot initiative concerning a tenant-ownership program] was very effective, especially since many renters were "conditioned" against it. . . . SMRR is a golden name. Lots of people are selfish; they save a lot of money. They're not progressive at all. But these are quality-of-life issues, and it takes a progressive approach to have these things in the first place.[71]

Thus, from a cost-benefit point of view, democratic participation did not "measure up"; its function was more to provide solidarity incentives that kept activists energized. Computerization, on the other hand, once initially acquired, was easier to carry out and easier to fund than ongoing organizing.

Critics of this view saw the technology employed by SMRR campaign managers as seductive in its suggestion of a neat, calculable solution to a complex problem. They also worried that it gave managers a heady, intoxicating sense of power that discouraged "nonexpert" grass-roots participation. Campaign managers such as Poffenberger were fully aware of these problems. They also noted that the return that SMRR received from this technology waned over time. On the one hand, it raised the financial stakes in each campaign since opponents tried to outmail each other; on the other, it created the eventual danger of an "oversaturated" direct-mail market (Snow et al., 1986). Poffenberger also admitted that each year it became harder to get volunteers out:

> What we're failing in is bringing in new people. The campaign is hard work; it's not exciting. The first few times they're willing, but there's a limit to how to do it differently. We try to think of ways, but it's hard. In '79 the excitement did it, but now. . . . In the last campaign, for example, intellectually everyone realized Prop Y [a ballot initiative rescheduling local elections to coincide with national elections] was terribly important, but not emotionally. The dichotomy exists, although it shouldn't.[72]

While this could be interpreted as a general problem experienced by all aging social movements, this explanation would ignore the many statements of discouraged movement activists who felt they still had energy to give, but found their chances to do so virtually eliminated. The 1983 loss may have proved that targeting is not enough and that a desire to participate arises out of "soft incentives" (Opp, 1985) or social relationships with other people, as well as out of a sense that community is important and necessary for successfully accomplishing progressive objectives (Klandermans, 1984). Although pragmatic SMRR campaign directors—along with their disconcerted political opponents—assumed that the overriding self-interest of rent control would automatically motivate voters, the ground-swell of support for SMRR and the energy in the early movement went far beyond this; it also came from the possibility of active participation in changing history and one's community. When this opportunity vanished, energy waned and progressives themselves became cynical about manipulations of "the base" by SMRR's experts:

> I've been surprised about their attitude toward informing their "base," as they would call it. They're never people, did you notice that? "Their base," "our base"...it's not the *people*.[73]

Perturbed over this kind of depersonalization, then mayor and SMRR candidate Ken Edwards perhaps put it best when he exclaimed: "Is there some guy named Base in the community? Who the fuck is Base?"[74]

These comments from rank-and-file grass-roots activists as well as from leaders point to a common conclusion: A social dimension was missing in the movement by 1983. At the outset, the movement emphasized community and democratic face-to-face interaction. There was also a greater emphasis on transformation rather than computer outreach to those who were already "converted." Responding to electoral losses in 1983 and 1984, and hoping to revitalize the movement, SMRR activists were forced to deal with the crisis by reorganizing SMRR in 1985. In the November 1988 election, progressives recaptured city hall with renewed energy, giving SMRR community activists a voting majority once again and appointing Dennis Zane to be mayor of Santa Monica. The debate over people power versus technology, however, persists.

## Generations and Levels of Activism

> The people who are involved in local politics there [in Berkeley] still have strong identifications with the antiwar movement—with major national issues—that our coalition doesn't have and never will have. We are ordinary working people who live in Santa Monica. —Ruth Yannatta Goldway (*Evening Outlook,* April 29, 1981)

At the same time that the forces of urban development were changing the demography of the city, many sixties activists found their way to the Ocean Park section of Santa Monica in search of a pleasant and inexpensive place to live. They began to build a "community" for themselves...and, most important, they turned their organizing skills to local political issues....—Derek Shearer (1982c)

We noted above the importance of "chains of opportunity" that resulted from prior social movements, some of them perhaps failed, but leaving openings for future movements. We began by considering the significance of tenant-organizing issues— such as those taken up by CHAIN—prior to and outside of the movement in Santa Monica, which left opportunities and resources in existence that could be picked up by the movement. "Resources," as social movement theorists have recognized, include the strategic location of certain people (or networks) at particular points in time with a collection of past biographical experiences that can become tools for social change (Braungart, 1984; Ross, 1983; Snow et al., 1980; McAdam, 1986). A Dennis Zane, a Jim Conn, a Ruth Yannatta Goldway, or a Derek Shearer thus become invaluable resources because they are structurally available and experienced in movement tactics. It is of particular significance to a sociology of tenants' movements to consider the experiences of the core group of activists in the city.

The Impact of the Sixties

We have noted the tendency among critics of the tenants' movement in Santa Monica to assign responsibility for the progressive agenda to local resident and sixties activist Tom Hayden and his then wife Jane Fonda. While both kept a low profile in Santa Monica, their past histories of activism during the Vietnam war continued to rankle conservative citizens. For example, in 1985, years after the rent-control victory and the election of progressives to office, Hayden—then assembly representative for Santa Monica's district—proposed a memorial to patriotic war protesters in the 1960s. In response, a local letter to the editor suggested a memorial to Hayden: a large hammer and sickle— below it, a skunk holding its nose (*Evening Outlook,* May 8, 1985). This anger was not, however, directed only at Hayden, but against the protesters of the 1960s, whom he had come to represent. While there is a danger in assigning too much significance to the role of this generation in Santa Monica, to ignore it would be an equally grave error. Hayden was crucial in Santa Monica as a "movement entrepreneur," and the significant impact of the skills, tactics, and experiences of the generation that he represents can be documented. Although the progressive movement considered it strategically important to play down any "sixties" connection—this being one of its less legitimate identities (Turner and Killian, 1972) in the community—its critics have been right to point up its significance.

In 1981, a *Mother Jones* article asked, "Here is the question: How typical an American city is Santa Monica, California?" (Mankin, 1981:66). The quotes from Ruth Yannatta Goldway and Derek Shearer, above, give different answers to the question. Goldway emphasizes Santa Monica's "average American city" image, playing down a legacy of radical activism. Shearer's quote serves as a reminder of the role of the sixties activism that provided key players for an eighties movement. Among the younger generation of progressive community activists in Santa Monica, many first became socially and politically active during the 1960s through civil rights and anti-Vietnam protest activities. Senior activists drew on some additional layers of generational experience (see below), all of which laid an important base for the subsequent movement in Santa Monica.

In the 1970s and 1980s, a pattern emerged of 1960s activism being translated into a less sensational, more pragmatic, community-oriented politics. Once most well known as a member of the Chicago Seven, in the 1970s and 1980s Tom Hayden himself came to be considered a pragmatist. Despite popular stereotypes, a significant portion of that generation retains a strong commitment to social change. Emphasis was placed on finding pragmatic alternatives to the existing system and testing them out at a local level. Much of the initial excitement of the Santa Monica campaign arose from the fact that real data were being collected for an alternative urban model. As SMRR activist Roger Thornton recalled:

> I remember reading Marx's *Theses on Feuerbach,* and the notion that material things create people, but how do you break out of that cycle? It seems to me you give concrete examples. That's how I saw Santa Monica politics.[75]

He was not alone. While not all activists worked from a Marxist-inspired model, many were influenced by a critical perspective of U.S. society and a progressive value set. They were interested in realizing theory at the local community level, which made a great deal of sense in terms of an entire generation of experience, beginning with the local community emphasis of the civil rights movement (Cloward and Piven, 1986; Morris, 1984; McAdam, 1986).

It is important to note that while sixties activists may have changed tactics many of the resources they accumulated are generational, arising out of pragmatic experience. Charles Tilly (1978) has argued that movement "repertoires" are historical constructions; up to a point, each generation engages in a typical form of collective behavior that is characteristic of that era. SMFHA and SMRR's willingness to use tactics of confrontation and to organize noisy, disruptive demonstrations at landlords' homes or at the local bank was drawn from a Saul Alinsky-inspired model for attaining community power (Alinsky, 1971) as well as from experience with civil rights and Vietnam protests.

At the same time, repertoires change continuously through interactions with new situations and groups and through the interaction between movement and countermovement (Mottl, 1980; Zald and Useem, 1987; Gale, 1986). This was as true of landlords in Santa Monica as it was of tenant activists (see Chapter 4). When landlords decided to hire a tank and drive it to city hall festooned with "Soviet Monica" signs, they were expanding their repertoire by learning from their opponents. Turkle (1975), Piven and Cloward (1979), Castells (1983), and others have stressed the importance of innovative elements in movement repertoires and the need to break away from institutionalized forms or habits of interaction. When networks are built, or when experience is traded between generations, the information base is multiplied many times over. In Santa Monica, networks were built and resources were discovered and created, all of which made the coming together of progressive energies in 1981 more possible.

As we noted earlier, by the time that rent-control activists achieved a winning campaign, they had worked their way through many losing elections, accumulating experience along the way. Thom Poffenberger became SMRR campaign manager in 1983 after acquiring irreplaceable experience from working on the earlier Hayden Senate campaign:

> When Hayden ran, I was hired as deputy campaign manager in charge of field operations. It was great—bigger than Santa Monica, and so much money was spent that you could really see just about anything you could do. I got to try lots of new things—computer, TV, which was unheard of at that time.[76]

Poffenberger came to CED already a seasoned activist, having participated for years in the grass-roots organization Massachusetts Fair Share. Similarly, Ruth Galanter—who became an elected Los Angeles city councilmember in 1987—focused on this building up of skills as she recalled the 1979 election:

> By this time they [rent-control opponents] were dealing with any number of people who had lived through one or another kind of political experience, either regular Democratic campaigns or civil rights stuff or antiwar campaigns or stuff in the army...just a lot of us had a lot of experience. The folks who had been here longer didn't, and they chose the route of digging in and resisting.[77]

Much of the progressive repertoire drew on the sixties experience, although it underwent significant changes. The personal involvement of Derek

Shearer, one of Santa Monica's primary "movement entrepreneurs," illustrates this experience well. Himself politicized by the 1960s, Shearer became interested in economic democracy at the grass-roots community level, and how it could be accomplished through an interaction between community organizing and voter mobilization (Carnoy and Shearer, 1980). Over the course of the 1970s, he was part of a group that constructed a nationwide network that explored progressive structural alternatives for social change. The network consisted of moderate radicals accepting an electoral context and minimizing ideological hairsplitting, yet strongly influenced by their experiences in the 1960s.

An organizational manifestation of this network was the Conference on Alternative State and Local Public Policies. As Shearer (1982a) described it:

By the beginning of the 1970's, many activists had matured in their views of the electoral system and had begun to involve themselves in urban electoral politics, initially in university towns like Berkeley, Austin, Ann Arbor and spreading into major urban centers like Cleveland, Detroit, San Francisco and New York. Some activists ran for and won local offices. As representatives of community-based organizations, these "new urban populists" began to develop a set of programs which would alter (in their view) the biased operation of city government and create a city government which would serve all the residents of a city, not just the owners of property and the upper middle class.

Meeting annually in various cities begining in 1973, this network promoted the sharing of information.

Another organizational effort was the Planners' Network (PN), which provided a medium of exchange for the practical experiences of progressive planners who are in diverse geographical areas, some outside of the United States. Because Shearer was involved in the Santa Monica movement and because he had access to these networks, SMRR was able to multiply its resources as an effective urban social movement organization. For example, some local members of PN, at the outset of the rent control campaign, briefly became involved in supporting research for rent control before shifting their interests to direct mobilization.

Shearer was not the only individual in Santa Monica with these kinds of links, but partly due to his own flamboyance, partly due to his marriage to Santa Monica's controversial progressive mayor Ruth Yannatta Goldway, and partly due to the visibility of his ideas in the book that he coauthored with Martin Carnoy, *Economic Democracy* (Carnoy and Shearer, 1980), he played a major role in the Santa Monica movement intellectually and as campaign manager of the 1981 election. Because they "put Santa Monica on the map" through their nationwide connections, Ruth Yannatta Goldway and Derek Shearer became spokespersons for the progressive movement. Along with Tom Hayden and Jane Fonda, they also personally provided important fund-raising capacities for the progressive movement. This brought Santa Monica a great deal of positive and negative publicity, creating mixed feelings among community activists there. Some felt that grass-roots activists did not get the recognition they deserved as the "guts" of the movement:

> Derek was always a kind of gray eminence behind all of this. There was a period during the campaign when I thought *Derek* was running for city council, his name was in the paper as much as the candidates—it was inappropriate.[78]

This tension was heightened by the progressive commitment to democratic structure. Chastised by a radio talk show host for not having read her "leader's" book, SMRR activist Cheryl Rhoden retorted: "Actually, Derek Shearer is not a major leader of our organization. He is acting as our campaign manager. The leaders, so to speak, if you speak in those terms, are members of the organization themselves" (*Los Angeles Times,* March 19, 1981).

Other negative feelings came from an impression that publicity about the city was drawing activists to Santa Monica as a kind of new radical playground, activists who demoralized others by leaving when their particular idea of what should take place there was not actualized.[79] Some grass-roots activists felt that Shearer's national articles and his book *Economic Democracy* contributed to this outcome and helped to mobilize SMRR's opposition. Because it was a pragmatic blueprint for social change, the book clearly frightened SMRR's opposition, in part due to the content of the ideas and in part due to its pragmatic suggestions, which helped fuel a conspiracy theory. As sociologist Ralph Turner (1969) has noted, the less naive and the more sophisticated a social change group is, the less likely they are to be viewed as legitimate according to the "folklore of protest" in the United States. The suspicion in which Shearer's book was held by the opposition was rivaled by only one other book. This was *The Cities' Wealth,* written by a number of progressives who raised the idea of public municipal ownership (Bach et al., 1976).

Despite the controversy, it is clear that the informal network that was created by individuals such as Shearer functioned as an effective form of resource mobilization for the progressive movement. Apart from providing information, it drew to Santa Monica both scholars and seasoned activists with a progressive orientation. On the positive side, this created a genuine excitement about sharing experiences and ideas. A former city councilmember recalled this as being one of the most stimulating outcomes of having a city labeled as progressive.[80] At the same time, it was extremely valuable information, which, when combined with the right strategic timing, could make or break the movement. As Shearer recalled, "I knew what had happened in some other places, and so I pushed for things, such as inclusionary zoning."[81]

In a recent book on Santa Monica, Mark Kann (1986:264) quotes sociologist Maurice Zeitlin's remark that "Almost in absent-mindedness the movement in Santa Monica did invent a radical new governmental forum." Zeitlin was referring to the creation of a democratically elected rent-control board that came out of the 1979 rent-control charter amendment. While the progressive program certainly had its inconsistencies and improvisations, all of the evidence from the early part of the movement indicates that, far from being "absentminded," it represented a highly deliberate, calculating, rational effort that drew on nationwide experience. The rent-control law is a case in point (see Chapter 5).

After rent control lost at the polls in 1978, its theorists deliberately drew on resources offered by CHAIN and the National Tenants' Union (NTU), whose 1982 annual meeting was held in Santa Monica. As a result, they were able to take a more rational approach to tightening up the rent-control initiative for the second election:

> It was never a single person, or if so, a single person cribbing from a lot of sources. Myers took liberally from Berkeley and then through the people in Berkeley, the people out on the East Coast, especially in New Jersey, Fort Lee. That's also where we got the vast bulk of our information on rent-control economics. None of us even knew this stuff existed before all this got started.[82]

The construction of a network made the rapid sharing of information possible and helped activists to gain experience and knowledge that on their own might have taken years to build. This was a progressive strategy to counterbalance the traditional "old boy" networks that existing elites had built up over the years.

The development of these various networks not only helped the progressive movement to survive, but enabled it to take an aggressive offensive posture toward urban policy rather than a more passive stance. The individual "entrepreneurs" such as Shearer who draw these organizational resources together are vital to social movements. Yet the tensions over democracy are not surprising. As one SMRR activist recalled:

> People don't understand; they resent the attention to Ruth, Derek, Tom. The kind of coordinated thinking they were doing and the balancing work they did on the politics of it were *essential*. Others probably couldn't have pulled it off. They pulled stuff together. Sure, they made mistakes, a little bit of arrogance. . . .[83]

William Gamson (1975) has noted that one of the benefits of a coalition structure is that it can shelter certain interests indirectly, presenting a more bland face to public view. However, it is clear that some individuals are more sheltered than others and that their presence can affect the scope of a social movement. This was the case with Yannatta Goldway and Shearer. As movement entrepreneurs with a national network, neither their experience nor their career possibilities was linked solely to Santa Monica. The politics of Santa Monica were significantly affected by the presence of at least a few such "risk-takers" (Staggenborg, 1988; Oliver, 1984) who raised the stakes and challenged the system further than was customary. Musing on this aspect of the movement, city councilmember Dennis Zane remarked:

> Derek Shearer has confidence in his judgment. Most people don't. He displays some recklessness. It's like my own experience with students in college, in the antiwar movement. Militancy was recklessness, really. It wasn't so much having stronger convictions—it was knowing that if you fell down, someone would pick you up. You feel like you have things to fall back on. Derek Shearer is like that; he has lots of things going. He's got other places to go, lots of political options. Therefore, he can take risks. Risks have to be taken. He can say, "Why do it if you're not really going to have a left-wing government? It isn't worth it; I'll go somewhere else." For others of us, this is an exclusive, limited opportunity to do something real. I don't stand outside the system the way he does. I don't have the resources. I want to be more careful, do it well. I don't want to antagonize people unnecessarily. But I've got a clear objective, and it's hard, hard, hard work.[84]

According to McCarthy and Zald's (1973, 1977) conceptualization, movement entrepreneurs are not likely to be found at the grass-roots level, but in a more directive role. Tom Hayden, who "acquired" the movement after the seniors in Santa Monica began it, is another case in point. Rather than being the function of individual personalities, the tension over democracy appears to be a sociological, structural feature of social movements.

## Relations Between Generations: Senior Activists

One of the significant organizational accomplishments of the progressive tenants' movement was the joining of efforts of "senior" and "junior" activists. As we have already noted, there was a significant presence of seniors in Santa Monica, veteran activists of the 1930s, 1940s and 1950s, for whom rent control was yet another cause in a lifelong series of commitments. For example, one senior testified that:

I joined the Southern California Women's Strike for Peace, which was
related to the Vietnam war. The peace movement drew me in. We formed
a group, and I was a coordinator. It was a very vital organization. When
the war was over, that fell off. Then I began working locally, in the
community. The vital issue then was rent control.[85]

Having been involved in various struggles elsewhere, such individuals had
no lack of experience with politics or organizing. Some unique resources were
created as a result of blending different generational repertoires, and the
movement was more broadly grounded in the overall community. While in
many cases younger and older activists worked together very well, interactions
between the generations were not always smooth.

While not lacking in socially radical ideas, the repertoire of the older
generation of progressive activists was tempered by experiences of political
persecution during the McCarthy era. Disagreements with younger activists
often took place squarely in the context of different generational experiences.
As one senior mused:

People don't necessarily learn from history; it's hard to apply, and people
often react on the level of their own anger. For many young activists,
the central issue is rent control, which equals the struggle. They focused
on the proper definition of the alignment of people politically. For many
old timers, alignments are flexible and rarely permanent. It's one incident
in a widespread series of developments. They [younger activists] don't
perceive things as a whole. I came of age during the depression, which
was a far more significant school than the students of the sixties.[86]

"Immature political arrogance" was a phrase sometimes applied to the younger
activists by seniors.

This had far more than symbolic consequences. Much of the dissension
between two SMRR coalition groups, the CED and the Democratic Club, had
to do with generational differences. As Dennis Zane recalled:

Sometimes if some of the older people in the Democratic Club think
the younger activists are up to something, "younger activist" equals
CED. Lots of times it was just a rumor, but it takes on a level of
significance that is quite unbelievable.[87]

In fact, a major attempt to restructure SMRR in 1983 foundered on the
Democratic Club's refusal to give up its veto power. According to testimony
by activists on various sides of the issue, the Democratic Club drew on its
own historical and generational experience to justify this protective gesture.

Had these issues not been present, the SMRR coalition might have been injected with new life and active democracy in 1983.

Stereotyping was practiced in both directions. Cheryl Rhoden and others noticed a tendency of younger activists to categorize older people in what appeared to be a kind of "ageism":

I like sitting in meetings with a real age mix, and it was absolutely hysterical to watch these young people sitting there reacting to some of the older people who were coming out with some of the most *outrageous* political statements, you know, total radicals, right? And these young people had somehow been treating them as though they needed to be coddled and nurtured, right? And these people were lifelong activists who had been in far more serious situations in their lifetime than Santa Monica's politics! These people were treating them like their grandparents, when actually they were more radical than a lot of the younger folks in the coalition. But their life experiences had taught them that. It was really funny; we have such a segregated society.[88]

Because of problems such as this, people of different generations were sometimes quick to judge each other. As we noted above, younger activists saw themselves as more organizationally astute and capable of sophisticated mobilization tactics. This resulted in a strong feeling among many people that when CED came into the picture, it "rewrote" the city's history in such a way that it took credit for rent control and progressive activism.[89] There are those who bristle at the idea of history being rewritten in a way that bypasses the crucial role played by Syd Rose and the senior activists, who in fact began the movement. A 1979 article in the *Los Angeles Times* picked up some of this sentiment, remarking that the successful passage of rent control was claimed by CED as its victory "with only a slight nod of recognition to such senior citizens as Syd Rose, who initiated the issue and campaigned vigorously for it" (*Los Angeles Times,* September 7, 1979). A senior is quoted as saying, "They're kids, a bit carried away with themselves, a little arrogant, but they did work hard, brought in a lot of money and certainly helped us win. I don't care who gets credit, as long as I get a rent reduction."

Another source of tension was a feeling among seniors that younger activists—the sixties generation in particular—were not so committed to long-term movements for change as older activists were. Some felt that the young people chose their involvements almost as a recreational activity to be engaged in and dropped after a time. As one senior activist observed:

When we were young, in our struggles, we had a vision of the future. Here they don't. They lose one battle and they get demoralized. They talk about burnout. We never talked about burnout; we didn't know what it was because we had a long-term vision of our work.[90]

Seniors often seemed surprised at the implication of choice when asked about how they became social activists. Typically, they responded with comments such as, "Growing up in that period, you had to be touched," or "Well, you just can't escape those things," or "Well, you just have it in your blood. You either care about people or you don't."[91] For many, it was the radicalizing experience of the depression that galvanized them into action. Asked about how she became involved in her union work, one woman simply responded, "It was the depression. The situation was bad, and it became necessary to organize."[92] Like many others, this woman found herself involved in tenant politics as an extension of her other commitments to social justice. Another found her way into tenants' issues through a commitment to peace and antiwar work. These activists felt that, in contrast to themselves, younger activists did not have a lifelong commitment and were too ready to "move on" to something else.

Critics might suggest that this was an idealistic or romantic reconstruction of past experience by older generations. Yet there is convincing evidence of actual differences between the life-worlds and experiences of various political generations (Ross, 1983). The puzzled reaction of older activists may in part be explained by generational differences in the approach to social movements. New social movement theorists in particular have pointed to "submerged networks" of activists that surface in response to various issues, but do not otherwise demonstrate a sustained presence (Melucci, 1985). They also characterize recent generations of activists as being more likely to engage in cross-class, shifting alliances and preoccupations with "self-production" of identity (Touraine, 1985). McCarthy and Zald (1973), on the other hand, have analyzed the shifts in the larger political economy of social movements in the 1960s and how these have altered the environment within which activists move. Taken together, these theories suggest the possibility that what seniors characterize as "burnout" or lack of commitment may be a misperception; younger activists may be committed to an ongoing battle for social justice that is different in structure from the repertoire of older generations, and thus not judged accurately. We will examine this issue in greater detail below since perceiving it correctly is crucial for the analysis of future social movements.

## Opinion Survey of Santa Monica and Houston Tenants

In Chapter 2, we noted in our review of the literature that the relationship among housing tenure, political consciousness, and social activism is theoretically disputed and underresearched. We became intrigued with this relationship as a result of our acquaintance with the theoretical literature, on the one hand, and our interactions with social movement activists on the other. The above-mentioned accounts offered to us by activists, for example, suggested that political generations strongly influenced repertoires of behavior and consciousnes about social structure (Mannheim, 1972). Analysts argue that the sixties had a major impact on U.S. culture (Flacks, 1988; Whalen and Flacks, 1989; Cloward and Piven 1986). Did the sixties have a lasting impact on U.S. politics? Did the sixties influence some cities more than others? According to Whalen and Flacks (1989:258):

It is often forgotten that the women's movements, the environmental movement, movements of gays, the handicapped, and other stigmatized groups, movements for community control and neighborhood revitalization, for tenants' rights, and seniors' needs, began to mobilize in the seventies, to a considerable extent the result of efforts by veterans of the sixties to carry forward the identity and vision they had developed as students into a larger society.

We decided to round out our study of tenants' movements in the United States by incorporating additional empirical data that would permit us to explore questions related to political culture as well as a number of other variables suggested by the social movements theories reviewed in Chapter 2. The empirical analysis, summarized below, builds on and challenges prior theoretical work in the area of tenants' movements and urban sociology.

As we pointed out in Chapter 2, Allan Heskin (1983) conducted one of the most exhaustive opinion surveys to date regarding why tenants supported rent control in Santa Monica. His survey of tenant attitudes was conducted shortly after Santa Monica passed rent control in 1979. The intent of the survey was to explore Manuel Castells's (1977) proposition that urban social movements result in greater political class consciousness. Heskin based his empirical analysis of interviews with Santa Monica residents and with residents in non-rent-controlled Los Angeles County.

While Heskin's history of the tenants' movment was excellent and the development of the dependent variable—tenant consciousness—creative, the overall statistical analysis lacked sophistication and was redundant. The statistical analysis was a comparative study between Los Angeles and Santa Monica using bivariate and trivariate techniques comparing percentage responses. Since these two cities share the same housing and media market, it is not surprising that Heskin found no difference between the two cities in terms of tenants' consciousness. Only two or three independent variables were simultaneously examined. Regression and logit—which would have allowed for simultaneous examination of the net impact of numerous variables—were not used in his study (Pindyck and Rubinfeld, 1976:247–254). More importantly, Heskin never analyzed as a dependent variable the question of whether or not the respondent supported the Santa Monica rent-control law.

As we noted above, Heskin's data analysis provided no support for Castells's contention that social movements are an independent source in the creation of radical political consciousness. Heskin (1983:158) found that "a worsening rental housing situation and landlord-tenant conflict in one form or another are necessary first elements in the emergence of a tenant movement." In addition, Heskin (1983:95–119) argued that certain demographic character-istics mold tenant consciousness: Individuals who were English-speaking, female, young, and low income were most radical in their beliefs about landlord/tenant reform.

Heskin's technique and results suggested to us the need to reanalyze his data using regression and logit analysis. We believed that regression/logit analysis could shed light on our hunch that the underlying causes of tenant support for rent control have more to do with political culture than with demo-graphics. In order to continue testing the work of Castells (1977, 1983) and Heskin's (1983) theory of urban social movements, we reanalyzed the data using logit analysis and replaced Los Angeles as the comparative non-rent-controlled city with Houston, the quintessential "free enterprise city" (Feagin, 1988).

Houston and Santa Monica are polar opposites in terms of how cities are organized and arranged in America, and their comparison presents a fresh approach to analyzing the causes of urban social movements. Securing a research grant from the Social Science Research Council, Gilderbloom and Rodriguez (1988) used many of the same questions from Heskin's (1983) Santa Monica survey to examine the political attitudes of tenants in Houston. Replicating the rigorous methodological standards of Heskin's study of Santa Monica renters, Gilderbloom and Rodriguez carried out over one thousand interviews with tenants in Houston in 1987. Roughly 50 percent of the questions from both studies overlapped, and Gilderbloom and Rodriguez combined these questions into one master data set.

The data yielded some surprising findings that challenge conventional wisdom. We begin our analysis with an examination of the bivariate tables. In both rent-controlled Santa Monica and free enterprise Houston, two thirds or more of the renters supported rent control. Santa Monica had a slightly higher percentage (83 percent) of renters supporting rent control compared with Houston tenants (68 percent) (Table 3-1). A higher percentage of renters in Santa Monica (47 percent) compared with Houston renters (29 percent) felt that a tenants' organization can be very successful (Table 3-2). The stronger support for rent control and tenant organization can be attributed to the fear that the rental situation in Santa Monica will continue to worsen (Table 3-3). In Santa Monica, one half of the renters felt the situation would worsen,

TABLE 3-1

Tenant Support for Rent Control by City

| Response Category | Santa Monica % | Houston % | Chi-Square |
|---|---|---|---|
| Vote for rent control | | | 24.3** |
| No | 17 | 32 | |
| Yes | 83 | 68 | |
| (N=) | (310) | (705) | |

Significance Levels:
* ≤ .05
** ≤ .01
Note: May not add up to 100% due to rounding.

TABLE 3-2

Tenant Attitudes Toward the Potential Success of Tenant Organizations by City

| Response Category | Santa Monica % | Houston % | Chi-Square |
|---|---|---|---|
| | | | 33.2** |
| Very successful | 47 | 29 | |
| Somewhat successful | 45 | 55 | |
| Not very successful | 6 | 12 | |
| Not at all successful | 3 | 4 | |
| (N = ) | (332) | (724) | |

Significance Levels:
** < .01

while only one fourth of Houston's tenants had a similar view. This "fear" was fueled by escalating rents in Santa Monica; half the renters in Santa Monica compared with one fifth of Houston's renters believed that rents were increasing in their neighborhoods (Table 3-4). The lack of homeownership opportunities in high-priced Santa Monica resulted in almost half the tenants believing they could not afford to buy a house in the next three years (Table 3-5). In Houston, on the other hand, two thirds of the renters believed they could purchase a home in the next three years.

Santa Monica's strong desire for and support of tenant organizations and rent control are not related to quality of housing (Table 3-6). The survey data indicate no substantive difference between housing conditions in Santa Monica and Houston. As Gilderbloom and Appelbaum (1988) have previously noted, the overall quality of American housing is excellent for the vast majority of

TABLE 3-3

Tenant Attitudes Toward the Future Situation for Tenants by City

| Response Category | Santa Monica % | Houston % | Chi-Square |
|---|---|---|---|
| | | | 96.1** |
| Situation will improve | 34 | 37 | |
| No change in situation | 16 | 41 | |
| Situation will get worse | 50 | 23 | |
| (N = ) | (329) | (747) | |

* ≤ .05
** ≤ .01
Note: May not add up to 100% due to rounding.

TABLE 3-4

Tenant Knowledge of Area Rent Fluctuations in Neighborhood by City

| Response Category | Santa Monica % | Houston % | Chi-Square |
|---|---|---|---|
| | | | 91.4** |
| Increasing rents | 50 | 17 | |
| Decreasing rents | 10 | 22 | |
| No change in rents | 40 | 61 | |
| (N = ) | (187) | (710) | |

** < .01

TABLE 3-5

Tenant Prospect of Buying Home in the Next Three Years, by City

| Response Category | Santa Monica % | Houston % | Chi-Square |
|---|---|---|---|
| | | | 20.6** |
| Yes, will buy home | 56 | 70 | |
| No, will not buy home | 44 | 30 | |
| (N=) | (344) | (798) | |

** < .01

Americans. Our analysis of Houston and Santa Monica shows that less than 5 percent of the tenants felt their housing was in poor condition; a fourth felt their housing was only in fair condition.

TABLE 3-6

Housing Conditions for Renter Occupied Households, by City

| Response Category | Santa Monica % | Houston % | Chi-Square |
|---|---|---|---|
|  |  |  | 3.6 |
| Very good condition | 31 | 32 |  |
| Good condition | 40 | 40 |  |
| Fair condition | 26 | 23 |  |
| Poor condition | 3 | 3 |  |
| Very poor condition | 1 | 2 |  |
| (N = ) | (344) | (798) |  |

Note: May not add to 100% due to rounding.

We then proceeded to examine the political attitudes of Houston and Santa Monica renters. We found that over 80 percent of the tenants approved of government support for low-income housing (Table 3-7). Interestingly enough, a slightly higher percentage of renters in Houston supported this proposal.

TABLE 3-7

Tenant Attitudes Toward Government Support for Low-Income Housing, by City

| Response Category | Santa Monica % | Houston % | Chi-Square |
|---|---|---|---|
|  |  |  | 4.3* |
| Approve | 80 | 86 |  |
| Disapprove | 20 | 15 |  |
| (N = ) | (329) | (745) |  |

* < .05
Note: May not add up to 100% due to rounding.

Seventy-three percent of Houston's tenants felt that escalating rents were caused by "greedy landlords"; 88 percent of Santa Monica's tenants agreed with this viewpoint (Table 3-8). According to Gilderbloom and Appelbaum (1988), this belief in the "greedy landlord hypotheses" is mistaken, but has important implications for how housing policy becomes constructed in the minds of tenants, landlords, and the government. Support for rent control could also be attributed to tenants in Santa Monica who tended to be more liberal (Table 3-9) and better educated (Table 3-10) than those in Houston.

While bivariate analysis provides interesting descriptive data, it should not be used to infer correlations among variables. A major problem with the

## TABLE 3-8

Tenants Who Feel Rent Increases Due to Greedy Landlords, by City

| Response Category | Santa Monica % | Houston % | Chi-Square |
|---|---|---|---|
| | | | 27.9** |
| Yes, landlords are greedy | 88 | 73 | |
| No, landlords are not greedy | 12 | 27 | |
| (N = ) | (332) | (798) | |

** < .01

## TABLE 3-9

Tenant Political Views, by City

| Response Category | Santa Monica % | Houston % | Chi-Square |
|---|---|---|---|
| | | | 21.3** |
| Conservative | 22 | 33 | |
| Moderate | 34 | 36 | |
| Liberal | 29 | 19 | |
| Progressive | 15 | 11 | |
| (N=) | (305) | (697) | |

** < .01
Note: Does not add to 100% due to rounding.

## TABLE 3-10

Level of Tenant Education, by City

| Response Category | Santa Monica % | Houston % | Chi-Square |
|---|---|---|---|
| | | | 33.0** |
| 12 or fewer years of education | 25 | 43 | |
| 13 or more years of education | 76 | 57 | |
| (N = ) | (343) | (768) | |

** < .01
Note: Does not add to 100% due to rounding.

previous research has been the use of bivariate analysis to establish complex theoretical arguments (see Heskin, 1983). In order to test our initial bivariate relationships, we ran a multiple regression analysis using both ordinary least squares and logit approaches. Unlike Heskin, who concentrated on predicting support for a variety of landlord/tenant reform measures, we chose to concentrate on just one question: support for rent control. Because our dependent variable (approve of rent control yes = 1; no = 0) is dichotomous, we used the more conservative logit results to decide if an independent variable was statistically significant. Statistical theory argues that logit is the most appropriate and sophisticated approach to analyzing dichotomous dependent variables. The logit analysis indicates that many of the initial bivariate relationships wash out in terms of their impact when we control for other intervening variables. The data show that support for rent control is unrelated to a person's age, years at current address, ability to purchase a home, Spanish language spoken, sex, future housing situation, or monthly rent (Table 3-11).

Of particular interest is the finding that a tenant's rent is unrelated to his or her support for rent control. It has become conventional wisdom that high rents lead to support for rent control, yet our data show that this is not the case. A tenant's fear that the housing situation might worsen is also a poor predictor of support for rent control. The data also found no empirical support for both Ron Lawson's (1986) and Allan Heskin's (1983) pronouncements that the renters' movement garnered a disproportionate amount of support from women and Spanish-speaking persons.

Our analysis of which factors led to support of rent control reveals some interesting lessons for urban social movement theory. We found that the following factors were statistically related to supporting rent control: (1) government support of affordable housing initiatives; (2) liberal political attitudes; (3) perception of housing condition, rent fairness and landlord; (4) viewing tenant organizations as important; (5) low incomes; and (6) more highly educated people supporting regulation. The fact that low-income tenants tend to be more likely to favor regulation than do higher income tenants turns Kann's (1986) major hypothesis that Santa Monica is simply a "middle-class revolt" completely on its head. The test of Castells's theory of urban social movements leading to higher consciousness concerning issues of class is given strong empirical support in this study (Table 3-11).

A separate logit analysis of Houston and Santa Monica found several significant changes in the statistical relationships. The most important change was a separate analysis of the Santa Monica data that found baby boomers to be strong supporters of rent control (Table 3-12). The Whalen and Flacks (1989) argument, that young individuals who were politically socialized during the sixties tend to be more progressive, needs to be put within a geographic context. Also, in Santa Monica a tenant's housing condition appears to be unrelated to support for rent control.

TABLE 3-11

Factors Influencing Tenant Support for Rent Control: Santa Monica and Houston

| Independent Variables | Ordinary Least Squares Regression | | | Logit Model | |
|---|---|---|---|---|---|
| | b | SE B | Beta | b | SE |
| Age | .0003 | .007 | .002 | −.01 | .01 |
| Government housing | −.82 | .16 | −.18** | −.67** | .13 |
| Fairness of rent | .37 | .16 | .08* | .34* | .16 |
| Years at current address | −.008 | .01 | −.02 | −.015 | .011 |
| Home purchase in 3 years | −.03 | .12 | −.01 | −.002 | .116 |
| Spanish language | −.06 | .24 | −.01 | .35 | .31 |
| Gender | .21 | .11 | .07 | .13 | .10 |
| Political views | .28 | .06 | .18** | .24** | .05 |
| Greedy landlord | −.42 | .14 | −.11** | −.42** | .12 |
| Future tenant situation | −.01 | .07 | −.003 | .005 | .066 |
| Housing condition | −.18 | .07 | −.10** | −.11* | .06 |
| Success in tenant organization | .27 | .08 | .12** | .17* | .07 |
| Monthly rent | −.0006 | .0004 | −.06 | −.0005 | .0003 |
| Income | −.04 | .02 | −.09* | −.04* | .02 |
| Highest completed grade in school | −.04 | .02 | −.08 | −.08** | .02 |
| City (Houston = 1, Santa Monica = 0) | −.11 | .09 | −.06 | −.27** | .09 |
| R Square | .21 | | | | |
| F | 11** | | | | |
| N | 693 | | | 677 | |

\* ≤ .05
\*\* ≤ .01

Why were Santa Monica's baby boomers—in contrast to Houston's—more supportive of rent control? As we shall show later in this chapter, a key determinant influencing the chances of a city adopting rent control was intensive antiwar activity during the 1960s. Los Angeles was a major staging ground for protests against the Vietnam war while Houston's record of protest, concerning Vietnam or civil rights, was largely nonexistent. In terms of urban folklore, Santa Monica was known as the home of numerous antiwar activists including Jane Fonda, Tom Hayden, Derek Shearer, and Leonard Weinglass (Chicago 7 defense attorney), while Houston had a reputation for being the home of redneck cowboys whose Texas-born son—Lyndon Johnson—was the president of the United States and commander in chief of American forces during the Vietnam war. Even Houston's large black community was seen

TABLE 3-12

Factors Influencing Tenant Support for Rent Control: Santa Monica

| Independent Variables | Ordinary Least Squares Regression | | | Logit Model | |
|---|---|---|---|---|---|
| | b | SE B | Beta | b | SE |
| Age | −.04 | .01 | −.23** | −.033* | .017 |
| Government housing | −.74 | .27 | −.17** | −.87* | .33 |
| Fairness of rent | .33 | .27 | .07 | .85 | .51 |
| Years at current address | −.14 | .04 | −.29** | −.13* | .05 |
| Home purchase in 3 years | −.08 | .20 | −.03 | −.02 | .28 |
| Spanish language | −.27 | .59 | −.03 | −.58 | .78 |
| Gender | .23 | .19 | .08 | .14 | .26 |
| Political views | .31 | .10 | .20** | .51** | .15 |
| Greedy landlord | −.84 | .30 | −.18** | −.67 | .37 |
| Future tenant situation | .19 | .11 | .11 | .18 | .15 |
| Housing condition | −.16 | .12 | −.09 | −.27 | .18 |
| Success in tenant organization | .28 | .14 | .13* | .16 | .17 |
| Monthly rent | −.0008 | .0007 | −.08 | −.001 | .001 |
| Income | −.06 | .03 | −.12 | −.11** | .04 |
| Highest completed grade in school | −.001 | .037 | −.003 | −.08 | .05 |
| R Square | .26 | | | | |
| F | 4.8** | | | | |
| N | 218 | | | 204 | |

* ≤ .05
** ≤ .01

as hawkish toward Vietnam. As Parker and Feagin (forthcoming) note, Houston is unique because "there have not been fundamental changes between 1960 and 1990." In a review of the political history of Houston, Shelton et al. (1989:135) claim that the city is extraordinary compared to other cities for its lack of "significant grassroots...input into local politics."

The antiwar movement had a significant impact on the lives of the young people that it touched, giving them a new set of values and skills in community organizing. Prior social movements are often a necessary condition for lighting the fuse for subsequent collective action. In Houston, few were trained to help light that fire, yet in Santa Monica, former antiwar activists were highly visible, fighting for women, disabled and gay rights, environmentalism, historic preservation, consumer protection, antinuclear initiatives, and so on. These groups—which also contained seniors who had experienced social activism in the 1930s, 1940s, and 1950s—challenged mainstream notions of what is fair and unfair, right and wrong, just and unjust. In this regard, the impact of the sixties was seen everywhere in Santa Monica and almost nowhere in Houston. The baby boomers in Santa Monica directly experienced the countercultural movement, whereas the young in Houston seemed little affected by the sixties.

Given our interest in the correlation between protest activity in the 1960s and the rent-control movement in the 1980s, and to study why certain cities enact rent control and whether or not this is related more to ideology than to material conditions, our next step was to merge a data set developed by Gilderbloom and Appelbaum (1988) that examined 140 non-rent-controlled cities and all rent-controlled cities over 50,000 population. Given the fact that Gilderbloom and Appelbaum's original data set was composed of government census defined urban areas of 50,000 or more, we added every rent-controlled city in America over 50,000. This resulted in twenty-one cities being added to the field. We again used logit regression analysis because the dependent variable under consideration (rent control) was dichotomous—cities were either rent-controlled or non-rent-controlled. Although this is only a preliminary analysis of the data, we found these results significant enough to include in this book.

Using variables that measure social and economic conditions in cities, we found that only two variables could predict the likelihood of a city adopting rent control (Table 3-13). The first variable was the percentage of tenants in a city. The larger the percentage of tenants, the greater the chance the city will adopt rent control. The second variable that predicts passage of rent control is whether the city had been jolted by protests against the Vietnam war during the sixties. This variable measures degree of antiwar activity by a city's closeness to a major antiwar protest activity. Table 3-14 shows that rent-controlled cities were within forty-three miles of a major antiwar rally of 50,000 or more during the sixties, compared with non-rent-controlled cities that were approximately 1,317 miles away. When we attempted to replicate our results with different measures of antiwar activity (number of colleges closed during the bombing of Cambodia and total number of people attending an antiwar rally within fifty miles of a city between 1967 and 1970), the results remained statistically significant. It is interesting to note that the average number of colleges closed during the Cambodian crisis was eleven in rent-controlled cities compared with zero in non-rent-controlled places. Similarly, the total attendance for an antiwar activity within fifty miles of a rent-controlled city was in the hundreds of thousands compared to only 480 persons in non-rent-controlled cities.

While neither geographical proximity—traditionally an ecological variable—nor percentage of tenants—a structural variable that taps material conditions—can be used to make inferences about "consciousness," the personal histories and accounts by activists that we presented earlier in this chapter indicate that many of the tenant organizers were former antiwar and civil rights workers from the sixties. This suggests that the culture of the sixties is playing a powerful role in the shaping of politics in the eighties and nineties. With this additional information gained through our qualitative case study, it is not a coincidence that the urban areas with the greatest amount of antiwar activity during the sixties (the Boston to Washington, D.C., urban corridor, the San Francisco Bay area, and Los Angeles) also have the vast majority of American cities with rent control and progressive urban movements. It is the culture of the sixties, not the material conditions of the present, that is transforming cities in a radical new direction.

TABLE 3-13

Factors Influencing Support for Rent Control in Cities

| Independent Variables | Ordinary Least Squares Regression | | | Logit Model | |
|---|---|---|---|---|---|
| | b | SE B | Beta | b | SE |
| 50 or more units at one address | .0009 | .0009 | .05 | .05 | .09 |
| Level of education | .0004 | .003 | .006 | .04 | .08 |
| Percentage of housing units for rent | .007 | .002 | .21** | .13 | .06** |
| Total population | .00000001 | .00000005 | .01 | .000 | .000 |
| Percentage of rental units lacking plumbing | .02 | .01 | .09 | .36 | .52 |
| Percentage voted for McGovern | .0008 | .002 | .03 | .05 | .04 |
| Median rent | .001 | .0005 | .13* | .004 | .008 |
| Population density | .00004 | .000006 | .46** | .00026 | .00024 |
| Percentage below poverty level | .009 | .005 | .11 | −.11 | .16 |
| Number of miles from major antiwar activity | −.0001 | .00005 | −.16** | −.01 | .004** |
| R Square | .67 | | | | |
| F | 30.3** | | | | |
| N | 161 | | | | |

\* ≤ .05
\*\* ≤ .01

A close look at Table 3-14 shows that many of the ecological conditions found in the two city types are virtually the same. These data further support our contention that Kann's (1986) interpretation of the rent-control movement as "middle class" is without empirical support. In fact, the rent-controlled cities appear to be somewhat poorer in terms of income, on the one hand, and have slightly higher housing costs, on the other. A cross-class alliance was crucial to the accomplishment of rent control, as was the hands-on experience and political consciousness fostered by participation in earlier protest movements in the 1960s.

TABLE 3-14

Factors Influencing Support for Rent Control in Cities

| Independent Variables | National Sample | | New Jersey Sample | |
|---|---|---|---|---|
| | RC | NRC | RC | NRC |
| Total population | 307,665 | 254,397 | 36,924 | 19,924 |
| Age | 29.4 | 29.1 | 33.6 | 32.5 |
| Median income 1980 | 18,568 | 19,550 | 20,193 | 22,566 |
| Percentage below poverty level 1980 | 13.7 | 9.5 | 6.9 | 5.0 |
| Percent completed college | 16.5 | 16.3 | | |
| Number of miles from major antiwar activity | 42.6 | 1,317 | | |
| Number of colleges closed by antiwar activity | 10.7 | .21 | | |
| Total attendance at antiwar activity 1967–1970 | 359,891 | 480 | | |
| Percentage voted for McGovern | 47.1 | 35.8 | 70.1 | 49.7 |
| Median rent 1980 | 218 | 186 | 252 | 267 |
| Median rent 1970 | 110 | 101 | 125 | 123 |
| Housing costs 1980 | 34,077 | 47,593 | 61,194 | 68,013 |
| Housing costs 1970 | 22,000 | 15,678 | 24,240 | 24,217 |
| Vacancy rate 1980 | 4.3 | 7.9 | 4.0 | 4.6 |
| Vacancy rate 1970 | 3.4 | 8.3 | 2.19 | 2.25 |
| Number of rooms | 3.7 | 4.0 | 5.24 | 5.89 |
| 50 or more units at one address | 16.3 | 12.6 | 10.6 | 9.4 |
| Percentage of units boarded up | 0.6 | 0.4 | | |
| Percentage of units built after 1975 | 4.43 | 17.3 | 5.3 | 8.2 |
| Percentage of housing units for rent | 55.8 | 36.3 | | |
| Percentage of rental units lacking plumbing | 3.5 | 2.4 | 2.94 | 2.53 |
| N | 21 | 141 | 26 | 37 |

## Conclusions

In this chapter, we have attempted to capture a social history of the progressive tenants' movement in Santa Monica from its initial mobilization through the election of progressive activists to public office on a platform of community control. We began by examining some of the structural and historical features of Santa Monica as a setting for the movement, including the insistence on a free market model by the city council, the destruction of vulnerable communities, and the gradual emergence of "free spaces" in particular neighborhoods that reasserted the rights of "community" in the face of "commodity."

In our effort to capture the process of the movement as it developed over time, we relied on the accounts of various activists—both in leadership positions and at the grass-roots level—to "tell the story" of the movement. These individuals placed a great deal of emphasis on features that are conducive to analysis using the resource mobilization perspective: the construction of viable social movement organizations and the competition and cooperation among them; the changes in the social movements sector that provided resources externally; the role of "movement entrepreneurs" such as Syd Rose, Denny Zane, Parke Skelton, Derek Shearer, or Tom Hayden; the growing sophistication and formalization of the movement along with the tension that this produced with the grass-roots activists; and the role of generational repertoires in the movement.

We ended our chapter with an empirical anlysis that further explored— in a different medium—the questions raised by earlier chapters and by the tenants' accounts themselves. We conclude, on the basis of our quantitative and qualitative analyses, that there is compelling evidence that individuals with a particular generational experience and protest repertoire have a crucial impact on social movements above and beyond other factors traditionally used to explain such movements. We have observed how the "sixties generation" provided practical experience, political savvy, and intellectual ideas for the progressive program, beginning with rent control and expanding into community control. The role of consciousness and exposure to a particular political culture was essential, whether in the case of the younger activists in Santa Monica or the seniors whose political experience was garnered in earlier movements. Likewise, the lack of exposure to such a culture appeared to lead to passivity in such cities as Houston that had no protest tradition. While Santa Monica began by taking a free market stand, community protests forced it to change its approach to politics and the shaping of urban space. Houston, on the other hand, remains wedded to the free market tradition (see Chapter 6).

Our data also support a resource mobilization perspective, which argues that neither sheer numbers of people nor grievances/strains will guarantee a movement; rather, this will depend on the creation of organizational opportunities and resources (Dreier, 1982:191). Santa Monica clearly demonstrates that an 80 percent tenant population does not mobilize itself (the closest that it came to doing so was after the letdown of Proposition 13), but rather relies on what frequently amounts to a handful of activists or "movement entrepreneurs." Parke Skelton, manager of numerous SMRR campaigns, affirmed both the role of political culture and resource mobilization when he recalled:

> The majority of people mobilized to work in these campaigns—and there were lots of them, unbelievable numbers—they came out of just a general left perspective, and they wanted to participate. They didn't come out of the tenant unions for the most part. They were young, left, progressive people who wanted to be involved, who may or may not have had bad situations on their own hands.[93]

The SMRR organization provided them with the opportunity to act out their convictions, which for the most part were already formed through prior involvements in other movements.

Our combined evidence also indicates that, contrary to the assumptions of a number of senior activists in Santa Monica, the younger activists did not drop out of the "struggle" for social justice, but defined it more broadly rather than through allegiance to one particular issue or organization. Not only did activists from the sixties turn up in the tenants' movement in the seventies and the eighties, but many continued their involvement through related issues later. A common ground for their various experiences is suggested by new social movement theorist Alain Touraine (1985), who emphasizes the right to define one's identity and goals rather than having these foisted on one by powerful others. There are many examples of movement activists pursuing this human right, demonstrating that the repertoire is ongoing. Parke Skelton was involved in fighting the statewide anti-rent-control intitiative, helped to orchestrate the Santa Monica campaign, and went on to be campaign manager for the victorious West Hollywood rent-control and cityhood campaign in 1984, which depended on a working alliance between young gay activists and senior citizens. Cheryl Rhoden became a senior staffperson for Senator Alan Cranston; Ruth Galanter was elected to the Los Angeles city council in 1987; Dennis Zane remained as city councilman and was reelected in November 1988, becoming mayor of Santa Monica. There are many other examples. Each of these people continued to work for an expanded, nonelite definition of human beings and/or urban spaces and for new possibilities for responsible, democratically controlled communities. While the monetary rewards for this type of work are seldom high, the commitments shaped by their generational experience led them—along with many others—to make sense of the world in a manner consistent with progressive activism. On the other hand, their career paths are different from senior activists since they blend individual career advancement with social justice issues. Many of these possibilities have to do with the professionalization of social movements and career possibilities that did not exist at an earlier time (McCarthy and Zald, 1973, 1977; Touraine, 1985).

While the resource mobilization perspective has proved valuable in generating insights for the analysis of the Santa Monica movement, there are aspects that need to be explored further using theories more attuned to the symbolic tasks of the movement. Even in our current findings concerning the importance of generational repertoires, resource mobilization is better at handling the material resources and formal skills constituting this repertoire than the ideas, consciousness, or symbolic behavior associated with it. Yet, it remains very important to ask: How did tenants construct new notions of "fairness" in Santa Monica? How did they recruit bystanders who were not direct beneficiaries to the movement? How did they help to redefine values in a private property culture so that their grievances were perceived as valid and their solutions perceived as just? In Chapter 4, we will turn our attention to these questions.

# Symbols and Collective Definitions of the Santa Monica Movement

## Introduction

The study of social movements has shifted increasingly toward examining the resource base from which collective behavior is able to emerge, rather than giving weight to the goals, frustrations, or legitimating symbols of challenging groups—nuts and bolts have replaced hearts and minds (Wuthnow et al., 1984:1).

In recent years, there has been an emphasis in social movements literature on the resource mobilization perspective in the United States. As we pointed out above, this theoretical orientation is especially useful for understanding how movement participants are able to establish control over a variety of material and organizational resources in order to build a movement. In Chapter 3, we examined the construction of a tenants' movement in Santa Monica and its expansion into a broader urban progressive movement. We noted how the structural availability of particular individuals as well as a supporting organizational infrastructure such as government policy created mobilization opportunities for tenants. We observed how the entry of groups such as CED and CHAIN and urban progressive networks rationalized the movement and allowed it to be proactive rather than reactive. We also raised the issue of community-building and social interaction in progressive movements, noting the tension over "people power" versus technology. This theme led us into an area about which resource mobilization theory has little to say—the symbolic and interactional processes that go into the making and maintaining of social movements.

As we pointed out in our review of critiques of resource mobilization theory in Chapter 2, this theory begins with interested, calculating groups of actors, and the level of analysis at which it treats interaction is between groups rather than within them. And above all, attention is directed toward strategic material rather than nonmaterial resources. By contrast, theorists such as Touraine (1985) and Melucci (1985) suggest that the symbolic control of information is becoming an increasingly important facet for social movements in modern societies. Domination and protest cut across many spheres and a large part of the struggle between social groups is over the right to "name" and define such basic categories as space and to construct a new kind of rationality (Portes, 1971). Opp (1985) and others have also noted the importance of "soft" or nonmaterial incentives for movement participation, such as social solidarity. We believe that it is essential to understand the strategic social uses of symbolic resources—from creating a sense of community to the important task of translating progressive issues into acceptable electoral terms. At certain critical junctures, these aspects had the power to make or break the movement in Santa Monica.

## Symbolic Mobilization Tasks

Several clues point to the importance of a symbolically oriented perspective on the Santa Monica movement. Among the most important is the vehement debate over regulation taking place in the United States. In this regard, the Santa Monica case raises an interesting question: Why, during a time when the general mood of the public was pro-Reagan and antiregulatory, did the usual tactics used to discredit such options not work? Why did the negative connotations surrounding regulation not "stick" in Santa Monica?[1] To vote for citywide regulation of rents is to depart from a tradition of individualism and to vote for a systemic solution that places curbs on the free market. This marks a shift in the collective definition of the situation, an outcome that presupposes some crucial symbolic work.

While opponents of rent control tend to characterize it as a "pocketbook" issue based on self-interest, they overlook the fact that many people in Santa Monica were also voting for a social construction of fairness that incorporated the tenant as an individual with community rights that were historically new. Certainly homeowners, who provided an important percentage of the swing votes, did not have anything personally to gain from doing so.[2] This type of redefinition is at least in part a symbolic social act and needs to be studied as such. Rent control became as sacred as motherhood in a city that had always relied on the growth model and opposed regulation. The most visible sign of this was that after 1981 no one dared run on an anti-rent-control platform (particularly since, as our data showed in Chapter 3, over 90 percent of tenants supported rent control). As one irate landlord put it, rent control was a "dirty, filthy appeal to motherhood and family" (*Evening Outlook,* September 14, 1983). People on both sides of the rent-control movement felt that politics in the city were being redefined and that rent control was at the new political center. A number of SMRR's opponents, for example, made statements such as, "I went all the way from liberal to reactionary without ever once changing my views."[3] How was this collective redefinition accomplished, and what were the successful strategies of the rent-control movement that permitted this to happen?

Tenants, because they were asking for the regulation of private property, had an uphill battle for legitimacy in the city. We suggest that in order for progressives to be effective at a symbolic level, they had to accomplish three primary tasks. First, they needed to gain access to information that was ordinarily unavailable to nonelites in the community, in order to unmask and reveal the "backstage" operating areas of their opponents.[4] This "information gathering" (Marx, 1979) was linked to a second task: to become public custodians of the community's identity, acquiring the power to shape public perceptions of the various social groups in the city. This role has usually not been accorded to tenants. It encompasses not only a reconstruction of the perception of tenants in the community by nontenants, but also a reconstruction of how tenants view *themselves* in relation to their community. In Chapter 2, we documented the grievances of tenants as a social group and remarked on their persistent low status in a private property culture. How did tenants in Santa Monica generate enough self-confidence to occupy civic and political life more securely? Third, they had to give attention to framing their issues and information in such a way as to render them more credible to the public than the claims of their opponents according to the "folk-concept of just protest" (Turner, 1969; Snow et al., 1986). Accordingly, progressives and tenant supporters had to learn to manipulate some points of cultural ambiguity in order to derive a legitimate position for the new traditions they were trying to create from more established cultural sources. Crucial to this task was claiming the legacy of "democracy," a heritage both sides were eager to appropriate. Below, we will examine these movement tasks in order.

Unmasking the Opposition: Backstage Work

> Our appearance, because we strip away all illusion, produces the total revelation of our oppressors as well. —Tom Hayden (1970:49)

Assembly Representative Tom Hayden has toned down his rhetoric since the 1960s, yet this statement from his past is symbolically appropriate for understanding the Santa Monica setting and, more particularly, the strategies of SMRR in that setting. One of the most effective tasks undertaken by SMRR to consolidate public opinion and mobilize voters was the "stripping away" of masks worn by city power elites and rendering the relationships in their starkest— and most blatantly economic— form. Normally, a distinguishing feature of elite groups is their ability to function as custodians of information, deciding what will and will not be public information (Suttles, 1972). By organizing research efforts and finding ways to share knowledge, tenants were able to go "backstage" and to acquire the discretionary choice over public and private information. This was all the more powerful given that the culture of capitalism respects, indeed mandates, privacy regarding one's economic investments. A "code of silence" governs investments and incomes in the United States (Čapek, 1985); tenants in Santa Monica who broke the code were at the same time extraordinarily effective and exposed to extraordinary risk due to the vehemence of the backlash they created.

One of SMRR's strategies was to make public in their campaign literature the financial contributions that funded their opposition. This was public information by law in California, yet for the most part the public had never laid eyes on it. The progressive contributions revealed, as is typical in such campaigns, financial support in small amounts from many different individuals. Contributions for the landlords and the anti-rent-control forces, on the other hand, tended to come in large sums from wealthy individuals or corporations, many of whom were not located in Santa Monica. For example, a 1979 SMRR mailer shows the opposition receiving $1,500 from the California Real Estate PAC and the Beverly Hills-based Board of Realtors PAC, and $3,540 from Moss and Company Apartments in Los Angeles. SMRR had the advantage of framing the conflict as a kind of David versus Goliath battle—an image that, among the many twists and turns of Santa Monica politics, small landlords later claimed for themselves against the "monster" of rent control.

The fact that many contributions came from outside Santa Monica helped to play up the image of outsiders gambling with the community's fate. Although landlords often attempted to portray the pro-rent control forces as motivated and directed by outside agitators, in this case it was easy for tenants to show that the "real" outside agitators were real estate interests and coalitions that prominently included bankers and developers. The theme of "Is Santa Monica for Sale?" proved to be highly effective for prodding beneath the placid, taken-for-granted surface of social life in the city. Moreover, it continued to be effective in electoral issues not relating directly to rent control, as in the June 1984 campaign for Proposition Y, whose passage was considered a victory for SMRR.

Proposition Y was a proposal to combine local with national elections in order to increase voter turnout locally. Because this would favor tenants' rights, opposition to it attracted vast sums of money (SMRR was being outspent by its opponents four to one) and created some new splits in the community.[5] Some of the heaviest contributors against Proposition Y were the Standard Investment Company, in which developer Larry Kates was a partner ($50,000), Kates himself ($25,000 twice), and the Shell Oil Company ($3,500), which was involved in litigation with the progressive government over costs due on their underground gas pipeline. SMRR once again exposed these financial interests. Even SMRR opponents were offended by the high-powered electioneering of outsiders.

SMRR thus made it a conscious policy to expose the community's economic structure. By merely providing financial information about its opponents, it hit upon a "damaging action" (Marx, 1979) that raised costs for its opponents, forcing them to take a defensive posture. It should be noted that the results may have been quite different in a culture that did not experience ambiguous feelings about the interaction of democracy and private property (see below). As it was, SMRR's information gathering helped to convince the community that there was a systemic problem that could not be solved individualistically. The strategy was particularly effective in a city where most people felt that developers and speculators had added to the city's woes. As we noted in Chapter 3, almost nine out of every ten tenants viewed landlords as "greedy."

The *Santa Monica Fair Housing Reporter,* a SMFHA newsletter, collected local as well as national information on rent control and additionally provided documentation about the structural features of the landlord-tenant relationship in the Los Angeles area. The May 1978 issue reported finding that one individual had made seventeen separate contributions to the anti-rent-control campaign by channeling them through the thirty-seven separate buildings he owned. It further pointed out that:

> Mr. Eisler is a relatively small operator compared to Francis Mariani and Jerry Buss. Mariani and Buss, who have offices at 2116 Wilshire, are involved in over 80 limited partnerships which own real estate in the area. Each limited partnership has a separate name—bizarre names such as Gomar, Aumar, Shi Five, Shi Four, Shi Forth, Shi II, MP, MPC, MPD, MPE, Fission, Fashion, Fusion, and Tiebreaker. (They are to be commended for their inventiveness.) So far, this incestuous family of businesses have made 11 contributions to the "No on P" campaign. These contributions total over $8,000!

Another article in the same issue observed that:

> Banks, of course, reap tremendous profits from the financing of real estate speculation. The higher rents go, the more money the banks

make....According to David Schulman's [sic] article in the Santa Monica Independent Journal, the real force behind the No on P campaign is the California Housing Council. This rather elite group is comprised of 200 landlords from throughout the state. These 200 landlords, however, own close to 500,000 units statewide, or, on the average, 2,500 units apiece!...The Los Angeles PR firm that has been hired to run the No on P campaign has worked closely with the California Housing Council before.

This backstage work functioned to discredit symbolically SMRR's opposition. It was not always easy to carry out, particularly since a maze of subsidiaries might make ownership research difficult (*L.A. Reader,* April 1, 1979). However, it was effective, judging by the outraged response of those who were targeted for these revelations, which damaged their "public face." In 1983, developer Larry Kates filed a $30 million libel suit against SMRR and the city, alleging that he was exposed to "hatred, contempt, ridicule and obloquy" in two campaign pamphlets (*Los Angeles Times,* March 13, 1983). Kates had contributed $4,200 to SMRR's opposition and over $75,000 toward the passage of an initiative that would permit tenants to purchase their apartments. The basis of the suit was that the revelation of personal information about him, including his wealth and his real estate holdings and campaign contributions, was damaging. He added that he was not a public figure, merely a contributor. As such, he invoked the economic code of silence that in U.S. culture defines the boundaries between public and private.

However, Kates was a public figure in the sense that he personally controlled the fates of large numbers of tenants. Allegedly, he deliberately maintained vacant units in his buildings in a protest against rent control; he also made public appearances to testify against rent control, as in the community of Thousand Oaks, California, where he had invested heavily in real estate. Robert Myers, Santa Monica city attorney, insisted on recognizing the public nature of his role. As he bluntly put it, "For Mr. Kates, one of the largest landlords in the city and the state, to claim the right not to have facts about him disclosed is a perversion of the Constitution" (*Los Angeles Times,* March 13, 1983).

The same violation of the code of silence surrounding private property holdings caused landlords to rebel against the rent-control law provision that demanded that they provide information about their apartments through a registration process (see Chapter 5). SMRR's exposure of the large campaign contributions made by landlords made their complaints of being brought to the edge of bankruptcy appear to be "crocodile tears."[6] In this way, SMRR used information gathering to symbolically pry apart the values of free enterprise and democracy, which in U.S. culture are unusually strongly and uncritically welded together. In order to do this effectively, SMRR needed to know where the weaknesses and ambiguities were in the culture.

Apart from relying on public information and documents, tenants also relied on interactional strategies. Infiltrating the backstage, or the "gotcha" school of politics, as councilmember Christine Reed referred to it, was a game played by both sides.[7] Attempts were made to find settings where social interactions were unguarded and where a construction of the other group's "public face" was being undertaken.[8] Both sides had their victories. For tenants, who worked hard to present their regulation issue as economically rational and all-American (see below), it was disconcerting to have their opposition obtain a tape of one of SMRR's leading spokespersons, Derek Shearer, addressing a conference on the virtues of using the term "economic democracy," which "unlike that 's' word [socialism]" could be "sold door to door like Fuller brushes." A tape with selected excerpts of the speech was mailed out to voters by SMRR's opposition in the 1983 campaign, damaging SMRR's credibility. SMRR, on the other hand, obtained information prior to the same election that Christine Reed, an SMRR opponent who was running on a platform of not opposing rent control, had appeared in two anti-rent-control campaign ads in Minneapolis. She, in turn, had to defend herself to the public.

All sides participated in these "backstage actions," which contributed to the local political drama in the city. One landlord boasted of having been part of a group of "stool pigeons" in Syd Rose's group.[9] In 1984, landlords infiltrated the progressive Mid-City Neighbors community organization, then used their status as "members" to persuade the city council not to give funding to the group. In every case, information gathering was used in order to try to prove that one's opponents were motivated purely by political interest while maintaining a public face of sincere interest. Tenants generally stressed economic conspiracy, while their opponents emphasized political conspiracy (see below).

## Tenants as Custodians of Image

We have said that a crucial element in the symbolic reorientation of the city would be to create the potential for tenants to have power over the public construction of their own image. Every community has a particular set of "custodians" who control the image and sense of identity of the community (Suttles, 1972). Especially important are newspapers and public officials since both can create a public forum for themselves. This gives them a tremendous power to shape public perceptions and helps to explain how it might occur that 80 percent of the population of the city would not have control over construction of its own image. John Walton (1984b:79) has defined culture as a "collective self-portrait" that is influenced in its presentation by groups that have power over others. We noted in Chapter 2 that, as a result of their powerlessness in the United States, tenants have been in most cases pictured in their communities as "second-class citizens" (Heskin, 1981b, 1983). The public portrait is not theirs to make, but its consequences are theirs to live with nevertheless. By studying the tenants' movement in Santa Monica, we can observe the effect of a social movement on urban culture.

Although it is little discussed, the change in the identity of tenants is one of the most tangible results of the social movement in Santa Monica. This fact may be overlooked when a resource mobilization perspective is employed that focuses only on material and organizational resources of the progressive movement. A revealing example of the change is the manner in which Santa Monica's relatively large senior citizen tenant population has been redefined several times over in response to structural changes in the city. By observing this, we can capture changes of meaning associated with the words "tenant," "senior citizen," and human rights generally.

Whereas at one time seniors were considered to be highly desirable, reliable, nondisruptive tenants, as the apartment boom developed in the 1960s and the freeway was constructed linking Santa Monica to Los Angeles, a new, more affluent tenant began to be sought. Seniors, many of whom had fixed incomes, were suddenly—through no doing of their own—reclassified from model tenants to "undesirables."[10] The rent-control movement publicly took up their cause and returned to them a positive status. Seniors emerged as a legitimating symbol of the movement, as the overlooked victims unable to defend themselves against those who wanted to turn "community" into "commodity." The displacement of older residents in Ocean Park was taken up as an example of what happened if profit-making went unregulated.

Seniors figured prominently in photographs on early rent-control fliers and placards, engaging in demonstrations or carrying packed suitcases (indicating eviction or economic pressure to relocate). On one hand, this emphasized their spirit and verve, while on the other, it played up their physical and economic frailty. The fates of the elderly were personalized as much as possible in order to appeal to bystanders, including a growing population of young professionals who lived apart from their own extended families and experienced a guilt typical in a country that has not come to terms with what to do with its elderly. As one flier reminded the population:

> To start a new life in a totally different location at 70 or 80 years of age is no small thing. Since the eviction notices were posted [at a trailer park] on April 1st, one elderly tenant has died of the shock and stress and two more have had strokes. 20% of the residents of Santa Monica are senior citizens. When will we learn to care for our elderly as they have cared for us? (*Santa Monica Fair Housing Reporter*, May 1978)

Another 1978 flier called attention to the fact that half of Santa Monica's elderly had incomes under $600 per month:

Many have lived here for years. This is their home. Where do you go when you are 65 and you can't pay the rent?

Conceptually, these pieces drew public attention to how the economic system subverted "home" and "community" even for long-term residents. The rent-control movement and the seniors' role in it led to a symbolic restoration of their standing in the community and to a generally sympathetic evaluation of them as a social group. Yet, having gained this standing, the elderly were to become targets of a new onslaught that was an unanticipated consequence of the movement. While the community in general, chastened about neglecting its seniors, evaluated them positively, this was not true of landlords. Angry about being regulated and having their anticipated profits reduced, organized landlord groups singled out the most needy subgroups of tenants, including the elderly and the disabled, as people they would not rent to. They claimed economic motives, but an additional motivation was symbolic—to show the public that regulation does not work and that rent control hurts most those whom it tries to help. The consequence was that, once again, through no doing of their own, the elderly began to be labeled undesirable. Landlords were careful to issue disclaimers about their responsibility for this, setting the blame squarely on rent control. As one landlord put it:

The biggest change that has happened with me and with most of my friends is that we will not rent to families; we will not rent to anyone who's old; we will not rent to anybody who's crippled. . . . Now, I built mine for a family building. I had eleven different families; they were all with children. Now when I have vacancies I've only rented each one to one person. I have a heart specialist living in one, a real sharp attorney who's on our side living in another one. I kicked out one of the other tenants and moved my daughter in—so therefore, the very people they claim they're supporting are being the most damaged. . . . I'm ashamed of the maintenance on my building. . . . but I say, don't look at *me*![11]

Another landlord concurred:

I used to rent to a different kind of person than I do now. I mean, I used to deliberately look for the older ones, the retired ones, the ones who were enjoying being down here at the beach, and today it's just the reverse of that, you know. I no way would rent to an old person. Not because I'm concerned that they can't pay the rent—I'm sure they can. But I'm not looking for anyone who's gonna sit in the apartment eight hours a day looking for trouble. I want someone who's working, who's not in the place. I don't want people who sit in the apartment all day long running my water and flushing the toilet. I know that sounds ridiculous, but I'm paying the bills. I want the ones that are making the bucks, busy enough that they're not hanging around.[12]

As we pointed out in Chapter 2, tenants in the United States have been allocated a different set of rights than those belonging to homeowners. Indeed, the concept of "home" seems to apply only to property owners. As evidenced by the above quote, tenants generally rent a "shell" in which to put their belongings—something that keeps the rain off, but not necessarily a place where one can feel secure and "at home."

Landlords are accustomed to justifying their actions by linking them to the values of the free enterprise system. This system directs them to be guided by their "pocketbooks." At the same time, they speak with scorn of tenants who vote in favor of rent control, also as a pocketbook issue.[13] In the United States, this makes cultural sense. According to the theory of capitalism, landlords take a risk by investing in private property that is rented or sold on the market. In Chapter 2, we observed that it is traditional in U.S. culture to speak of risks inherent in ownership. Not customary, however, is the application of the language of risk to tenants when they buy, on trust, the temporary right to live somewhere.

Speaking of rent control, James Baker, a leading landlord activist in Santa Monica, remarked:

If anyone's left standing, I can assure you that it'll be us, because these are people's homes and security that we're talking about, and they're never going to give those up.[14]

Baker exemplifies the tradition of applying these words only to property owners, but not to those who rent from them. The new application of the language of risk to tenants had to await the social reconstruction of fairness accomplished by tenant activists in Santa Monica.

The language that different groups use about themselves and others is always revealing of social relationships in communities. As Benjamin Barber (1984:221) has suggested, "Major shifts in ideology and political power are always accompanied by...paradigmatic shifts in language." The tenants' movement was able to orchestrate a change in social relations in Santa Monica that was reflected in public discourse, associating with tenants a new language of rights that had been traditionally denied them. The semantic shift signaled a rising prestige of tenants in the community.

Landlords, on the other hand, lost a great deal of credibility in the community. This is not to say that they had the best of images to begin with; as Ron Lawson (Lawson, n.d.:9) has observed, "... leaving aside the owner of the sweatshop, the landlord has a worse reputation in American urban mythology than the employer." But as property owners, landlords have been accustomed to a certain status that has sharply declined in recent years. The best evidence of their wide recognition of this is their attempt to remove the word "landlord" from public use in favor of a more neutral term.

This is illustrated in a 1976 meeting where California landlords were found educating each other about the undesirable connotations of the word "landlord" and were attempting a reconstruction:

> And just for the record, I would like to strike the word tenant from my vocabulary. I hope all of you will attempt to do the same. Our vocabulary is owners and renters, and the eastern vocabulary is landlord/tenant. And most of the problems that I ran into in California are created by eastern immigrants to California, who come here understanding landlord/tenant law as they learned it in New York and expect to transplant it here in California...(Gilderbloom, 1976:VI–16).

Landlords recognized that their "cultural portrait" as a group had been covered with all sorts of undesirable grafitti, and it was becoming too expensive to keep exerting the effort to sponge away the evil mustachios and horns that the public conjured up at the word "landlord." They preferred instead to construct a fresh portrait. This is the best indication that the rent-control movement left tenants with more power as custodians of identity in the community, to a large extent due to their newly found voting power. Landlords had to resort to the invention of a new language to sidestep their own inability to shape their identity, just as the rent-control movement had to construct a new language to incorporate the rights of tenants.

Tenants: Symbolic Redefinition of Self

> There is a movement in Santa Monica. It is unprecedented in the history of our city. It is quiet, strong and inevitable. The movement is your neighbors. The movement is you. —1978 rent-control flier

The symbolic work that social movements carry out in communities can be analytically divided into two parts. One type of symbolic work is done to convince a general public, including bystanders, that an issue is legitimate and deserving of support. Another type of work is done to convince those whose rights would be protected (the direct beneficiaries) that they have the right to ask others to support them. In Santa Monica, a strategic problem for the progressive movement was not only to convince bystanders that renters' rights should be supported, but to persuade tenants themselves—who were accustomed to being bystanders in their own community. Social identity is an emergent phenomenon, and its construction is crucial to any movement (Turner, 1983; Melucci, 1985). Tenants' images of themselves needed to be strengthened and reinforced in order for them to seek any rights at all, including accountability from landlords (Scott and Lyman, 1968). Some of this symbolic work was done through the construction of small-scale "free spaces" where tenants could interact and produce their own definition of their identities.

As has been pointed out by Zurcher and Snow (1981) and McAdam (1988), "micromobilization" issues have been neglected by the resource mobilization perspective, particularly the role that symbolization and face-to-face encounters play in the generation and maintenance of a social movement. Ralph Turner (1983:178) has suggested that an appropriate model for social movements

> ...must address the generation of self-confidence and mutual support necessary to risk challenging the established order of things. It must address both the structures and the processes that facilitate the communication necessary to formulate and disseminate these challenging conceptions of reality.

These suggestions are valuable for interpreting the Santa Monica movement. Although a situation existed there that, numerically, seemed to favor tenant power, it was far from automatic. Many tenants had to "learn by doing" how to be public actors (McAdam, 1986) and how to transform passive into active democratic behavior. As we noted in Chapter 3, for seniors as well as for younger activists, feelings of solidarity that emerged out of being together were important for generating confidence in the movement's ability to produce social change (Heskin, 1983; Klandermans, 1984).

Symbolic activity in Santa Monica took place at several levels. The propaganda and image work turned out in connection with elections did not have to be a social endeavor; it could be the work of a skilled technician. However, the symbolic reconstruction of the identity of tenants was for the most part a social task. The new symbolic identity and the frame that would legitimate it both emerged from this group interaction, building a sense of the possible out of being together. Tom Hayden acknowledged the importance of this when he observed of activists in CED that their participation was probably "the most meaningful thing they are doing in their lives" (*Los Angeles Times*, September 7, 1979).

How were tenants able to gain control over their own image construction and that of other groups in the community? To begin with, they had help from their opposition. We have already observed how opponents of rent control participated in highly visible acts that violated a public sense of fairness held by many residents of the city. These were newsworthy events, and tenants benefited from their exposure. To ensure that these problems remained visible, however, tenants had to work to continuously create new public arenas for themselves and to imaginatively "seize" public urban space (Gottdiener, 1985).

Recalling Saul Alinsky's adage that power comes in many forms, including targeting one's opposition for public embarrassment, tenants used a repertoire of "attention calling" tactics (Gamson, Fireman, and Rytina, 1982). Senior citizens collected signatures at grocery stores. If a landlord mistreated a tenant, movement activists, including many senior citizens, were willing to picket the apartment complex in shifts, turning away prospective tenants and achieving media attention. City hall became still another forum. The news media became a free publicity tool, which at the same time provided public cues that tenant activities were legitimate. As one landlord remarked:

> On the weekends they'd get news coverage, and it was all staged, and the cameras would be there. For hour after hour you'd hear about awful landlords. And we'd say, "Where are they?" And they wouldn't give us equal time; they'd say, "These are just news events."[15]

It was a coup for tenants to be able to present their message through the cost-free, supposedly neutral, and very public medium of "just news events." Landlords in their turn learned to use the media, taking their cue from tenants. As landlord activist and property owner John Jurenka observed in 1984:

> You can see how we both learned from one another. We had this done to us first. It started with the Pier, where you'd see all this staged protest— kids, merry-go-round, lollipops, balloons, you name it. Then it was rent control. On the weekends they'd get demonstrations going, and it was all staged, and the cameras would be there. . . .Well, we learned. One time we had the tanks up at city hall. We've learned to stage, to rehearse. We all learned that if you carry a sign you get on camera. We've learned to get press by being outrageous. Now when we want to organize a dog and pony show, we make no bones about it. We sit down and we have a speakers' task force. We review the whole subject so that everyone understands it, and these people can either pick out their own subjects or if necessary you can get an outline so that we can stay in sequence and we don't repeat ourselves. . . .hell, we can produce fifty speakers in no time at all, these people that were never taught to stand up before. The tenants are just

amazed. These last couple of meetings they've sat there, and hell, we can dominate the whole thing, take it over, and they can't even come up and say anything.[16]

Both tenants and landlords had the experience at different times of an "outgroup" symbolically binding itself together through an act of protest. Moreover, both groups learned to have fun and to be playful while protesting, creating solidarity among themselves. Landlords, as did tenants, accumulated their own folklore during the movement (Čapek, 1985). However, an additional task that each group had was to try to make its symbols part of the legitimate folklore of the city. As Wuthnow et al., (1984:4) have observed, "Social movements make use of symbolism and ritual and themselves become figments of the cultural world as they are given public definition and historical meaning." A case study of Santa Monica reveals the *process* of two conflicting social movement groups trying to claim justice and legitimacy from a bystander community (Turner, 1969). The social movement itself becomes an artifact, a prop for a larger system of beliefs. The ongoing symbolic warfare in the city also takes place at this level.

We should note that symbolic action in Santa Monica was rendered more complex by the fact that the city played to a national audience. Due in part to the controversial nature of the events there, and also due to the national networks to which some of its key activists—both progressive and conservative—belonged, Santa Monica received enough publicity to become a national symbol. When *60 Minutes* did a segment on the city, it highlighted the controversy, contributing to polarization in the community.

There was, as a result, a great deal of "public theater" in the city. Over time, these actions were spearheaded less by the sixties actors—who gained access to city hall in 1981—than by their opposition, who learned from their direct action tactics. This 1985 scenario is a prime example:

A Santa Monica apartment building has a new look and an odd name to symbolize what owner Chuck Jones calls his "private hell". . . . More than 40 property owners from the landlord group ACTION [A Committee to Insure Owners' Needs] joined Jones Tuesday with brushes and rollers to paint his light gray building black. In the words of the group's pamphlet, the gesture mourns "the most oppressive rent control and blatant confiscation of (our) private property" (*Evening Outlook,* May 8, 1985).

Tenant Shelly Davis observed that:

They painted the front of the building black, took down the American flag, sang the national anthem and put up red communist flags. . . . Then they strung red and black crepe paper along the railings and painted an X on the name of the building. They say rent control is like communism. So now instead of Mar Villa, the sign reads Marx Villa (*Evening Outlook,* May 8, 1985).

One of the landlord activists suggested another name: "Hayden's Hades." A progressive activist—who recalled being shouted at to "go back to Russia" when she testified in favor of more affordable housing in 1982—remarked: "It's landlord guerrilla theater!"[17]

Ten years after the passage of rent control, this protest activity still surfaces. In 1989, as Mayor Dennis Zane and tenant supporters celebrated the tenth anniversary of the rent-control law, the landlord group ACTION staged a protest, allegedly bringing about forty homeless persons to the celebration:

About 40 landlords, wearing hard hats and carrying picket signs, marched along the sidewalk in front of City Hall. Repeating a tactic from a previous demonstration, they drove a small armored tank into the parking lot next to City Hall. An American flag waved from one side of the tank while a sign reading "In Defense of Freedom" was draped from the other side. . . . "Hey Myers [city attorney and author of the rent-control law], come down here. You're responsible for this homeless mess," [landlord] Kovach shouted, referring to Myers' refusal to prosecute homeless persons sleeping in city parks. . . . Pickets carried signs reading, "Help the needy, not the greedy," and "Rent Control does not help the needy." To dramatize the theme, picket Don Howland, wearing a top hat, depicted an affluent tenant harnessed to bedraggled "landlord" Tony Alvarez who carried a can of paint and a brush (*Outlook Mail,* week of April 19, 1989).

In Santa Monica, had landlords or the city council been conciliatory at the outset of the progressive movement, they would have taken symbolic and real power away from it. In their refusal to confront tenants' problems in any realistic fashion, however, they prepared the population for SMRR's message. As former head of the chamber of commerce Robert Gabriel acknowledged:

If we had foreseen the problems, we never would have had other than free enterprise thinking people in there . . . and convincing people who are supposed to be our friends to vote with them on a pocketbook issue.[18]

### The Power of Solidarity

Through this sort of grass-roots ferment, a different, older and more participatory understanding of ''democracy'' develops. Democracy seems real only when ordinary people develop a sense of communal

responsibility and engage in a continuing civic action, learning the skills
and values of public life, building the tools to gain political power (Boyte,
1984:476)

Apart from claiming public arenas in which to call attention to landlord
behavior, another avenue that tenants used to gain power over image construction was through the social relationships that they developed among
themselves. Social relationships proved to be the key to activating the structural
resources that were available both to landlords and to tenants (Gilderbloom,
1985a). Tom Hayden, feared and praised by traditional politicians for his ability
to build CED into a formidable political organization, recognized the role of
not only material mobilization, but also the social interactional factor:

> It is organization that teaches people how to be citizens rather than private
> souls, and how to work together instead of at one another's throats.
> Without organization, people will not commit their lives to social change
> (Hayden, 1981:212).

Similarly, in their own group context—whether through free spaces such as
tenant unions or organizations such as SMFHA—tenants had a positive, solidary
image reflected back to them that helped them to rehearse their power and
to perceive themselves as potentially powerful actors.[19]

The solidarity produced through mutual social interaction was especially
valuable in the hostile setting in which some of the earlier progressive
community activists functioned. Cheryl Rhoden described how much courage
was needed to take advantage of existing opportunities for participation. At
Coastal Commission hearings, she recalls being alone with one other activist
in a sea of hostile faces, the two of them clinging together in order to have
the courage to speak.[20] There was a similar hostility at city council meetings:

> And the atmosphere then was so much more formal and intimidating
> and if you came there speaking about the words "low- and moderate-
> income housing" or "renters' rights," worse yet, you were just treated
> like dirt. It was really awful. It angered me so much; I think it fueled
> my keeping involved.[21]

During the early stages of the movement, a concerted effort was made
by progressives to support each other in public and to create incentives for
solidarity. This was especially true at rent board meetings, where a hysterical
atmosphere prevailed throughout the summer months of 1979 after rent control
was passed. As Rhoden remembered:

It was like every Thursday night we'd all go to the rent control board meeting, showing our solidarity, and it was the most nerve-wracking experience. Lynda and Dora and I were Bob's [Myers] bodyguards. Most of the hate was focused on him because he had written the law. We had the theory that they wouldn't attack him if he was surrounded by women. Well, we were wrong.[22]

The same solidarity was expressed at city council meetings. An older woman who gradually became involved as a supporter of the movement, recalled how the first time she rose to speak at a city council meeting "my buttocks were shaking so hard that I was afraid somebody would see." But she persisted because the issue was important to her and because she was receiving support from people in the movement.[23] The fear passed.

This sense of mutual support could also draw people into the movement. The activist cited above recalled her early impressions of SMRR activists:

I said, isn't this exciting, and it was, to see these grass-roots people—I didn't know that word then—but these ordinary people take over a city that had been run by real estate people and bankers and the chamber of commerce. I couldn't believe it. I went over to the Retail Clerks Union building for the election, and they were a ratty bunch, very scruffy looking, with lots of old people there too. But I remember some young women so sweet and nice—they called me by name and made me feel like somebody. I had a feeling like I was working in a worthwhile cause. And they were nice to one another—honest, straightforward, hard-working. I went to other SMRR events, and I always had the same impression of interesting, bright, hard-working people concerned about city issues and supporting a good cause.[24]

As an older professional who had not been previously involved in such a movement, it was very important to her to see how people treated each other. The system of social support that she witnessed left a strong positive impression.

Many SMRR activists perceived the progressive movement as their first authentic chance to participate in civic life in the United States, despite being lifelong residents. Accustomed as they were to a more remote kind of democracy, this was a new and vital experience. While some of the seniors who became involved in the rent-control movement had a long history of activism, others discovered their powers for the first time. Aside from a core of activists, many of the younger progressives were also relatively inexperienced in the political arena. They were pulled into the activity by a broad social support network that encouraged them to feel that their contributions were worthwhile. This "micromobilization" aspect (Zurcher and Snow, 1981; McAdam, 1988) was critical for the success and growth of the movement.

The democratic participation accomplished in the early phases of the movement extended into city hall when the progressives won in 1981. Speculating on its role, Cheryl Rhoden observed:

> The one thing I think that this council has done to a great extent that's different from any previous council is that they've involved people in more substantive ways than any other council has done....I mean they have really dragged people, almost unwillingly....''No no no I won't do it.'' ''You will, you will.'' Democracy. And I think that's been incredibly painful because of the many hours that it takes to do it that way, but the result has been that so many more people have become part of the process. And are participating in this, in government. We live in a city that 20 percent, 15 percent of the voters used to elect the city council and now we've got 55 percent. There's no other city in this country that's turning out like that.[25]

Even in the face of some cynicism that surfaced as a result of disappointments regarding democratic opportunities to participate in the progressive agenda, many activists were willing to admit transformative results in their own lives and identities. An Ocean Park activist, pausing to consider how his life had changed when he became involved in his community through rent control and the Ocean Park Community Organization, concluded:

> I've learned a lot about organizing skills. OPCO *does* do empowerment. They get people to speak, overcoming fears. Whatever the issue is, this city has more participation than anywhere else. The personal benefits to me have been being involved working with someone who is a good organizer. I really learned a lot of important skills which I can now take with me for other things. Community organizations really get you out there. I even sit back and observe myself a lot. I can see how the situation is ''manipulated.'' I've been manipulated myself [he laughs], but I know how to do it too. They're interesting skills. Lots of people don't know how to mobilize. I learned a lot. I'm better, stronger, for having done this in public, gotten ''sucked out'' of my house.[26]

Initially, support networks in the movement were informal and spontaneous, as was the impulse that threw together the Santa Monica Fair Housing Alliance in an Ocean Park living room. The early days of the movement are remembered with affection by most activists. Part of this has to do with the smallness of the original group, the frank interactions, and the feeling of togetherness. As one activist recalled, ''Those meetings at Cheryl's house I remember much more vividly than what came after. The camaraderie, the trust, the frankness...*that* went down the tubes later."[27] Cheryl Rhoden herself recalled the informality and the closeness of the original group as they sat around with glasses of wine on her living room floor.[28] The early movement was strongly influenced by personal feelings and interactions that provided the foundations for the later resolution of more technical problems of resource mobilization.

Settings such as this one provide a true instance of a free space, where people can meet together and carve out their own definitions of who they are, engaging in "self-production of identity" (Touraine, 1985) and a resistance to the "colonized" imagery imposed on them as second-class citizens (Memmi, 1967; Habermas, 1971). At the same time, they participate in the social interactional process of learning roles that generate structures of support for social change (Evans and Boyte, 1986; Klandermans, 1984; McAdam, 1986). Rather than sharing merely strategic knowledge, progressives gained "soft incentives" in this setting—feelings of solidarity that mitigated the impact of outside efforts to control them (Opp, 1985; Touraine, 1985; Eder, 1985). These are the types of interactional resources that have been generally ignored by the resource mobilization perspective.

In Santa Monica, then, meanings emerged out of this social context that permitted a changed relationship to the community as a whole. This interactional dynamic received more explicit attention than it may have in some other groups since participatory democracy was an important part of the value system of the activists. Great emphasis was placed on doing away with hierarchy and instead encouraging consensus decision making. Many were the times when some cynic criticizing somebody's "agenda" stopped to say, "You have to trust that *dialogue* between people works. There's a lot of people I don't trust personally, but I trust them in a group situation."[29] This trust itself formed an important social bond in the early movement.

People were drawn together by being an "outgroup" and also by being members of a similar generation and life-style. They shared values and knew how to have fun together. Activists of a slightly different generation or experience found participation a bit more difficult. Ruth Yannatta Goldway, for example, recalled that the whole style of socializing at the Circle Bar in Ocean Park—another free space that emerged spontaneously and became an informal institution for progressive political activists—was not inclusive of people like herself with children at home.[30]

Social interaction helped to build what Lawrence Goodwyn has referred to as "movement culture," which is based not only on people's similarities, but on the transformative possibilities that emerge out of their coming together. He emphasizes that this incorporates a new way of looking at things, as well as a construction of individual and collective self-respect that promotes the "shaking off of inherited forms of deference" (Goodwyn, cited in Boyte and

Evans, 1985:74). The resulting emergent culture gives rise to new social possibilities in a community context, including groups celebrating together and sharing "exhilaration" (Lawson, n.d.).

A regret expressed by some progressive activists in 1984 was that this element no longer seemed to be present for them. If anything, the groups *opposed* to SMRR became adept at celebrating their own identities. Although this could be explained in part by virtue of the more recent mobilization of SMRR's opposition as a countermovement, the criticism hit home for many progressives. As one SMRR activist, now distanced from the movement, suggested, "We don't have our festivals. Politics is a culture, you learn it. . . . They should have reached out to people, done something that was more culture."[31]

The passage of time brought a new formalized context into the activist group, as it went from a feeling of "family" to "organization." In the new organizational context, attempts were made to formalize mechanisms that would build in an emphasis on the same face-to-face democracy that was found more informally earlier in the movement. However, within a formal coalition structure with representatives and a number of groups, this became more problematic. In-groups and "inner in-groups," as one activist put it (or "the inner enclave of the in-club" as another dubbed it), developed and eventually created rifts in the movement.[32] Yet, people in SMRR did spend an extra-ordinary amount of time struggling over how to be socially supportive with each other. The wish to do this was heightened by their realization that an unusual opportunity existed in the city to do something truly innovative. From the earliest days of the movement, when all-day meetings were held about "how everyone related to everyone," to SMRR restructuring efforts in 1983 and 1985, the desire not to "blow it" raised the willingness of the group to attempt to rebuild a sense of solidarity:

> When the loss occurred, we had a chance to learn from it. The hope was there, since everyone was there sitting together in one room. We filled a large room with butcher paper all the way around and tried to figure out how to fix things. . . .[33]

Although this meeting resulted in a stalemate, and the hoped-for SMRR restructuring did not take place at that time, the effort revealed a high degree of commitment among activists who, after years of the ups and downs of movement involvement, were willing to come together in an energetic fashion to try to rebuild the group. The issues raised—copied by an activist from the butcher paper covering the walls at the meeting—provide a catalogue of almost all possible permutations of social, human, organizational, and political considerations important to social movements.[34] As a group, SMRR activists could not be accused of being naive or inexperienced about organizational questions.

The negative side of social solidarity incentives showed itself when criticism was defined as non-support. This was always an area troubled by the ambiguity of having elected one's "friends" to public office (Čapek, 1985), friends who were not linked to any of the previous elites and thus theoretically in need of all the support they could get. Whether this help should take the form of healthy criticism or supportive silence was never comfortably resolved, and the movement paid the price through attrition of its activists.

### "Framing" as a Movement Resource

As we noted above, framing actions are those that strive to affect the social interpretation of events and identities (Goffman, 1974; Snow et al., 1986). Snow et al. (1986:472) have observed that each type of framing activity corresponds with a "micromobilization task" that involves aligning values with participation in movement activities. A symbolically oriented perspective toward social movements directs our attention to the use of available cultural symbols as a wellspring for legitimating group identities. Two separate but related framing tasks are generally undertaken by social movements to build public support. One focuses on an affirmative, nonthreatening presentation of the movement's identity to the public (Turner, 1969). The other places the movement's opponents and their actions in a negative light, or constructs an "injustice frame" (Gamson, Fireman, and Rytina, 1982).

#### Appropriating "Democracy"

The past does not speak only to conservatives. America offers its children both Paine and Hamilton, both Jefferson and Madison.... A democratic community is inevitably obliged to create its past no less than its future.
—Benjamin Barber (1984)

As we are approaching the April municipal election, there is some talk of issues as though there were many. But it seems to us that there is just one issue—democracy.... Shall our city be governed by majority vote of the population of ordinary folks such as have cast the majority of votes in the last several elections. Or indeed, shall the city be governed by the tiny group of realtors—landlords, real estate developers, their cronies and hangers-on—who have been ruling our city [of Santa Monica] for many years. —Saul Larks, *The Independent* (1979)

In reference to struggles over the acceptance of new values, Ralph Turner (1983:180) has observed that "How American society came to be vulnerable to such transformations and why counterideologies took the forms they did are among the most important questions for students of social movements." The question of vulnerability or "conduciveness" is one that we have attempted to explore at a number of different levels. In Chapter 3, we carefully examined the historical development of some of the structural features of Santa Monica that, as an urban setting, made it vulnerable to a movement espousing the progressive value system. In our present chapter, we consider some of the features of a culture centered around individualism and respect for private property in a free market context and the obstacles and opportunities that it presents for the mobilization of a tenant constituency. A social movement is produced in part by the interlocking of different levels of conduciveness, assisted by framing activities undertaken by social groups to produce a desired public response.

A history of radical or challenging social movements in the United States shows that the most typical symbolic challenge faced by many of these movements is an identification with "alien," non-American forces (Adamson and Borgos, 1984). The "outside agitators" identity imposed on such efforts has been an effective way to discredit them by eliciting an emotional response from the general public. This is especially likely when a movement makes an attempt to challenge the private enterprise system in any fashion; as we have noted, it is a feature of U.S. culture to weld together the values of free enterprise and democracy.

Any movement that wishes to present a challenge and still function in a legitimate framework must be cautious about its presentation to the public. As Turner and Killian (1972) remarked, movements often retain several identities, some public and some private, in order to maintain legitimacy. A question that the resource mobilization perspective does not address is how organizations come to be perceived as legitimate in the first place. We have already mentioned the importance of public cues supplied through the media; in some cases, a small handful of actors comes to be identified as legitimate merely through their public visibility. However, a far more significant strategy for cultivating legitimacy and a "respectable" identity in the community is to establish a link to sanctioned traditions. As has been the case with many social movements (Snow et al., 1986), in Santa Monica the right to associate the concept of democracy with one's movement became the most highly contested symbolic battle.

"Democracy" can be counted on to have powerful emotional connotations, in part because, although it is highly valued, it is an ambiguous and disputed term. As one critic put it, "Democracy is the most promiscuous word in the English language" (Crick cited in Plant, 1974:17). Its very ambiguity makes it desirable because it permits maneuverability of the sort that is useful in the political arena. Progressives in Santa Monica attempted to appropriate the term "democracy" and cause the public to reflect on how far the United States had come in practice from a truly participatory understanding of the word, even though popular culture glorifies such participation as part of the "American dream." Recognizing the ambiguity surrounding the term "democracy," they resolved the ambiguity in the direction of the popular image of direct, participatory democracy in their rhetoric. In this manner, they hoped to tap public dissatisfaction with a remote kind of democracy that favored elite actors. The progressive appeal to direct, face-to-face democracy and the power to shape one's community was pitched to those who had a reverence for democracy, but felt a large gap between the ideal and the practice in the early 1980s. Snow et al. (1986) have suggested the concept of "frame amplification" to define this process of revivifying an existing set of values or beliefs. Accordingly, the social movement task for SMRR was to call attention to control of the city by large outside actors, to construct institutionalized public space for community debate, and to present itself as the appropriate vehicle for realizing a vital democracy.

Change often occurs when existing rights are extended into a new area, legitimating them on the basis of what has already become acceptable practice (Scotch, 1984). Snow et al. (1986) refer to this type of activity as "frame bridging." A crucial and culturally perilous task for the broader progressive movement was the attempt to extend the political concept of democracy into the economic arena. Economic democracy—increased democratic control over economic decisions—was a favored concept among movement ideologues such as Tom Hayden and Derek Shearer. When rent control was passed in 1979, Hayden announced that "In Santa Monica, the first coalition explicitly favoring economic democracy has come to power."[35] This concept caused particular outrage among opponents because they considered it an attempt to steal the rights to democracy and to put a red, white, and blue coating over a "socialistic" principle.

It was conscious strategy on the part of progressives to construct a bridge between political and economic democracy by using a rational language tied to familiar concepts. Theorist George Rudé (1980) argued that an important ideological social movement task is to find the right combination of inherited traditional beliefs, ideas shaped by direct experience, and new ideas that can transform the combination. Progressives in Santa Monica endeavored to create this combination. As Shearer remarked about the progressive program: "What we were actually talking about were references that people recognized from high school civics classes."[36]

Examples of this abound. Syd Rose argued at the outset of the tenants' movement that certain forms of regulation have always been regarded as necessary to the ongoing function of democracy. Traffic lights are less controversial than movements for environmental protection and consumer rights once were; yet today all three are an accepted part of the democratic landscape, having arisen out of the need to regulate forces that present a danger to democracy. Using this kind of a bridging argument, progressives built their case for increased economic democracy.

Numerous other examples illustrate the same frame-bridging principle. Mayor Ruth Yannatta Goldway argued that housing rights can be perceived as an extension of consumers' rights. The renter, who is buying a certain product (in this case, use of housing), has the hard-won right to be protected. Another activist, who argued from a legal perspective, justified rent control out of a similar extension of basic rights:

> There's a growing legal consciousness over rent control. In the 1850s, you had child labor, and the Supreme Court would say that there's no constitutional issue there. After thirty or forty years, they found one.[37]

Evidence from the courts upheld this argument. Baar and Keating (1975, 1981) have documented the shifting legal acceptance of rent control from an emergency basis to rational proofs of need. A former rent board member emphasized that Santa Monica had not broken radically with past traditions of regulation in the United States, pointing out that land-use controls have been in existence since 1900 and that anyone who develops property knows the role of the government and the risks, particularly large developers.[38]

Along similar lines, Ruth Yannatta Goldway made the following case for the controversial developer agreements (see Chapter 5) during her administration:

> Years ago it was considered radical to require developers to provide adequate parking for the auto traffic their building generated. Now it is commonplace.... The generous tax breaks the Reagan administration has lavished on business makes it difficult for government to afford to clean up the mess the private sector leaves in its wake. So in Santa Monica, we are planning ahead, requiring developers to agree in advance to share social costs (*The Sacramento Bee,* December 12, 1982).

Much of the progressive agenda was conceived in line with such a rational extension of democratic rights. It was not an irrational idea that city hall should represent 80 percent of its constituents; it simply had not been tried before in practice. Emphasizing the rationality of the progressives' approach in contrast to their opposition, Dennis Zane would claim, "We argue, 'What are the consequences of unregulated private property?' We're utilitarian. They argue on principle."[39]

Opponents of the progressives were highly threatened by these constructions of economic democracy. Attempts to debunk them often surfaced in the *Evening Outlook*:

> This subversion of factions by the "New Left," particularly Hayden and the CED, is what "economic democracy" is all about. From the Hayden literature any old group will suffice. You name it: Tenants, labor, women's, peace, consumer and, although not listed, any liberal church as well as the Boy Scouts could be exploited. It's a free country, so who will fault a caring politician for supporting worthy voluntary associations in a community?

> This is exactly what is projected outwardly, but make no mistake: inside each American apple-pie group is concealed the convoluted worm in the shape of the big "S," so close to the delicious recipe, so full of protein it takes an expert cook to find it. One can read the New Left for days without stumbling on the word "Socialism," and yet their only argument is how to convert private concerns into public bureaucracies, a la Marx....However, if the big "S" is taboo, the word "democracy" bubbles out all over the pie (*Evening Outlook,* February 21, 1985).

The author of this letter recognized with dismay that the "halo" of democracy could be appropriated by a range of groups, including the New Left, if framed appropriately. Opponents therefore used their own kind of "belief amplification" to invoke traditional stereotypes and "negative typifications" (Snow et al., 1986:470) regarding critics of the free enterprise system. In this way, they hoped to appropriate democracy and to label their opponents as conspiring to destroy it.

Challenging the Culture of Capitalism: Constructing an Injustice Frame

Among the most important symbolic tasks of the progressive movement was to show that democracy and private property do not necessarily go hand in hand. Although progressives were concerned, as we noted above, with a rational extension of democratic rights into the economic sphere, they also contested the generally uncritical belief that respect for private property fosters democracy. This presupposed a frame "breaking" or frame "disassembling" process rather than an attempt to bridge or amplify values. Ultimately, it posed a radical challenge to existing belief systems. As Snow et al. (1986:473) point out:

When such is the case, new values may have to be planted and nurtured, old meanings or understandings jettisoned, and erroneous beliefs, or "misframings" reframed (Goffman, 1974:308) in order to garner support and secure participants. What may be required, in short, is a transformation of frame.

Progressives were particularly concerned to interpret nonregulated capitalism through an "injustice frame." As Gamson, Fireman, and Rytina (1982) point out, an important aspect of constructing an injustice frame is to show that a particular existing system, if allowed to operate without interference, will cause injustice. This was the crux of the progressives' argument about private property, particularly in the form of urban land development and housing. To make this into an acceptable fairness issue, however, they had to pinpoint the consequences of nonregulation.[40] In Santa Monica, this was not difficult to do. Framing it in such a way that regulation would be acceptable was, however, another matter.

Firmly in place was a culture whose ideal of freedom embodied the capitalist system. The symbols attached to this system are powerful, sharply cutting the world up into acceptable and nonacceptable beliefs and practices.[41] For example, the absence of capitalist organization is seen as producing either anarchy or excessive regulation, which brings chaos and injustice into a set of relations as nearly perfect as can be expected with imperfect human beings. Bureaucracy springs immediately to mind, an image repugnant to the majority of Americans.

As we pointed out in Chapter 3, anti-rent-control forces were able to make use of this folklore of regulation in their campaign literature in 1979: "Proposition P a Bureaucratic Nightmare!" is emblazoned over a photograph of crumbling buildings in New York, purporting to represent the future of Santa Monica under rent control.[42] Elsewhere in the same newsletter, an apartment owner poses with his eleven-page income adjustment form dramatically spread out over the ground to show its cumbersome length.

Traditional arguments against rent control assume that regulation itself creates any negative consequences in the system:

> It must be reiterated, however, that there is nothing improper about landlords per se, absentee or not. Their antisocial and uneconomic acts are the result of rent control. They were unknown before the advent of this legislation and will disappear after decontrol (Block and Olsen, 1981:299).

Like the justifications used by Santa Monica landlords in interviews above, this is an effort at systemic attribution, in this case blaming the system of rent control for going so far as to change human nature. Ironically, these proponents of individualism were unwilling to accept any individual responsibility for their actions once placed in the context of rent control. All negative qualities appeared to show up only in government, rather than in the competition for economic profits, where one might just as naturally look to find them.

Progressives undertook to dismantle some of the fallacies of the culture of capitalism, such as its inherent link with democracy. They were aware of the fact that they had some symbolic leverage. There was, and is, plenty of evidence that despite strong beliefs favoring a rather ruthless capitalism, a degree of moral ambivalence accompanies it (Čapek, 1985). Progressives could play on this uneasiness in the same manner as they could raise the issue of participatory democracy. It was no coincidence, for example, that even as the country abandoned support for New Deal policies, theorists of free market capitalism were giving it an ethical facelift. Even in an atmosphere of antiregulation, the moral ambivalence existed. Although the New Deal arrangements lost credibility with voters, to say that the waters closed over that period and left no mark on the contemporary political dialogue would be incorrect: the experience served as a historical marker, defining, among other things, points in the social and political dialogue beyond which it was inappropriate to go. Even as Ronald Reagan dismantled systematic protections, he had to at least appear to trade in fairness; his message to the public was moral and ethical at the core, although his vision of fairness was radically different from what came before. His successors pay even more attention to the public perception of fairness.

The contemporary concern with ethics in capitalism, whether found in the writings of Michael Novak or the Catholic Bishops, indicates a moral tension. Some critics of socialism have argued that, if so-called socialism were truly democratic, there would have been no need to invent the term "democratic socialism." When Novak's (1982) book on "democratic capitalism" appeared, it indicated a similarly troubled concept. Thus, to SMRR's opposition, people like Tom Hayden and Derek Shearer were all the more dangerous because, by applying intellectual and emotional arguments about the shortcomings of capitalism to this area of moral discomfort, they hit a nerve.

To an extent, progressives could rely on these areas of uncertainty to gain a hearing. They offered an explanation that made sense to residents of a city marked by speculative investments. To many ordinary U.S. citizens, capitalism is associated with fairness and freedom, which includes the right of the "little guy" to compete. As various theorists and organizers have perceived, the discovery that these rights are not in practice embodied by capitalism can be powerful and transformative. We noted earlier that one of the most effective SMRR strategies was to go backstage, behind the language of fairness ("I'm just trying to get a fair return on my investment") and to shed light on the actual legal and financial relationships obtaining in the community. This "raising of the curtain" was a rational strategy that produced a highly emotional result because of violations of notions of fairness and community control.

However, there was more to the new social construction of fairness than this. Baring existing power relations was an important first step. But framing, or the presentation of the issue, still mattered greatly. Rent control eventually won largely as a consequence of broad disillusionment over what was perceived to be a breach of faith, or common standards of fair play, between landlord and tenant; tenant activists, however, had some concerted symbolic work to do in order to socially construct and maintain this interpretation. A "bridging" technique that they used was to draw an analogy between their activities and the civil rights movement. Since many rent control supporters were involved in movements of the sixties, they saw regulation as playing a role similar to that of the Civil Rights Division of the Justice Department enforcing the law in the South in the 1960s: "Everybody in the South complained about 'uneven justice,' and that's what the landlords don't like now."

A key element in the construction of an injustice frame was the linking of landlords in Santa Monica with greedy behavior. Although many of the landlords could be considered small "mom and pop" owners, it was important to extend the injustice frame to include them and to create one large category or "class" of landlords. Militant landlords who protested against any form of regulation made this task easier. Without the creation of this all-embracing category, tenants would have been likely to think of their particular landlords as exceptions and to rely on their personal relationships with them as sufficient to take care of problems. SMRR's efforts, on the other hand, were aimed at showing that there was a systemic bias operating. SMFHA, in one of its early newsletters, made a special point of cautioning renters that "Even renters who have fair landlords should realize that the building that they live in could be sold tomorrow" (*Fair Housing Reporter,* May 1978).

At the same time, in order to resist the efforts of landlords who would try to impose an injustice frame on rent-control supporters, tenant activists in Santa Monica, as in every other city, exempted from the law the "mom and pop" owners (this applied to apartment buildings that were owner-occupied and consisted of three or less units). This was strategically important for symbolic reasons because tenant leaders could argue that only big professional landlords would be affected. However, small landlords were frequently mobilized into landlord organizations and remained strongly opposed to SMRR.[43]

Although landlords claimed to be "sick" of hearing about the imaginary wrongs they committed in the wake of Proposition 13, it was clear that abuses were widespread enough to fuel a spontaneous wave of resentment. However, the actual extent of abuses by landlords at this time has been much debated. Enough landlords raised rents to give rise to the impression among tenants that they were not acting in good faith, and to help produce a public image of injustice. On the other hand, the Santa Monica Rent Control Board's statistics showed that 55 percent of renters received no rent increase at all in the year following Proposition 13. Although landlord behavior was interpreted as a kind of ground swell of abuse, an early SMRR activist recalled that there probably was no actual increase in abuses, although the population was ready to interpret the situation in this way.[44] While the media helped to create the impression of a major problem, it also generally capitulated to the argument that regulation does not work. Because of these ambiguities, the issue of framing became highly significant for both tenant and landlord groups.

The image of greedy landlords and large corporate interests gobbling up the city contained selected pieces of the truth. It was an effective symbolic strategy for several reasons. First, the image of a large, solid bloc of corporate interests was threatening to the prototypical "little guy" who believed in the possibility of getting ahead through competition under the capitalist system. Such restriction of choices for those who were less economically powerful could easily be defined as nondemocratic. This drove the needed wedge between capitalism and democracy and helped to disassemble the accepted "frame." Second, one of the ways to counter Olson's (1968) classic "free-rider" problem—where people choose not to participate in fighting for a collective good such as rent control because they benefit from the actions of others—is to make each person feel that their contribution is individually significant to the realization of the whole public issue (Klandermans, 1984). The "big money and powerful interests" imagery of landlord cartels against poor tenants helped to foster a sense of urgency. In terms of sheer numbers, the impression was given that each and every tenant and democratic individual was needed because the existing power structure was so entrenched—and yet poised for a fall. Allied with the fact that rent control was an issue calculable in pocketbook terms, this raised the likelihood of individual participation.

Knowing that SMRR had constructed an effective injustice frame from selective evidence increased the resentment of many landlords in Santa Monica. As one of them said:

It makes me angry, all this talk about rich landlords. Where are they? The Rent Control Board has all of the figures. They took all the registration forms and computerized them, and they discovered that 55 percent didn't raise rents after Prop 13. They don't like to talk about it because they find that we don't have too many nasty landlords. But it's PR, the word "landlord." We ended up filling that role, and I guess we did a job of it. It annoys me—I do this for a living.[45]

Landlords felt their loss of prestige in the eye of the public and bitterly resented their change of status, particularly when they surmised that it was used for political purposes. Many of them felt like scapegoats, singled out to pay for society's ills; trapped by their regulated property, they were the most visible element among the powerful urban actors who had created a crisis situation in the city. Many of them felt that the true villains, the large-scale speculators, remained invisible. As one moderate-scale landlord put it, "We did have a period where people did work over property, they'd buy, raise rents—not many. It's a terrible problem. But I'm not sure the solution is to dump it on *me*."[46]

The Opposition: Symbolic Resources

The symbolic response of SMRR's opposition was quite consistent, although its rhetoric was toned down over time for pragmatic political reasons. This opposition, however, should not be perceived as monolithic. This was no more the case than it was with SMRR itself (for a more detailed discussion, see Čapek, 1985). SMRR's opposition was mobilized in stages, beginning with landlords and broadening to a coalition structure that included homeowners, downtown business groups, real estate interests, and liberals who were critical of SMRR's strategies. This coalition faced similar organizational and motivational problems as did the progressives, with a slight time lag.

Unlike large-scale landlords, small landlords were at first only loosely organized until a local grass-roots group was formed—A Committee to Insure Owners' Needs—with ties to regional, statewide, and national real estate groups. The first and second rent-control campaigns were opposed by a real estate sponsored group called the Santa Monica Taxpayers and Residents Committee. After rent control was voted in, a predominantly landlord group called the Citizens' Congress (CC) formed to defeat SMRR at the polls. Another group called Concerned Homeowners of Santa Monica (CHOSM) mobilized against SMRR in 1981 in reaction to proposed zoning changes that would have permitted the construction and renting of "granny flats" in single-family home neighborhoods. The Commercial and Industrial Properties Association (CIPA), formed in 1982, militantly fought for downtown business interests. Finally, a broad coalition called the All Santa Monica Coalition (ASMC) was formed in 1983 to pull together groups opposed to SMRR. Although eventually disbanded, it was this coalition that defeated Ruth Yannatta Goldway in the 1983 election.

A framing device that was especially employed by landlords in Santa Monica was the insistence that SMRR politics were merely a front for CED, and hence for socialism in general. Although local residents Tom Hayden and Jane Fonda generally kept a low profile, both of them had their pictures in the paper during rent-control rallies and used the word "our" when referring to the victory. Among the opposition, however, there were different levels of recognition of the structural situation in Santa Monica as a cause of the tenants' movement, rather than the machinations of Tom Hayden. On one extreme could be found people such as Charles Isham, president of the Greater Los Angeles Apartment Owners' Association, who claimed that the housing crisis existed merely "in the eye of the beholder." Such individuals saw CED as totally responsible for constructing the rent control issue. Many of SMRR's opponents, however, did not share this conservative view. John Bambrick, former mayor, wrote the following in response to an article that called "sleepy" Santa Monica a "Berkeley for the 80's":

> . . . [it] makes us seem like a bunch of bumpkins who've been captured by the "city slickers" [the CED] through "a power grab by the radicals of the Tom Hayden-Jane Fonda machine. . . ." This, of course, is just not true. There may be a hundred or more arch-conservatives to the right of Attila the Hun who will be convinced [of this]. . . . But I am privy to the goings-on in this city and I can tell you categorically that Santa Monica is not being run by Tom Hayden & Co. . . . My view is that Tom Hayden and the CED rode into town on the crest of the wave of the renters rebellion of 1979. And they will be a potent force so long as they curry the favor of our burgeoning tenant population (*The Independent,* November 20–26, 1980).

Bambrick and others represented an effort to debunk the conservative framing of the issues and to distance themselves from a conspiracy theory.

Concerned Homeowners of Santa Monica, formed in 1981, consisted largely of professionals, some of whom were similar in age to SMRR activists, but who had taken more traditional career paths. Although willing to employ some imagery suggesting a CED conspiracy to destroy free enterprise, a more important ingredient in their framing devices was criticism of SMRR for unprofessional conduct and for dividing the community. A medium that captured the evolving process of labeling directed at SMRR was the newsletter put out by CHOSM. In the same manner as tenants had targeted earlier city councils, the newsletter engaged in "attention-calling" tactics (Marx, 1979), catching SMRR city councilmembers at awkward moments. A diverse selection of political cartoons appeared on selected themes, some of which materialized in a special "coloring book" ridiculing the progressive administration. Scenarios included the following:

1. In a restaurant, Derek Shearer, in chef's garb, cooks up the "special of the day," Economic Democracy. Ruth Yannatta Goldway brings it out

(in the form of an S-shaped cobra on a platter) to an unsuspecting, rather tattered client, saying, "Don't worry, Derek dear, they'll swallow anything if we make it sound good."

2.  The SMRR city council, with Shearer peering out from behind Goldway, is dressed in lab coats, pouring beakers of Socialism, Increased Density, Redistribution of Wealth, and Increased Bureaucracy into the Santa Monica Experiment. Under the table lie two dead rabbits labeled the "Hartford, Conn. Experiment" and the "Berkeley, Cal. Experiment"[47]

3.  Foreign leaders including Fidel Castro, Menachem Begin, Margaret Thatcher, the Ayatollah Khomeini (and even E.T.) cluster in the city council chambers to shake Ruth Goldway's hand.[48]

4.  Ruth Goldway as the Pied Piper leads transients and robbers to Santa Monica.[49]

5.  Energy police drag away a woman who didn't have enough money to insulate her house.[50]

6.  The CED octopus destroys the city with its tentacles.

While drawing on some strong traditional community sentiments, these accusations were generally more toned down than those of landlord groups and centered on stigmatizing the nonprofessional behavior of SMRR councilmembers. Although the specter of socialism was raised, the homeowners generally ridiculed what they perceived to be amateurish and dangerous efforts, with a focus on local disruptions to community sentiment. An incident that revealed that CHOSM was committed to a frame that would be perceived as moderate and rational was the departure of their cartoonist over issues of freedom of expression. In a Christmas cartoon, the CHOSM cartoonist wanted to put a hammer and a sickle bulb on the SMRR tree, but was "censored."[51] Interestingly, the newsletter changed around the time of the city elections in 1983, and a more moderate piece was subsequently produced. This in part indicated the desire of the homeowners' group to avoid such crude constructions and to cultivate a more moderate image.

Emotions ran high in Santa Monica, but over time a number of things became clear. One was that rent control showed no signs of going away. This became clear after the battery of initial elections that all yielded the same result: support for a strong rent-control law. Another evident conclusion was that the city as a whole was becoming tired of the bitterness of existing divisions. The most clear-thinking among the strategists opposed to the progressives used this knowledge to frame their arguments and to mobilize constituents.

Claiming to support reasonable regulation (the anti-SMRR ticket in 1983 confused voters by presenting itself as "the *real* renters' rights team"), the opposition also played up its image as moderator of the city's disputes. Even the Citizens' Congress, a landlord group mobilized relatively early to fight SMRR electorally, attempted to cultivate this image. Using the language of community, respect, and nonpartisanship, one of their letters began:

Dear Friend of Santa Monica:

SANTA MONICA IS IN TROUBLE. Single-issue politics and dogmatic approaches threaten our traditional community spirit. At the same time, respect for individual accomplishments and their earned rewards is eroding.... Can we build on our common interest to promote better communication and overcome fragmentation? Can we foster a political process in which citizens with diverse beliefs can exchange views and settle differences by majority rule? Moved by these concerns, a group of us has put together a nonpartisan organization called Santa Monica Citizens' Congress....

The Citizens' Congress, however, was rather easy to discredit because of its broadly perceived link with landlords. This proved to be a stigma it could not shake.

More effective was the construction in 1983 of the All Santa Monica Coalition, which acted as a bland, moderate front for a diversity of property interests in the city. Its name was inclusive, and it made an effort to present itself as a group of rational, democratic, civic-minded individuals. Upon their electoral victory in 1983, one of their spokespersons remarked, "We managed to keep our right wing at bay. The other side [SMRR] didn't do the same with their left wing." The implication was that they had won through an image of moderation and "putting the community back together" for which the city was eager.[52] They also worked to incorporate effectively an image of balanced democracy and community fairness into their public presentation of self, a set of appealing symbols that SMRR had more problems appropriating the longer that it stayed in office.

When Concerned Homeowners organized in 1981, it came the closest to having a new "motherhood" issue in the city since it mobilized over the protection of family-oriented neighborhoods. Progressive advocates had to tread softly in the vicinity of this issue, realizing that rent control would lose if an antifamily label could be made to stick to it. They withdrew the proposed zoning change, but generally remained unreconciled with homeowners, a stance that some progressives felt to be mistaken. SMRR did learn to carry out some symbolic repair work with its various constituencies in the city. For example, in 1984, during public hearings regarding the content of an upcoming ballot measure to plug loopholes in the rent-control law, some important compromises were made (see Chapter 5). As a SMRR council-member put it:

> One of the landlords told me yesterday that they don't think they can organize opposition to our charter amendment because of what we put in it. As a gesture, we put in an incentive for renting to low-income people and an exemption for single-family homes.[53]

He presented this as an example of an instance where SMRR learned from its past mistakes, both in terms of packaging its propositions and in realizing the symbolic value of particular responses to the community.

Of all the groups, landlords most lacked a "motherhood" issue. Searching through the cultural storehouse for some legitimating symbols of their own, their resources proved meager. Having attempted unsuccessfully to discredit rent control as "socialism," they focused on other symbolic strategies, some of which draw on deep-seated beliefs about fairness. One was to play up the plight of the "mom and pop" owners, a number of whom were having financial difficulties with rent control.[54] Another was to emphasize the wealth of many tenants in relationship to landlords—a strategy that was less effective because it was common knowledge that landlords bragged about deliberately renting only to upper-income tenants. It did, nevertheless, draw on the cultural preoccupation in the United States with defining the "deserving poor," and thus carried some legitimacy. Landlords were also somewhat effective in their comparisons between rent control and Prohibition, claiming that it was unenforceable and went against human nature ("Anytime you regulate like that, you're just asking for bathtub gin.")[55] When all else failed, landlords made a direct appeal to self-interest, highlighting the costs of rent control to tenants and throwing in a reference to unmanageable bureaucracy.

Symbolic attribution remains an interesting problem in Santa Monica, if only for its diversity. Tenants blame greedy landlords and the system that encourages them; landlords blame greedy tenants and the (rent-control) system that encourages them, as well as "outside agitators" such as CED; and real estate developers blame environmental and quality-of-life activists for down-zoning and making apartment construction "unprofitable." Perhaps most paradoxically of all, foreign investors, who flocked to Santa Monica in the 1970s and were often taken advantage of due to their unfamiliarity with the rent law, blame the rent-control administrators rather than the real estate agents who victimized them. The facts by themselves do not explain these attributions of blame, but rather the framing devices employed by each social group and their shifting power in relation to each other.

A Note on the Media

One final actor deserving to be mentioned at least briefly in this game of symbolic definition is the media. We have given some attention to national coverage and publicity, but local newspaper coverage in Santa Monica was also significant. The *Evening Outlook* and the *Los Angeles Times* both cover Santa Monica. The *Outlook,* the hometown paper, appeared biased against SMRR and its policies, with occasional surprises, such as its endorsement of popular SMRR candidate Ken Edwards. SMRR tended to neglect cultivating a relationship with the paper since, as one activist put it, "It was war from day one." Another explained:

> It's rare that we ever get a good story in the *Evening Outlook.* A poll showed that a very low number of respondents say they read the paper. But if we don't do anything, over time it permeates; there's a psychological effect. But dealing with it gives a low rate of return. It's better since it became a Copley paper. There's a de-emphasis on Santa Monica now. . . . But it has an impact.[56]

The newspaper was present at crucial contentious moments, such as the effort to restructure SMRR in 1983, and its presence, activists felt, had an adverse impact. Its definition of an interesting story leaned toward "growth machine" interests (Logan and Molotch, 1987) and the coverage of sensational issues. Like any form of media, it had a distortive impact on local communication. As SMRR activist Barbara Jo Osborne recalled:

> We watched the news media when they used to come to city council meetings. We asked them to cover a story, which then doesn't materialize because everyone finds out the press is coming, and the council makes the issue die. On a slow night, the newspeople play it anyway—they'd show the meeting and do a voiceover, and you'd come home and watch it on the eleven o'clock news, and they'd say something happened, and it didn't at all.[57]

Selective focus and framing devices give the media a particularly fateful power (Gitlin, 1980). As one city official commented in regard to media coverage of Santa Monica:

> Someone once said to me, "This is socialist revolution." I said, "No, this is good progressive government." I couldn't *believe* it. Rent control is a radical shift, a big deal, but it's not revolution. Some people have talked about this in an earth-shattering way, and did us a disservice.

You can see from the City Needs Assessment Survey that people here
are not very revolutionary. There are structural features that lead to rent
control....It's happening in other places too, especially Southern
California. They'll fight high-rise development there *if it's not talked
about in a revolutionary way.* It has to do with the responsibility of the
developer to the public. There is a movement to curtail them. Many rent-
control militants don't care about social services. That's not a radical
issue, but it's important to the community.[58]

This individual was very sensitive to the need to frame the issue appropriately
and worried about media coverage that would reinforce sensational or negative
stereotypes. SMRR Mayor Ken Edwards had similar observations. Battling
to keep a rational public perception of the progressive administration in place,
he remarked that, with all of the media attention, "We got the reputation for
being an activist city with outsiders. We became the Ellis Island of the eighties
for progressive causes. You get a flaky label and it ruins your credibility."[59]

Thus, newspaper and television media were additional actors engaged
in symbolic framing work, constructing a reputation for groups in the city as
well as for the city as a whole. Although the local paper leaned toward the
traditional elites in the city, it exerted an additional and independent influence
on a symbolic community portrait that was only partially under the control
of actual residents. Frustration with this imposed identity led many people—
on all sides of the issues—to resent the limelight created by media coverage
of Santa Monica.

## Symbolic Resources: Conclusions

Drawing on suggestions made by social theorists who emphasize symbolic
processes and the role of ideas in social movements (Turner, 1969, 1983; Snow
et al., 1986; Klandermans, 1984; Evans and Boyte 1986; Rudé, 1980; Melucci,
1985; Touraine, 1985; Habermas, 1971), we began this chapter by outlining
three crucial symbolic movement tasks that SMRR had to accomplish in order
to become an effective and legitimate public actor in the city. These included
unmasking the opposition through backstage work, achieving the position of
custodians of identity in the community, and framing the movement's
propositions and public "presentation of self" in a manner that would draw
on legitimated cultural resources to defuse the opposition and gain adherents.
We stressed that a successful accomplishment of these tasks relied on a social
interactional context and an understanding of the "cultural storehouse" of
meanings that could be plumbed for precisely those symbols that would help
to create an appropriate frame for movement issues.

We have found support for the importance of the face-to-face interaction in free spaces that yields emergent identities and meanings, including the social construction of confidence to challenge an existing system. We noted that collective definitions change through group interaction—in this case, for both tenants and landlords—and through the appropriate choice of a symbolic frame for public presentation. In our discussion of framing, we singled out the progressives' attempt to demonstrate that the accepted cultural fit between the concepts of democracy and capitalism was an awkward one; playing on an ambivalence built into both of these terms (particularly the contrast between theory and practice), progressives attempted to legitimate their own social movement by fitting it into a cultural context with a "respectable" past. Briefly, we also examined some of the frames constructed by SMRR's opposition in response to progressive strategies. Finally, we observed the power of the media to subvert or strengthen the framing presentations of the various groups in the city. The evidence supporting the importance of symbolic framing processes in the tenants' movement is consistent with our finding in Chapter 3 that there was a major difference in political attitudes of tenants in Santa Monica and Houston.

Given the complexity of group interactions in Santa Monica, this is but a brief examination of aspects of the social movement not grasped by the theoretical tools offered by the resource mobilization perspective. Even so, it reveals the numerous symbolic dimensions of the movement that functioned independently and in their own right to make it possible. Without them, material resources represent only a partial answer to the puzzle of how organized social change takes place.

# III

# Free Enterprise
or Regulation?

# 5

# Progressives in Office:
# Santa Monica

## Introduction

In Chapter 1, we pointed out that to understand tenants' movements as a social force we need to examine their outcomes. Specifically, what are the consequences of social movements? The evolution of a tenants' movement into a more general progressive urban movement provides a unique opportunity to evaluate structural constraints and opportunities for social change movements in the United States. In addition, it gives a taste of the day-to-day atmosphere in which challenging movements try to carve out "insurgency spaces" in a private property culture. What does our case study reveal about the possibilities for urban social change movements?

In Santa Monica, the transformation of the movement from a "mobilization" to an "administrative" phase was marked by the April 1981 municipal election, when, amid general euphoria on the part of their supporters, SMRR candidates Dolores Press, Dennis Zane, Jim Conn, and Ken Edwards joined Ruth Yannatta Goldway on the Santa Monica city council. For the first time, progressives had a voting majority. As low- and moderate-income residents who were not recruited from traditional urban elites, they represented the kinds of people who had never been elected to city government in Santa Monica—nor in most places in the United States. The movement was certainly not over at this point; SMRR supporters had high hopes for the candidates they elected and for the democratization of city politics, evidenced by the fact that over six thousand residents actively participated in the election work through such activities as telephoning, door-to-door canvassing, and community meetings.

For close to ten years, progressives have been elected to the city council in Santa Monica, sometimes in the voting majority and at other times in the minority. In April 1983, the SMRR majority was reduced to 4-3 when Ruth Yannatta Goldway lost her seat.[1] In November 1984, another seat was lost, and SMRR candidates Dennis Zane, Jim Conn, and Ken Edwards were left to function in the minority by one vote.[2] In August 1985, the death of Ken Edwards, who had been battling cancer, changed the voting balance to 5–2 in favor of SMRR's opponents. SMRR supporter David Finkel was elected to the city council in 1986, but SMRR candidates were a minority on the city council from 1984 to 1988. In November 1988, the progressives again regained control of the city council with the election of Judy Abdo and Ken Genser. Dennis Zane easily won reelection and became mayor of Santa Monica. In 1990, continuing its commitment to expanding electoral choices away from the traditional pool of white, upper-class males, SMRR fielded, and elected to the city council the following candidates: Judy Abdo, a lesbian activist; Tony Vasquez, a Hispanic; Kelly Olsen, a taxi cab driver, and Ken Genser, a disabled activist. Black candidates were also elected to the school board. The rent board elections, in the meanwhile, continued the tradition of only SMRR-endorsed candidates winning since passage of rent control in 1979.

From the vantage point of ten years, it is possible to measure some of the actual consequences of progressive policies as well as the extent to which a progressive agenda made Santa Monica a different kind of urban place. SMRR candidates won the right to pass laws affecting the city, to appoint people to controlling positions in city office, and to have discretion over city funds. While tenants' rights and rent control were their initial and most influential platform, progressives had a more general program ready to implement when voters became disillusioned with free market solutions. Where were new frontiers created, and what were the limits discovered in the attempt to alter urban space, material relations, and political culture in Santa Monica? Progressives provide a new answer to R. E. Pahl's (1975) question, "Whose City?"

To put the progressive movement in perspective, it is useful to recall that it functioned according to different levels of meaning depending on the various activist networks involved. For CED, Santa Monica meant a step toward "economic democracy"; for the network of urban progressives, it meant control of development and land-based assets to capture returns for the city locally and to promote a human-scale, participatory environment; for neighborhood activists, it meant community-based control through participation in decision-making; for those who focused on housing or on senior issues, it meant a struggle to keep their own city living space affordable.

There was also a difference of opinion in the movement regarding the extent to which the movement was expected to be "transformative." Some activists felt that the public could be converted into supporters of progressive options through education and experience. Others felt that this was a utopian goal and that within the limits of a reformist movement, the best alternative was to rely on a structural solution—making a rent-control law, a participatory arrangement, or rules about land use and development an institutional part of the city's structure. This was the attitude of hard-nosed City Attorney Robert Myers, who said of rent control that "With or without their [landlords'] cooperation, it's going to work and it's something they'll have to live with" (*Evening Outlook,* June 12, 1979). After the 1981 election, the pragmatist strand of the movement came to the fore. With Ruth Yannatta Goldway serving as mayor and Derek Shearer on the planning commission, energy was directed toward using the tools of urban planning to design a structure appropriate for a progressive city.

In this chapter, our primary focus is on the urban agenda in Santa Monica as an outcome of the social movement. Since the progressive program has been analyzed at various stages by a number of sources from a variety of perspectives (Shearer, 1984a, 1984b; Moberg, 1983a; Heskin, 1983, 1984; Kann, 1983, 1986; Daykin, 1987; Clavel, 1986; Walton, 1984a; Fulton, 1985; Boggs, 1983, 1986; Čapek, 1985), our intent here is not to present a complete outline or a detailed overview. Rather, we will give our attention to some selected areas that should act as touchstones, or "barometers," for any progressive program. Among these will be rent control and housing, development, and the status of minority communities. In addition, some of the detail and complexity of the issues are reflected in our notes (see also Čapek, 1985).

## Rent Control Law

When you do it, it seems like a reform movement; the left criticizes it. But when you intimately experience the struggle in Santa Monica, you know it's a very *radical* proposition. To sustain our effort has taken very bright, committed, energetic people working eighteen hours a day for four years, sixty such people. That says the system doesn't want rent control. —Bill Allen[3]

I think that Adolf Hitler and Josef Stalin could be elected on the SMRR ticket by promising to give money to tenants. —a landlord quoted in the *Evening Outlook*

The item on the progressive agenda that has had the strongest force in the community is Santa Monica's rent-control law. The law is less negotiable than any other aspect of city politics because tenant organizers presented it as a city charter amendment on the 1979 ballot. It continues to be administered by a tenant-elected rent control board. The elected rent control board is one of the strongest features of the law. This removes it from some of the pressures that cause political compromises in other areas. In a number of other cities, rent-control laws were undermined by hostile city appointees to rent boards; activists knew this and created a different structure. As we noted in Chapter

3, it is no accident that the law is unusually strong; it is a result of nationwide progressive networking engaged in by movement activists, who learned from the experience of other cities with more moderate rent-control laws. Gilderbloom (1986) found, for example, that New Jersey's moderate rent-control laws did not result in a redistribution of rent from landlord to tenant and were largely symbolic. Thus, the rent-control amendment is at once a legal document and a testament to networking among movement activists.

Recognizing that the housing crisis (see Chapter 3) as well as those forces willing to exploit the shortage for personal gain "endanger the public health and welfare of Santa Monica tenants," the rent-control law passed in 1979 had the following provisions (Gilderbloom, 1981b:303). As a first step, it instituted a rent freeze of one hundred twenty days, to be followed by a rollback of rents to April 1, 1978. Yearly rent adjustments were to be made on the amount of rent charged in this base year, when the free market was assumed to be operating and giving landlords fair returns on their investments.[4] An appeals process was available to landlords on an individual basis if their circumstances were exceptional. Owner-occupied buildings with three or fewer units were exempted from controls, as was all new construction.

The city charter amendment provided for a ninety-day interim rent-control board, whose duty was to register the rent-controlled units in the city and to enforce criminal sanctions in cases of noncompliance.[5] Subsequently, a rent-control board was to be elected, whose responsibility was the adjustment of rents yearly: upward to account for utilities, maintenance, or property tax increases; downward to reflect any decreases in costs to landlords.[6] The rent board had the power to hire its own staff, to conduct hearings, and to seek penalties. It was to be funded through the annual registration fees charged to landlords. Landlords were required to report vacancies, a list that the rent board would make available to the public. Security deposits to landlords were to be placed in interest-bearing accounts out of which landlords were to offset operating expenses. The law also contained a "just cause" eviction clause, treble damages for rent overcharges, and rent decreases in the case of improper maintenance. Landlords were required to obtain a permit from the rent board for any demolitions or conversions (not for new construction, however); they could only obtain such if their alteration did not produce a negative impact on housing availability in the city or adversely affect low- and moderate-income tenants. Rents were affixed to the unit, rather than to the tenant, meaning that no "vacancy decontrol" of rents was allowed with the departure of a tenant (in cities with vacancy decontrol, tenants were often evicted so that landlords could raise rents in the apartment). The rent board was required to act within one hundred twenty days or forfeit its discretion.

These provisions were quite stringent, leading one observer to remark that the law appeared to be written with an almost complete distrust of landlords.[7] One of the most controversial portions of the rent law stated that, while landlords had to be guaranteed a fair return, *no* increase would be authorized merely because a landlord had a negative cash flow as a result of refinancing, if the landlord could have reasonably foreseen a negative cash flow based on the rent schedule then in effect.[8] In an effort to remove buildings from the speculative cycle, the rent increase formula was based on "historic investment," that is, the amount of money actually paid for a piece of property, rather than current market value. Concurrently, "debt service" was not taken into account in rent increases. The reasoning for this was based on a number of studies that found that, while about 50 percent of the rent dollar goes into debt service, many buildings were purchased at fixed-rate mortgages, leading this expense to remain constant (Gilderbloom and Jacob, 1981).[9] To peg rent increases to the consumer price index, as landlord groups wished, would be to reward landlords for double the amount of their expenses.

Challenges to the Law

It appears now that the city wants to own the property and this is the wrong country for the government to own the housing. —Anonymous note scribbled on the back of a rent board agenda, summer 1984

What constitutes a "fair return" legally and socially has been the most contested portion of the law. In one such case, the owner of the Inn at Santa Monica claimed a loss of $184,000 per year on a 97-unit apartment next to the hotel after his mortgage interest rate went from 10.0 percent to 17.5 percent. He sued the rent board on the grounds that their formula ignored debt service. The rent board's response was that the law was not formulated to "insulate landlords from the risks" of business, including variable interest rates. Their decision was bolstered by actions of courts in New Jersey and Massachusetts that supported excluding debt service as an operating expense in determining a fair return.

A similar controversy arose over the Osio case, in which a landlord was denied increases on the grounds that his purchase was "speculative." The owner claimed that he was losing money, while the rent board calculated that he was making a 9 percent profit.[10] The decision was upheld by one court, then overturned and called unconstitutional. In 1981, a superior court judge ordered the rent board to appear before him for sentencing for contempt of court after the board refused to grant the landlord an increase. He told the board that they based their decisions on:

...innuendo, gossip, conjecture and political persuasion. There are enough commissars and juntas in the world to make decisions on the basis of personal philosophy. A rent control system must be just, reasonable and governed objectively, for the good of the whole community (*Evening Outlook,* June 27, 1981).

Rent board member David Finkel responded that these comments were "totally unnecessary, inflammatory and biased" (*Evening Outlook,* June 27, 1981). The rent board was forced to comply with the decision, however. This experience highlighted the fact that the rent board had to be concerned about the symbolic environment of the court system and its reputation in legal and political circles. The level of tension was raised by the incessant efforts of real estate groups to pass a statewide law pre-empting local rent controls (see below).

The most comprehensive challenge to the rent law is the (James) Baker case, filed the day after rent control was passed in Santa Monica in 1979. It challenges the fair return formula and the restrictions on demolishing buildings. It is slowly working its way to the highest court in the nation. During one phase, a judge ruled that the rent board was not entitled to prevent demolitions; this was overturned by a temporary restraining order. In a related case, Thomas Nash—a landlord who was making a profit, but decided that he wanted to demolish his building and go out of business—sued the rent board for interfering with his constitutional rights. The city's right to regulate demolitions was upheld, however, since the U.S. Supreme Court refused to hear the Nash case (the first to reach that level of the court system).

In March 1981, in a phase of the Baker case, a judge struck down the Santa Monica rent board's original formula, Regulation 4040, ruling that its "historic investment" basis was confiscatory.[11] He also struck down the provision denying rent increases to landlords with a negative cash flow. The rent board and the city council were required to come up with a new fair return formula.[12] In June of that year, the same judge, in a more favorable move, refused to give landlords a temporary injunction prohibiting the rent board from controlling rents on vacant units while the new formula was being developed. Using evidence from all over the country, the rent board asked its attorneys to design alternate models demonstrating the impact of different formulas on the city. After receiving an extension on their deadline, they presented a new formula, which then stood up in court.[13]

In 1983, the rent board received a series of setbacks at the hands of the Southern California Legal Foundation (SCLF). Based in Santa Monica, the SCLF was a spin-off of the Pacific Legal Foundation, a conservative "public interest" firm that described its priorities as fighting "government abuse."[14] Claiming that Santa Monica was more abusive than almost any other city, it targeted the city through its "Santa Monica Project," asserting that the "people of Santa Monica have a particularly pressing need to be represented against the abuses of their government." In the person of its legal director, David Shell—who ran a losing race against Tom Hayden in the 1984 California assembly campaign—over one hundred suits were filed, largely focusing on procedural issues intended to chip away at the rent law indirectly. Many of these won favorable rulings in 1983.

One in the series challenged the independence of the rent board in setting its own budget and hiring legal staff. Originally financed by a city general fund loan, the rent board has faced many budgetary crises. The original progressive idea was to fund it through a $12.50 per unit annual registration fee to be paid by landlords. Flooded with requests for help as well as lawsuits, and also facing the social noncompliance of landlords, the board in its 1980–82 budget proposed a $48 fee, which would be passed through to tenants at the rate of $4 per month.[15] This was raised in 1981–82 to $72, which translated into $6 per month. In 1991, it was $132. Original estimates had vastly underestimated financial expenditures. Critics charge that the rent board is a "swollen bureaucracy," while supporters point out that the flood of litigation that is unique to Santa Monica has immensely driven up the cost of rent control.[16]

In December 1983, a superior court judge stripped the rent board of powers to set its own budget and hire its own legal staff, saying that it had usurped the rights of the courts and should be subject to budgetary control by the city council.[17] Other victories for Shell and SCLF included the board's loss of the right to hire a lobbyist and to hear rent decrease petitions, something that had constituted one of its major tasks (between 1979 and 1983, it heard two thousand cases). Shell also won restrictions on enforcing penalties for nonregistration and rent overcharges.

While many rent board members believed that favorable rulings would be returned, the situation was demoralizing and injected confusion into an already difficult situation.[18] As Susan Packer Davis (at the time an ex-member of the rent-control board, later reelected) observed in 1984:

> They're [Shell's group] *incredibly* destructive; they spend a lot of money just trying to jam up the courts with cases. The Supreme Court will hopefully lay it to rest, but while waiting it's debilitating. And the tenants feel helpless. Right now the rent board just *takes* abuse, and it's terrible to do that. Nowhere does it say that you have to take personal attacks.[19]

The year 1984 did bring the overturning of many of these decisions. The budget and legal staff were restored, the state supreme court upheld rent law restrictions on condominium conversions, and a state high court upheld provisions blocking apartment demolitions. The board's right to hire a lobbyist was reinstated, and the formulas for determining rent increases were upheld in an unpublished decision by a court of appeal. The rent board also won back its right to lower rents for buildings that were not maintained.[20] As a rent board staffmember pointed out, the fact that two out of the three judges claimed that they took these decisions reluctantly showed the strength of rent control's legal position.[21]

## Recent Amendments to Rent Control

In November 1984, a new charter amendment was put on the ballot in Santa Monica and passed by voters. It was intended to strengthen provisions and fill loopholes in the rent-control law.[22] At the same time, it reflected some pragmatic compromises achieved between SMRR movement activists and their opponents in urban politics. Like the original charter amendment, its text reveals the process of emerging collective definitions of fairness resulting from group interaction. Thus, in response to court decisions challenging the rent board's independent right to formulate its own budget and hire staff, the amendment institutionalized these rights. In a move to placate homeowners, it exempted from controls single-family homes and condominiums that were not on the rental market as of June 1984. On the other hand, it limited apartment owners to one eviction per building for a relative (the rent-control law had not restricted such evictions, prompting landlord activist John Jurenka to move his relatives into seven apartments in one of his buildings and to brag about outwitting the rent board with his "seven-bedroom home"). A much-debated clause allowed the board to set higher rent ceilings or to remove ceilings altogether on vacated units for buildings in which 15 percent of the units were reserved for people of low or moderate income. This constituted a limited form of "vacancy decontrol," a move generally opposed by tenants. On the other hand, it provided the "means test," which SMRR opponents charged was lacking in the rent law. Exemptions were also provided for nonprofit uses and residential social services, such as child-care. The amendment affirmed two other rights of the board that had been challenged in the courts: It would be allowed to hear rent reduction cases and to hire a lobbyist to work for rent control in Sacramento, the state's capital. In administrative hearings for excess rents, the penalty was limited to $500, as opposed to the earlier treble damages. The rent board was also empowered to enact replacement regulations for sections of the law invalidated by the courts (*Evening Outlook,* November 1, 1984; also city council hearings, summer 1984).

In preliminary hearings during the summer of 1984, a controversial provision was removed that would have denied rent increases to landlords deliberately holding units vacant. Although the extent of this activity is not empirically measurable throughout the city, many tenants (and landlords) have testified of personal knowledge of such situations in their buildings.[23] When this particular provision was struck, Mayor Ken Edwards asserted that he did not want to impose an "economic penalty for a noneconomic act." Yet landlords boasted of their acts of noncompliance, making their social circumvention of the law a significant problem.[24] Moreover, they defined their acts as economic. As one landlord activist stated:

It's not symbolic. It costs me $1,000 to put an apartment in good shape, and I've done that in the past. But I won't do it now. I've got one tenant now who has two burners that don't work, and the gas company says it could be dangerous. So I've got an old junker down here I'll replace it with. . . . If you invest in something, you don't just get your money *back*. In savings accounts or in bonds I'd get interest, so why should I do *this* with my money? It's just economics. And there's no way in the world they can force me to rent to someone I don't want. There is *not*. When they came out with the ordinance that says on it that we're supposed to notify the rent board— well, there's not one single owner who would *ever* tell the rent board if he ever had a vacancy.[25]

Such "civil disobedience" has a devastating effect on tenants.[26] However, the rent board overlooked this and other forms of social noncompliance. In order to address landlord threats of a decrease in maintenance expenditures, rent board members decided in 1984 to ignore a staff recommendation to give an annual rent increase of only 2.26 percent based on their fair return formula. Instead, they approved a 4 percent increase, claiming that they hoped this would function as an incentive to repair Santa Monica's deteriorating apartment stock (*Evening Outlook,* June 29, 1984). Landlords scoffed at the increase, and tenants were angered. OPCO staffperson Pete Sevino, who has worked with tenants throughout the Los Angeles area, remarked that "landlords always get something, a lot more than tenants, and it doesn't pacify them. Tenant organizations would survive on such gains for *years,* but the community doesn't get these things."[27] Tenants were also angered by a pilot program for capital improvements that contained a pass-through of expenses to tenants on a voluntary basis.[28] In 1989, the rent board approved a 2 percent annual rent adjustment. The search for a simplified "fair return" formula continues, with recent suggestions that the consumer price index be used more extensively (Gilderbloom, 1981b).

While Santa Monica's strong rent control has generally remained intact despite numerous challenges in the courts, landlords have attempted to circumvent the law by supporting preemptive state legislation that takes the teeth out of local rent control. In general, the bills seek to turn strong rent-control legislation into moderate rent-control laws. Moderate rent-control laws are characterized by vacancy decontrol, higher allowable rent increases, and weak administration. Most studies indicate that these kinds of laws have very little impact on overall rent levels (Appelbaum and Gilderbloom, 1990).

With one major exception, these attempts have been unsuccessful, thanks to the persistent efforts of Senator David Roberti, who, as leader of the senate, has caused most of these bills to die before they reached a vote in the full senate. It is generally acknowledged that these anti-rent-control bills have the support of the majority of senators, assembly persons,, and the current Republican governor Pete Wilson. Should Senator Roberti lose his position as leader of the senate, the future of Santa Monica's tough rent-control law would be in jeopardy. One bill that did get past the senate and was signed by the governor was the Ellis Bill, which allows landlords to remove their buildings from the rental-housing market and replace them with condominiums. This is one way for landlords to elude regulation. As a result, by the end of 1990, Santa Monica city officials estimated that over 1,000 apartment units had been taken off the market.

In 1989, the rapid loss of apartment units due to the Ellis Bill alarmed SMRR, the city council, and the rent-control board. By the winter of 1990 an average of 12 units a week were being lost. Most of the apartment units taken off the market had rents under $500 and were being replaced by posh $400,000 condominiums. The response to the Ellis Bill came in several local government actions to encourage landlords to stay in business.[29] In the fall of 1989, the rent-control board passed an "inclusionary housing plan" that would allow rents in vacated units to rise to market levels with a ceiling ranging between $400 and $900. This allowance was contingent on a landlord providing evidence of having another unit in the building with a very low-income person residing at a fixed rent, ranging from $266 for a studio apartment to $361 for a two-bedroom apartment. Following this, the rent board granted a 6 percent allowable increase and a simplified cost pass-through system. In November of 1990 SMRR sponsored and passed an initiative that required that 30 percent of all multifamily residential housing newly constructed must be affordable and occupied by low- and moderate-income persons. These measures were designed to subvert the state-sponsored Ellis Bill, which has wreaked havoc on Santa Monica's strong rent-control law. The 1990 SMRR initiative has resulted in a significant drop in the number of apartment units being taken off the market. It should be noted that it is not strong local rent controls that caused the dramatic loss of affordable housing units, but the intervention of the state legislature. If the Ellis Bill had been defeated, Santa Monica would not have lost 1,000 affordable units.

Of interest here sociologically is the uncertainty of the legal and political definition of the limits of private property rights and the fragility of some of the political alliances that challenge the status quo. The history of rent control in the United States reveals this ambiguity. It does show, however, that the progressive movement was right to assume that rent control could be rationally extended from other basic rights. Many of the rent-control decisions have been legally upheld. At the same time, the climate of the court system continues to be highly volatile and is closely watched by all factions.

In contemplating the role of the state, the lesson for progressives is how an urban grass-roots movement can be circumvented by forces outside the city limits (see Savitch, 1979:234–35). The state legislature has been a major foe of strong local rent controls and other progressive legislation that put restrictions on the property rights of owners. More recently, the U.S. Congress has gotten into the act by proposing legislation that would deny federal housing funds to any cities with strong rent-control laws. Progressive urban social change is subject to many forms of attack. Even when citizens democratically choose a progressive form of government, elite interests will mobilize their resources by using the courts and the legislative branches of state and federal government to challenge it. This has implications for rent control as a housing strategy (see Chapter 7).

Social Interactional Consequences of Rent Control

The institutionalization of rent control in Santa Monica is interesting not only in legal terms but also as a social interactional process. A testimony to the revitalization of democracy in Santa Monica was the fact that ninety-eight people applied for the interim rent board, while sixty-four took out papers to run for the permanent rent-control board. The names of people wanting to take part in the process (either to protect or to oppose rent control) took up entire pages of Santa Monica's *Evening Outlook* newspaper. In a special municipal election in June 1979, the permanent board consisting of five members was elected. All five represented the SMRR slate.[30] The unruliness of the early meetings became legendary. For example, a landlord rally to discuss "survival" issues that June drew a boisterous crowd of eight hundred.[31] The local newspaper noted that "even ministers who talked of reconciliation and good will were hooted and jeered by some members of the audience" (*Evening Outlook,* April 8, 1980). In this atmosphere, as we noted in Chapter 4, progressives had a strong interest in keeping the dialogue about rent control rational. As board member Neil Stone observed, "Our responsibility is to show what the law means factually; that the board is committed to implementation of the law and that being pro-tenant doesn't mean you're anti-landlord" (*Los Angeles Times,* July 5, 1979). However, progressives who wanted to evaluate the assets and flaws of the Santa Monica rent-control law rationally, and thus add to the existing stock of knowledge about progressive options for all cities, had difficulty doing so. Former rent board member Bill Allen recalled that dialogue with the landlords was desirable, but the atmosphere of the meetings led to a "circus."[32] Susan Packer Davis concurred:

> It doesn't lend itself to dialogue; it's like a shoot-out. My disappointment was the climate of hysteria. I used to take a deep breath and look at what I wanted to accomplish. Sometimes that wasn't possible. I was not prepared for the degree and intensity of the attack on the rent-control board. In the city council, a person is allowed to address the public on the same topic only once and has to submit the rest in writing. But it didn't get the votes for the rent board. The landlords say the same thing all the time.[33]

Because the meetings have the latent function of being institutionalized release mechanisms for community hostility, many rent board commissioners supported the norm that allowed landlords to have their say, even if this included personal insults to the board itself. For example, when the rent board decided on one occasion to ignore the recommendations of its staff and made the annual permissible rent increase larger, a landlord taunted them and told them to follow their staff blindly "like trained pigs" (*Evening Outlook,* June 29, 1984). One rent board member defended his attitude of tolerance, saying, "I'd rather hear them say it in here than out there." A tenant observed, "That just gives them [landlords] permission to do it in *both* places."[34]

The situation reveals clearly who is accustomed to having power in the society. Even though the rent board is an elected body, given the legal right to regulate landlords economically, landlords behave confidently as a privileged elite, drawing on their understanding of American culture. Many tenants are critical of the rent board for allowing rude behavior, feeling that it makes all too clear the uncertainty and tentativeness that progressives feel in their unaccustomed position of power. They argue that the wrong signals are being sent; the symbolic message sent to landlords is that they are right to draw their inferences from the old set of relations.[35] As a tenant activist observed of progressives, "They're so *apologetic* for the law. I don't think that a lot of these people believe that we actually *have* the right to regulate landlords. Personally, I have no problem with it at all."[36] Progressive rent-control administrators, on the other hand, claimed that the complexities of the law were far greater than could be recognized by neighborhood activists.

The fault for the polarization did not lie exclusively with landlords. Renee Gould, an early rent board member who was supported by SMRR although "not really part of it," had bitter feelings about being "ostracized" by SMRR for attempting to engage in a dialogue with landlords:

> There were a lot of problems among that group [the rent board]—a kind of lack of—well, certainly manners. Which have to do with living in

a society with other people who aren't like you. When you have a political objective, it seems to me that everything you do you have to keep that objective in mind. If it means working with people you ordinarily don't like, in order to make things happen, that's your primary objective. Part of the rent-control law was to educate people, give them information about what was happening in their lives. I said early on that we must discriminate between the different *kinds* of landlords in the city, especially the moms and pops. These were your *allies,* as opposed to the Jerry Busses [a reference to large-scale landlords] who smile all the way to the lawyer's and have all the resources. . . . So I met with [landlord] James Baker. I get a call from my supporters who say they're seriously insulted that I talked to the opposition, that landlords are exploiters. I said, "Nobody's going to tell me what to do. This is *not* a class war; there are some people living as tenants in this community who own apartments elsewhere and live here because it's so cheap. . . . " After that, it was all over; I was excluded from everything.[37]

This viewpoint revealed some of the tensions within SMRR and between SMRR activists and other groups in the city. One of the consequences of the siege atmosphere in which rent control operated was interpersonal tension among progressive activists and sometimes an outright fear of democracy. Clearly, the social construction of fairness was not something that could be resolved on paper; instead it presented complex issues when it came to face-to-face interactions in the city.

### The Redistributional Impact of Rent Control: Who Benefits?

A major question regarding the goals of the progressive tenants' movement in Santa Monica concerns the economic redistributional impacts of Santa Monica's rent-control law. Astonishingly, Mark Kann's (1986) "left" analysis of Santa Monica fails to address this crucial issue. The question is important: What can tenants gain in real dollars by participating in an urban grass-roots movement?

Santa Monica's strong rent-control law resulted in substantial income redistribution between landlords and tenants. In a study of Santa Monica, for example, Shulman (1980) estimates that under rent controls rents increased from $281 to $320 in 1980—a rise of 14 percent. If no controls had existed during that same period, he estimates that rents would have risen to an average of $446 a month—an increase of almost 59 percent in two years. Shulman (1980:13) calculates that, as a result of rent control, the amount of rent lost by landlords and the amount of income gained by tenants has been roughly $108 million over a twenty-four month period.

Similar evidence was found when Appelbaum (1986) directly compared the effects of strong and moderate rent controls in different cities. Strong rent controls permit no vacancy decontrol (increase of rents when tenants move out of a controlled apartment), are administered by elected boards, and use rent increase formulas of partial consumer price index or net operating income. Moderate rent controls have some vacancy decontrol provisions, are administrated by appointed boards, and use rent increase formulas of full CPI, with provisions for hardship appeals. Appelbaum compared a ten-year forecast of rents (1987 to 1997) and affordability under certain cities' current strong rent-control laws with the probable results of more moderate ordinances that would have permitted vacated units to be temporarily decontrolled. Appelbaum estimates that under Santa Monica's strong rent-control law, average monthly rents would increase from $458 to $631—a ten-year increase of 37 percent. On the other hand, under a vacancy decontrol provision, average rents would rise to about $1,123—an increase of 145 percent, as landlords take advantage of tenant turnover to raise rents in vacated units to market levels—a difference of 78 percent.

Appelbaum (1986), using current government standards of a household paying no more than 30 percent of its income into housing, finds that in 1986, 48 percent of the rental units were unaffordable and by 1997 this would fall to 29 percent. If the law were changed to a moderate rent-control ordinance with a vacancy decontrol provision, the number of unaffordable units would increase to 55 percent by 1997. Santa Monica's strong rent-control law could lead to the creation of 6,000 additional affordable units—significant when one considers that this represents almost 20 percent of the total rental housing stock. Appelbaum estimates that tenants in Santa Monica under a strong rent-control ordinance will save a cummulative total of $1.1 billion between 1987 and 1997. Strong rent control, in other words, would produce a substantial redistribution of wealth from landlords to tenants.

The most recent study of the impact of strong rent controls in Santa Monica was carried out by Ned Levine and Gene Grigsby (1987). The study used many of the same questions asked by Allan Heskin (1983) in his 1979 study, when rent control was first enacted in Santa Monica. Using 1979 as a baseline, Levine and Grigsby (1987) found very few negative impacts and many positive impacts. First, they found that the length of residence had increased for many residents, indicating greater neighborhood stability. The number of tenants who had lived in the same rental unit over a ten-year period had doubled, and the number of tenants who had moved after a six-month period had fallen by a factor of three. Second, 14 percent of the renters surveyed felt that the condition of their rental unit was in poor or very poor shape, a small increase from the 1979 baseline, where only 6 percent complained of this problem. On the other hand, tenants reported fewer problems or disputes with landlords. The results are fairly dramatic: While in the 1979 survey, 32 percent of the tenants reported problems; this fell to 18 percent in 1987. Third, Levine and Grigsby (1987) estimate that strong rent controls have resulted in a $160 a month saving compared with non-rent-controlled cities in the Los Angeles area. An alternative model estimates that the savings could be as high as $190 a month, but it is not reliable due to a smaller sample. Based on the more conservative estimate of a net savings of $160 a month, the authors argue that rents are about 25 percent below current market rents in adjacent non-rent-controlled areas. They also point out that the proportion of income going into rent has fallen from 34 percent in 1979 to 30 percent in 1987. Finally, contrary to the claims of Kann (1986) and Devine (1986), that rent control is a subsidy aimed at benefiting the middle class and hurting the poor, Levine and Grigsby (1987) report that the economic composition of Santa Monica renters—including the percentage of poor renters—has remained the same since the enactment of rent control.

These findings support the argument that strong rent control laws work to the advantage of tenants. Additional evidence is provided in a study conducted by Ken Baar and Gary Squire (1987), which found that rents in the Los Angeles area went up by 113 percent between 1978 and 1987, whereas in Santa Monica during the same period they increased by only 46 percent. Moreover, a study of multifamily construction between 1980 and 1986 ranked Santa Monica second among seven coastal cities in the Los Angeles area in multifamily construction per square mile, undermining real estate industry claims that rent control leads to shrinking construction and therefore more severe housing shortages than a regulation free atmosphere. Attempts by landlords to discredit the rent board by making tenants angry about lack of maintenance have not been successful, as evidenced by an article in the Santa Monica *Evening Outlook* on April 30, 1985:

Despite all theories and claims to the contrary we do not find significant renter dissatisfaction with the Rent Control Board. . . . Whatever view supporters of rent control have of the deterioration of their apartments, they do not appear to have a lesser view of the Rent Board because of this belief.

To answer the question "Who benefits?" then, the evidence points to low- and moderate-income tenants and to the fact that urban space is made more accessible to mixed-income groups as a result of strong rent controls. While 1,000 units have been taken off the market due to state legislation, according to Appelbaum's (1986) study, 6,000 units will have eventually become affordable because of strong rent control.

Ownership Programs

An avid debate over private property and its relationship to individual and to collective rights was engaged in not only between progressives and their opponents, but among progressives themselves. As we discussed in Chapter 2, the Marxist and Weberian arguments linking homeownership to decreased political radicalism represent contemporary views of many progressive activists. For example, a number of SMRR activists assumed that one's *class* perspective would be changed through ownership. These same individuals felt that if, for example, SMRR supported condominium ownership it would be supporting a luxury use that did not fit the progressive agenda. This presented an interesting problem, particularly when an initiative designed to allow tenants to negotiate with landlords for ownership of their apartments was nearly passed by voters in 1983.[38] Realizing the strength of the vote, SMRR became involved in negotiating a compromise initiative with landlords in 1984 (Proposition X) that contained many more protections for tenants. Nevertheless, it caused significant disagreement in the SMRR coalition.

CHAIN activist Cary Lowe recalled an earlier conversation with Dennis Zane, who at this time became SMRR's chief negotiator for the agreement:

Some think it's a sellout. . . . I used to argue with Denny Zane. "Ownership shouldn't be looked down on as an enemy. Homeowners voted for you too. It's not bona fide representation of your constituency to tell them they must remain renters. You preserve them in a relation you say is bad." He said, "We need mass public housing." I said, "It won't happen." He said, "Then it's better to stay renters with political power." So this was quite a switch for him, Prop X, a giant turnaround.[39]

Ed Kirshner, a former planning commissioner with a history of nationwide involvement in housing issues (Clavel, 1986), noticed a similar problem, in this case a reluctance on the part of key city administrators to become involved in housing co-operatives:

It was a *strange,* naive view. I got this view organizing in the East with people too. It's a strange view: Renters are the proletariat (no matter what their income level is), and owners are the bourgeoisie. Anyone who becomes an owner changes into the "enemy." *That's* very bad in this town. Homeowners are enemies— that's crazy! Luckily it's not in too many places— I was surprised to find it here. It's *not* in Berkeley. They have a strong tenants' union, but they'll go to the wall for limited equity co-ops. They quickly realized that part of the alliance was black, a 25 percent black population, and upwardly mobile. They displayed realism, unlike Santa Monica, which is a never-never land. In Berkeley, tenant ownership is important. In Sweden, any place that's gone through a tenants' movement invariably becomes oriented toward tenant ownership. This was also a problem in Cambridge, New Jersey, New York. Property ownership versus not owning was to them the key, as opposed to *class*. They mix up real estate with the means of production. That got translated here as "landlords are the enemy, they own property, therefore homeowners are too." It got polarized along certain lines it never should have.[40]

SMRR's involvement in the negotiated agreement for tenant ownership was therefore seen as a strong symbolic statement. Opinion was divided as to its progressive nature. A group calling itself "Nix on X" split off from the coalition and claimed to have shaved off 5 percent of the vote in the election. Their concern was similar to that articulated by Allan Heskin: that the new law would "put a price tag on every tenant's head" (*L.A. Reader,* May 25, 1984). Intensive outreach to tenants was required; many recalled the SMRR campaign against the ownership initiative in the previous year, and were confused.

However, there were significant differences, in a progressive direction between the two initiatives, including stronger social protections for tenants and for the city in general. Two thirds of tenants had to agree to the conversion of their buildings. Maintenance records had to be provided; tenants had an exclusive two-year option to buy; and the disabled or elderly could not be forced to leave. Further, the city had the right to review the agreement and to get equity participation in return for providing financial assistance. It could also attach conditions to the resale, such as antispeculative provisions. A fund would be provided to assist low- and moderate-income tenants from a conversion tax on sales. In this form, Proposition X appeared on the 1984 ballot, and it won a resounding victory. Although a symbolic victory, Proposition X led to few apartment complexes being converted to condominiums or cooperatives.

The lack of interest on the part of tenants to become homeowners is a by-product of the strong rent-control law. Attempts to convince tenants to convert their apartments to limited equity cooperatives have been unsuccessful. Because rents are dramatically lower under Santa Monica's rent-control law, cooperative ownership—at least for the short term—would be significantly costlier. While the city's nonprofit housing development corporation has built and rehabilitated hundreds of rental units, no limited equity cooperatives have been produced. In 1988 the Community Corporation of Santa Monica (CCSM) estimated that a conversion from a rental to a cooperative dwelling would result in mortgage payments $65 per month higher. Although CCSM (see below) is technically capable of producing cooperatives, it sees no tenant "demand" for this kind of housing. The gamble that tenants are making is that Santa Monica's law will remain strong in the future, which seems rather shaky.

Federal funds play a key role in most city housing programs, however. A traditional means of dealing with housing has been through government HUD Section 8 programs, which were slashed by 78 percent during President Reagan's administration (Gilderbloom and Appelbaum, 1988). For example, Santa Monica used general revenue sharing money that it obtained in 1982 to set up a housing rehabilitation program that provides grants to landlords with low-income tenants to bring buildings up to habitable standards.

To these traditional options, progressives added a number of other avenues for obtaining housing. One of these was the developer agreement, where trade-offs were given to the community in exchange for the right to build (see below). While this adds directly to the housing supply, targeting the low- and moderate-income population, quantitative gains are small. Another option was the founding of a nonprofit community development corporation, Community Corporation of Santa Monica, which concerned itself with the purchase and renovation of housing on a nonprofit basis, contributing to the "decommodification" of housing (Achtenberg and Marcuse, 1983). CCSM— founded and originally headed by Allan Heskin—is partially dependent on federal money for projects, but also contributes on the other end to assuring long-term affordability.

While these projects are necessarily small-scale, they provide evidence of the positive impact of re-creating "community" in areas of the city that have been systematically neglected. In one such effort, tenants in a 12-unit building in the Pico neighborhood compared the new owners favorably to prior owners, who had let the building change hands often and did not attend to maintenance or safety problems. CCSM immediately began crucial repairs, including the removal of abandoned cars and attention to security measures.[41] A Neighborhood Watch group and pride in the increased maintenance have brought tenants together. As one said, "We know each other, talk to each other, help each other with problems. Our kids play together. It's nice now because the kids can go back outside" (*Santa Monica Seascape*, January/ February 1984). As we will discuss below, however, there are many constraints on such programs, including a limited field in which to operate and vulnerability to the curtailing of federal funds.

## Development Programs

I think we've shown that development can occur in a way that meets both the public balance sheet and the private balance sheet of the investment community. —John Alshuler

The city has lost a lot of its values, such as social progress and meaningful participation. The progressiveness has been bought off, and they're delivering the city to the developers. Our success makes it possible for them to exist within the context of progressivism, rather than just *being* progressive. —Ken Genser[42]

When SMRR progressives were elected to the city council in 1981, there was a general fear in the city that real estate developers would transform Santa Monica into a city of high-rise buildings and high-income residents—as we noted earlier, a Miami Beach of the West Coast. Evidence included investor Lawrence Welk's eleven-story building near the oceanfront, plans to construct the "largest condominium development in California," and a history of redevelopment plans that targeted low-income communities. Surrounding communities just outside the boundaries of Santa Monica were already full of tall buildings. Although negative public sentiments in the early 1970s resulted in down-zoning and swept in a more moderate city council, this was not enough to prevent large developers from targeting Santa Monica. Exercising local control over development was an idea shared by progressives and a majority of the population.

Dealing with growth and development in a progressive manner became a major preoccupation of SMRR city councilmembers. As William Fulton (1985:4) concluded in his assessment of the Santa Monica experiment, "planning, not El Salvador or the nuclear freeze, was the centerpiece of their 'progressive' administration." In particular, progressives wanted to preserve "community" at the expense of "commodity," challenging the traditional urban script that automatically gives developers broad leverage (Judd, 1984; Feagin and Parker, 1990). One of their first acts on achieving office was to institute a six-month moratorium on all construction in the city. They did this in order to stop the development process while buying time to institute a progressive agenda that would resolve questions of growth, land use, and zoning. Their act was met with outrage by the business community, which argued that this was an unacceptable interference with private property rights. Not all projects were stopped "cold" by the moratorium, however. Some developers had viable "vested interest" arguments that could have withstood a legal test.[43] To resolve this situation, the city council used the concept of the "developer agreement," a solution that brought widespread notoriety as well as praise to Santa Monica.

Development agreements were not by themselves a new idea. They put into practice the concept of a "public balance sheet" (Smith, 1979), whereby it is assumed that since developers impose significant costs on communities by using municipal resources, subsidies, or creating social problems, they should give something back to the community in exchange for their right to build and to make money. Traditionally, city officials have encouraged growth, arguing that as the pie gets larger, everyone gets a larger slice. The "pie" is often presented as consisting of new jobs, higher land values, increased tax revenues, and greater consumer spending. However, growth is frequently accompanied by problems such as higher housing costs, a rise in crime, more pollution, and traffic congestion. Because these costs are frequently invisible to the public, the balance sheet strategy is used to make the costs visible so that corporations and businesses can provide trade-offs to the community to make up for the stress that they are placing on it. For progressives, the task is to minimize negative aspects of development and maximize those that are positive.

Trade-offs with developers were put into practice with much less controversy in cities such as San Francisco and Boston.[44] In Santa Monica, however, the controversy resided in two features. First, instead of asking for fees, the progressives asked for "social goods" that would benefit low- and moderate-income residents rather than traditional elites. Second, during the time of the six month moratorium, there were no fixed rules for negotiating such agreements. Negotiations were a way for developers to resolve their situations out of court; for SMRR, a way to push agreements in a progressive direction. However, each situation was handled on a case-by-case basis. Progressives knew they had unusual leverage due to Santa Monica's attractive and desirable location, but even they did not know in advance what the limits of the bargaining process would be. As they groped to find what was socially possible under the circumstances, they faced a great deal of hostility. Their agenda represented a complete break with existing rules and expectations in the community, and the resulting tension was enormous.[45] A developer interviewed on *60 Minutes* referred to the situation as "legalized extortion." Moreover, some progressive neighborhood activists themselves criticized the process since SMRR candidates and City Manager John Alshuler went behind closed doors to negotiate instead of through genuine participation from the neighborhoods to be affected.

Development agreements have been around in Santa Monica for over a decade, and thus, it is possible to look beyond the emotional rhetoric that surfaced in the early 1980s and carefully to assess results. Furthermore, the "free-form" negotiation of agreements no longer exists. With the approval of the final version of the Land Use Element in the fall of 1984, the guidelines for such agreements were formalized, except in the cases of very large or complex projects. The document institutionalized some progressive principles while bowing to some pressures from traditional elites. The final product was modified by prominent participation of the Commercial and Industrial Properties Association, which attacked the original version as "no growth." Hiring a consultant, CIPA involved itself deeply in the revision process.[46]

The end result gained a favorable reaction from business leaders, healing a two-year-old rift over the document. Thus, like the rent control law, the city's Land Use Element is both a formal document and an embodiment of a social process emerging between various groups over time. Below, we will briefly examine the features of the development agreements.

Give Backs to the Community

The most well-known development agreement, in part because it was publicized by *60 Minutes,* was the Welton Becket agreement. The Colorado Place development was projected to be a massive $150 million project. With office condominiums, retail functions, and a hotel, it was intended to serve as the international headquarters of Welton Becket, a major architectural firm.[47] While it had secured preliminary approvals, the project was stopped by the six-month moratorium after an unsuccessful appeal for exemption. It was further halted by the negotiation process with the city, adding up to a delay of about one year.[48] For progressives, the challenge was to transform a huge office complex into something that socially served all elements of the community. As a result, they bargained for 150 units of affordable housing, a 150,000 square foot public park, a 2,000 square foot day-care center with improvements including play equipment and furnishings, affirmative-action hiring, an accessibility plan for the disabled, and an arts and social services fee for the city.

After hostile exchanges with Welton Becket, an agreement with the city was concluded. The retail and office space was constructed, along with 150 units of the promised low- and moderate-income housing.[49] One of the surrounding neighborhood organizations, Mid-City Neighbors, successfully negotiated with the firm over the design for a park.[50] However, with Phase II, which included the hotel, financing troubles began. Although the city applied for funding for the firm to save the project, it was unsuccessful in obtaining it. In the summer of 1984, Welton Becket announced its inability to complete the project. Spokespersons for the firm insisted that the provisions of the development agreement had nothing to do with the decision, but SMRR's opposition loudly protested the "business climate" in the city, which they viewed as being responsible. The project was bought out by Southmark Corporation, which intended to see it through completion after seeking some minor amendments in the agreement. Paul Silvern, planning director for the city in 1984, insisted that there are certain "inviolates" in the agreement, such as the remainder of the housing, the open space, and the design frame.[51]

The Welton Becket agreement became a benchmark for future development projects. Progressives were willing to support office and commercial developments only if they complied with the following conditions:

1.  a 1.5 percent arts and social service fee based on the total cost of the development;
2.  one housing unit for every 5,000 square feet of floor area for any development of 7,500 square feet or more;
3.  encouragement of the use of public transportation, bikes, and walking for every development of at least 20,000 square feet or more;
4.  an affordable day-care center for all developments with at least 40,000 square feet;
5.  provision of parks for developments of 70,000 square feet or more;
6.  developments should not exceed six stories and should be mixed-use, containing community enterprises on the first floor (bookstores, restaurants), offices on the middle floors, and housing on the top floor.

Another developer agreement known as the Kendall project resulted in substantial "give backs" to the city. The Kendall project was a nine-story office building almost directly across from the ocean and the Santa Monica Pier. It is a generally admired small-scale, mixed-use project, with retail tenants on the ground floor and a small number of affordable housing units (6–8) on the upper floor. Ordinarily, such units would be unavailable there at an affordable price since the project is in such a prime location. Progressives have pushed for mixed-use projects because they keep city spaces "alive" at night instead of creating empty, dead space that attracts crime (Jacobs, 1961).

An example of this approach is the Third Street Mall project. Before progressives took office, the Third Street Mall was representative of many decaying downtown areas: Many stores were boarded up, and much of the mall was empty, shunned by middle-class shoppers for the enclosed mall (Santa Monica Place) across the street. (As we documented in Chapter 3, Ocean Park activists fought a losing battle against this mall.) The challenge for progressives was to revitalize the old mall without significantly displacing existing businesses and their clientele. Their approach was to produce housing above the shops, to encourage a major movie complex to open a theatre, and to encourage the placement of additional restaurants. Moreover, the planners decided to allow automobile traffic through the mall to create a more lively appearance.

Several other projects resulted in developers making substantial concessions to the city. The Greenwood Center office complex is a five-story development undertaken in part by a subsidiary of the Campeau Corporation of Canada. It has 20 units of affordable housing off-site, as well as a public park and day-care space. Another project at 2701 Ocean Park Boulevard was altered by a development agreement into a slightly less dense neighborhood-commercial and office project than originally projected.[52] A cash-in-lieu fee based on the approved formula in the new Land Use Element was permitted as a substitute for housing. An unusually large and bulky condominium development, the Toibb project, was scaled down and included provisions for 6 to 8 affordable units off-site.[53] If one were, in a drawing, to superimpose the originally envisioned projects over their renegotiated versions, one would see a physically different city. This gain is sometimes forgotten because the alternative has to be imagined.

Although controversial within the progressive community itself, the most successful "give back" negotiated by the progressives was the $300 million, 1.26 million square foot development called the Water Garden.[55] According to an agreement made on March 23, 1988, this development will be built on a seventeen-acre site around a two-acre pond. Over 65 percent of the acreage will be landscaped to provide a parklike atmosphere. The buildings will be human-scale (six floors) with a pedestrian orientation featuring atriums, courtyards, restaurants, and a health club. The project will have a 3,500 square foot day-care center and elevators to two and a half levels of subterranean parking. More importantly, progressives were able to get the developers to donate $7.2 million toward improving low-income housing and parks, $300,000 for a homeless shelter, and $150,000 for a citywide art program. Developers expect the project to generate $1.2 million in annual revenue and 5,000 jobs. Consequently, they are paying a $6.5 million traffic improvement fee (*Los Angeles Times,* February 28, 1988). *The New York Times* recently highlighted the project, declaring it a "creation from Fantasyland." *Los Angeles Magazine* declared the developer, J. H. Snyder Company, "the city's favorite developer" (Wilson, 1989:19).

An overview of these projects reveals several things. First, as far as housing is concerned, due to the scale of the construction, the proportion of affordable housing obtained is small relative to the city's shortage. The largest batch of housing obtained was the initial 150 units through Welton Becket. Without progressives in office, however, no housing would have been created at all since this is not part of the institutionalized dialogue between cities and developers.[55] Demands for social "give backs" ask developers as significant urban actors to recognize the needs of the community, including lower-income residents. In principle, this is a broadening of public discourse toward nonelite priorities in the city.

In practice, the development agreements raised some troubling questions in the city with reference to broader progressive goals. As noted above, the initial case-by-case resolution led to private negotiations between the city manager (John Alshuler) or city councilmembers and the developer. Although formally neighborhood input was to be included, it was often overridden. Ken Genser, SMRR appointee to the planning commission and future elected city councilmember, had strong words on this subject:

> The Becket agreement, that was *classic.* Their rep told me that the city
> was negotiating with them *months* before anyone had heard of the project.
> I know someone on the *Times* who told me that the *L.A. Times* was

getting pressure from the city and the developer before it even went to the planning commission about how wonderful this would be for the city. They're good at that. Also with Martin Cadillac [a negotiated deal that later fell through] the deal was cut without input. The planning commission was not listened to. The city manager went directly to the city council and told them that the planning commission was being unreasonable. There's been no neighborhood input, no public process. The city manager [Alshuler] negotiates on behalf of the developers. He also targets individuals and groups— he tried to withhold funding for Mid-City Neighbors, because they rightly opposed him.[56]

Some of this tension was due to the emergence of a staff of experts in city hall who began to define the city's agenda in spite of public input (Čapek, 1985). Despite being progressives, they were characterized by their own faction as nondemocratic. From a social movements perspective, the movement was fighting its own formalized bureaucracy (Staggenborg, 1988).

Liberal planners charged that the progressives arbitrarily traded off hard-won zoning stipulations against the "deals" made behind closed doors with developers. Herb Katz, who spent many years on the planning commission, and who was later elected to the city council, said:

I don't believe in deals behind closed doors. The Welton Becket was a *badly* dealt thing. They [WB] wanted a million square feet and a hotel. There's *no* way they would get it under existing zoning laws, no way. They were asked to make trade-offs, and gee, they thought they'd been had, but they never would have gotten *close* to it, if it had been an open process. They couldn't even solve the traffic problems. But [City Attorney] Myers said the planning commission had no right to hear it. . . . There shouldn't be any one group of people exclusively in power. Then you're just Nixon talking to Ehrlichman.[57]

Former Planning Commissioner Frank Hotchkiss had a similar view. Remarking on a project in Ocean Park where SMRR councilmembers ignored zoning, community testimony, and even the vote of the planning commission to pursue their negotiations, Hotchkiss said, "The lesson is that you can participate as long as you agree with what they say."[58]

Thus, people on both sides of the issues had complaints about the nondemocratic aspects of the negotiations when one set of experts was replaced by another. The negotiators themselves had their own rationales for behaving this way. According to progressive councilmember Dennis Zane, who came under fire from neighborhood groups:

Developer agreements are a way to maximize public benefit from private developers, but there are costs involved, including political ones. . . . The city staff find themselves in an awkward position. Developers are not typically owners of the land, caught between all of this. If it doesn't look like it will work for them, they don't build, and they go elsewhere. They seek their best options, and they especially don't want to be raked over the coals in public. If you get that agreement, you get it only because the developer believes that the staff will then advocate it. Their advocacy is *structural*, not dispositional.[59]

Much of this has become a moot point, however, since such negotiations have been practically eliminated. Prefaced by a statement that its purpose is to make the rules clear in order to increase predictability in the city, the 1984 Land Use Element includes formal guidelines. Developers are asked to pay a standard fee per square foot for housing and parks, with the fee increasing above 15,000 feet. The role of citizen participation is explicitly preserved in the document.

The development agreements did leave behind a legacy of social concern. Before progressives took over, community development programs were aimed at middle- and upper-income neighborhoods.[60] According to Nancy Desser, former Santa Monica planner, precious community development money was spent on installing "lawn bowling" in an upper-middle-income neighborhood. Elites traditionally viewed community development as a "gimmick" to provide tax breaks for a firm, free land for a corporate relocation, employee-training programs, and recreational opportunities for the well-to-do. Progressives challenged these priorities. They attempted to involve ordinary citizens in agenda-setting and decisions about how money was to be spent to benefit low- and moderate-income people. Attractive and citizen-friendly packets were put together to promote outreach. Despite troubled relations with some of the community groups—such as Mid-City Neighbors—progressives provided a climate in which corporate actors needed to consult these groups. For example, prior to the progressive administration, hospitals used an "eminent domain" argument with neighborhoods when they expanded and dismissed the need to discuss housing, saying: "We are not in the housing business." In 1984, however, a hospital negotiated a satisfactory agreement with the Mid-City Neighbors community organization. Progressive pressures made this possible, although these did not always come from elected SMRR officials.

Likewise, Santa Monica's community development program was aimed at meeting the needs of low- and moderate-income citizens. The program was drawn up in two major parts: community/neighborhood improvements and community service projects. Community/neighborhood projects were aimed at the following kinds of beneficiaries for 1988–89:

1.  Community Corporation of Santa Monica; $270,000 to support a local nonprofit corporation for the development of low- and moderate-income housing;
2.  Pico Neighborhood Housing Trust; $576,000 for the purchase and renovation of low- and moderate-income housing in Santa Monica's largest minority neighborhood.

Community service projects were of the following type for 1988-89:

1.  Latino Resource Organization; $106,625 to provide public awareness activities for Latino residents;
2.  ADEPT; $33,514 to assist disabled persons with employment and training;
3.  Low Income and Elderly United—Community Action Project; $105,625 for advocacy and assistance for low-income persons.

When Congress set up the Community Development program, the intent was to serve low- and moderate-income persons. Yet without effective grass-roots strength, these funds are often poorly targeted and fail to meet the needs of the poor (see Chapter 6 on Houston for examples). The progressive movement in Santa Monica mobilized the less advantaged population and raised their entitlements in the city. This continued to be the case even when SMRR candidates lost their voting majority.

Social versus Economic Values

A progressive item in the 1984 Land Use Element was the creation of an industrial conservation district, where the city would attempt to retain the disappearing industries that employed blue-collar and unskilled workers.[61] This was an acknowledgment of the needs of Santa Monica's less privileged neighborhoods. Like other cities in the United States, Santa Monica has seen a long-term trend toward the departure of many of its leading industrial employers. Beginning with the closing of the McDonnell Douglas plant in 1975 and its relocation to Huntington Beach and Long Beach, a number of large firms have left. Also typical of broader regional urban trends was the fact that when Douglas left the site was replaced with a business park catering to newer industries, such as research and development and high tech.

Other losses included the Systems Development Corporation (SDC), which provided between 300 and 400 of its 1,400 jobs to residents of Santa Monica.[62] When it left, it claimed problems with recruiting professional employees due to a housing shortage and also a lack of space for expansion. When the General Telephone Company of California decided to move its headquarters out of the city in 1985, it gave the same reasons. Middle-level professionals in particular had difficulties finding housing. As David Shulman put it, "the labor force can't live in the Westside" (*Evening Outlook,* January 15, 1985).[63]

Not one of the firms relocating out of the city cited its relationship with the city as its reason for leaving. In fact, public statements were made by representatives of each firm that this was specifically *not* the case. General Telephone, for example, claimed that there was nothing the city could have done to make the situation better and that plans had been made long ago. Privately, however, many in the business community felt otherwise. As Aubrey Austin of the Santa Monica Bank contended:

There's one major corporation in town that said, "How in the hell can you do business with this group?" What is the effect on business? They want to find someone else. Also, General Telephone—they were treated shabbily here. It started under Ruth Yannatta Goldway. Slamming their need for an increase. They started saying, "How soon do we get out?" Yet in the meantime they kept supporting the YMCA, et cetera; they poured money into the community, and still do.... Many of the phone company people—and there are some that aren't working there anymore—who will honestly come up and say, that the reason is, Long Beach bent over *backwards,* gave them concessions like Santa Monica would never give them, and they still wanted to be in Santa Monica because of their territory. I wouldn't have come here. I have to take *that* from this city, when I go to Long Beach and get everything I want? But they stayed here and still are going to keep their people here because of the location geographically.[64]

Robert Gabriel, former president of the chamber of commerce, had a similar view:

We lost GT. They say it wasn't the city. But this didn't just happen. Who knows why they first started talking about it. Now they say the other deal was so good...but they may not even have thought of moving if the attitude had been different. The Peoples' Republic—*Big business sees it that way.* I know of one corporation that wants to come into town because they've got the site available, but they don't want to use the Santa Monica address; they want to maintain they're in L.A.[65]

While the above quote confirms both the desirability of Santa Monica as a place and also the importance of doing business in a familiar community (Gilderbloom, 1978:9), members of the business community insist on the importance of the cues that are sent out by a city. If these are read in the broader, nationwide networks as unfavorable to business, there may be a blacklisting of the city. Particularly since Santa Monica signaled a strong stand against "pass-throughs" of any sort and provided a climate in which the social value of particular businesses might be challenged, the portrait of the city could be quite negative in business circles. Individuals who were part of this network claimed to know of instances where decisions had been made on this basis not to locate in Santa Monica. However, the city's desirable location has always exerted powerful pressure in the contrary direction. Generally speaking, local businesspeople, while they have no love for the progressive council and are particularly bitter about the first progressive (Goldway) administration, have recognized that in most ways "business will go on as usual." Aubrey Austin's threat to the progressives that "You're going to be held fiscally responsible for the bankruptcy of this community" in 1981 proved overstated and unfounded (*Evening Outlook,* July 3, 1981). On the contrary, despite over a decade of rent control and developer agreements, Santa Monica receives high marks on economic and fiscal indicators; it is one of a handful of California cities with a double A bond rating, and regularly receives awards from the Society of Auditors for sound financial reporting (Dennis, 1990).

Santa Monica's attractiveness, while providing a kind of insurance for progressives, also raised difficult questions for them. Although there was concern in the community when General Telephone left, the newspaper immediately noted that:

Because Santa Monica has the advantage of being part of a dynamic and diversified economy in the L.A. region, the space being vacated by General Telephone will probably find a ready market. The desirability of the Westside means the new tenants may bring an even higher income level than the employers currently occupying the GTC buildings (*Evening Outlook,* January 18, 1985).

The city has been eager to cash in on these possibilities. Aside from the "industrial conservation zone" set up to protect traditional industries, the other half of the zoned commercial district in the Land Use Element was reserved for "garden offices," where the city hoped to capture some of the new high-tech land uses. Hotel construction was for the first time encouraged close to the oceanfront, with an eye to the revenues generated for the city (this move was also opposed by the liberal planners since they had fought developers who wanted to do this very thing). Some progressives, however, claimed that, in addition to supplying revenue, the hotels would supply more of the vanishing low-skilled jobs in the city, the loss of which particularly hurt the demographics of minority neighborhoods. Residents of these neighborhoods, however, have been very critical of many of the priorities outlined in the Land Use Element, seeing a drift toward an acceptance of a higher-income population despite statements to the contrary. For them, the progressives' choices are still too consistent with past administrations (see below).

Considerable debate took place over the last major piece of undeveloped land that the city had at its disposal, approximately 40 acres at the site of Santa Monica's airport. In 1985, Jim Conn, SMRR councilmember at the time, suggested that the "social value" of the uses for the land should be considered, perhaps emphasizing a mix including blue-collar employers to replace vanishing jobs for unskilled workers. SMRR opponent Christine Reed, on the other hand, argued for a "cash-cow" approach to the land, getting the maximum amount of money for it from developers and allowing it to "trickle down" to fund social services (*Evening Outlook,* February 20, 1985).

This is yet another example of the urban debate we have traced throughout this book, where concerns of "community" (preserving people's ability to stay in their community) tend to be upheld by a progressive agenda, as opposed to the traditional precedence given by urban administrations to "commodity"— the economic benefit to the city's coffers. Both views address questions of economic benefit, but the latter—Reed's solution—means accepting job displacement and people being forced to leave the city while waiting for social service funds to trickle down. Conn's solution acknowledged the city's social role in altering people's lives and its responsibility to them if it disrupts their lives. Providing social service funds when it takes away jobs is not an even exchange. Over time, Conn himself became a target of progressive criticism for allegedly moving toward a "commodity" view of the city.

Before progressives came into office, social value and social costs for the community as a whole were not figured into the planning formula for the city. SMRR's opposition, when it regained a voting majority, attempted to erase this objectionable and "irrational" rhetoric from the traditional business ledger. Although polarization does not exist on all issues, the social and political aspects of the decision-making are a continuous reminder of the fact that one vote can determine an entire city's policy; in 1983–84, when the progressives had a majority by one vote, there were many 4–3 votes on the city council.[66] Not only did this indicate a paper-thin division between possible and actual urban scenarios, but it also predicted which elements would be the first to go if the voting balance changed.[67] High on the list of SMRR's opposition was any sort of social worth rhetoric, such as that found in the developer agreements. While forced to be sensitive to social problems, SMRR's opponents addressed them in a different kind of language, avoiding terms like "social justice."

Progressives themselves were tested on their commitment to their "social value" principles during the period of their majority. One such instance arose when the Jonathan Club, a private club contiguous to a public stretch of Santa

Monica beach, requested an expansion permit from the planning commission. The club allegedly discriminated against blacks, Jews, and women in its membership. The club did get its permit due to a decision by the city's experts that the city could be successfully sued. However, the votes were divided between those, such as William Jennings, who rationalized the decision, claiming that it was improper for the planning commission to take up discrimination, and several of the progressive members, including Derek Shearer and Ed Kirshner, who refused to give a vote of approval. As Kirshner put it, "I cannot, in my public or private role, ever support an institution like this no matter how technically legal the application may be" (*Los Angeles Times*, January 10, 1985).

This disagreement makes salient a crucial symbolic task of the progressives: to extend the language of social justice into the neutral language of city policymaking. The effort was continuously labeled inappropriate by their opponents, who saw it as the introduction of an unsuitable element into an otherwise rational economic calculus. This was reflected citywide; for example, a couple came before the rent-control board in 1982 seeking permission to tear down the apartments they owned, claiming they wanted to put their property to the "highest and best use." Their definition of this was economic; the rent board's definition took account of social consequences.[68] The couple's attorney, however, refused to provide information to the board concerning his clients' financial position, arguing that a decision must be made in the abstract.

Thus, the appropriateness of using a "social" or an "economic" standard for the evaluation of city priorities was an ongoing battle between SMRR and non-SMRR officeholders, with each side attempting to present its formula as the more rational. Each side mustered its own battery of experts to lend credence to its position. Ultimately, as we illustrated in Chapter 4, larger symbolic values were at stake, including whether or not raising the issue of social costs was socialistic. Although progressives had some leeway due to changing conceptions of fairness, their hope that a progressive program might be judged for its own sake on "rational" grounds (Moberg, 1983b) was only partially realized.[69] This symbolic strife did leave an indelible mark on city policy, however; never again would it be assumed that the city should be defined only as a commodity.

## Minority Communities

A litmus test for any progressive government is how it treats its minority communities. It was part of the progressive platform to empower communities that had been previously underrepresented by city government. This included both organizational assistance to facilitate their democratic participation and structural protections to ensure that the most vulnerable segments of the population, particularly minorities and elderly, would no longer be priced out of their communities. As we have noted, the "trickle down" theory espoused by prior city administrations both permitted and encouraged a systematic neglect of the residents of these communities when political and economic decisions were made. When their neighborhoods appeared on the city agenda, it was as commodity, not community; the land under the people and houses was the concern, rather than the people themselves. The progressives attempted to displace the concerns back in the direction of "community" and to facilitate a participatory structure. What can we conclude about their success from examining the progressive record for minority communities?

To begin with, progressives arrived on the scene after considerable damage had already been done to these communities. Minority populations have been present in Santa Monica since its inception (see Chapter 3), although, as "invisible communities" once the area became predominantly white, they were not recorded in the history of the city. Older white residents who were not affluent could also become invisible; we referred in an earlier chapter to the high likelihood of displacements in both the Pico and Ocean Park neighborhoods. These neighborhoods were targeted by the city administration for revitalization projects on the basis of their official designation as "blighted."

Today, Santa Monica has a small minority population. The two largest groups are the Latino (13 percent) and black (3 percent), both of which are concentrated in two census tracts in the Pico neighborhood (Levine and Grigsby, 1987). Within the Pico area, residents are 40 percent Latino and 17 percent black (1980 Census; Hernandez, 1983).[70] According to census data, the Pico tracts are notably different in other ways from the rest of the city: Median household income is lower, and the population is younger. As a working-class area, dominant occupations there include manufacturing, industrial repair, crafts, and service occupations. As Bluestone and Harrison (1982) have documented, these are precisely the categories threatened most by the current economic restructuring that is altering urban areas throughout the United States. The neighborhood's plight is worsened by the fact that housing is measurably more crowded, the educational level is lower (62 percent of the population has graduated from high school), and large numbers of the population speak little or no English.[71] A growing undocumented population has added to these figures.

The progressive agenda for the neighborhood included empowerment on several levels. One priority was to help create a community organization that would mobilize the population in its own interests and speak for the neighborhood in city hall. Although the Pico Neighborhood Association was not founded until 1980, as we noted in Chapter 3, efforts to organize the community began out of the black churches in 1978, largely through the efforts of Ellis Casson, pastor of the First African Methodist Episcopal Church located in the Pico neighborhood.[72] In a newspaper interview, Casson recalled that the genesis of the organization came when he "called ten people together who were committed to community concerns" (*Evening Outlook,* June 22, 1981). Expansion of the organization relied on a block structure, while leadership was provided by an elected board of directors of which Ellis Casson was the first chair.

A direct accomplishment of the PNA was to claim the neighborhood's share in Community Development Block Grant funds. Although the poverty of the Pico neighborhood was the justification for the city receiving federal money, as in many other cities the funds were used for general purposes, not for that neighborhood. It was Casson who helped uncover the fact that less than 2 percent of the CDBG money was going into the Pico neighborhood. The money had been used elsewhere in the city for such things as fixing potholes, subsidizing malls, and building lawn bowling greens in middle-income neighborhoods.

After PNA—which had visibly and effectively organized by that time— pointed out this contradiction in 1981, the city agreed to give 20 percent of the money to PNA in that year and 80 percent in the next. Since then, CDBG funds have provided money for such key elements of the progressive agenda as the Housing Trust Fund, which goes toward purchasing and renovating buildings in the Pico neighborhood. In 1988, city government officials estimated that up to 80 percent of the CDBG funds were going to housing for low- and moderate-income persons.

Efforts to empower the Pico neighborhood organizationally, although philosophically supported by progressives, did not mean that the PNA's relationship to SMRR would be cordial, nor that serious organizational problems would not arise.[73] Some of these problems were internal; others had to do with the relationship to SMRR. Although minorities did participate significantly in the tenants' movement, neither minority organizers nor candidates figured prominently in the broader progressive movement. There were also tensions between blacks and Latinos in the Pico neighborhood (Daykin, 1987). According to one Latino participant, some of the problems arose from the fact that by the time the Pico neighborhood began to get political power most of the blacks were gone, leaving a majority Latino population that was willing to accept worse living conditions.[74] The PNA power structure was mostly black, with strong tension between the two groups. This has led to accusations that there is a greater interest in providing housing for middle-class blacks than for poor Latinos. In addition, in the early and mid-eighties, PNA was directed by Fred Allingham, a white male. Note was also taken of the fact that there was no Latino organizer, although 38 percent of the population was non-English-speaking. An organization with only English speakers guarantees a low rate of participation among Latinos, especially large undocumented populations (Gilderbloom and Rodriguez, 1988).

Blacks, on the other hand, perceived a loss of jobs to the undocumented population, which, apart from the language difference, caused resentment between the communities. Black activists also criticized Latinos for being nonparticipants. Yet they were also critical of the PNA structure:

> The board that Fred Allingham allows to exist is not balanced intellectually. It doesn't understand the more technical issues. Rather than let people know that they don't understand, they just go ahead. . . . The board must be balanced. People must understand, if they are helped to. Take the housing issue. PNA has some expertise, but it doesn't do outreach. Fred surrounds himself by people he can control. There are professional whites on the board, while the blacks are community people. He has the responsibility to make things under-standable. . . . We're now down to 4 percent blacks in this city, and I think that they think that we just don't exist. I truly feel that this administration. . .how can I say this. . .I think city staff, John Alshuler [city manager] talks out of both sides of his mouth. I think that the whole concept that the city uses when they say they want to empower the neighborhood is just something that looks good on paper to submit to the federal government. I don't think they mean it. When it comes to empowering the neighborhood, there's always a reason why they can't.[75]

The same individual admitted, however, that "we have practically forgotten Hispanics. We need to put them on the board." The conclusion was that while PNA vocalized the concerns of the community, it did not represent it.[76]

Housing Programs for the Minority Community

Although certain other issues such as jobs and youth programs have been raised, the primary preoccupation of the PNA has been housing and, in some instances, neighborhood development. Many pressures have been placed on the neighborhood that led to a decreasing stock of affordable housing. Revitalization projects and "spot zoning" permitted the replacement of single-family areas with manufacturing, industrial, and multifamily zones. Residents were also indirectly affected by accelerating property values. As PNA Director Fred Allingham commented, rising property values prior to Proposition 13 led to higher taxes, which many residents could not pay; consequently, many sold to apartment developers (*Santa Monica Seascape,* July/August 1983).

As a response to the housing crisis, the implications of rent control have always been mixed for lower-income communities, a fact that helps to explain the mixed electoral support that SMRR gets there. While rents are regulated, many are already too high for the income structure of the poorest neighborhoods. Furthermore, these areas generally experience more deteriorated conditions in their housing; a common fear—frequently realized—is that landlords will curtail what little maintenance they are already doing if controls are instituted. Finally, the argument is also made that in some cases controls "rationalize" the process for landlords, giving them guaranteed rent increases (Marcuse, 1981b, 1981c). Under such a structure, some of the landlords who previously kept their rent levels low respond to the "cue" sent out by the yearly general adjustment process and raise their rents (Mollenkopf and Pynoos, 1973; Gilderbloom and Appelbaum, 1988). For residents with low or fixed incomes, this can make the difference between being able to stay or having to leave a community.[77]

Since residents were being driven out by the "free market" rents in Santa Monica, for the most part rent controls froze the situation as it was in 1978. However, even rent-control advocates know that it is only a holding measure. Unless accompanied by a more comprehensive housing program, it will only slow the exodus of the lower income residents. Examining the impact of rent control over a seven year period in Santa Monica, Levine and Grigsby (1987) report that rents have fallen relative to noncontrolled areas and that the class composition of renters has remained the same. The authors claim that the proportion of low- and moderate-income renters has remained the same; thus, the phenomenon of gentrification has been halted in Santa Monica. However, the percentage of black renters has fallen from 5 percent to 3 percent and Latinos from 18 percent to 13 percent. Levine and Grigsby do not blame the decline in the black and Latino renter population on rent control, but on other factors related to declining fertility levels for both groups and for blacks' declining incomes.

Efforts by the Community Corporation of Santa Monica (CCSM) to provide affordable housing in the Pico neighborhood must transcend some difficult problems, including perceptions of the CCSM itself. The Community Corporation and its projects have suffered from "turf" issues that are both organizational and racial.[78] Since CCSM was initially linked to the Ocean Park Community Organization, and since Ocean Park was viewed by many as white, middle-class or "voluntary poor," "hip," and strongly linked to the SMRR power structure, PNA was suspicious when efforts were made to draw it in. It was also wary of becoming involved with developers. On the other hand, PNA exercised control of the Housing Trust Fund disbursed by the city, which necessitated getting its approval each time CCSM wanted to buy a building. PNA was accused of not reporting back to the community or educating them on the issues, which fueled criticisms of the Community Corporation "ripping off the community." This interneighborhood suspicion combined with interracial tensions to complicate the groups' projects.

The first five buildings bought in the Pico neighborhood made use of federal Section 8 Moderate Rehabilitation money. Bedrooms were added for crowded residences, which particularly benefited Latinos. According to a participant, the subsidy more than paid the cost of bedrooms, carrying the purchase and the rehabilitation as well. However, many problems were evident, particularly from a social movements/social change perspective:

> There isn't anyone to organize. PNA secures money from the fund, and it has approval power. It is essentially a regulatory body, and an organizer in this situation becomes a "cop" for the city as opposed to organizing new people. We did rehabilitation with people living right in the apartments. To do it at all was an achievement, but we don't bring new people in. Expectations rise, and people complain of the "cops" aspect. In one year, we did 64 units, spent enormous time and energy. But we ran into turf issues. There are five Community Corp. buildings, one in Ocean Park. There is nothing more there to buy. OPCO has its own problems, and PNA always had to be checked back with. With the second building, we saw serious problems, including racial ones. The second building was ideal. It had 19 units, 15 of which were low income; 75 percent of the building was to be low income. It was rejected by two black board members because there were too *many* low income. *The conclusion may be that empowering people may not work.* How do you keep people who have their own agenda from destroying an organization?[79]

The structural limitations placed on progressive attempts at housing innovation, particularly in the low-income communities, become evident. Both developer agreements and CCSM projects, while conceptually providing innovative alternatives for adding to much-needed housing stock, are currently far too limited in scope to address the housing problems of the community as a whole. Developer agreements provide a small percentage of low-income housing in proportion to more luxury-oriented uses. CCSM currently owns a total of five properties containing 64 units. Although effective on a small scale, its efforts are hampered by availability of land and funding.[80] Federal funds have been drastically curtailed, leaving major sources of funding through general revenue sharing funds and CDBGs precarious at best. In the context of the attack on the welfare state, the PNA projects are inevitably affected by the trend toward privatization. Here the limits of a progressive municipal government become evident; as long as they rely on federal programs, local areas are subject either to national political priorities or to the whims of the private sector. This renews the cycle of problems since the private market has never been willing to channel funds into lower profit areas such as low- and moderate-income housing. Thus, while some housing is targeted by progressives to those in need, the systemic crisis continues.

Jobs and Community Control

As we noted above, jobs are an immediate issue for the Pico neighborhood, given the gradual phasing out of the traditional manufacturing sector. Approximately 58 percent of Latino heads of households work in Santa Monica, for the most part as "craftsmen, repairmen, operatives, service workers and gardeners" (Ortiz and Fastiggi, 1983:61-2, cited in Daykin, 1987). Data from the city's land use plan have projected growth in all major sectors except manufacturing and agriculture. Small locally owned businesses are expected to decline, accompanied by a feminization of employment in the office sector (Daykin, 1987). Employment statistics for the Pico neighborhood reveal that individuals employed in manufacturing dropped from 39.00 percent to 12.33 percent between 1970 and 1980 (Hernandez, 1983). In addition, 2,303 manufacturing jobs were expected to be lost by the year 2000. Hernandez (1983) claims that, given the high number of non-English-speaking, unskilled residents in the Latino community, job loss would selectively discriminate against Latinos at a higher rate than blacks.[81]

According to these critiques, the serious problems of the most vulnerable populations in Santa Monica—the elderly and racial minorities—are not being adequately addressed by progressives.[82] To one alienated progressive critic, "Ruth Yannatta Goldway's biggest issues were bourgeois planning issues. . . cosmetic planning, sign ordinances, low-rise buildings, a farmers' market."[83] Such critics charge that, although the Land Use Element attempts to preserve some of the vanishing occupations in the city, it also appears to accept as "natural" the process of regional restructuring, thus defining minority residents as economically expendable.

Amid all of the criticism, however, it is recognized that progressives did set the tone for changes by making public issues out of problems that were never raised before, such as community control by the Pico neighborhood.[84] As a result, the PNA found itself in a position for the first time to negotiate with a developer over give backs to the community. One such agreement led to a financial partnership between the PNA and the developer of a commercial office project. PNA's involvement was to be a 2 percent limited partnership, with additional provisions for a percentage of the hard costs of the project to go to the city and to fund housing in the Pico neighborhood, as well as social services and improvements in the community. A crucial inclusion was the training and relocation of workers being displaced from their jobs by the development. Although the agreement fell through for other reasons, it set a precedent for future negotiations.

While based on an "exchange" model of fairness, this kind of negotiation was categorically dismissed by prior administrations as being too unpredictable for the business climate.[85] Furthermore, such interference offends those dedicated to a "laissez-faire" urban model. In Santa Monica, the Commercial and Industrial Properties Association (CIPA) refused to accept the give backs as "fair" and was extremely vocal against the agreement:

> This is a revolutionary concept—to give 2 percent to an organization. We believe there may be some constitutional problems with this type of thing. Being party to this is repulsive to us (*Evening Outlook,* March 21, 1983).

Critics of SMRR policies often qualify their criticism by recalling that, even if results fall short of progressive expectations, participation of the Pico neighborhood used to be "zero"; more people have been brought into the process, and progressive policies were a prerequisite for this. As one activist observed:

> I don't want to make them [SMRR] sound like the other side. There are things that would never happen without them. There *is* money going into housing, there *is* money going into the neighborhood organizations, and people are being listened to who have never been listened to before. The first time they [PNA] asked for the CDBG grant money there were about three hundred people. You don't normally see many black and brown faces in city hall. It was pretty dramatic.[86]

This served as a public cue, a reminder to the community that its invisible populations were becoming visible.

Finally, it should be noted that the Pico Neighborhood Association is in a peculiar, and somewhat ironic, position in the city. Because it functions in the most economically deprived neighborhood in Santa Monica, it has been perceived by SMRR's opposition as the most legitimate among the community organizations to which SMRR provided city funding. It also serves as a legitimating symbol of social concern for SMRR's opponents. A belated obligation was recognized to the Pico neighborhood, in part as an ongoing construction of the dialogue of "fairness," in part for the electoral votes this would generate. When SMRR initially lost its voting majority in the fall of 1984, the PNA was the only neighborhood organization that did not lose its city funding. Ironically, the greatest adversaries in theory were bound together in practice, at least for the short term.

Keeping the funding constitutes a kind of affirmative action for the neighborhood. As PNA Director Fred Allingham told the *Evening Outlook*:

People in the neighborhood will lose a valuable resource—people who can spend time talking to city staff to find out what's going on. . . . In really affluent neighborhoods that kind of interaction occurs at the Rotary Club or at luncheons. Low and moderate income areas might not be able to protect those interests.

Ultimately, however, the organization is vulnerable to outside forces that operate at a national level. To the extent that organizing has been deemphasized while networking with the city has been encouraged, the organization is increasingly vulnerable to political winds that blow from Washington. This once again provides important testimony that grass-roots mobilization is crucial for initiating social change and sustaining definitions of fairness.

### Disabled Rights and Accessibility

An important area of minority rights where progressives have made a lasting mark is that of accessibility for the disabled. Led by SMRR city councilmember Dolores Press, progressives have transformed Santa Monica into the most accessible city in the nation. Through intelligent and farsighted planning, an array of programs were put together that allow disabled persons to move freely, independently, conveniently, and safely within the city. In 1982, the progressives established an Office for the Disabled, which serves an important advocacy role and coordinates a range of programs. The city of Santa Monica has developed a path-breaking Home Access Program, which provides the free installation of grab bars, handrails, bathroom safety equipment, audible and visual alarms, lowered thresholds, and wood entry ramps into the homes of disabled low- and moderate-income persons. In terms of transportation access, every street in Santa Monica contains a parallel sidewalk with curb cuts for wheelchair users. The city even installed a popular wooden sidewalk that runs from the street down to the beach and allows wheelchair users to touch the ocean water. This sidewalk provides an important symbolic gesture of Santa Monica's commitment to persons with disabilities. According to Audrey Parker, "Physical barriers are, in fact, visible evidence of attitudinal barriers. You can't see attitudes, but the results of attitudes are all around. By focusing on the removal of physical barriers, attitudinal barriers will also be decreased."[87]

While no regularly scheduled buses were wheelchair accessible during the 1970s, progressives made 75 percent of them accessible by 1988, and by 1992, 100 percent of the buses will have wheelchair lifts. In addition to this program, Santa Monica has also put together a door-to-door transportation service for elderly and disabled persons, which takes them from their homes directly to any other address in Santa Monica. Santa Monica's Office for the Disabled also provides additional services for the disabled including an architectural barrier-removal program, library services, recreational opportunities, employment programs, and community service opportunities.

All of this indicates an important symbolic and actual commitment to empowerment for the traditionally disenfranchised members of urban communities. This has always been an important goal for progressives. In Santa Monica, the first progressive administration set the tone for these commitments and institutionalized them. The city now has a stated commitment to social services and tolerance of minority viewpoints. Evidence for this was provided when progressives regained a voting majority in 1988 with the election of Judy Abdo, OPCO activist, avowed lesbian, and aide to the mayor of West Hollywood, and Ken Genser, SMRR activist and disabled community planner. Thus, the search for an appropriate definition of community fairness continues to thrive.

## Conclusion

This chapter reviews the impact of the grass-roots tenants' movement in Santa Monica as it became a broader progressive urban movement with its own elected officials. Electing progressives to public office permitted the exploration of the limits of the authority of city government and the tools of urban planning—when held by a very different set of people—to reshape urban space and social relations within that space. We found that major gains can be made in the area of housing, urban design, and service delivery to the disadvantaged. Grass-roots organizations were able to redefine and redirect the urban agenda away from the traditional exchange value and "commodity" emphasis toward use values and "community" priorities.

In terms of physical space, they achieved a reduced-scale, less-dense environment and a more accessible city. The city has a different face as a result, free of many common urban blights such as pollution and lack of green space. Regional and long-term trends, however, continue to operate in the city. The Land Use Element, a product of political compromise, retains a progressive character, but job displacements grow side by side with some of the new revenue priorities of the city. This remains a challenge to any progressive agenda. In the area of social relationships in the city, the progressive administration acquired concessions from developers that never would have made their way into the city's public dialogue under a different group and in the absence of a progressive movement.[88] Many of these were oriented away from traditional elites and toward the less-privileged communities in the city, which were thus rendered socially and politically visible.

We found that the rent-control law contributed significantly to affordability in the city, although it needs to be supplemented with a broader progressive housing program. We pointed to the danger of overreliance on the law itself since it is vulnerable to interference at the state and national levels (see Chapter 7). Without a well organized tenants' organization that keeps tenants mobilized and without the creation of new housing, even a strong rent control law quickly reaches its limits.

While reviews of the progressive administration are mixed, and relations with neighborhood groups sometimes downright hostile, the climate for neighborhood community participation was created by progressives and continues to shape expectations in the city. We found evidence of a healthy debate about community fairness and the responsibilities of urban government to residents, a debate that retains its vitality due to an active grass-roots presence in the city originally linked to the tenants' movement.

In our next chapter, we will examine the contrasting scenario of Houston, Texas, the quintessential "free enterprise" city. We will argue that Santa Monica's success in establishing a more equitable and democratic city is not representative of other cities' experience, even those with rent controls in place. The principal reason for this is that most tenants' movements have failed to develop an effective and powerful grass-roots organization.

# Cities without Urban Grass-Roots Movements: The Case of Houston

Santa Monica presents a radical alternative to the conventional American city. It poses the question: What is the good city? This question has been debated by Plato, Leonardo da Vinci, Rousseau, and others. Size by itself does not make a city great; for progressives the ideal urban place has an active, democratic citizen movement that plays a role in the defining of space. As Castells (1983) has noted, an authentic grass-roots movement in a city has three general characteristics: (1) a demand for greater citizen involvement and control; (2) policies that reflect the needs of collective consumption (use over exchange values); and (3) defense of community cultural identity. According to Castells's definition, Santa Monica represents one of the few American cities that would meet this definition of an urban social movement.

Santa Monica is important because it demonstrates both the possibilities and the limitations of a well-organized urban movement and how cities can be affected in a progressive direction. Important quality-of-life gains were made in Santa Monica as a result of the tenants' movement: Housing became more affordable; environmental quality improved; government became more accountable; and tenants were no longer second-class citizens. More important, Santa Monica provides a model for progressives in other cities to emulate. If Santa Monica represents the extreme form of a "planned" city, Houston represents the antithesis of this model: the free enterprise approach. Both cities are on opposite ends of the continuum of how the modern capitalist city can be governed. A comparison of Houston with Santa Monica is instructive in showing the possible consequences of each approach. From a Weberian perspective, Houston and Santa Monica represent "ideal types" that provide important analytical lessons. Houston is important because it demonstrates the negative consequences of not having a grass-root movement to force city hall to be responsive to the needs of the disadvantaged—whether poor, elderly, or disabled.

Houston is also interesting because, in the battle over rent control or any government intervention in the marketplace, real estate interests frequently cite the Houston free enterprise miracle. Joe Feagin (1988:3) writes in his path-breaking book on Houston:

By the late 1970s Houston not only had become one of the largest cities in the United States but also had achieved the status of a widely cited model of the positive consequences of a free enterprise, laissez-faire approach to economic development. Conservative think tanks such as the Adam Smith Institute in Great Britain utilized the Houston case as a primary example of the economic prosperity that comes from an unrestrained free enterprise ("supply-side") approach to economic investment and development.... For a time, thus Houston was more than a place in urban space; it had become a symbol in a resurgent free enterprise ideology.

With the election of Ronald Reagan as president in 1980, conservatives frequently cited Houston as a model for cities around the world to follow. Houston became known as the free enterprise capital of the world. Former mayor and chamber of commerce president Louis Welch argued that the Houston free enterprise approach has been the best approach to solving the problems affecting the poor:

The free market place has functioned in Houston like no other place in America. It has a method purging itself of slums. No city is without poor people, but the opportunity not to be poor is greater than in most cities. The work ethic, and opportunities, are strong here (Feagin, 1988:424).

For Houston, the business of government was to accommodate the needs of capital. Community became a commodity.

Houston, which is the same size as the state of Delaware and the nation's fourth largest city, is also unique because the social movements of the sixties never found any expression in the city. While Houston has a large black population, the civil rights movement was basically nonexistent. According to Robert Fisher (1988:4–6)

Houston experienced no sense of crisis and little insurgency in the 1960s and 1970s. Unlike other Southern cities, Atlanta and Montomery, Ala., for example, it was not wracked by racial conflict. It was one of the few large American cities with a large black population which was relatively quiet. The citizen-action movements which developed in other cities in the United States and Western Europe in the 1970s only appeared in Houston in modest form.

Martin Luther King made five trips to Houston between 1958 and 1967, and the response from the black community was at best tepid:

Much of the Houston black community did not embrace King: By opposing President Lyndon Johnson's handling of the Vietnam War, King had lost the support of many black Democratic Party activists aligned with the Texan in the White House (Bernstein, 1988:8).

Black activist Pluria Marshall declared King's visits to Houston "a complete disaster" (Bernstein, 1988:8). When King was assassinated in Memphis, racial riots broke out in cities across America, but Houston remained quiet. In fact, no ghetto riots occurred during the sixties and late seventies in Houston (Feagin 1988:275).

As we showed in Chapter 3, most tenants' movements came out of cities where there was a lot of civil rights and antiwar activity. The social movements of the sixties provided individuals with a set of new values and, most importantly, a set of organizing skills that could bring together individuals around common problems. Antiwar activity was almost nonexistent in Houston. While Chicago, New York, Washington, D.C., Los Angeles, and San Francisco drew antiwar demonstrations of between fifty thousand and four hundred thousand individuals, the largest demonstration against the Vietnam war in Houston numbered in the hundreds. Even during Nixon's Cambodian invasion during the Spring of 1970, where thousands of universities were closed down and spontaneous demonstrations reverberated throughout the country, Houston newspapers reported that all local colleges and universities remained open and that only one small demonstration of a dozen students was held at a local college.

The lack of any major social movements in Houston during the sixties helps explain why the neighborhood empowerment movements of the late seventies and eighties that swept across American cities never took hold in the Bayou city (see also Shelton et al., 1989:135; Parker and Feagin, forthcoming). According to Joe Feagin (1988:149):

Houston has rarely had major grass-roots input into local political decisions, and there have been no immigrant political machines. For virtually all of its history, and without any major interruptions since the early 1900s, the local business elites have been able to dominate governmental decisions and nondecisions about most major issues, including determinations on planning and zoning mechanisms.

While hundreds of civic clubs exist in Houston, their primary goal is not advocacy but to promote and enforce deed restrictions in neighborhoods

(Feagin, 1988). The civic clubs were politically reactionary in that many of the deed restrictions—even today—prohibit racial and ethnic integration, among other things. San Francisco, Boston, Chicago, New York, and other major cities are known for having neighborhood groups battling downtown interests and trying to preserve community. These organizations have played a pivotal role in council and mayoral elections; Houston's neigbhorhood groups are largely invisible. During the seventies and eighties, Houston only had one poor peoples' organization, the Alinsky-inspired The Metropolitan Organization (TMO). Although the focus of the organization has been on improved infra-structure and greater police activity against drugs, the response from Houston's establishment has been unfavorable: Newspapers have run negative stories, the business community has denounced it as radical, and city councilmembers have asked churches to withdraw support.

The absence of any significant urban social movement between 1960 and 1990 has made Houston the most unlivable city in the nation for the disadvantaged. The consequences of having virtually no neighborhood groups organizing, advocating, and defending their needs against downtown interests have been devastating to the quality of neighborhood life. Some analysts have labeled Houston as a "soulless Los Angeles" (Melosi, 1987). It is a city characterized by rampant crime and pollution; poor schools and parks; a severe homeless and hunger problem; and an urban aesthetic in neighborhoods that is tawdry. Some of the poorest neighborhoods have houses that are reminiscent of shanties from a typical Mexico City slum. In 1978, Paul Recer of *U.S. News and World Report* described Houston in the following graphic terms:

Left behind in Houston's headlong flight toward growth and economic success are an estimated 400,000 people who live in a 73 square mile slum, that, says a college professor, "has an infant mortality rate that would have embarrassed the Belgian Congo" (Recer, 1978:47).

According to Joe Feagin (1988:424):

Houston has some of the largest and most oppressive poverty areas in the United States. The free market city has not only not purged itself of "slums" it has actually created grinding poverty, unemployment and subemployment, which are more difficult to bear in Houston than in cities with substantial social programs. . . . The local government and State of Texas programs for the unemployed and the poor vary from minimal to nonexistent.

When Democratic presidential candidate Jesse Jackson visited on February 28, 1988, he equated the conditions of Houston's largest black slum to that of segregated South Africa. According to Jackson (Conlon, 1988:A–1):

The poor are left to squat and then forced out by developers. It is forced removal as opposed to urban renewal. They do it slower here because of the laws but it's the same process used in South Africa. The government can arbitrarily move people from one area to another, the mentality is the same.

While the Fourth Ward has received a tremendous amount of media attention, the Bordersville neighborhood in northern Houston has even worse slum conditions. Bordersville is a former slave camp that contains over eight hundred black residents. The neighborhood is without sewage, many of the streets are unpaved, water was only recently installed, 30 percent of the housing units are dilapidated, and 80 percent of the residents live in poverty. Drug use is rampant and the streets at night are deserted. Police rarely patrol the neighborhood. The city has only provided $200,000 in Community Development Block Grant funds to Bordersville. According to Doug Samuel, who is executive director of the Bordersville Community Center:

No grass-roots organization; we can't get the citizens together. Bordersville residents don't feel it's worth the effort; they have a sense of helplessness and resentfulness: We are not worth it.[1]

These kinds of conditions result in Houston having one of the worst reputations in the United States in terms of quality of life. In 1988, a poll of eighty-three urban affairs experts from around the country found that Houston has the third most bleak future among fifty U.S. cities (Williams, 1988:1–26). The poll also named Houston the fourth worst managed city. These experts pointed to high unemployment, traffic congestion and lack of planning and zoning.

## Poor Planning

The lack of citizen grass-roots organizations in Houston is also reflected in the lack of planning in the city. Conventional planning would interfere with the rights and privileges of the elite. Consequently, Houston is the "planless city." It is the only large American city without zoning and a master plan. In a city of three million, Houston has roughly the same number of planners (twenty-seven) as Santa Monica with a population of around one hundred thousand. The lack of planning results in a city that is second class when compared to other American cities. Consequently, you have a city where a cement factory can be found next to a school, a muffler shop in the middle of a residential neighborhood. Planner and architect Peter Brown (1988:E3) describes Houston in the following way:

There are some beautiful parts of Houston. But there are plenty of unattractive areas also—ribbons of strip commercial property marred by incompatible land uses, the lack of landscaping and proper setbacks, all tangled in a web of billboards, signs, utility poles and congested streets. We have neighborhoods threatened by blight, ill-placed strip joints, run-down industrial areas, freeways choked by cars and open-ditch streets that flood and don't go anywhere...all signs of an unplanned city.

The lack of properly designed public spaces, historic preservation, human-scale architecture and street-level commercial enterprises make Houston the textbook example of a poorly planned downtown (see also Whyte 1988). This is compounded by a maze of elevated and underground walkways that connect one skyscraper to another so that employees never have to walk outside. It is not uncommon to walk in the downtown during regular business hours and not see anyone else on the sidewalks for blocks at a time. The often monotonous postmodern architecture of concrete, steel, and glass reaching as high as seventy stories is cold and faceless. Houston lacks the warmth and character of its neighboring city to the west, San Antonio; to the north, Austin; and to the east, New Orleans, which despite the oppressive heat and humidity are successful pedestrian-oriented cities. While these cities have had successful historic preservation laws that have protected many important structures from the 1800s to 1900s, Houston is without such regulations. In the seminal book, *The Death and Life of Great American Cities,* Jane Jacobs (1961) argues that great cities provide a mixture of old and new architecture for their citizens to see and feel. By Jacobs's criteria, Houston will never be considered a great city in the same category as Chicago, San Francisco, New York, Boston, Washington, D.C., and, of course, New Orleans. Houston's corporate monumental buildings make citizens feel overwhelmed, small, and unimportant.

Houston's planning is so haphazard that the foundations of buildings are often within inches of major boulevards. Not only does Houston have more billboards and peep shows than any other major city, but these activities can be found within residential neighborhoods (Grondolfo, 1988:1). A common characteristic of most neighborhoods is the lack of sidewalks—which effectively prevents the disabled, elderly and families with baby carriages from taking strolls. Gilderbloom, Rosentraub and Bullard (1987) estimate that over 70 percent of the neighborhoods lack sidewalks and/or curb cuts.

Houston is a city that lacks the soul of citizens actively involved in the political process. Within a framework of operating in an unrestrained free market, business sets the agenda for city hall. Below are some of the problems that have resulted due to a lack of neighborhood movement and proper planning: **Toxic Waste Disposal:** According to Charles Reinken (1988:E–1), Houston's three largest chemical and refinery complexes in the ship channel released over ninety-two million tons of toxic pollutants in the air, water, and land in 1987. This would average out to twenty-five pounds of toxic waste for every citizen in Houston. William Ruckelshaus, then chief of the Environmental Protection Agency, declared that Houston ranks among the worst cities in the nation concerning the disposal of hazardous and toxic wastes. Houston has over one hundred toxic waste sites. Additionally, a recent helicopter search of the Houston area found two sites where low-level radioactive waste had been illegally dumped. The city's ship channel, which is without plant or fish life, is so toxic that residents are warned not to let the poisonous water come in contact with their skin (Feagin, 1988).

**Sewage Disposal:** Millons of tons of raw sewage are dumped into the Buffalo Bayou—which flows through the city's best park and within blocks of the city's gleaming downtown skyscrapers (Feagin, 1988:351). Garbage sites are located in areas that are largely minority (Bullard, 1987).

**Air Pollution:** Houston is ranked second in the country in ozone pollution problems by the Environmental Protection Agency (Dawson, 1988:24). According to Feagin (1988:358), Houstonians are exposed to unhealthy air at least once a week. Air pollution is considered a major reason why lung cancer rates are twice the national rate.

**Subsidence:** Because Houston has relied on underground water supplies for much of its drinking water, parts of southeast Houston have sunk a much as eight feet and downtown locations supporting huge megastructures have subsided by as much as five feet since 1943 (Feagin, 1988:352). Most homes commonly have foundation problems that take an average of $5,000 to repair.

**Flooding:** Due to the lack of planning, one-fifth of Houston's real estate development is on a floodplain (Feagin 1988:353). In certain Houston neighborhoods, seven major floods occurred between 1973 and 1983. The cost of these floods averaged $30 million in annual losses during the seventies and eighties.

**Traffic Problems:** The Federal Highway Administration has ranked Houston as having the worst traffic problems among thirty-seven metropolitan areas (Feagin, 1988:363). For several years during the 1980s, Houston had the highest death rate on highways among major cities. Part of these hazardous driving conditions were contributed by the over two million potholes in the city streets—more than any other city in the country. The traffic problem has also led to rapid gentrification in the city's older inner-city neighborhoods.

**Parks:** Compared to other cities, Houston has very few parks. A 1977 study by the Interior Department ranked Houston 140 in park land per capita (Feagin, 1988:380). The parks that do exist are worn and unkempt in terms of upkeep and restroom facilities. Many of the parks are also experiencing criminal activities. According to Susan Chadwick (1988:D-10):

Some of the city's largest and nicest parks have been nearly abandoned by the parks department due to staffing and funding problems. Others have not yet been developed. Most of the city's smaller, inner-city parks are dreary and worn-out, while others are overdone, gaudy, and artificial, lacking a sense of balance and harmony.

Fights and heavy drug use characterize the city's largest parks. Former Mayor Louis Welch once remarked, "Houston doesn't need parks, they have big backyards."[2]

Houston's downtown area, where fifty-, sixty-, and seventy-story skyscrapers compete with one another has very few spaces to accommodate the public. As a result, downtown Houston is empty, cold, and unimaginative in terms of being people-oriented; after five on the weekdays and during the weekends, the downtown is practically barren of any human activity.

**Crime:** Houston also has a well-earned reputation of having a high crime rate. One out of every four households has been a victim of crime (University of Houston Center for Public Policy, 1988). Houston has one of the highest murder rates in the country (Boyer and Savageau, 1981). Houston's murder rate is almost 50 percent higher than New York or Los Angeles. Of 277 urban places surveyed, Houston had the fifth highest rate of rape, the seventh highest robbery rate, and the tenth highest burglary rate (Boyer and Savageau, 1981). Crime is so frequent in Houston that it is not uncommon to drive through middle-class neighborhoods and see burglar bars on the windows and doors of almost every house. Fear of crime prevents about 70 percent of the residents from taking walks in their own neighborhoods.

### The Use of Federal Poverty Funds in Houston: Business Wins Big

Unlike Santa Monica and other liberal cities where poverty funds are spent to eradicate the problem, Houston spends its federal antipoverty funds to support business interests. While no report exists that provides a detailed accounting of how community development funds are spent, the city's major newspapers have uncovered scandals over the expenditure of these funds. For example, in 1986 the federal government provided Houston with $41 million in community development money. HUD yanked $2.6 million from the city for not spending it fast enough. The intent of these funds is to be used to attack poverty faced by low- and moderate-income persons. Houston only spends 10 percent of its CDBG funds on housing, while other large cities spend a great deal more in this category (Friedman, 1988 A–20). In Boston and Santa Monica, 75 percent of CDBG funds go into housing programs (Friedman, 1988:A–20).

Houston has been irresponsible in its targeting of CDBG funds, investing in ventures that have little to do with combating poverty faced by low- and moderate-income persons. The priorities of Houston are significantly different from those of Boston, Pittsburgh, Santa Monica, and other American cities. The city council gave serious consideration to giving $800,000 in CDBG funds to build a new dog kennel. The city also seriously considered using $10 million in federal poverty money to finance partially a one thousand room Hilton Hotel next to the convention center. Both of these dubious plans were abandoned after being brought to the public's attention by the press and an uproar ensued. The private sector has done very little as well to participate in any public/private venture. Another quarter of a million dollars in federal poverty funds was given to the sister of the mayor's top adviser to finance an art center (Thomas and Downing, 1988:3–A). Several million dollars were used to remodel an old Sears store into a shopping center. The council also voted to provide a $700,000 loan to a fast-food chain restaurant that was facing bankruptcy, despite the fact that the company owed over $1.2 million in unpaid loans and $200,000 in unpaid federal, state, and local taxes. In 1988, the city council agreed to give $15,000 in community development funds to a nonprofit organization headed by the wife of a city councilmember (Benson, 1988). Another $1 million was used to pay for a sewage treatment plant (Friedman and Thomas, 1988:A–1). The city also provided a $300,000 loan to an air-conditioning filter manufacturing plant that would supposedly employ fifty persons, yet only five were employed and no payments were ever made on the loan (*Houston Post,* 1988:E–1).

## A Private-public Partnership:
## The Houston Economic Development Council[3]

Virtually all public-private partnerships in Houston's history have been generated from and dominated by the city's powerful business elite. Virtually all such arrangements have in effect been *private*-public partnerships. Houston has not, of course, been strictly a free market city, its image in the conservative literature notwithstanding. The close relationship between the local, state, federal, and business elite is one of the less well-known aspects of Houston's prosperity. For example, there has been much governmental aid for infra-structure projects eagerly desired by the business community, such as federal money for highways, substantial military-industrial aid for the local petrochemical industry during World War II, and the millions for the Johnson Space Center. This aid was aggressively sought by the business elites that have, as a matter of fact, long controlled and actually staffed the city government. Although this city is frequently advertised as *the* free enterprise city, actually its business leadership has regularly taken major government assistance for projects that assist private profit-making.

As hard as it may be for analysts familiar with public-private partnerships in other major cities to believe, Houston's leadership waited until the 1980s to consider seriously a public-private partnership specifically designed to recruit corporations to the city and to stimulate economic development and diversification in the city. Only slowly did the implications of the economic bust that the city experienced in the 1980s penetrate the thinking of the business leadership organized through the local chamber of commerce. They realized that in the future, the city's economy would be battered by the negative swings in the capitalist business cycle that had been avoided in the past. Given the extraordinary weakness of the local city planning departments, the chamber has traditionally been the effective local planning agency that has developed business-oriented solutions for city problems that have become too serious for them to ignore.

In the troubled 1980s, when the economic recession in Houston generated a growing apprehension about the need for greater economic diversity, the chamber created several investigative committees to assess economic development. Belatedly, in 1984, the chamber's leadership established the Houston Economic Development Council (HEDC). Initially headed by a major local developer, HEDC had as vice-chairs the top executives of the two local papers and the four largest banks, an oil executive, a business leader heading up a city booster group, and a token union official. It is noteworthy that the Houston mayor and the chief county executive were appointed by the private sector officials, the chamber leadership, to serve on what was ostensibly a public-private partnership. In reality, this was a *private*-public partnership (Feagin, 1988).

Where did HEDC funding come from? In the beginning, the chamber's HEDC generated $6.3 million for the first two years from the local business community. A second two-year budget was for $7.2 million. HEDC was created by the business community, but local governments have played a considerable role in financing the organization. Houston city government put together a $150,000 grant for the first budget; in 1986, the city council voted to match private contributions, to $1.25 million annually. Mayor Kathy Whitmire tried to stop this subsidy because of the new taxes required, but she was defeated. Not recognizing the irony, business leaders called it the "first true economic wedding of the public and private sectors" in the city's history. This was not true; the city's business leaders have often utilized state aid for their business needs. But what they were thinking was that this was the first aboveboard, public-private partnership for general economic development and reorientation of economic direction in the city's history (O'Grady, 1987:1F).

Because of this new character of the public-private partnership, there has been conflict and struggle over the exact dimensions of the bureaucratic structure. There has been debate over the relationship of HEDC to the chamber; some have argued that it should be an entirely separate organization. Others have argued that it should be kept with the chamber. This was finally resolved in 1987, when HEDC became officially separate from the chamber, although it still utilized chamber research resources. There have also been squabbles between the public partner and the private partner. For example, during the summer of 1986, city councilmembers became irritated that HEDC had not signed a contract with the city government to fund a portion of the public-private partnership. One problem was that HEDC leaders were afraid that such a money linkage to local government would necessitate too much surveillance of the sometimes secret HEDC and chamber operations and expenditures (Gravois, 1986:1A). Nonetheless, by 1988 the relationship with the local governmental authorities, including the city government, the county government, and the Port of Houston authority, appeared to have stabilized; HEDC, now with a staff of thirty employees, was securing one third of its total funding from these governmental sources, with the remainder coming from private sources, including the chamber.

There has been some shifting of goals in this unique public-private partnership. Initially, HEDC laid out these categories of sought-after economic development: (1) biomedical research; (2) research laboratories; (3) instruments, medical, and computer equipment; (4) communications equipment; (5) chemicals; (6) materials processing research; (7) computers and office machines; (8) engineering and architectural services; and (9) distribution services. When these target categories were proclaimed, some analysts criticized the listing. For example, the lead priority of biomedical research seemed naive because Houston's medical center had not yet spun off a major med-tech firm (Clark, 1985:9–11).

Moreover, the Center for Enterprising of Southern Methodist University prepared a commissioned report that counseled Houston's business leaders to reject the national obsession with biotechnology and computers and to examine instead traditional manufacturing areas that had potential but that had been overlooked in the quest for diversification ideas, especially processing of paper, agricultural and food products, printing, and pharmaceuticals. Looming above diversification was the problem of insufficient educational institutions in Houston to support a high-tech economic base. Gradually, business leaders acknowledged that metropolitan areas with high-tech industries tended to bankroll first-rate educational institutions and research labs. So HEDC suggested that its parent, the chamber of commerce, create a task force to work to improve research and training in local universities and to press for greater federal funds for the medical center and NASA facilities. Moreover, HEDC's

1986 revised agenda targeted energy, biotechnology, space enterprises, international business, and tourism as areas of emphasis for economic development (Crown, 1986:1; HEDC, 1986:4). By 1987, HEDC had a new chief executive, Lee Hogan, a local engineer and entrepreneur who adopted an even more pragmatic approach to economic development, focusing corporate recruitment and diversification efforts on Houston's strengths and specifically targeting aerospace, petrochemicals, and med-tech as the principal areas in which to work for corporate recruitment.

While some efforts have been put into the nurturing of small businesses, HEDC has for the most part functioned as a public relations and booster organization for Houston. Much money and effort have been expended on marketing efforts, especially on the city's image. Business leaders have attacked the national media for depicting Houston negatively. HEDC has conducted a number of national advertising campaigns to improve the city's image and to attract enterprise. HEDC officials sponsored a European trade mission, attempted to secure the proposed General Motors automated Saturn automobile facility, and worked hard to secure a major Navy homeport for the Houston-Galveston area. Military-industrial corporations have been the target of recruitment. In October 1986, HEDC took some credit for recruiting the military-industrial firm Grumman to the NASA area in south Houston. The incentive package that attracted Grumman included $20 million in tax abatements from the city government. Although as of early 1988 Grumman had not actually moved into the site because of shifts in the national space program, it was still expected to come to the southern part of the city. In 1987, HEDC proudly proclaimed its role in getting twenty-two companies to locate or expand in the city, adding three thousand new jobs. HEDC officials were also proud of attracting two of Australia's largest firms and several large Japanese firms to the greater metropolitan area, in part the consequence of the falling dollar. By the late 1980s, Houston's business leaders proudly proclaimed that they were learning to play the "economic development game" (Brubaker, 1986:1).

El Mercado del Sol: A Real Public-Private Project

One of the biggest boondoggles the city engaged in was the financing of the El Mercado del Sol Center. The city contributed approximately $5 million to renovate an old mattress factory into a modern Mexican theme shopping center in the heart of the city's sprawling barrio. This celebrated public-private sector venture would go bankrupt within a few years and today is boarded up. The project hoped to emulate the success and precedent set by San Francisco's Cannery and Boston's Faneuil Hall, along with other Mexican-style marketplaces successfully attracting tourists in San Antonio and Santa Barbara, California.

The idea for the center emerged from discussions among white and Hispanic business leaders and certain city officials, especially the city's chief planning officer. In 1983, city officials contributed $500,000 from a Community Development Block Grant for a $13 million public-private partnership project to help minority business leaders revitalize an old Mexican-American section. The project called El Mercado del Sol was a marketplace with 400,000 square feet, located on the edge of a Mexican-American barrio two miles from downtown. The development would provide space for eighty stores and restaurants with Mexican cultural themes (Downing, 1988:1D; Downing and Friedman, 1988:1A).

If El Mercado worked, it would have become one of the nation's largest Hispanic commercial centers. This project involved a public-private partnership, one that combined the goals of neighborhood physical improvement and Hispanic business growth. El Mercado represented the first serious attempt of local government to improve conditions in a run-down area where a large portion of Houston's three hundred thousand Hispanics reside. Moreover, it was the first major attempt by local government to display the contributions made to Houston by Mexican-Americans. Given the barrio's blight, El Mercado was seen by some city administrators, especially Efraim Garcia, the city planning director, as crucial for local business revitalization by locating in the Hispanic community, with benefits trickling down to the poorest residents. But the dream of economic and neighborhood improvement turned into a nightmare when, in 1987, El Mercado's owner, Encore Development Corporation, filed for bankruptcy, the financing bank went into receivership, and the FSLIC foreclosed on the shopping center. After a delay, it was sold to new owners, Mercado Partners II, with the city of Houston injecting $5 million in federal CDBG money into the center in 1987 to prevent total collapse (Downing and Friedman, 1988:1A).

There are a number of factors explaining why the El Mercado public-private enterprise never reached its goals of being profitable and neighborhood-enriching. The project was flawed by poor timing; it opened in the midst of Houston's dramatic economic decline, which brought a drop in disposable income and retail sales. On the center's opening day, fewer than five stores were opened; the large crowd had few places to shop. Some critics of the city government involvement argue that El Mercado's premature opening with so few shops was politically timed by the mayor, Kathy Whitmire, to draw Hispanic votes to her campaign and to upstage her opponent's announcement of candidacy in a upcoming election.

Other critics point to the lack of planning to lessen the negative image of the marketplace's barrio setting. The city never came through with its promise to provide an additional $2.5 million in CDBG funds for parks and access roads. The street that leads to El Mercado from the downtown area, a critical source of shoppers, winds through blocks of dilapidated warehouses, bars, and run-down hotels where vagrants and prostitutes congregate. There is no exit ramp at a nearby freeway that could bring large numbers of shoppers from suburban areas nor is there an effective public transportation system to bring customers from the downtown area. If a trolley had been installed, El Mercado would have had better business. Although San Antonio's Mexican-style marketplace is outside of the downtown area, a trolley makes the marketplace easily accessible to the city's downtown crowds and tourists. Given the problem of accessibility, critics suggest that El Mercado should have been located downtown in one of many historic brick buildings alongside the Buffalo Bayou. This has worked well in Santa Barbara, where the Mexican shops and restaurants are integrated into the downtown area, or in San Francisco, where the Cannery is adjacent to Fisherman's Wharf. A few store owners have sued the new owners of El Mercado and the city's planning director for mismanagement of the project (Byars, 1988:1–18; Urban, 1988:1–3).

All factors cited above have contributed to El Mercado's failure as a neighborhood revitalizing project. But there are also other underlying problems. Houston's city government lacks tradition, experience, and skill in public-private partnerships and in minority economic development. This is a direct consequence of the enduring free enterprise philosophy that economic development can be accomplished by unhindered privately driven capitalism. The second underlying problem is that the Hispanic and black communities have been viewed by the city's white growth coalition as labor reservoirs and low-priority areas for development. For over one hundred years, these communities have received little attention or assistance from the business elite and have thus remained foreign areas to the white leaders and affluent residents of the city. For example, business and government leaders have never felt the need to build effective street systems leading into the eastside barrios. In a sense the problems of El Mercado are more than a problem of attempting a rare public-private partnership in this free enterprise city. More fundamentally, the problem is the pernicious racial and ethnic discrimination, the persisting neglect and exclusion.

## Houston's Housing Crisis: A Free Market Model

Real estate interests often cite Houston as the only American city without a housing crisis. Rents are cheap relative to cities on the two coasts and the homeless rate is the lowest for any large American city (Siegan, 1972; Johnson, 1982; Tucker, 1987). During the 1980s, Houston was cited by Reagan administration officials as a model for the production of affordable housing. The key ingredient to affordable housing according to the President's Commission on Housing (1983) is the free market: no zoning, little planning, lax environmental regulations, and no rent control.

Houston serves as a model for providing affordable housing to the rest of the nation, according to conservative economist Bruce Johnson (1982). A top Reagan official declared that Johnson's book, *Resolving the Housing Crisis,* is a "valuable complement to the efforts of the President's Commission on Housing."[4] Similar praise for Johnson's book was given by conservative planner George Sternlieb, director of the Center for Urban Policy Research, and Anthony Downs, senior fellow, Brookings Institution. Johnson (1982:14) declared that only the free market is capable of producing affordable housing:

> Houston's lack of land use controls is actually a more efficient system in protecting neighborhoods than the scandal-ridden, bribery-prone zoning boards found elsewhere. . . . The market works in Houston because Houston has no zoning and, thus, cannot use zoning ordinances to restrict supply and exclude "undesirable" developments and people. With the fastest-growing population of any large city in the land, house prices in "unenlightened, nonprogressive" Houston have risen but a fraction of the distance California's prices have risen.

Johnson is joined in his book by other well-known conservative urbanologists such as Bernard Frieden, Richard Muth, and Bernard Siegan, who argue the superiority of the unfettered market as a mechanism to produce affordable housing and good neighborhoods. During the campaign for rent control in Santa Monica, Houston was often cited by real estate interests as a model for the city to pursue in terms of planning and housing.

The extraordinary claim made by conservative housing analysts, that Houston has "resolved its housing crisis," is without any empirical support. Even with a 20 percent rental housing vacancy rate, no zoning, and little planning, Houston has a major housing crisis. Houston's housing problems are just as severe as the rest of the nation: 10,000–15,000 homeless persons, 18,000 persons waiting to get into public housing, 500,000 low- and moderate-income persons making unaffordable housing payments, one-fourth of the low-income persons living in overcrowded housing, and a zero vacancy rate for housing accessible to the disabled. Despite this enormous emergency, in the late eighties thousands of rental units were demolished every year because of the virtual nonexistence of community organizations trained to convert these units into co-ops.

Despite this crisis, landlords have almost free rein in the city. The apartment owners' association was able to convince the mayor to have the number of city building inspectors examining apartments for code violations cut from twenty-six to six. According to the *Houston Chronicle* (Cobb 1987:1–12):

The Houston Apartment Association is patting itself on the back over anticipated layoffs among city building inspectors after lobbying that inspectors were harassing association members. . . . Field inspectors say they have focused on apartment complexes because so many are dilapidated and poorly maintained because of the city's economic problems.

Houston's high apartment arson rate is partly due to the lack of proper code enforcement. In addition, Houston also has the most inequitable landlord/tenant laws of any major American city. Landlords deny tenants just-cause eviction rights, often the standard apartment lease stipulates that the first $50 of any repair is charged to the tenant, and landlords inhibit minorities from renting moderate-income apartments by charging a $50 application fee for all prospective renters (Bullard, 1987). The rental application form typically asks questions that could be used to infer race by identifying hair and eyes. Consequently, several apartment complexes in the inner city are virtually all white. According to a local consumer rights official, landlord/tenant conflicts are the number one complaint in Houston. Moreover, most civil rights experts believe that landlords play an important role in keeping Houston a highly segregated city (Massey and Denton, 1987; Bullard, 1987; see also Gilderbloom 1985a).

Quality of Housing

Despite the relatively large number of new rental units built over the past ten years, major problems with quality and affordability remain for the poor and disabled. In 1987 and 1988, one-third of Houston's 400,000 apartment units went into foreclosure. In 1987, between 5,000 and 15,000 apartment units were torn down, with only 500 units built (Bivins, 1988:5–1). Real estate analysts predict that another 24,000 apartment units will be demolished by 1995 (Bivins, 1988:5–1). It is estimated that over 10,000 buildings containing close to 100,000 apartment units have been abandoned and are unsafe (Benson, 1988:A–4). Each year Houston gets 2,500 new complaints about dangerous buildings that should be torn down. A recent study by Gilderbloom et al. (1987) found that 15 percent of low- and moderate-income families live in substandard housing. One out of every ten Houston renters live in overcrowded housing, with close to one out of every three Hispanic renters living under these conditions.

The quality of housing is especially bad for Hispanic renters (Gilderbloom and Rodriguez, 1990). Poor Hispanic renters (earning less than $10,000 a year) have problems with: incomplete kitchens (14 percent), roof leaks (17 percent), toilet breakdown in the previous ninety days (14 percent), cracks and holes in walls and ceilings (27 percent), and mice and rats seen in the previous ninety days (43 percent). Poor Hispanic renters were five times more likely to have household rodents than were poor white renters. While many housing deficiencies decrease as incomes increase, Spanish-speaking Hispanics earning between $10,000 and $20,000 still face problems with "mice and rats" (27 percent) and roof leakage (22 percent).

A substantial number of elderly and disabled persons require architectural modifications in their homes. One out of every ten Houstonians requires such special architectural modifications. One third of Houston's seniors and more than one half of the disabled need grab bars in their homes. At least 20 percent of the elderly and disabled want ramps placed in their homes. Not surprisingly, the need for ramps and rails increases with age and severity of disability.

Outside of the house, Houston remains an invisible jail to the disabled and elderly. Over 70 percent of the disabled and elderly do not have sidewalks with curb cuts to give them access to buses. The elderly and disabled want certain amenities within the house and the neighborhood in order to live independently. Houston is, perhaps, the least accessible city of any major city in the country. Even San Francisco with its steep hills is a more hospitable place for the disabled (Gilderbloom et al., 1987). Given these problems, it is not surprising that approximately 25 percent of the disabled and elderly population would like to move from their current residences in the next year.

Affordability Problems

The crisis of unaffordable housing for low- and moderate-income families exists in every American city—including Houston. Most analysts predict that the problem of high housing costs will escalate in the 1990s (Gilderbloom and Appelbaum, 1988). Barton Smith, senior associate at the Center for Public Policy at the University of Houston, predicts that rents might increase two and a half times in the next four years. In 1983, the Annual Housing Survey indicated that median rents in Houston were higher than most U.S. cities. Houston's median rent was $77 higher than the rest of the southern region (Gilderbloom, 1985c).

The federal government has traditionally determined that a tenant is paying an excessive amount of rent whenever the proportion of rent to income is more than 25 percent (Comptroller General, 1979). According to this rule of thumb, more than half of Houston's renters—most of whom are low- and moderate-income families—are paying an excessive amount of rent (Gilderbloom, 1985:149). The Annual Housing Survey also shows that close to one third of Houston's renters pay more than 35 percent of their incomes into rent, and almost one fifth pay more than 50 percent of their incomes into rent. Black renters have even greater affordability problems, with three fifths paying more than 25 percent of their incomes into rent and almost one third paying more than 50 percent of their incomes into rent. Gilderbloom et al. (1987) found that 36 percent of disabled households and 27 percent of elderly households in the Harris County area paid an excessive amount of their incomes for rent.

Homelessness

The number of homeless persons is estimated to be between 10,000 and 15,000 (Feagin, 1988:425). Houston's homeless population represents a tremendous problem. According to Feagin (1988:425):

The city's shelters for the homeless were overflowing, with significant numbers of families seeking refuge there. The Star of Hope Mission's family shelter had 180 beds, but was housing 240 people, including 90–95 children, each night. This was in addition to the 500 plus single men housed in the Mission's main shelter. This was at the time the largest mission shelter for the homeless in the United States. In addition, many others stayed in the Salvation Army facilities, also the largest such shelter in the country. Other Houstonians lived under bridges or in the Tent City, a makeshift community of unemployed adults and families living out on the edge of the metropolitan area.

Officials predict that the problem of homelessness will continue to grow in Houston as well as in the rest of the nation. Houston has never committed any tax dollars to the city's large homeless population (Grandolfo, 1988:21A).

Public Housing

The free market has failed to provide a decent, affordable, and suitable living environment for Houston's low- and moderate-income population. The city's business and government leaders have never made affordable housing a human right that should be provided regardless of the cost or political consequences. Houston's business elite has historically opposed the construction of public housing (Feagin, Gilderbloom, and Rodriguez, 1989). During the depression, only a modest amount of public housing was built.

Houston has approximately 3,000 public housing units, down from 4,000 a few years ago (Houston Housing Authority, 1987). This contrasts sharply with New York's 207,000 units, Chicago's 47,000 units, Los Angeles's 26,000 units, and Philadelphia's 23,000. While Houston ranks as the nation's fourth largest city, it ranks twenty-fifth in the number of public housing units (Stuart, 1989:35). In Texas, Houston ranks third behind Dallas and San Antonio in number of public housing units. The Houston Housing Authority has a waiting list of thirteen thousand for public housing units.[5]

A similar situation exists for other kinds of federally subsidized housing. Of those Houstonians who qualify under government guidelines for Section 8 aid, merely 6 percent of low- and moderate-income families received help, while 9 percent of the disabled and 5 percent of the elderly were given government aid.[6] The percentage of persons receiving Section 8 assistance in Houston is well below other cities. The President's Commission on Housing (1983:13–15) estimates that, nationally, 27 percent of all persons who qualify for Section 8 assistance receive help (see also Gilderbloom et al., 1987; Huttman, 1987:12). Houston has not received its fair share of Section 8 certificates. Historically, Houston has not been aggressive in pursuing its "fair share" of the federal housing assistance pie. According to sociologist Elizabeth Huttman (1987:12), 45 percent of the San Franciscans eligible for Section 8 assistance have received aid. The process of allocating federal assistance is based not on need but on politics. Houston has largely been passive concerning these funding inequities, allowing HUD to give greater assistance to those cities that lobby the federal government.

Including the Section 8 rental housing program, Houston subsidized only 11,754 housing units—a fraction of the amount of housing assistance needed. Houston ranked thirteenth out of eighteen public housing agencies surveyed in its subsidized housing programs (Houston Housing Authority, 1987). This survey found that New York had 256,129 subsidized units, followed by Chicago with 49,155, Philadelphia with 30,816, and Los Angeles with 30,554. San Francisco, which has a population that is one fifth the size of Houston, has a housing subsidy program almost equal to Houston's. Houston ranks fourth in Texas in terms of susidized units, behind Fort Worth, Dallas, and San Antonio. The survey also showed that Houston ranked second to last in the number of specially designed disabled/elderly housing units. By 1988, it was estimated that over 18,000 Houstonians were on the waiting list for some kind of government housing assistance.

Despite the enormous housing crisis and the relatively scarce public housing units in Houston, city officials are planning to demolish the largest public housing project in Houston. Allen Parkway Village (APV) is a two-story low-rise public housing project containing 1,000 units spread out over 37 acres. While city officials argue that Allen Parkway Village is obsolete and cannot be rehabilitated, numerous professional planners and social scientists disagree (Cuff, 1985; Fisher, 1985, Bullard, 1985). They point out that Allen Parkway Village could be rehabilitated at roughly one half the cost of building new public housing. Additionally, APV recently was added to the National Register of Historic Places for its architectural significance. APV represents a perverse form of public-private partnership where the government acts to eliminate needed public housing to meet the needs of real estate interests.

Opponents point out that the true reason for wanting to demolish APV is its prime downtown location, within three hundred yards of gleaming glass skyscrapers and jogging paths. For the developer, Allen Parkway Village would be an ideal site to construct upper-middle-class condominiums (Griffiths, 1985). According to Tom Armstrong, formerly in charge of HUD's southeast regional office, "That was without doubt the most valuable piece of property in that metroplex...developers were applying significant pressures on Washington and area (HUD) offices to acquire properties that were located in highly appreciated situations" (Flournoy, 1985:435). While business has increasingly pressured government to demolish public housing near prime downtown locations throughout America, Houston is unique in its almost total cooperation with those real estate interests.

The desire of city officials to demolish Allen Parkway Village is a classic case of the conflict involving values of development capital in opposition to community values. The demolition of Allen Parkway Village is the cornerstone of the city's ambitious plans to redevelop the entire Fourth Ward—Houston's oldest black neighborhood that dates back to the days of slavery. The overall plan is to demolish over 2,500 homes in the neighborhood and sell the tract of 90 acres to a developer to build office towers, condominiums, and shops (Flournoy, 1985:435). It is estimated that the value of the land could be in excess of $250 million. Kenneth Schnitzer, chairman of Century Development Corporation, the nation's tenth largest developer, has been known to be a prime mover to get the city to redevelop the Fourth Ward (Flournoy, 1985:437). At the time of this writing, close to 900 units have been boarded up. In a dramatic reversal, the Houston city council in the spring of 1989 voted to withdraw its application to HUD to demolish Allen Parkway Village. This victory, due to an unprecedented grass-roots effort to save the Village, could be a turning point for grass-roots politics in Houston.

Urban Homesteading

The problem of abandoned housing in Houston could be greatly reduced and turned into an important resource to combat homelessness and unaffordable rents with the introduction of an urban homesteading program. While many low-income persons are interested, the program run by the city is miniscule (Gilderbloom, Rosentraub, and Bullard, 1987). Accordingly, thousands of units are abandoned yearly, but less than forty homes have been turned over to "urban homesteaders" despite close to two thousand applicants who would like to participate in the program. Close to 10,000 apartment units were foreclosed in Houston in January 1988—with thousands of units being demolished. The production of affordable units can be increased dramatically. This involves residents providing "sweat equity" in the rehabilitation of an abandoned or foreclosed unit. Sweat equity generally involves exerting physical labor to rehabilitate the housing unit and ranges from replacing or repairing major structural elements to improving the plumbing, heating, electricity, and other necessities. Also involved is contracting out material, equipment, and labor expenses. In addition, because the cooperative acts as its own contractor, permits must be applied for from city hall as well as housing assistance contracts. When self-help rehabilitation is done, the cost of bringing multifamily housing up to code can be 50 percent of the cost of conventional rehabilitation by private developers.

## Roots of the Housing Crisis

Most progressive American cities like Santa Monica have used Community Development Block Grant funds and other HUD special demonstration grants to remedy the housing crisis. Houston remains the major exception. Houston has given little or no support for such middle of the road programs as house sharing, equity conversion, cooperative housing, and urban homesteading. Landlords have been successful in Houston in keeping the government out of the housing arena and protecting the profitability of the private market. This lack of action on the part of Houston's government has resulted in a severe housing crisis.

Additionally, Houston's housing crisis is further fueled by the concentration of ownership and management of apartment units. According to documents from the Houston Apartment Owners Association, 116 companies control one half of the total rental housing stock in the metropolitan area; just twenty-six firms control one fourth of the total rental stock. Three firms control over 10,000 housing units each. This concentration and control of apartment units in the hands of a small number of companies results in noncompetitive pricing practices (Gilderbloom and Appelbaum, 1988).

This helps explain why in Houston—with a vacancy rate of between 16 percent to 20 percent—rents declined by only 17 percent (from $375 to $313) during the collapse of the oil-based industry. In Dallas, where vacancy rates ranged from 9 percent to 14 percent during 1983–86, monthly rents actually *increased* by 11 percent (from $400 to $443). Gilderbloom and Appelbaum (1988) found in their study of 140 urban areas in the United States that supply factors such as vacancy rate, percent rental, and level of construction activity had no statistically significant relationship with intercity rent levels. Their work suggests that vacancy rates will only begin to impact rents at about 15 percent— not 5 percent as conventionally believed. The impact of vacancy rate is small relative to other factors, such as changes in the interest rates and tax laws that encourage rapid turnover of property in order to maximize properties and at the local level through the social organization of landlording and the economic position of tenants (Gilderbloom and Appelbaum, 1988). Rent is a social result in which the market plays only an intermediary role in a process that is constructed by institutions and actors representing special interests.

## Community-Based Housing Programs

While it is estimated that cities such as San Francisco, Los Angeles, Boston, Chicago, and New York have hundreds of community-based nonprofit corporations, Houston has only five. Neighborhood-based non-profit development corporations are a key to the revitalization of low- and moderate-income neighborhoods. While Boston or New York nonprofit organizations can rehabilitate abandoned housing for approximately $70,000 a unit, Houston has the potential to develop anywhere from 5 to 10 units at that cost (Hensel, 1988; Gilderbloom et al., 1987). As we discuss in more detail in Chapter 7, cooperatives can rent out units well below market levels.

Despite the tremendous potential of these programs and the likely direction of Bush administration housing policy for cities, Houston has resisted the concept of co-op housing. For example, the Enterprise Foundation attempted to organize a Neighborhood Development Foundation to assist and develop nonprofit organizations for housing co-ops. The Neighborhood Development Foundation has been successfully organized in twenty-seven cities around the nation and has served as a catalyst for "progressive" urban renewal. For two years, the Enterprise Foundation pledged $100,000 to the city of Houston for a Neighborhood Development Foundation, but was unable to get any matching funds from the Community Development Block Grant, private foundations, or corporations (Gilderbloom, Rosentraub and Bullard, 1987). In 1987, the Enterprise Foundation discontinued its efforts in Houston. The loss was a tremendous defeat to efforts to create more affordable housing and better neighborhoods for low- and moderate-income persons.

While the future of housing low- and moderate-income persons looks bleak in Houston, some hopeful signs have developed during the late eighties. Private Sector Initiatives (PSI) provide some services for nonprofit organizations in creating development proposals. During the fall of 1987, Private Sector Initiatives presented a series of half-day seminars on organizing nonprofits in Houston. PSI has established a $850,000 community investment fund for community development by neighborhood-based groups. It has also organized thousands of volunteers to repair and paint approximately 100 homes a year.

Finally, the last group to make a positive contribution in the development of affordable housing is the Houston Housing and Transportation Advisory Committee. Originally organized by progressive city councilmember Eleanor Tinsley to develop affordable and accessible housing for the disabled, the committee has become one of the most powerful housing and transportation organizations in Houston.

The committee, comprised of government and community leaders, began in 1986 to study the housing and transportation needs of the elderly, disabled, and poor. These efforts resulted in a detailed report and large conference on urban housing and transportation policy for the disadvantaged (Gilderbloom, Rosentraub and Bullard, 1987). The committee has seen government policy grow out of many of its recommendations to increase the amount of affordable and accessible housing. On the federal level, HUD is seriously considering doubling its allocation of housing vouchers for Houston to remedy past inequities. Second, HUD is giving serious attention to providing $500,000 for a special demonstration grant to provide 100 housing units for disabled people. At the local level, the Department of Planning and Development has pledged $500,000 from Community Development Block Grant funds for co-op housing developments by local nonprofit organizations. METRO (the region's public transportation agency) has given preliminary approval to develop an "accessibility corridor" that would allow the disabled to ride on a regularly scheduled bus route. This bus would have special wheelchair lifts, and the route would have sidewalks with curb cuts, specially designed shelters, and increased police protection. The infrastructure for this development would be funded by Community Development Block Grant funds, METRO physical improvement funds, and HUD demonstration grant monies. Tax incentives and specially targeted housing vouchers are also being developed to encourage housing cooperatives along the accessibility corridor.

While the committee has developed respect and support among government and community leaders, the private sector—with a few notable exceptions—has been unwilling to support its recommendations. Initially, the Apartment Owners Association supported the formation of the committee to provide "help" to house the disabled. However, when the committee expanded its agenda to include housing problems of the poor, the Apartment Owners Association no longer participated in committee activities. The spokesperson for the Apartment Owners Association claimed that the organization was uninterested in tenants with Section 8 certificates and modifying housing for the disabled. When the Center for Public Policy sponsored a conference on designing, locating, and financing housing services for the disabled, elderly, and low-income persons, only ten of the two hundred participants were landlords. The Apartment Owners Association refused even to announce the conference in its monthly newsletter, which goes out to thousands of landlords. This is ironic, given the fact that a 20 percent vacancy rate exists for *abled* persons and close to zero for disabled persons.

## Conclusion

The lack of an effective urban grass-roots organization to counterbalance the power and influence of real estate interests has caused Houston to be one of the worst cities in the nation in terms of quality of life. Houston—like most other cities—has failed to plan for the needs of its disadvantaged residents. This can be reversed. Reliance on the private sector, however, to provide affordable housing and stable communities is virtually useless. On the other hand, government can play a major role in facilitating citizen rights to essential resources such as housing, health care, transportation, safety, and food.

In many ways, the struggle to build community becomes a fight against *houstonization.* In comparing the progressive city (Santa Monica) and the free enterprise city (Houston), we find distinct differences in how disadvantaged citizens are treated.[7] In Santa Monica, the disabled have almost complete access to shopping, government, work, and educational activities (see below). Contrast this experience to Houston, where the public bus lines are without lifts, 70 percent of the streets are without sidewalks, and ramps are haphazardly built and placed. For renters, Santa Monica attempts to turn second-class citizenship into first class. In Houston, tenant protection laws are almost nonexistent. Community development in Santa Monica is aimed at low-income renters, whereas in Houston it is a gimmick to support commercial enterprises. Santa Monica represents a spectrim of interests, whereas Houston is run by wealthy elites. Which is the better city?

In 1950, M. Emmett Walter of the Houston City Planning Commission declared that Houston's greatest shame was "mediocrity in planning" (McComb, 1969:158). He told the Kiwanis Club:

> We have an opportunity in Houston to develop a magnificent city; a city that will be adequate to the economic demands and also provide facilities needed to make it a satisfactory place in which to live. Such a City can be built, if a little attention is given to planning, and it will cost less in the long run than a haphazard development. Surely a program that will . . . satisfy every man's [sic] craving for the beautiful should receive the support of all citizens.

Walter's call for a "magnificent" Houston needs to be renewed. A city is judged great, not by the number of monumental buildings or the people living within its borders, but by its ability to provide justice and civility: How well does a city address the needs of its citidens—whether they are rich or poor, black or white, old or young, able-bodied or disabled? Great cities are measured by the kinds of jobs, housing, education, and aesthetic and spiritual opportunities offered to their citizens. All urbanites should live with dignity and without fear. Great cities provide for all; great cities exclude no one.

IV

Conclusion

# Tenants' Movements and the Progressive American City

Can we have hope about the future of American cities? Are ghettos and homelessness inevitable? Do urban social movements matter? Is government intervention harmful to the workings of the market, or will economic democracy generate the "good city"? And what do tenants' movements reveal about the answers to any of these questions? As we head into the 1990s, can a more comprehensive, more engaging, and perhaps more optimistic theory of the city be embraced? These are the kinds of questions we should be addressing as we seek to develop an urban paradigm with greater explanatory power.

## Social Movements Theory and Tenants' Movements

In this book, we have explored tenants' movements in an urban setting as a subset of social movements in general. Our case study methodology has enabled us to examine, both qualitatively and quantitatively, how a tenants' movement becomes possible, how it evolves over time, and what its consequences are. While a case study always has limited generalizability, we feel that our detailed study of Santa Monica enables us to make a contribution to the systematic study of social movements.

In Chapter 2, we reviewed a broad range of theories bearing on tenants' movements, from Marxist and Weberian analyses of tenants, the state, and housing status, to the resource mobilization perspective and its various critics. Our purpose has not been to find one theory that works, or to construct an ultimate theory of urban social movements. Instead, we explore the theoretical implications of each tradition for tenants' movements and suggest directions for the future.[1] We are convinced that urban sociologists need to utilize a variety of perspectives to understand the totality of urban social change. At the same time, we are not advocating a smorgasbord approach or suggesting that all theories are equally useful. Some are clearly more useful than others.

Resource Mobilization

We begin with the dominant—and much debated—resource mobilization perspective. Resource mobilization theory suggests that the crucial factor for the emergence of a movement is organizational resources rather than structural strains or grievances. Indeed, our data revealed that structural conditions in the housing market in Santa Monica and Houston were very similar. Certainly resource mobilization theory (a perspective actually reflected in the thinking of many movement activists) was highly effective in analyzing the organizational appropriation of various resources—from computer technology to experience with other social movement repertoires—that transformed SMRR into a formidable social movement organization. With its predilection for rational and organizational behavior, resource mobilization theory lends itself to the analysis of conscious strategies undertaken by the movement in order to maximize its material and organizational gains. Thus, we were able to pinpoint cost-reducing mechanisms undertaken by a tenants' rights organization that was vastly outspent and faced a deeply rooted community elite with dense networks at its disposal. In Santa Monica, a base was constructed through the incorporation of existing blocs among the population, such as the Democratic Club, CED, organized labor, and the seniors' movement centered around Syd Rose. This base was gradually expanded as the movement became more electorally focused. The results were striking: Six thousand renters participated in the Santa Monica movement by donating money, distributing leaflets, or making telephone calls.

Of vital significance was the movement's ability to mobilize activists from other causes, some of them dating back to the 1960s or even further. Tarrow (1983) has suggested that "cycles of protest" are often centered around a key originating movement, such as the civil rights movement, which provides a mold for other protest activities (see also Whalen and Flacks, 1989; Boyte, 1980; Mannheim, 1928/1972). This argument is certainly borne out in our case study, which revealed that social networks, material support bases, and sheer experience of a sixties protest culture became resources to be mobilized for an eighties movement. The CED organization in particular was likely to attract such seasoned activists. These submerged networks from earlier social movements were ripe for mobilization around tenants' rights. Chains of opportunity left in place by prior movements, government funding for programs such as VISTA, "biographically available" activists, and progressive networks linked to prominent movement entrepreneurs were crucial for constructing a powerful tenants' movement.

Our empirical survey data corroborated these findings. They clearly revealed that the formation of a protest culture had a great deal to do with propensity for activism in Santa Monica as opposed to passivity in Houston. Thus, a key explanatory variable was the impact of the sixties movements, which varied across location as well as generation. This is a partial vindication of resource mobilization theory, but only if it is further combined with insights from its critics.

A resource mobilization perspective also calls attention to the perishable quality of certain resources as the legal, economic, and technological environment of social movements changes. Government funding of VISTA volunteers, SMRR's ability to supply a photocopied and reduced version of the rent control amendment to all voters, the fairness doctrine giving equal television time to opposing views—all of these would have been impossible at a later time.

One of the most important debates that we uncovered was over the appropriate balance between interactional "people power" and "automatic outreach" computer technology. This debate is being experienced by grassroots progressive movements nationwide and is deeply divisive. An over-saturated direct-mail market has prompted the invention of some new outreach strategies (Snow et al., 1986) that are more personalized, including thank you notes and phone calls. By identifying these types of changes in the "social movements sector," resource mobilization theory proves valuable in practice as well as in theory; its findings can become a handbook of successful mobilizing strategies that are transferrable to other settings. It can also identify strategies that have diminishing returns.

## Structural Strain

Of course, organizing skills alone do not explain the emergence of tenants' movements if the situation is not conducive in other ways. Certainly, popular anger over Proposition 13's perceived failure was crucial. In addition, we documented many structural strains relating to the housing crisis in Santa Monica that gave tenants a rising tide of grievances and a perception of injustice. Yet in our study of tenants' movements, the "worsening conditions" argument is given only partial support. We noted that housing conditions (both quality and cost) did not significantly differ between cities that enacted rent control and those that did not. Perceptions and attributions were what mattered. Public actions of the Santa Monica city council made tenants feel that they were second-class citizens compared with property owners, and helped to foster a sense of "relative deprivation." As Fainstein and Fainstein (1974:240-1) have observed, relative deprivation has been a particularly important factor in creating a common consciousness about shared structural positions in urban social movements. Tenant organizers in Santa Monica could use these perceived inequalities as a basis for organizing tenants. In Houston, where no public dialogue about tenants' rights took place and where no culture of dissent existed, tenants remained quiescent. Thus, we found that housing conditions did not necessarily have to be deteriorating, but tenants *did* have to perceive themselves as unjustly treated.

## Framing Ideas

As William Gamson (1988) has pointed out, movements respond not only to "structural conduciveness," but also to "cultural conduciveness." A culture that has certain fundamental tensions and disturbing ambiguities is ripe for a challenging movement, if the movement can frame its claims in a manner that "resonates" culturally with the population it seeks to mobilize (see our discussion in Chapter 4). Ideas compete with each other for the conscience of the community. Using both rationally analytical and emotional appeals, Santa Monica's movement entrepreneurs were very effective at framing their demands in a way that caused a community to rethink the fairness of the position of tenants and landlords. This was true both for prominent and energetic spokespersons, such as Derek Shearer and Ruth Yannatta Goldway, and for grass-roots participants and alternative media at the neighborhood level. Their ideas were critical for framing the movement, drawing on ambivalence about greed and "dog-eat-dog" capitalism, and invoking beliefs about the need for regulated behavior to preserve democracy, the rights of the "little guy" to get ahead, and the appropriateness of protecting senior citizens.

As we documented in Chapter 4, movement leaders were able to draw on and expand existing notions of justice and fairness and to ward off the symbolic efforts of the countermovement. By presenting tenants' rights as a human rights issue, movement strategists could also invoke the "master metaphor" of the civil rights movement (Tarrow, 1983; Snow and Benford, 1988), which not only carried a great deal of credibility, but which many had been deeply influenced by or had personally participated in. Without these skills that mobilized bystanders, the movement could have faltered under the barrage of criticisms hurled at it by well-funded property interests. We therefore agree with Snow et al. (1986:478) that "interpretative resources in general...seem as crucial to the temporal viability and success of an SMO as the acquisition and deployment of more tangible resources."

## New Social Movements

While we agree that there is room for debate concerning whether or not "new social movements" are new, NSM theories were salutary in directing our attention to the symbolic manipulation of information, cross-class mobilization, nontraditional alliances, submerged networks of activism, and the non-political achievements of social movements. In their emphasis on the self-production of identity, they proved crucial to our analysis of the tenants' movement in Santa Monica. An essential movement task for tenants was taking control (or custodianship) over the construction of their own identity in the city instead of having it imposed on them by existing elites. As we documented, they accomplished this through utilizing the media and public demonstrations for "attention calling," through backstage research, and through their skill at framing the fairness debate. The end result was a legitimate identity in the city. The measure of their success was the opposition's appropriation of tenants' language (for example, SMRR's opponents billing themselves as "the real renters' rights team," or landlords wishing to be called "owners") in public discourse. These were far more than political victories; they led to a broader debate about fairness in "civil society" among people who were not themselves tenants.

The Importance of Social Interaction

Much of the success of tenants' efforts depended not only on framing skills, but also on their ability to come together interactively, to express solidarity, to network with activists elsewhere, and to construct a feeling of confidence about their movement. It was this "perceived efficacy" arising from social interaction (Klandermans, 1984) that was particularly lacking in Houston. In alternative subcommunities in Ocean Park or in the black churches in the Pico neighborhood, activists protesting against the "commodity" definition of Santa Monica were able to construct "free spaces" from which they could rehearse their challenging repertoires and build feelings of solidarity. While some of these free spaces eventually led to accusations of "in-clubs" and a new elitism, they permitted social constructions of identity early in the movement that won tenants new respect and political clout. The free spaces were also used as forums for becoming informed about progressive experiments elsewhere and creating a shared vision of a more humane city. Our qualitative methods in particular permitted us to see the ongoing construction of such a vision and to observe how over time social learning took place in the movement.

The social interactional dimension has been highlighted by social-psychological critics of resource mobilization theory, who emphasize not only cognitive definitions of the situation, but also interactional processes and "micromobilization." We found these suggestions to be essential to an understanding of the success of the movement and, on the other hand, of its failures. As tenants achieved a new successful identity in the city, we were able to document the interactional process through which it was accomplished. As the debate over "people power" versus technology unfolded, we found that it was orchestrated in social interactional terms—movement leaders were quintessential resource mobilization theorists, while the grass roots wanted participation. Over time, for reasons we feel went beyond an "aging movement" life-cycle argument, the grass roots distanced itself from the entrepreneurs.

## Construction of Urban Space

Finally, a social construction of urban space perspective not only highlights the "community versus commodity" theme, but calls attention to the social groups that struggle for power over the very definition of urban space. We have observed throughout that tenants' movements are urban movements. In Santa Monica, the tenants' movement broadened the public dialogue concerning the control of urban space. It was able to draw on existing environmentalist sentiments that had mobilized a cross-class, citywide, slow-growth coalition protesting the proposed demolition of the Santa Monica Pier (see Chapter 3). The overabundance of tenants in Santa Monica was itself a "growth" issue, one that traditional elites came to regret. The social construction of urban space perspective, along with NSM theory, draws attention to the fact that space is produced—literally and figuratively—by social groups that have power. However, challenges to power need not come through the working class or workplace mobilization favored by traditional Marxist theorists. Communities under twentieth-century capitalism are equally contested terrain, and they may create new alliances and enmities in which the middle class plays a prominent coalition role. Our case study bears out the validity of this perspective. As a potential subset of *growth-questioning movements*, tenants' movements are on the cutting edge of social movements of the 1990s (see below), along with the environmental movement. They are a potentially powerful force that provides a vehicle for questioning the supremacy of commodity over community.

## A Summary of Our Urban Social Movement Findings

Unlike Engels, to whom housing movements were reformist, we find that urban social movements—including tenants' movements—can mean real change in terms of quality of life and the ongoing definition of human rights. Although the significance of community movements has been hotly debated (Fisher and Kling, 1989; Gottdiener, 1987; Katznelson, 1981), urban tenants' movements in capitalist societies can make a difference. Structuralist Marxists are wrong to dismiss them as inconsequential in terms of distribution of power and wealth. The goal of progressives is to change the ideological emphasis of development from commodity to community. Progressives in Santa Monica successfully negotiated with developers for additional affordable housing units, day-care facilities, parks, affirmative-action hiring, accessibility plans for disabled persons, and improved homeless programs. Moreover, Engels's "iron law of wages," which argues that housing movements—even when successful in lowering shelter costs—will not result in an economic gain by the working class, cannot be supported in our study. We found that tenants in Santa Monica stand to save $1.1 billion in housing payments under the strong rent-control law. Without such controls, most tenants in Santa Monica would be paying an extra $400 to $700 in monthly rent—with working-class tenants being the first to feel the pinch. Studies also show that strong rent controls in other parts of the country can lead to substantial rent savings. While rent-control laws are not without flaws, and while capitalism as a system limits the degree of change, the parameters are wide enough to allow a significant amount of change.

We do not share the traditional Marxist perspective that all urban reform—save class struggle between worker and capitalist— is doomed to fail and provides only symbolic reforms. Santa Monica is a beacon of hope for neighborhoods struggling to create community over commodity. Progressive change is obtainable, but as our study indicates, it is a difficult, fatiguing, often personally painful struggle that demands constant vigilance.[2] Movement organizers make errors that can stall the movement and in some cases put it in a tailspin. Yet when progressives lost their voting majority in Santa Monica's city council from 1984 to 1988, they learned enough important lessons to come back and win the majority from moderate growth machine interests.

Some of our surprising findings included the discovery that, contrary to "commonsense" views, radical beliefs are unaffected by homeowner or tenant status, which should make tenant organizers rethink current as well as proposed housing strategies. We also found that housing conditions do not necessarily have to be deteriorating in order to spark a social movement; rather, a key factor was symbolic framing of perceptions about fairness. While we expected this to be important, its degree of importance was further dramatized by our comparison with Houston. Finally, a major explanatory variable for urban tenants' movements was the existence and strength of previous social movements from the 1960s. Although prior movements could be expected to have some effect, we were surprised by the strength with which they manifested themselves both in our qualitative and quantitative data. This connection needs to be researched further, particularly in view of the stereotype that sees 1960s activism as a passing adolescent fad of little future significance. Our finding also has implications for other movements; in Chapter 1, we asked ourselves whether tenants' movements have created possibilities for future social change action, as participants make their way to other organizations and related causes. Through our qualitative data, we saw the beginnings of such a transfer of resources, as one movement feeds into another.

Our findings thus challenge some traditional assumptions about social movements and indicate some directions for future research. The interaction of groups over housing is still a remarkably underresearched phenomenon in sociology; therefore, our work helps to fill this gap in the literature. In conducting our qualitative and quantitative analysis, we have found patterns that have implications for a more general analysis of social movements, in particular the interplay among ideas, resources, and structural conditions. We hope our work will stimulate further research on housing relations and urban social movements.

This brings us to our final point about social movements theory. Often underplayed in the social movement literature is the role of academic research. In the case of rent control, academic research has played a major role in challenging and demystifying landlord-sponsored research, as well as debunking one of our most powerful cultural myths: the myth of a "free market" where collusion does not take place. Many credit the research of Piven and Cloward (1971, 1979) with laying the essential groundwork for the welfare rights movement in the 1960s. In addition, Michael Harrington's (1962) work is often cited as the book that convinced President John F. Kennedy and the nation to begin the war on poverty. On the other hand, William Tucker's (1987, 1989) attacks on rent control (see below) have fueled protests against regulation and social intervention in the economy. To some degree, academic research increasingly seems to be used to sway the minds of opinion-makers such as the media, elected leaders, celebrities, professors, and elites. In writing this book, we have borne in mind the relationship between ideas and social outcomes. We hope that our effort to incorporate this dimension, and to be self-conscious about our role in the process, is a further contribution to a full analysis of social movements. For this reason, we devote the remainder of this chapter to exploring the social consequences of traditional versus progressive paradigms for the housing crisis in the United States, concluding with some practical suggestions.

## America's Housing Crisis

During the 1990s, one of the most important domestic problems facing America will be affordable housing. The amount of tenants' income going into rent has reached record levels, with over half paying rents that are unaffordable by government standards. Over one quarter of the renter households devote at least one half of their household income to rent. Since 1970, rents have tripled, with tenants' income only doubling. Ownership and control of rental housing are increasingly concentrated, leading to uncompetitive practices. Growing waiting lists for public housing have forced two out of three cities to close their lists to new applicants. A million homeless people sleep in our cities' streets and shelters. For individuals over seventy, one out of every two require barrier-free designs, such as ramps, rails, or wide doorways. The percentage of American households owning homes has steadily fallen since 1980. Looking into the future, some analysts estimate that the number of households paying unaffordable housing payments will reach eight million by the year 2003 (Appelbaum, 1990:258).

Ordinary citizens have often been ahead of government administrations in perceiving these problems. As we pointed out in Chapter 2, a recent national opinion poll found that next to AIDS, inadequate housing was considered the most important domestic problem facing America. Moreover, seven out of every ten Americans feel that the Bush administration has not shown enough concern for the homeless (Gilderbloom, 1990a). Belated and somewhat limited recognition of the problem has led to at least symbolic efforts to respond to homelessness and housing affordability, in part to ward off grass-roots responses such as those in Santa Monica.

## Conventional Explanation: Competitive Housing Markets and Government Interference

Housing analysis in the United States has been dominated by free market economists. Accordingly, government has been blamed for any housing problem: Government zoning laws, building codes, historic preservation, public housing, tax shelters and rent control distort the market, which, in turn, results in high rents, homelessness, and low homeownership rates. While conservative economists tend to favor demand-side strategies and liberal economists support supply-side programs, few question the assumptions of the free market. In part, this reticence to criticize supply/demand theory was influenced by a belief that no housing crisis existed during the past ten years.

Social scientists have played an important role in developing this perspective. They have assumed that the rental housing market is competitive, with little collusion between landlords. This conception of how housing becomes priced, while grounded in human ecology and neoclassical economics, is shared by the popular press, lawmakers, real estate interests, and even some tenant organizations. According to Logan and Molotch (1987:4), the "centrality of markets and the assumption of a free market system have been major elements in the reasoning of urban social science since it first began." Human ecology, which is the dominant urban sociological perspective in America, presupposes that markets are freely competitive—"a school of thought so deeply immersed in free market reasoning that its practitioners seem not to have been aware that there was even an alternate approach" (Logan and Molotch, 1987:4). Park (1952:228; see also 150) saw the urban land market as little different from the competition that exists in plant and animal communities.

Given the vested interests, the lack of diversity in paradigms, and the cultural biases evident in mainstream analyses of housing problems in the United States, we argued in Chapter 1 that there is a special need for more sociological research into this subject. We have responded by focusing on tenants as a pivotal social group whose efforts to control urban space and to emphasize community over commodity bring together issues of democracy, economic systems, and grass-roots citizens' movements for social change. We believe that social scientists bear a heavy responsibility: They either help societies and governments to deny their problems or they risk debunking myths that penalize large numbers of people who are hurt by those more powerful. Social science should work for more humane and democratic systems and, in doing so, should be willing to reach beyond conventional paradigms.

The Social Consequences of Denial:
Federal Government Cutbacks In Housing Programs

Conventional social-scientific explanations of housing markets in the United States have made it easy for government administrations either to deny that a problem exists or to blame the problem on excessive government interference. Thus, while rents have been rapidly rising, Presidents Reagan and Bush have slashed housing assistance funds by more than two thirds during their administrations.[3] These deep budget cuts are justified by the assertion that, in reality, no rental housing crisis exists. In fact, the President's Commission on Housing (1983:xvii, 9–11) optimistically concluded that "Americans today are the best-housed people in history, with affordability problems limited to the poor."

The budget knife has cut especially deeply into housing programs targeted for the poor. During the pre-Reagan era, government was subsidizing about 350,000 units a year; by the end of the 1980s, this fell to roughly 80,000 units annually (Kuttner, 1990:24). HUD hopes to sell or demolish 100,000 public housing units over the next five years, and previous commitments for some 250,000 low-income units have been canceled. Public housing tenants must now spend 30 percent of their incomes on rent (rather than the previous 25 percent), while recipients of rent supplements will also be required to devote higher proportions of their incomes to housing. Currently, it is estimated that only 27 percent of the households that qualify for low-income housing supplements get assistance from the government. Compare these housing expenditures for low- and moderate-income persons with the generous $47 billion a year subsidy to middle-class homeowners in the form of mortgage interest write-offs, rollover on capital gains, and local property tax deductions. In fact, over 81 percent of these subsidies go to households that have an annual income of more than $50,000 (Institute for Policy Studies, 1989:19). In recent years, federal programs have dwindled down to a handful of approaches: publicly owned housing, a limited amount of subsidized new construction, and rent supplements to reduce partly the gap between market rents and what the very poorest tenants can afford to pay—with a budget appropriation of $8 billion a year.

A logical consequence of the belief system that produced these programs is U.S. Secretary of Housing Jack Kemp's view that the key ingredient for affordable housing is the unconstrained free market where government does not regulate zoning, planning, environmental factors, historic preservation, and building code inspections. According to Kemp (1990) in the Heritage Foundation sponsored *Policy Review,* these types of government interventions are largely the cause of the nation's housing crisis. He argues that government regulation has caused a 30 percent increase in housing costs. Only one city in the nation approximates Kemp's prescription for solving housing problems through lack of regulation: Houston. If Kemp is correct that government regulation and interference are the chief culprits in the housing crisis, Houston should be a conservatives' textbook example of a city without a homeless or affordability problem. Yet Houston mirrors other large American cities by having a major housing crisis, with most experts predicting a worsening of the situation in the 1990s.

Houston's Housing Crisis

As we discussed in Chapter 6, conservatives often point to Houston as a city that has "resolved its housing crisis." Such an argument is without any empirical support. It is, however, supported by the ideology that the free market solves all problems—a belief that died a slow death in Santa Monica and led to a massive tenants' movement. Even with a 20 percent rental housing vacancy rate, no zoning, and little planning, Houston has a major housing problem, with 10,000–15,000 homeless persons, 18,000 persons waiting for public housing, 500,000 low- and moderate-income persons paying unaffordable housing payments, one fourth of the low-income persons living in overcrowded housing, and a zero vacancy rate for housing accessible to the disabled. Despite this serious problem, up to 24,000 rental units will be demolished in the next five to seven years because of the absence of community organizations trained to convert these units into co-ops (Bivins, 1988:5,1). In 1987 approximately 10,000 apartment units were torn down (Bivins, 1988:5,1). Most analysts predict that the problem of high housing costs in Houston will escalate in the 1990s. Barton Smith, senior associate at the Center for Public Policy at the University of Houston, predicts that rents may double by 1992. More than half of Houston's renters, most of whom are low- and moderate-income families, are paying an excessive amount into rent.

Houston's plight is related to the domination of the city's agenda by business elites and the lack of grass-roots citizens' movements that could push for progressive options. As we noted in Chapters 3 and 6, housing and neighborhood conditions are worse in Houston, yet Santa Monica's tenants were more supportive of rent control and believed in the efficacy of grass-roots movements. We found that it was not objective conditions, but political culture and experience with other social movements—particularly those of the 1960s— that made a difference. In Houston, the few hopeful scenarios that we documented in recent times were the results of some incipient grass-roots movements that have begun to alter the city's agenda. Therefore, to the question "Do progressive urban social movements matter?" our answer is yes. The "life chances" of a tenant in Santa Monica are much better than they are in Houston. Yet, because progressive movements run against the tide of an established "free enterprise" culture, they are full of pitfalls, internal tensions, and external constraints, some of which are clearly visible in Santa Monica (see below).

The Progressive Paradigm

Conventional housing analysis came under attack in the 1980s, and an alternative paradigm to mainstream economics began to evolve. The progressive paradigm—rooted in power/conflict sociology—made the following arguments: (1) a housing crisis exists for many renters, seniors, disabled, and single mothers; (2) housing markets are the cause rather than the solution to the housing crisis; and (3) a community-based housing program is the most efficient, humane, and affordable approach to the problem. Contrary to some structuralist Marxist assumptions, the progressive paradigm views housing affordability as attainable under capitalism. Representatives of this perspective give "equal emphasis to organization and rules through which economic behavior is mediated. . .they assume that abstract laws of demand and supply are only one of the elements of economic behavior" (Quadeer, 1981:176).

This perspective can shed important light on housing processes that cannot be properly understood by the other major paradigms. As we noted in Chapter 2, this perspective is rooted in a Weberian analysis that examines how scarce and fundamental resources within a spatial dimension are distributed, who decides this allocation, and what impact these spatial arrangements have on an individual's life chances.[4] "Gatekeepers and managers" along with opposition groups become the focus in a Weberian urban analysis. In the case of rental housing, for example, the actions of bankers, landlords, public officials, and tenant organizations are central in the location, access, and price of shelter.

According to this paradigm, the housing analyst cannot "presuppose" that the market is perfectly competitive, without first assessing possible social and political interventions in the marketplace. The presence of these "market imperfections" is an important determinant of whether the unregulated market can produce relatively affordable housing. These concerns are, for the most part, ignored by mainstream analysts and are underestimated by recent government administrations. Yet they are part of the "structural strains" that can lead to the emergence of tenants' movements. Given the fact that the past two presidential administrations were buttressed by conventional economic analysis, it is not surprising that they were caught napping when it came to one of the nation's most severe problems—housing accessibility. Yet, as we pointed out above, their views do not reflect those of ordinary citizens; housing the poor is seen as one of the most serious domestic problems facing the United States.

## Santa Monica's Challenge

Just as Houston's problems are due in part to an unquestioned belief in free market solutions, Santa Monica's search for solutions flows from grass-roots pressures and a progressive paradigm. Until 1978, it was managed like any other U.S. city. A "growth machine" consisting of banks, real estate interests, the local newspaper, and commercial interests had the final say on most political matters—especially development issues (Molotch, 1976). Although the proportion of tenants living in the city rose dramatically, the city council viewed them as second-class citizens and believed tenants could have no political impact.

Contrary to these expectations, when rising rents became an issue, tenants in Santa Monica, beginning with senior citizens, organized for a voter referendum on rent-control. Initially, rent-control proponents lost by a narrow margin. Aside from the fact that the tenants' pro-rent-control campaign was poorly funded and organized, landlords were able to argue successfully that rent control was not the answer to tenant woes. Instead, the landlords contended that the answer was Proposition 13, which cut landlord taxes by at least half. When Proposition 13 failed to deliver the promised reductions, rent control was again put on the ballot, this time by a more experienced and resource-rich coalition of social movement organizations. Victory soon followed for the renters' rights coalition—which brought together old and young activists, tenants from different socioeconomic groups, and some homeowners. After the rent-control ordinance was enacted, a slate of pro-rent-control candidates was elected to the city's rent-control board and city council. The central theme of their campaign was the defense of the rent-control law from landlord court challenges.

As we documented, the tenants' rights activists who gained control of the city council won not only rent control, but also the chance to experiment with a progressive political program that provided tangible benefits for the city's eighty percent tenant constituency as well as other groups traditionally disenfranchised from local politics. Unlike the Houston approach to the housing problem, the progressive political program addressed the needs of tenants and inspired them to vote.

The renters' rights coalition, a politically progressive platform at the local level, campaigned for rent controls, cooperative housing, limited commercial expansion, inclusionary zoning programs, farmers' markets, food cooperatives, neighborhood anticrime efforts, and controls on toxic wastes. The city attempted to democratize city hall by funding numerous neighborhood organizations, appointing citizen task forces and commissions, and making extensive use of public hearings. The linkage policies institutionalized the idea of trade-offs between neighborhood groups and developers to preserve and balance community needs.

As we examined in great detail in Chapters 3, 4, and 5, Santa Monica's progressive agenda halted economic displacements and empowered new groups of social actors to enter into the debate about the appropriate use of urban space. At the same time, it propelled urban policy into a new set of dilemmas concerning housing, development, and the city's relation to its minority communities. In the sense that the progressive model moved beyond an inadequate free market solution, these were creative dilemmas, permitting urban theorists to examine a new set of problems and challenges. Yet the effort also reaped enormous bitterness and factionalism. Because it was a departure from traditional beliefs about tenants and urban spaces, it threatened some groups in the city and unrealistically raised the level of expectations for others. It also caused some elected members of the SMRR coalition to make hasty decisions that led to accusations of nondemocratic behavior. In view of these criticisms, the contrasting "ideal type" of Houston is a salutary reminder of the consequences for urban residents of a traditional free market solution. Below we will examine some of the new dilemmas raised by the social movement in Santa Monica, but first we will address the issue of rent control as a housing strategy and as a social movement goal.

### Rent Control in the United States as a Housing Strategy

In Chapter 1, we justified our focus on rent control as an outcome of tenants' movements. We noted its popularity as a grass-roots organizing strategy, and we found that its frequency enabled us to engage in comparisons and to assess a particular social movement goal. Because the rent-control issue can function both as a mobilizing tool and as a program addressing the housing crisis, we will consider these issues separately, beginning with the latter.

Evidence exists that the private market cannot produce affordable low- and moderate-income housing. Consequently, tenants' groups are looking to rent control to help solve the housing crisis. During the past fifteen years, over two hundred cities in the United States have enacted rent control— including Los Angeles, San Francisco, Washington, D.C., and Boston. Currently, 10 percent of the nation's renters are covered by some form of rent regulation. Cities that have adopted rent control recognize that the "market" is no longer free.

Concentration of ownership and collusion by landlord management firms are a growing problem in most rental housing markets. In New York and Houston 5 percent of all landlords control over 50 percent of the rental housing stock. In rent-controlled Boston twenty individuals own 40 percent of the rental housing stock. Increasingly, local apartment owners associations are telling their members "where, when, how and what dollar amount to raise rents" (Gilderbloom and Appelbaum, 1988).

Given these kinds of problems, rent control is a logical and reasonable alternative to the market. Yet, to present it as a viable alternative requires a good deal of framing work by tenant activists. Moreover, since it is an example of regulation of free enterprise, it generates controversy and an objective assessment is difficult—even in the "ivory tower" world of academia. Rent control has been alternately presented as a scourge that does more harm than "dropping a bomb" on a city and as a welcome solution to gentrification and rent gouging. As we pointed out in Chapter 1, it has been a contested strategy both on the right and on the left of the political spectrum—the right objecting to government regulation, the left arguing the futility of reformist movements in a larger capitalist structure. What does the evidence show, and what are its implications for social movements? Once again, one's paradigm as a social investigator makes a difference.

In purely economic terms, most modern rent-control ordinances serve primarily to avert large rent increases, bringing highly inflationary housing markets more into line with others. Rent control has also provided protection against arbitrary evictions, incentives for maintaining units, and reasonable rent increases. This is due primarily to the nature of most modern rent-control ordinances, which typically exempt newly constructed housing, guarantee a fair and reasonable return on investment, and allow for annual rent adjustments to cover increases in operating costs (Gilderbloom and Appelbaum, 1988).

Credible research concerning homelessness, rent control, and other important urban issues is often buried by an avalanche of pseudo-research orchestrated by landlord public relations firms. These firms work feverishly to convince the public that rent control and regulation in general are destructive. Yet, their claims have been empirically challenged repeatedly. A systematic review of twenty recently published scholarly studies of modern rent control finds that such regulations have not caused a decline in construction, maintenance, or taxable value of property relative to uncontrolled units (Gilderbloom, 1981a, Appelbaum and Gilderbloom, 1990). Studies arguing the reverse are generally funded by landlord organizations with a direct stake in the studies' outcome. Anti-rent-control research is "characterized by data rendered suspect because of nonrepresentative sampling and highly selective statistics" (Gilderbloom, 1981a). Moreover, not one of these anti-rent-control studies has appeared in a reputable academic journal.

Perhaps the most prominent example of this kind of erroneous and deceptive research was an article in the *National Review* by journalist William Tucker (1987), claiming that rent control causes homelessness. This article garnered national media attention in such publications as the *New York Times,* the *Wall Street Journal,* and *Parade* magazine, and led Congress to demand that HUD study the issue. A careful reexamination of the data shows no such relationship exists between homelessness and regulation. Tucker's analysis is flawed by numerous methodological and statistical errors. First, Tucker used the dubious estimates of the HUD survey of homelessness for sixty cities and proceeded to drop twenty-six of these cities from his analysis. Second, Tucker chose fifteen additional cities to include with the thirty-four cities from the HUD study. Third, Tucker mislabeled one of the cities he chose as rent-controlled. A regression analysis that examined the HUD data exclusively, controlled for appropriate variables, and correctly identified regulated cities found no correlation between rent control and homelessness (Appelbaum et al., 1990).[5] Furthermore, Tucker's own data do not support his conclusion. For example, three of the four cities cited in the study with the worst homeless problems are non-rent-controlled cities. Yet, Tucker's work won easy acceptance and was widely disseminated because it supports the "free enterprise is best" ideology and conventional explanations of the housing crisis.

Types of Rent Control

There are important differences between various types of rent control. Rent-control laws provide protection against extreme rent increases, unjust evictions, and poor maintenance. These kinds of protections usually do not exist for tenants in the absence of controls. Within the United States, three major forms of rent-control laws exist: stringent, strong, and moderate. The stringent rent-control laws (postwar New York is the classic example) virtually froze rents for over two decades. They set rents without regard for landlords' returns on their investment, and, most studies have found, resulted in such negative consequences as disinvestment in rental housing and a general decline in construction, maintenance, and overall rental property value.

Attempts to avoid these problems resulted in the introduction of moderate rent controls during the early 1970s. Moderate rent controls guarantee a "fair and reasonable return" competitive with other kinds of investments with similar risks. In order to meet this criterion of guaranteeing a "fair return," most moderate rent-control ordinances share the following features: exemption of new construction, requiring adequate maintenance as a condition of rent increases, guaranteed annual increases as necessary to cover increases in operating costs, and provisions for pass-throughs of major capital cost increases. Moderate rent control allows for rent increases that approximate increases in the consumer price index. The rent-control board generally consists of two landlords, two tenants, and one homeowner appointed by the city council. The administration of such laws is generally underfunded and understaffed.

A third form of rent regulation, known as strong rent control, arose during the late 1970s because moderate controls simply "stabilized" rents, resulting in the maintenance of excessive rent burdens for many tenants covered by moderate regulations. Tenant activists noted that moderate rent control had failed to produce a reduction in the proportion of income going toward rent. Strong rent control called for rent increases that were approximately one half of the consumer price index, no vacancy decontrol, and a well-funded administration. The rent-control board was made up of members more sympathetic to tenant needs than to landlord interests. Finally, strong rent controls were the *result of mass based tenant movements* that focused on assuming the reins of power for the entire city.

A sociologically accurate reading of rent control must take these differences into account, rather than lumping them all together under the heading of "regulation." The success or failure of rent control is generally dependent on the type of rent control enacted. Most of the cities that have adopted rent regulation during the past fifteen years have opted for moderate rent controls. Moderate rent control has not achieved significant rent relief. Gilderbloom (1986) examined the mean rents for 1970 and 1980 for twenty-six rent-controlled and thirty-seven non-rent-controlled cities from an earlier study (Gilderbloom, 1984). His data revealed that the average percentage rent increase between 1970 and 1980 was virtually identical for the rent-controlled cities (105 percent) and non-rent-controlled cities (106 percent). Similar results were arrived at by Heffley and Santerre (1985:22) in their study of 101 rent-controlled cities in New Jersey. These data suggest that the impact of New Jersey's rent-control law on rents has been simply to match rent increases with the non-controlled sector.

However, the evidence is different for cities such as Berkeley and Santa Monica that enacted strong rent-control ordinances. These cases reveal that redistribution of wealth between landlords and tenants has taken place. In an analysis of Santa Monica's strong rent controls, Richard Appelbaum (1986) estimated that the average percentage of income going into rent will fall from 23 percent in 1986 to 17 percent by 1997. He also concluded that the number of unaffordable units (renters paying more than 30 percent of their income toward rent) will fall by 39 percent in 1997—from 15,360 units to 9,387. Appelbaum estimated that the income transfer from renters to landlords over the next eleven years will be over $1.1 billion. Appelbaum (1986a) reached similar conclusions in his analysis of Berkeley's and West Hollywood's strong rent-control laws.

Strong rent-control ordinances operate to redistribute wealth from landlord to tenant, while moderate rent-control ordinances simply stabilize rent levels relative to other unregulated markets. The effectiveness of rent control as a strategy for tenants' movements, therefore, depends largely on the type of rent control enacted. As we documented in the case of Santa Monica, tenant activists learned from their networks in other cities about the failures of moderate rent controls and therefore lobbied for a strong law.

Academic research on the subject of rent control has impacts in the "real world." Appelbaum (1986), operating from a progressive paradigm, finds rent controls to be useful and effective. Tucker, on the other hand, operating from a conventional urban paradigm, associates rent controls with worsening urban problems, including homelessness. The Appelbaum research justifies movements for social change, while Tucker's research upholds the status quo and fuels countermovements. This was reflected in recent landlords' protests against rent controls in Santa Monica (see Chapter 4); they used homeless people as props, accusing progressive officials of causing homelessness.

Despite the gains for tenants in cities that have strong rent-control laws, the future of rent control by itself as a housing strategy is questionable due to outside interference and other aspects of the housing crisis. We will return to this issue below, but first we consider rent control as a social movement strategy.

### Rent Control as a Mobilizing Strategy: Outcomes for Social Movements

Rent control is not only a housing program; it is also a tool for mobilizing social movement participation for broader goals. Santa Monica provides an important case study of the kinds of political and economic gains tenants can make by organizing themselves as a collective force.[6] By "networking" with tenants' groups around the nation, Santa Monica's tenants were able to institute a strong rent-control law that had a redistributive impact and that halted the process of displacement. It also promoted a new social definition of fairness in the community and gave tenants first-class citizenship. The participation of tenants and their supporters—"bystanders" or "third parties" who had nothing immediately to gain from rent control but responded to the fairness issue—led to a very high mobilization and participation rate in the initial movement (see Chapter 3) and to broad electoral participation in future elections of progressive candidates.

Rent-control efforts are not only associated with protection against arbitrary rent increases, election of pro-tenant officials, and reform of landlord/tenant laws. In addition, a movement for rent control is associated with the building of a broad-based tenant coalition (Lawson, 1983; Baar, 1977; Čapek, 1985). As we pointed out in Chapter 2, this is often a cross-class coalition that includes seniors, low- and moderate-income persons, and minorities, among others. Women often have a prominent leadership role in tenant movements. During the past ten years, women have been elected presidents of statewide tenant associations in New Jersey and California, while many citywide organizations are also headed by women. The bringing together of individuals from a range of economic, racial, ethnic, and age groups not only breaks down stereotypes and creates new grass-roots alliances; it also teaches tenants that better housing conditions are accomplished through collective action.

Coalitions incorporating tenants' issues have been instrumental in electing progressive candidates in various parts of the country. In March 1981, the voters of Vermont's largest city, Burlington, voted out of the mayor's office a five-term conservative Democrat and elected Bernard Sanders, a self-proclaimed socialist. Sanders focused on the basic issues confronting Burlington's large blue-collar population: high rents, unchecked development, property taxes, and neighborhood preservation. Sanders's victory was largely attributed to his pro-tenant stance, which drew together a coalition of tenants, senior citizens, municipal unions, and liberal homeowners. During the election, Sanders appealed to their votes by proclaiming:

People are literally not eating in order to pay their rent and fuel bills. . . . The issue here is that people have been exploited, thrown out of houses. In Burlington a tenant has no rights at all. Hundreds of people have been forced to move from apartments in Burlington because of rent increases. It's about time tenants have legal protection (McKee, 1981:8).

Similar appeals to the "tenant vote" were used successfully in electing David Sullivan to the Cambridge city council and Peter Shapiro to the powerful position of Essex County Executive in New Jersey (Krinsky, 1981:10; Atlas and Dreier, 1981:8). In Ithaca, Santa Cruz, Berkeley, and West Hollywood, tenant activists have also been successful in electing progressive slates to city office. The election of Mayor Ray Flynn in Boston was due, in part, to his strong pro-tenant identification. A historic Tenants' Rights Bill was passed in 1987 by the city of Chicago. Because tenants have organized, their issues have become increasingly visible.

Tenants have also played a role in reforming archaic landlord/tenant laws. This has been especially true in New Jersey, which has the most progressive landlord/tenant law of any state in the United States today. The key has been

organized grass-roots activism. Through the efforts of the New Jersey Tenants
Organization (NJTO), over one hundred cities there currently have rent control
(Atlas and Dreier, 1981:34). NJTO has passed numerous pro-tenant laws that
affect security deposits, eviction for just cause, receivership, state income tax
credits, and landlord disclosure of ownership. The laws that have been passed
by NJTO have been used as models by other tenant groups and successfully
passed in cities and states around the nation. As a movement-building strategy,
therefore, this type of networking over issues of tenant laws and rent control
has been very successful.

In Chapter 1, we remarked that the issue of regulation reveals broader
tensions between beliefs about economic systems and democracy in U.S.
culture, with tenants playing an important social role as a "test case" for beliefs
about fairness. This led us to investigate the possibility of tenants' movements
being part of a general "cultural drift" toward redefining notions of justice
in our society, based on the housing problems' high visibility due to grass-
roots mobilizations. In this regard, tenants' movements have some general
implications.

The debate over whether a city should adopt a rent-control ordinance,
although centered around the rights of landlords versus the rights of tenants,
is about a broader set of issues. When people affirm the need for rent control—
through either referendum or their elected officials—they state that landlords'
private property rights are not absolute. Rather, the needs of the landlord must
be balanced with the needs of the tenant. The traditional sanctity of private
property rights falls under public scrutiny (Harvey, 1979), and the fairness
of the overall system is debated. As new social movement theorists such as
Melucci (1985) argue, this bringing of private issues into the public arena is
often an important accomplishment of recent movements. Where citizens
support rent control as fair, landlords no longer have the right to raise rents
to unlimited amounts. Instead, rents must be geared to rates reasonable for
both tenant and landlord.

Once rent control is enacted, the parameters of the discussion are changed
even further. According to John Atlas and Peter Dreier (1980a:11):

> In these areas where people have fought for rent control, it is always
> attacked as anti-free enterprise and anti-business. After victory the debate
> shifts to what level of profit the landlord deserves: for example, six years
> ago most New Jersey tenants believed landlords could charge as much
> as they wanted, just like any business (That's the way it has been, that's
> the way it is). Now many believe that a landlord's need for profit must
> be balanced against the tenant's needs for an affordable and decent place
> to live. These are important changes in people's consciousness.

The fact that progressive activists have successfully framed tenants' rights issues and rent control as positive measures reveals the ambiguity in U.S. culture regarding the "free market" and its fairness. Furthermore, the basis for tenants' rights leads back to an argument for community (people have a right to be respected as first-class citizens in their communities, whether they own property or not) and against commodity (neighborhoods are about more than economics, and therefore should not be sold to the highest bidder). The issue becomes human rights versus property rights; it raises important political and economic questions about how housing is to be produced and distributed, and how urban space should be defined.

Where strong tenants' movements have taken place, as in Santa Monica, the general population is often more willing to organize against the "commodification" of urban space than to be resigned to "that's just the way it is." Increasingly, there are environmentalist slow-growth and in some cases no-growth movements in U.S. cities that protest such commodification and that mobilize powerful, new cross-class coalitions (Gottdiener, 1985). Tenants' movements, by effectively tying growth issues to economic displacement of community residents, can prepare the way for these more general dialogues about "the good city."

Although a "reformist" measure, rent control has potentially radical implications as a challenge to the individualism and market arguments of a private property culture. Urban tenants' movements reveal that social policy is not simply an instrument of class domination, as the structuralist Marxist view claims; rather, social policy is contested by groups that are more or less successful at organizing themselves and gaining supporters. Government policies and programs, especially those of a distributional nature, are an object of struggle between propertied and nonpropertied groups. Consequently, the debate over rent control has had an important political impact. It has taught tenants that, in order for housing conditions to improve, they must get involved in the political system. They must vote for referendums and elect political candidates who represent their interests. Traditionally, tenants have been apathetic toward the political system, but when confronted with an issue that directly affects them, and on which they believe they can have an impact, they respond.

The struggle for decent housing links various disenfranchised groups into an organized body demanding greater economic and political change in all spheres of life. The participation of middle-income groups is often crucial (Feagin and Čapek, 1991), but solely to emphasize a self-interested "middle-class radicalism," as Mark Kann (1986) does, is to miss the point of tenants' movements. They are significant because they are able to create new coalitions around fairness issues that emerge from the contradictory heart of U.S. culture.

While it is certainly true that the economic gains made by the tenants' movement in most cities have been moderate, it appears likely that more radical

rent reduction programs will appear on future public agendas. It should also
be kept in mind that the tenants' movement in the United States is relatively
new. In 1969, there was very little tenant activity in the United States; only
a few cities had rent control or tenants' unions. Today, the tenants' movement
is a force that politicians are only beginning to address, as provisions for decent
and affordable housing continue to be limited. Given the willingness of the
courts to uphold enacted rent-control regulations (we observed in the Santa
Monica case study that opponents of rent control had to resort to interference
by the state legislature), there certainly appears to be a "cultural drift" toward
more economic democracy in the definition of housing rights. On the other
hand, tenants' movements do not spring up just anywhere; urban social
movement theory has helped us to understand why and how they take place.

## Limits of the Rent-Control Strategy

In Chapter 1, we noted the wide array of activity around rent control and
suggested that this constituted a potential general movement for expanded housing
rights. Although this activity has permitted tenant activists to learn from each
other and to disseminate successful models nationwide, this is still a far cry from
an organized national tenants' movement. According to Atlas and Dreier (1988:9):

> The strength of tenant activism is uneven. Real estate organizations can
> easily out-spend tenant groups in terms of campaign contributions,
> referendum ballot campaigns, and other aspects of political influence-
> peddling. Tenant activism is most successful where middle-income and
> low-income tenants work together; where tenants represent at least 40
> percent of a municipality's population; where tenants tend to live in larger
> (20 or more unit) buildings; and where tenant groups are able to form
> coalitions with community, religious, labor, and other organizations. So
> far, the tenant movement's strength is concentrated in a few places—
> New Jersey, New York, California, and Massachusetts, with some
> successes in other areas. . . . Efforts to organize tenants on a national basis
> have proven unsuccessful.

Santa Monica is a particularly interesting case because symbolic and
cultural resources were used to neutralize the material resources of real estate
groups. This was an inspiring example of the power of nonmonetary resources
and skilled organizing. Yet, the Santa Monica case, too, is fraught with
problems. Despite the concerns with social justice and with democratizing how
essential goods are distributed, the surest appeal to voters has been through
"pocketbook issues." While the progressive movement attempted to expand

the agenda, elections in Santa Monica often collapsed it into the more narrow issue of protecting rent control. As Derek Shearer (1984c) observed, "Narrow, pocketbook grievances, it seems, cannot sustain a mass political movement." SMRR electioneers became increasingly wedded to a proven formula (see Chapter 3). While the initial progressive administration truly did engage in "transformational interventions in space" and efforts to promote community self-management (Gottdiener, 1985), the later elections focused on the economic benefits of rent control. This meant that alternatives that would have created new affordable housing, such as housing cooperatives, went unexplored. While Santa Monica's politics had a transformative potential, then, they fell short of the promise. Over time, SMRR campaigns minimized ideology and maximized talk of economic benefits. This is not a problem unique to the tenants' movement in Santa Monica, however (Fainstein,1985:558).

The role of ideology in the tenants' movement in the United States is currently being debated nationwide among both grass-roots activists and academic theorists (Heskin, 1983; Fisher, 1984, 1987). Fisher (1987) has proposed that tenants' movements have suffered as a result of their emphasis on "nonideological" organizing and a narrow focus on the single issue of housing. He concluded that organizers, drawing on an Alinsky-influenced model that focuses on material self-interest, have seen ideology as an obstacle to organizing and have dismissed it. Thus, while "Tenant organizing has the potential to introduce a counterideology . . . . this has rarely occurred and with too little impact" (Fisher, 1987:16). Fisher claims, along with Boyte (1980), that mobilizing ideologies need to be grounded and framed according to day-to-day community traditions, with a focus on a larger vision that extends beyond material self-interest. We have seen that this lesson, drawing on the work of social movement theorists such as Gramsci (1971) and Rudé (1980), was taken to heart by Santa Monica progressives. "Framing" was responsible for some of their impressive victories regarding social policy, many of which have been quietly institutionalized. Nevertheless, the increasing concern with electoral politics minimized the ideological content of the issues. This debate over ideology puts tenants' movements at the focal point of discussions about appropriate strategies for social change in the United States today.

Santa Monica's strong rent-control law, ironically, contains yet another pitfall that can serve as a lesson to other movements. This is what Adamson and Borgos (1984) refer to as the "crisis of victory." Because Santa Monica's law included strong protections for tenants, it had a demobilizing function. Tenants felt safe and were lulled into believing that the law would protect them without their having to protect the law. Instead, the law has been under continuous assault since the day it was passed and most recently has been weakened by legislation signed by Republican governor Deukmejian of California. Unlike tenants, landlords have remained mobilized and have made a strong public showing at rent-control board meetings (see Chapter 5). This has weakened the position of the rent-control board and has led it to make some concessions to landlords, such as the discussion in 1984 of a pilot program that allowed landlord pass-throughs of fees to tenants for repairs, a 6 percent allowable increase in 1990 and in 1991 a likely 10 percent to 20 percent increase in rents on vacated units. Tenants felt betrayed; however, as rent board member Wayne Bauer observed, "There's not much of a social movement going on around rent control in Santa Monica...we wouldn't be *talking* incentives or pilot program if there was a strong, organized tenants' union in the city."[7] The lack of mobilization on the part of tenants also meant that there was no ongoing cultivation of leadership drawn from progressive constituencies that would match the scale of that provided by traditional elites.

There is also the question of "backlash" and the mobilization of countermovements. The rent-control concept has been threatening enough that it has caused communities attempting to institute regulation to be targeted by organized real estate coalitions. Where these have been unable to defeat initiatives locally, they have lobbied at the state and national level against rent control. The Ellis Bill is able to override some of the provisions that protect tenants even in the strong Santa Monica rent-control law, a reminder of the "fragile nature of most progressive innovations" (Bach et al., 1982:23). Meanwhile, real estate organizations have successfully enacted laws prohibiting rent control in a number of states such as Texas, Colorado, and Arizona. Progressive movements are still accumulating experience compared with elites that have made public decisions for years. Often the novelty of the situation and the atmosphere of siege contribute to tensions within progressive groups themselves. Moreover, gender inequality and racial tensions continue to plague even those organizations with progressive aspirations.

Rent control might continue to be a part of housing policy if the current federal administration continues to cut sharply back on low- and moderate-income housing programs that are aimed primarily at subsidizing the incomes of poor renters and building public housing. In addition, professional real estate analyses suggest that rents might increase anywhere from 15 percent to 20 percent in an effort to compensate for the loss of tax shelters. Landlords' efforts to have strong rent-control ordinances outlawed were defeated when the U.S. Supreme Court upheld the constitutionality of such laws. With sharp reductions in federal housing programs, tenants will have to seek local solutions. The existence of homeless advocacy groups in cities across the United States provides an important resource base for local advocacy as well as for mobilizing around legislation at the state and national level. Rent control should be one of the big issues in the next ten years, but the debate will simmer around the issue of whether it is symbolic or redistributive politics (Edelman, 1967).

Nevertheless, the benefits of rent control are often small—given the magnitude of unaffordable rents—and the efforts required to enact and maintain them are enormous (Stone, 1983). Many tenant organizers have come to question the efficacy of rent control as the chief objective of the tenants' movement, with many now advocating other innovative housing programs in addition to rent control. Large-scale cooperative housing programs for low- and moderate-income persons are becoming the main organizing theme of numerous tenants' rights groups (Gilderbloom, 1981b:212–60; Lawson, 1984; Bratt, 1989).

## Toward a Progressive Housing Program for the 1990s

### Community-based Housing Programs

The progressive paradigm puts a considerable amount of emphasis on democratic small-scale management of housing developments as the key to resolving the crisis. While a great deal of research has documented the extent of the housing crisis and the inability of the market to supply affordable housing, little work has been done to show that a community-based housing program is a viable alternative. [8]

Community-based housing programs are a decentralized housing strategy emphasizing empowerment of nonprofit community groups to produce, rehabilitate, manage, or own housing for low-income persons. Most of the decision-making is done by people who reside in the housing. Restrictions are placed on the resale price to insure that the housing remains affordable. The government facilitates community-based housing programs by providing technical advice and funding. Bratt (1989) finds that community-based housing is superior compared with other kinds of low-income shelter programs.

Cooperatives are perhaps the most effective way of reducing housing costs. [9] They have lower costs because interest rate payments are not subject to escalation and developer fees are eliminated. Cooperatives with resale restrictions offer a useful example of attractive multifamily community-based housing since they provide many of the guarantees ordinarily associated with homeownership. Such cooperatives are operated through a nonprofit corporation that holds a single mortgage on the property. The corporation is operated by an elected board of directors. Under a typical arrangement, each new owner purchases a share for a minimal down payment. In a limited equity cooperative, a resident might pay a $500 initiation fee to become a member. Monthly payments then include each owner's share of the common mortgage, plus a fee for maintenance and operating expenses. When an owner wishes to move, he or she sells the share back to the cooperative, which then resells it to a new owner. Since the whole process takes place within the cooperative corporation, no new financing or real estate fees are ever involved.

The cooperative is termed limited equity because the appreciation in the value of each member's share is limited by common agreement to a low level. Cooperative members cannot sell their shares for what the market will bear. In this way, the sales price of units quickly falls below the market price for comparable housing. While a typical home or condominium is sold and refinanced at ever-inflating prices many times over its lifespan, a limited equity cooperative is never sold. The original mortgage is retained until it is fully paid off, at which time the owners' monthly payments decrease to the amount necessary to operate and maintain the units. The principal difference between cooperative and private ownership is that, within cooperatives, owners may change many times without the cooperative itself ever changing owners. Owners share the full rights and privileges of private owners, including the tax benefits that are not available to tenants in rental housing. Ownership would rest in the hands of residents, public agencies, or community organizations. In all instances, management would be structured to promote resident involvement and to encourage resident control over the use of space. This structure self-consciously places the value of community above commodity.

Numerous countries (Canada, Sweden, Finland, France, and Italy) and cities (Boston, New York, San Francisco, Los Angeles, Berkeley, among others) have enacted programs to create cooperative housing. These actions have led to a dramatic decrease in the percentage of income paid into housing. Sweden stands as a model for this kind of program and the results have been very encouraging (Gilderbloom and Appelbaum, 1988). Sweden has no homeless problem, and slum areas have been eliminated. The average household pays half of what the average American household pays in rent. In Sweden, a four-bedroom modern cooperative unit with numerous amenities rents for $205 a month, yet a similar unit in Houston, San Francisco, Los Angeles, New York, or Chicago would cost two to six times that amount. Instead of advocating the "houstonization" of our cities, policy analysts should look to Sweden to provide America with a workable and pragmatic affordable housing program for the 1990s.

Cooperative housing would also result in substantially more control over the existing housing environment, leading to a greater sense of community. This sense of "we-ness" is translated into lower rates of crime in cooperatives after conversion from private rental housing. While it is difficult to predict how successful a community-based housing program would be, Ronald Lawson's (1984:87) evaluation of low-income housing cooperatives in New York City indicates that the level of satisfaction is quite high. Bratt also conducted a survey of residents of community-based housing and found that a majority indicated greater satisfaction with community and home life. According to Bratt (1989:199) "62 percent of respondents indicated that their home life is better since getting into mutual housing; 69 percent said that their ability to rely on neighbors when unexpected problems arise is better and a persuasive 77 percent reported that their hopes for the future have improved.'' In addition to supplying housing, some of these community-based housing programs provide important social benefits such as programs for the elderly and child care.

Community-based nonprofit housing organizations are increasingly responsible for a growing share of newly created low- and moderate-income housing. According to the Institute for Policy Studies (1989:54):

In Massachusetts about seventy-five nonprofit sponsors have created 7,000 affordable housing units since 1975, with another 2,000 down the pipeline. Total rehabilitation and construction by New York City neighborhood groups is estimated at 3,000 units annually. San Francisco's nonprofit developers, with a later start than many East Coast counterparts and an extremely speculative market, have produced 2,000 to 3,000 affordable units in recent years.

While little or no equity is earned, the cost of cooperative housing is substantially lower than market rate housing. Cooperative Services in Detroit is able to construct housing at 25 percent below market cost and rent out units 33 percent below comparable private developer units. In Middletown, Connecticut, the Legal Services Foundation has produced cooperative housing for low-income families at $220 a month plus utilities with no down payment (Franklin, 1981). In Hartford, Connecticut, the Bethel Street Cooperatives has used innovative financing mechanisms and special tax breaks to produce four-room apartments at $185 (Franklin, 1981). In Boston, the Methunion Manor, a 150-unit federally subsidized development, went into foreclosure and was sold to the residents as a limited equity co-op for less than $100 per unit. Currently, the monthly payment for each household is $56 to cover insurance, maintenance, and other expenses (Institute for Policy Studies, 1989:49).

Limited equity cooperative housing provides the best hope for supplying decent and affordable housing for low- and moderate-income persons. While rent control is useful for organizing tenants politically and for eliminating the most blatant abuses, it is vulnerable to numerous forms of attack from landlords; thus, the immediate gain seems short term. On the other hand, limited equity cooperatives, while not so ''sexy'' an issue as rent control, provide a solution that will eventually result in even lower housing payments than under rent control.

This is dramatically illustrated by developments in Santa Monica. When tenants in a Santa Monica apartment complex rejected conversion to a cooperative in 1987, they based this decision on a calculation that housing payments would rise an additional $65 to cover higher mortgage interest rates.

They failed to anticipate that a gradual weakening of the Santa Monica rent-control law due to landlord attacks would result in rent hikes that would eventually exceed projected co-op estimates. Moreover, by 1991, the California State Assembly is considering banning strong rent-control laws and allowing only moderate regulations resulting in catch-up rent increases of between $200 and $400. Finally, the federal government might make the continuance of rent control in any form (strong or moderate) impossible by withholding federal housing subsidies to these cities. If rent controls are discontinued in Santa Monica, rents will go up anywhere between $400 to $900 a month, depending on the unit size and location. Under these pressing political circumstances, limited equity cooperatives appear considerably more stable and affordable than a rent-control program that increasingly is a gamble for tenants.

Homesteading

The significant cost savings of cooperatives can be even greater when self-rehabilitation is utilized. This involves residents providing "sweat equity" in the rehabilitation of an abandoned or foreclosed unit. Sweat equity generally means exerting physical labor to rehabilitate the housing unit and ranges from replacing or repairing major structural elements of the house to improving the plumbing, heating, electricity, and other necessities. Also involved is contracting out material, equipment, and labor expenses. In addition, because the cooperative acts as its own contractor, permits must be applied for from city hall as well as housing assistance contracts. When self-help rehabilitation is done, the cost of bringing multifamily housing up to code can be 50 percent of the cost of conventional rehabilitation by private developers. For example, the problem of abandoned housing in Houston could be greatly reduced by the introduction of an urban homesteading program.

Churches, anti-poverty organizations, and nonprofits serving disadvantaged groups should begin sponsoring nonprofit housing development and rehabilitation. Abandoned and dilapidated units could be renovated by these organizations. New York and Boston have been able to revitalize many declining neighborhoods by developing innovative homesteading programs. These programs result in greater housing opportunities for disadvantaged persons, an increase in tax revenues, more jobs, and the renewal of neighborhoods. Coupled with this program would be the passage of a statewide receivership program. When a landlord repeatedly refuses to fix housing code violations, tenants can ask the court for help by applying their rent toward needed repairs. Housing receivership programs have worked well in New Jersey (Listokin et al., 1985). Poor neighborhoods could be dramatically turned around with the adoption of a large-scale homesteading and receivership program.[10]

## Conclusion

The private market alone cannot provide affordable housing for all citizens—especially for minorities, disabled, elderly, and poor. The conservative free enterprise approach has worked against the economically disadvantaged. On the other hand, reliance on the traditional liberal strategy of providing massive tax breaks and subsidies for builders and landlords has proven to be too costly and inefficient for solving the housing crunch. New and bold measures must be used to combat the housing crisis.

More government, not less government, is needed to resolve the nation's housing crisis. But calling for greater government involvement means adopting programs that have a proven track record. President Jimmy Carter did as much to fuel the nation's housing crisis as did Ronald Reagan by allowing interest rates to go sky high and supporting accelerated depreciation allowances, which meant rapid turnover of apartment ownership tied to higher interest rates (Gilderbloom and Appelbaum, 1988). Moreover, Carter's support of the traditional Democratic supply-side approach was as ineffective as the Reagan/Bush demand-side programs of increasing housing vouchers. Calling for more government also means honest government, one that is watched over and participated in by ordinary citizens. In an age of S&L and HUD scandals, it is clear that unmonitored government is bad government. It is also clear that the economically disadvantaged are harmed most by this misuse of funds.

Historically, housing policy in the United States has been shaped by landlords, builders, and bankers. Housing activists were virtually invisible in this process. In the 1990s, housing activists—including tenants—are becoming key players in housing legislation and are challenging government's accommodation to special real estate interest groups. Progressive leadership combined with grass-roots initiatives can turn the American nightmare of homelessness into the American dream of good and decent homes for everyone. When George Bush talked of the "thousand points of light" in his presidential campaign he was referring, in part, to the numerous nonprofit housing developers working in our nation's cities. These organizations need federal financial support in order to continue their important work of rebuilding our cities, creating jobs for the unemployed, and providing homes for the homeless. Opinion polls indicate that there is widespread national concern regarding the housing crisis and support for spending what is necessary on innovative measures that get to the root of the problem. We hope that our leaders will have the vision and courage to shake off the old shibboleths and to take decisive steps in support of progressive housing legislation.

Cities must be remade for all to enjoy. Goodman (1956:97) observed that an individual "has only one life and if during it he has no great environment, no community, he has been irreparably robbed of a human right."

Urban tenants' movements, with all of their limitations, have pushed forward the public dialogue centering on human rights and what constitutes a fair and just society. They have rendered problems and social relations visible that are often hidden from view by the heartfelt belief that a free market unleashed can solve all problems. Tenants' mobilizations dramatize the fact that, after all, rent control exists in every city. The question is whether rents should be controlled by a handful of landlords responsible to no one or by a representative government body accountable to the community. This question is symbolic of a much larger debate about democracy, community, and economic rights that will determine what kind of a society the United States becomes as it enters the next century.

# Notes

## Chapter 1

1. Marwell and Oliver (1984:6) have argued that "social movements are most usefully understood as complex aggregates of collective actions or events...in contrast to most definitions in the literature which tend to equate social movements with particular kinds of actions."

2. John Goering and Coulibably Modibo (1988) noted that Robert Merton (1948:167) warned sociologists about the difficulties of researching housing issues. The sociologist "must know that he is forsaking the relative calm and peace of his academic laboratory for the strife and embroilments of the institutional battlefield....He is volunteering for a hazardous reconnaissance in sociological no-mans land, where he will be exposed to pitiless cross-fire from all camps."

3. Exception must be made for the recent detailed studies carried out by Allan Heskin (1983) in the Los Angeles area and Ron Lawson's (1986) historical analysis of tenant activism in New York City.

4. Marwell and Oliver (1984:14) have called for the recognition of the value of territorial or "ecological" units in the analysis of social movements: "For any given public good there is a specifiable ecological unit that appears to make the most sense as a basis for organizing collective action to achieve that goal."

5. In emphasizing the urban character of tenants' movements, we are well aware of Hanspeter Kriesi's (1988:352) critique of the tendency for social scientists to label movements according to their own areas of specialization, for example, designating more general movements as "urban movements." Our decision to emphasize the urban character of tenants' movements is empirically based, and arises out of our observation that tenants' movements are about a broader set of urban and human issues, of which rent control is a subset and a symbol.

6. A high degree of personal risk may also have the opposite effect, functioning to promote mobilization and to build solidarity, as recognized by Rosabeth Moss Kanter (1972) and others (McAdam, 1986; Ferree and Miller, 1985).

7. The timing of this field research turned out to be important (for methodological details, see Čapek, 1985). Mark Kann (1986), who was in the field doing interviews approximately two years before Čapek (1985), observed in an informal interview that his research was affected by proximity to the election victory. Reporting that there was less criticism and openness and more of a "line," he invested much energy into

getting a frank assessment of the movement (interview with Mark Kann, August 10, 1984). By the time of Čapek's arrival, progressives had been in office longer and had accumulated more of a public history. Criticism and dissension were more common, as were self-examination and an attempt to find explanations for the evolution of the movement. On the other hand, Čapek also lost people due to timing. One of Čapek's few refusals for an interview came when the individual in question said that it was "all history" and had been "a miserable time," and he didn't want to talk about it. He added that had it been just six months earlier, he might have felt differently. His past had become closed history sometime during those six months (Čapek, 1985:463).

8. The "opposition" in Santa Monica was a complex amalgam of views ranging from conservative to liberal. For details and interviews, see Čapek (1985). See also Kann (1986).

9. Of the twenty-five SMRR members who consented to be interviewed by John Gilderbloom in July 1988, twenty-two supported Jesse Jackson's bid for the Democratic nomination for President of the United States. As of June 1990, a majority of the city council and rent control board members were supporters—although some of these elected officials asked not to be identified as such. Jesse Jackson coined the phrase "rainbow coalition," which signifies a diverse group of progressives who represent the interests of gays, feminists, disabled, nonwhites, poor, seniors, homeless, tenants, and environmentalists. Finally, we gave some consideration to calling our book, *When the Rainbow Rules: Prospects for the Good City,* but as the reader can see *Community Versus Commodity* won out. Perhaps someone can use this as a title for a future article on Santa Monica.

## Chapter 2

1. In actual practice, most U.S. homeowners are "renters" from the bank for long periods of time. However, the cultural respect accorded to the set of norms surrounding homeownership disguises this relationship and permits the homeowner to claim space with dignity.

2. Most recently this discussion of housing as a human right has been played out around the homelessness issue. The Carter administration moved toward the recognition of housing as a human right, while the Reagan administration moved away from it (Gilderbloom and Appelbaum, 1988). Many cities have engaged in symbolic and pragmatic efforts to recognize decent shelter as a human right. An example of this is the Chicago Tenants' Rights Bill passed in 1987.

3. According to Jim Kemeny (1980:372): "...among critical observers there is considerable agreement that owner-occupation constitutes a stabilizing factor in capitalist societies." Harvey (1976:272–3), for example, maintains that "a worker mortgaged up to the hilt is, for the most part, a pillar of social stability, and schemes to promote home ownership within the working class have long recognized this basic fact." Castells (1977:185) argues that owner-occupation gives workers a stake in the

system and that "... chronic indebtedness ties individuals into the job market and into society in general in a most repressive way". Others argue that owner-occupation divides the working class and gives owner-occupiers a vested interest in the system or that owner-occupation strengthens sectional divisions among workers and has been a key factor in the creation of the middle class (Saunders, 1978).

4. Saunders (1978) points out that Weber's work on classes could lead to an infinite number of classes since so many differences exist in terms of market situation. Weber (1947:425) seems to acknowledge this when he argues "Only persons who are completely unskilled, without property and dependent on employment without regular occupation, are in a strictly identical class status."

5. "Every homeowner, whether he or she likes it or not, is caught in a struggle over the appropriation of values because of the shifting pattern of external costs and benefits within the built environment" (Harvey, 1978:16).

6. New social movements theory may be a challenge to the notion that support for trade union activities is a measure of radical or progressive beliefs. NSM theory argues that traditional "class" variables are no longer so significant in social movements and that they are frequently combined with or overridden by other issues.

7. Although some conceptual confusion has existed over the definition of "resources" (Jenkins, 1983; Zurcher and Snow, 1981), they tend to be defined as material and organizational goods (Tilly, 1978; Marwell and Oliver, 1984) rather than ideas and skills.

8. As Zurcher and Snow (1981) note, numerous studies show that no simple correspondence exists, but rather that the relationship is "complex and indeterminate." Neil Smelser (1963) was careful to avoid assumptions of correspondence by developing a value-added theory and by noting that particular kinds of strain did not necessarily yield particular kinds of social action.

9. Opinion is divided as to whether resource mobilization theory can be stretched to incorporate the features of social movements that it has neglected, or whether this would too far distort the original model. The approach taken here is that the original model can be supplemented to take account of process and nonmaterial symbolic behavior.

10. Melucci (1985:813) has noted that collective action "Challenges the operational logic of technocratic-military apparatuses. . . . It makes the power visible. In systems where the power becomes increasingly anonymous and neutral . . . to make it visible is a fundamental political achievement. . . ."

## Chapter 3

1. A number of the seniors who were displaced from Santa Monica appear in Barbara Myerhoff's sensitive and insightful ethnography *Number Our Days* (1979),

which explores how displaced elderly Jews reconstructed their culture through participating in a senior community center in Venice, California.

2. Interview with Vivian Linder, August 7, 1984.

3. Interview with Roger Genser, July 30, 1984.

4. Interview with Dora Ashford, August 9, 1984.

5. Interview with Ernie Powell, July 26, 1984.

6. Interview with Dan Cohen, July 13, 1984.

7. This attitude has been firmly enshrined in national policy, which crucially
shapes urban outcomes. For example, the United States President's Commission on
Housing in 1982 found that "The genius of the market economy, freed of the distortions
forced by government housing policies and regulations that swing erratically from loving
to hostile, can provide for housing far better than Federal programs" (Hartman,
1983:13).

8. Interview with Frank Hotchkiss, July 23, 1984.

9. Anonymous interview, July 5, 1984.

10. Interview with Cary Lowe, November 23, 1984. Although Lowe was
instrumental in creating and fostering networks that built up the tenants' movement
in California, his role did not appear in Allan Heskin's (1983) account, *Tenants and
the American Dream.*

11. Interview with Cary Lowe, November 23, 1984.

12. Interview with Cary Lowe, November 23, 1984.

13. Interview with Cary Lowe, November 23, 1984.

14. Interview with Cary Lowe, November 23, 1984.

15. Interview with Moe Stavnezer, March 13, 1985.

16. Interview with Moe Stavnezer, March 13, 1985.

17. Interview with Cary Lowe, November 23, 1984.

18. Interview with Dorothy Merken, June 15, 1984. The role of the seniors is
a story in itself, but it is one that is vanishing as many of the seniors are no longer
available for interviews. We have tried to contribute at least a partial documentation
of their roles and viewpoints throughout our book.

19. Interview with Cheryl Rhoden, June 25, 1984.

20. Interview with Moe Stavnezer, March 13, 1985.

21. Interview with Parke Skelton, March 14, 1985.

22. Interview with Parke Skelton, September 30, 1982, from the files of Dale Eunson.

23. Interview with Parke Skelton, September 30, 1982, from the files of Dale Eunson.

24. Interview with Parke Skelton, September 30, 1982, from the files of Dale Eunson.

25. Interview with Hank Barnard, June 25, 1984. The Santa Monica CED chapter was an offshoot of a much larger Westside CED chapter, which split into a Santa Monica and a West Los Angeles chapter. Apart from creating more manageable numbers, the division also indicated a different local focus of interest.

26. Interview with Ruth Galanter, August 14, 1984.

27. Interview with Parke Skelton, September 30, 1982, from the files of Dale Eunson.

28. Interview with Moe Stavnezer, March 13, 1985.

29. Interview with Dennis Zane, August 2, 1984.

30. Interview with Moe Stavnezer, March 13, 1985.

31. Interview with Michael Tarbet, August 8, 1984.

32. Interview with Moe Stavnezer, March 13, 1985.

33. Interview with Parke Skelton, September 30, 1982, from the files of Dale Eunson.

34. Classic resource mobilization theory posits grievances as a constant, while mobilization is a response to organizational opportunities. In 1978, however, many activists testified that the organizations were running to catch up with the tide of grievances in order to be able to channel them. In the early years of the progressive administration, a Tenant Organizing Project (TOP) counseled tenants; by 1984, no organization was taking care of this need (interview with Roger Thornton, June 13, 1984; interview with Leslie Lambert, August 13, 1984; interview with Wayne Bauer, June 21, 1984).

35. Interview with Parke Skelton, March 14, 1985.

36. Interview with Cary Lowe, November 23, 1984.

37. Interview with Moe Stavnezer, March 13, 1985.

38. Interview with "Mark" Markovicius, August 6, 1984.

39. The stigma of this "outsider" identity was often attached to progressive activists, even prior to the entry onto the scene of CED. As Ruth Galanter recalled

270 *Notes*

the battles in the early 1970s to keep Ocean Park affordable, "There was the other bunch, 'us,' new, from New York, Jewish...they *did* worry about who we were and why. They found us very disturbing to the life of the community. But if it hadn't been us, someone else would have done it" (interview with Ruth Galanter, August 14, 1984).

40. Interview with Dennis Zane, June 30, 1984.

41. Interview with Moe Stavnezer, March 13, 1985.

42. Interview with Al Smith, July 28, 1984.

43. For example, the League of Women Voters suffered a bitter split when its former president narrated an anti-SMRR election tape that was mailed out to voters in 1983. This was challenged as an inappropriately partisan activity.

44. In retrospect, little information was available on this union because, as organizational entities, the tenants' unions were the least ongoing presence in the city. According to Parke Skelton, "...about 130 tenant unions were organized after the Prop P election and right before the Prop A election...about forty buildings went out on rent strike.... This group was formed called the Santa Monica Tenants' Union that joined SMRR for a while that was a coalition—a group of representatives from the tenant organizations throughout the city—at one point there were like twenty or twenty-five buildings. Active tenant associations represented in the Santa Monica Tenant Union that was a part of SMRR" (interview with Parke Skelton, September 30, 1982, from the files of Dale Eunson).

45. Interview with Dennis Zane, June 30, 1984.

46. Interview with Dennis Zane, June 30, 1984.

47. Interview with Cheryl Rhoden, June 25, 1984.

48. Interview with Hank Barnard, June 25, 1984.

49. In retrospect, given that the election showed such an outpouring of votes for SMRR, it appears that a third candidate could have won easily. This was a cause for some regrets later. In 1983, the opposite strategy was followed. SMRR ran a full slate for all seats and lost. Its opposition used this to bolster its arguments that SMRR was "taking over the city." Interestingly, a full slate was opposed not only by SMRR's opponents, but also by its supporters, 56 percent of whom stated that SMRR should not have all of the seats on the city council (interview with Parke Skelton, March 14, 1985).

50. Interview with Michael Tarbet, August 8, 1984. William Jennings dropped out of SMRR at the end of 1980, causing considerable public embarrassment to the coalition since he informed the newspapers of his decision before informing anyone in SMRR. He claimed that SMRR demanded narrow political loyalty.

51. The Santa Monica Taxpayers and Residents Committee was formed early to oppose SMRR candidates. The name it chose was part of the symbolic war over

"fairness," emphasizing that the group consisted of committed community residents. The name prompted a quip from a tenant: "Meaning what, that we're *not* taxpayers and residents?"

52. Interview with Cary Lowe, November 23, 1984.

53. Interview with Parke Skelton, September 30, 1982, from the files of Dale Eunson.

54. Although the selection of candidates has been presented as the most rational choice in view of the alliances that would be brought to the coalition, some activists provided a different backstage view: that the group of four candidates was "almost entirely second choice" and that the original "dream ticket" included Ellis Casson, a black minister in the Pico neighborhood who was also an organizer. Ken Edwards, winning SMRR candidate and future mayor of Santa Monica, recalled that "there was no miraculous outpouring from the community" and that many people had ambivalent feelings about the slate (interview with Ken Edwards, July 26, 1984).

55. Interview with Michael Tarbet, August 8, 1984.

56. Anonymous interview, July 11, 1984.

57. Interview with Michael Tarbet, August 8, 1984.

58. Interview with William Mortensen, March 15, 1985.

59. Interview with Moe Stavnezer, March 13, 1985.

60. Interview with Cheryl Rhoden, June 25, 1984.

61. Anonymous interview, July 23, 1984.

62. Interview with Parke Skelton, March 14, 1985.

63. Interview with Parke Skelton, March 14, 1985.

64. Interview with Parke Skelton, March 14, 1985.

65. SMRR was fortunate to benefit from this strategy at the time, since in later elections the legality of duplicating such a document and reducing the text to small print came into question.

66. Interview with Thom Poffenberger, July 11, 1984.

67. Interview with Thom Poffenberger, July 11, 1984.

68. Interview with Roger Thornton, June 13, 1984.

69. Interview with Karin Pally, July 18, 1984.

70. Interview with Thom Poffenberger, July 12, 1984.

71. Interview with Thom Poffenberger, July 12, 1984.

72. Interview with Thom Poffenberger, July 12, 1984.

73. Interview with Moe Stavnezer, March 13, 1985.

74. Interview with Ken Edwards, July 26, 1984.

75. Interview with Roger Thornton, June 13, 1984.

76. Interview with Thom Poffenberger, July 12, 1984.

77. Interview with Ruth Galanter, August 14, 1984.

78. Interview with Moe Stavnezer, March 13, 1985.

79. Interview with Dolores Press, June 29, 1984.

80. Interview with Cheryl Rhoden, June 25, 1984.

81. Interview with Derek Shearer, March 12, 1985.

82. Interview with Moe Stavnezer, March 13, 1985.

83. Interview with Ed Kirshner, March 14, 1985.

84. Interview with Dennis Zane, June 14, 1984.

85. Anonymous interview, July 5, 1984.

86. Interview with Dan Cohen, July 13, 1984.

87. Interview with Dennis Zane, August 2, 1984.

88. Interview with Cheryl Rhoden, June 25, 1984.

89. In interviews conducted by Stella Čapek in 1984 and 1985, assumptions were frequently made that nobody in the community was telling the story of Syd Rose any longer.

90. Anonymous interview, June 12, 1984.

91. Anonymous interview, July 9, 1984.

92. Anonymous interview, July 9, 1984.

93. Interview with Parke Skelton, March 14, 1985. There were "deserters" as well, including William Jennings and Gerald Goldman (Goldman was a fiery advocate for tenants when he was on the early rent-control board). Public denunciations of SMRR by those who no longer supported it were particularly embarrassing and painful. One activist had among her files on the movement one that was labeled, semifacetiously, "backstabbing file." On the other hand, a "holier than thou" politics among left activists also led to strife and ostracism, experienced by some activists when they came to be "on the outs."

## Chapter Four

1. Just as President Reagan was characterized by his opposition as the Teflon president, so Santa Monica's ability to shrug off the negative context of regulation was observed with dismay by rent-control opponents. Activists in Santa Monica found this significant and ironic during a time of mounting national conservatism and antiregulation sentiments. By contrast, Mark Kann (1986:261) has argued that this had little significance because "the relationship between local radicalism and national politics is indirect if not inverse," and that local radicalism is generally not threatening to, and may even benefit, elites.

2. Real estate interests have often viewed homeowners as the pivotal group in a rent-control election, arguing, with little empirical support, that rent control results in higher property taxes (Gilderbloom, 1983).

3. Penny Perlman of Concerned Homeowners remarked that "Much of their [SMRR's] opposition here is made up of liberal Democrats—but that *reads* more conservative here than it would elsewhere" (interview with Penny Perlman, July 31, 1984).

4. This helped to counterbalance the deceptive everyday language used in the community. Forester (1980:330) has raised this issue in connection with urban planners who face the consequences of interests that work to systematically violate the norms of communication: "Planners then face the results: a community group 'snowed' by a developer's consultant, an inquisitive citizen confused by apparently 'necessary' public works cut-backs, a working class community organization led to accept delays as 'better' neighborhoods receive more attention from city government."

5. For example, the League of Women Voters was split by a legal suit that questioned the propriety of unapproved electoral endorsements.

6. Empirical support for this conclusion is supplied by Gilderbloom and Jacob (1981).

7. Interview with Christine Reed, July 10, 1984.

8. Under previous city councils, no particular effort needed to be made to gain access to the backstage because, with the easy confidence of established elites, the council engaged in enough damaging acts "frontstage" to play into the hands of its opponents later.

9. Interview with John Jurenka, August 2, 1984.

10. Gilderbloom's interview data reveal that landlords consider income first, age only after, and thus suggest that a social redefinition of the elderly is a useful myth (Gilderbloom, 1985a). This varies with type of landlord, with the degree of personal relationship existing with tenants, and with whether high profits are more important than quiet, reliable, and long-term tenants. Expectations for raising rents and attracting

wealthier tenants changed after the freeway was built in Santa Monica. Landlord hopes that vacancy decontrol would be passed also led them to discriminate against the elderly, soliciting younger tenants who were more likely to vacate. As the economic stakes went up in Santa Monica, landlords took on more organized and professionalized behavior.

11. Interview with Donald Howland, March 13, 1985.

12. Interview with John Jurenka, August 2, 1984.

13. Confronted with a derogatory remark by a landlord who said that tenants only "vote their pocketbooks," a longtime tenant activist laughed and said, "Well, I hope so. After all, whose pocket is emptier, his or mine?" (anonymous interview, July 9, 1984).

14. Interview with James Baker, March 11, 1985.

15. Interview with John Jurenka, August 2, 1984.

16. Interview with John Jurenka, August 2, 1984.

17. Interview with Doris Ganga, July 31, 1984.

18. Interview with Robert Gabriel, March 12, 1985.

19. The landlord group ACTION, which mobilized local "mom and pop" landlords, had a similar experience later.

20. In 1972, a Coastal Commission was voted into being in California to protect beach communities. This included the preservation of low- and moderate-income housing. Twenty percent of Santa Monica fell under the jurisdiction of the Coastal Commission, including the Ocean Park area.

21. Interview with Cheryl Rhoden, June 14, 1982, from the files of Dale Eunson.

22. Interview with Cheryl Rhoden, June 14, 1982, from the files of Dale Eunson.

23. Anonymous interview, August 18, 1984.

24. Anonymous interview, August 18, 1984.

25. Interview with Cheryl Rhoden, June 14, 1982, from the files of Dale Eunson.

26. Interview with Roger Genser, July 30, 1984.

27. Interview with Moe Stavnezer, March 13, 1985.

28. Interview with Cheryl Rhoden, June 25, 1984. Also interview on June 14, 1982, from the files of Dale Eunson.

29. Anonymous interview, July 27, 1984.

30. Interview with Ruth Yannatta Goldway, July 6, 1984.

31. Interview with Karin Pally, July 18, 1984.

32. Anonymous interview, July 27, 1984. Also, interview with Cheryl Rhoden, June 25, 1984.

33. Interview with Michael Tarbet, August 8, 1984.

34. Anonymous interview, July 27, 1984.

35. In relation to this incident, city councilmember and SMRR opponent Christine Reed remarked, "Someone must have forgotten to give him his script." She was referring to Hayden's more typical posture of distancing himself from the movement in public.

36. Derek Shearer, remarks taken from a presentation at the University of Texas at Austin, April 1984.

37. Interview with Wayne Bauer, June 21, 1984.

38. Interview with Bill Allen, July 14, 1984.

39. Interview with Dennis Zane, June 30, 1984.

40. In regard to rationality, Mark Kann (1982:81) has pointed out that "radical activists have better understood that talk about religion and truth, good and evil, is an important line of communication to Americans, who temper their rationalism with the religious and secular verities that are a part of their everyday lives. . . . The point is not to eliminate rationalism but to augment it with the moral talk necessary for contesting elitist Lockean terrain."

41. An example of this was the response of an editor of *Business Week* when confronted with John Gilderbloom's empirical study of rent control. Gilderbloom's evidence was not included in an article on rent control. The editor's response when pressed was, "I made up my mind about rent control twenty-five years ago and I don't care what any college kid says" (Dreier, 1979; see also Dreier, Gilderbloom and Appelbaum, 1980).

42. Because of its legacy of strict rent controls and urban problems, New York functions in the rent-control mythology as a condensed symbol of all that is wrong with regulation. For example, in 1978, during the first rent-control campaign, a camouflaged landlord group called Opinion Associates engaged in phone surveys; one of their questions was, "Did you know that a New York syndicate is behind rent control?" When a New Yorker was appointed to be a rent control administrator in Santa Monica, James Baker remarked, "You stun us again with the deliberate choice of a young attorney from bankrupt New York City" *(Evening Outlook,* September 29, 1979).

43. Although small owner-occupied apartment complexes were exempted from the rent-control law (see Chapter 5), other "mom and pop" landlords were in some

cases unfairly penalized. An unintended consequence of the law was that it penalized the more fair landlords since it calculated a base rent using 1978 figures. Landlords who were rent gougers, consequently, had a higher base rate for collecting rents.

44. Interview with Parke Skelton, March 14, 1985.

45. Interview with John Jurenka, August 2, 1984.

46. Interview with John Jurenka, August 2, 1984.

47. Berkeley and Hartford were symbols of progressive urban policy. See also Pierre Clavel (1986), *The Progressive City.*

48. This represents a dig at one of the SMRR council's more embarrassing moments, when, without bringing it up for public discussion, they voted to support the Israeli invasion of Lebanon. This caused a furor and was seen as a blatantly transparent attempt to help Tom Hayden's image with Jewish constituents. An opponent at a public hearing christened the city "Santa Moronica."

49. Because Robert Myers, city attorney in the progressive administration, resisted prosecuting the homeless, and because opponents have claimed that rent control causes homelessness (for a refutation, see Chapter 7), the progressives were lampooned as attracting transients to Santa Monica.

50. Progressives made energy efficiency one of their issues. Homeowners were offended because they felt that the suggested policies were coercive and punitive rather than voluntary, and an interference with private property.

51. Anonymous interview, August 1984.

52. When SMRR lost its voting majority in November 1984, the new mayor, Christine Reed, sent at a local level public messages very similar to Ronald Reagan's "bringing America back" theme. She even repositioned her mayor's desk in the place where it had stood before the progressives won and Ruth Yannatta Goldway became mayor (interview with Ken Edwards, March 13, 1985).

53. Interview with Ken Edwards, July 26, 1984.

54. See note 43, above.

55. Interview with Herb Katz, July 13, 1984.

56. Interview with Thom Poffenberger, July 12, 1984.

57. Interview with Barbara Jo Osborne, July 22, 1984.

58. Interview with Vivian Rothstein, June 28, 1984.

59. Interview with Ken Edwards, July 23, 1984.

## Chapter 5

1. In this election, SMRR put up three candidates including minister Al Smith. All were defeated. Just as SMRR's electoral victory was important in convincing progressive activists that "you *can* fight city hall and win" (Mankin, 1981), so individuals involved in opposing SMRR claimed that their 1983 victory was a psychological breakthrough that showed them that SMRR was not invincible even in a city with such a high tenant population.

2. This election would ordinarily have been held in 1985, but SMRR had won an electoral battle (Proposition Y) to have local elections rescheduled to coincide with national elections, which would increase voter (read renter) turnout. Dolores Press fell several names short of the valid signatures required for having her name on the ballot and thus was forced to wage a write-in campaign. The campaign was impressive by write-in standards and received important support from the women's community. She lost, however, which left SMRR in the minority. Their opponents on the city council included former SMRR member William Jennings.

3. Interview with Bill Allen, July 14, 1984.

4. Recent studies on rent control (Gilderbloom, 1981; Gilderbloom and Appelbaum, 1988) distinguish between two generations of rent controls: an older, "strict" set of controls that did not offer landlords sufficient rent adjustments, and a new, more moderate generation of controls that legally guarantee a "fair return" to landlords. The Santa Monica law falls into the latter category, meaning that the rent board must define a legally acceptable formula for controlling rents and yet providing fair adjustments to landlords; without this the law could be declared confiscatory, as was Berkeley's in 1976. Fair return concepts differ around the country, but are commonly based on the idea of returns comparable with those on investments carrying similar risks. In this book, we expand upon this distinction.

5. Proposition P, the first (1978) rent-control initiative, did not spell out the powers of the interim board or specify the required annual adjustments. In addition, the rollback date was June 1, 1976, after a rent freeze of ninety days. With the powers of the interim rent board made clear, many landlords objected to the nonconfidentiality of the registration form and the fact that tenants could "check up" on them, and thus they delayed registering their units.

6. In actual practice, the downward adjustment has not been used. When rent board estimates of the general adjustment have yielded decreases, these have always been adjusted in some fashion.

7. Landlord activist James Baker's "horror list" in 1985 included: "no increases on vacancies; annual adjustments averaging 4.9 percent; frozen differences for identical apartments; no increase for added occupants; no increase for full utilities; no financing relief; renter-dominated, antiowner board; impossible, biased petition system; penalties and fines as tenant bounties; no escape permitted."

8. This was aimed at speculative investments undertaken since the passage of the amendment—foreign investors who had not bothered to find out about the local law were especially likely to be in this category. Seventy percent of the rent increase petitions to the board by 1980 came from landlords who had purchased their buildings between the spring of 1978 and the spring of 1979 (*Los Angeles Times*, April 20, 1980).

9. The Rent Board's explanation of its debt service figure acknowledges the difference between new and old purchases. It concludes, nevertheless, that "In consulting various sources, 40 percent appears to be a generally acceptable figure. It further appears that, if anything, the 40% figure understates the actual amount. . . . All available information, including information received at the public hearing, indicates that debt service expenses and property taxes (in light of Proposition 13) are constant. Variable interest loans have not been used in the City of Santa Monica on a widespread basis" (General Adjustment Subcommittee, 1979).

Landlord-activist James Baker called this a big myth that assumed that "nobody had to refinance in order to pay off thousands of second and third loans coming due. . . that adjustable rate mortgages do not exist. . . that sales triggered by death or incapacity never occur and that the cost of money is completely unaffected by inflation!. . . It would seem that this Alice in Wonderland thinking would be obvious to any rational person, but this has been the sole excuse in six years for reducing Santa Monica rents in real terms by almost 30 percent" (*Evening Outlook*, June 27, 1985).

10. However, the loss of money was not at issue; the verdict would have been the same.

11. A recent ruling in the case of the city of Cotati, California, allowed a formula basing a fair rate of return on landlord's original investment as long as rents were adjusted for inflation. The inflation adjustment was missing from the Berkeley law, which was pronounced confiscatory.

12. As we noted in Chapter 4, this basic challenge to the rent law helped to mobilize tenants to vote for SMRR candidates for the city council. Tenants packed the chambers as the rent board promised to fight the decision (*Evening Outlook*, March 13, 1981).

13. As Regulation 4100, it preserved a landlord's net operating income (NOI) based on 40 percent of the CPI (NOI is the amount left after a landlord's operating expenses, including property taxes, are subtracted from the building's gross income). The board assumed on the basis of its information that 90 percent of the NOI went into debt service, while the rest was profit. While discarding historic investment, it still used 1978 as a base year.

14. The Pacific Legal Foundation targeted Santa Monica, becoming involved in several lawsuits, one of which was by the United Brotherhood of Carpenters and Joiners to stop the city from collecting arts and social services fees from developers. The organization's board of trustees was comprised of lawyers and heads of large corporations. It was funded largely by private businesses, as well as individuals and foundation grants. Its list of accomplishments included opposing affirmative action,

fighting to stop bans on DDT and other pesticides, challenging California's nuclear power plant moratorium, and removing species from the endangered list when they stood in the way of government and private development (*Evening Outlook,* November 16, 1982).

15. Even this did not please landlords since they said that the city was making them act as its collecting agency. The rent control board was challenged by over three hundred lawsuits (*Evening Outlook,* October 1, 1984).

16. A comparative study of the costs of rent control found the Santa Monica administration to be much more costly than others; for example, Berkeley's is $30 per year, New York's is $10, and Los Angeles's is $7 (*Los Angeles Times,* April 8, 1984). However, Santa Monica's law is also among the strictest in the nation.

17. The state supreme court, however, suspended the deadline given to the board to surrender its authority until all appeals were resolved. In October 1984, a state appeal court struck down this decision, returning the rent board's powers. Judges ruled that the prior decision had mistakenly ignored the intent of the voters to set up an independent board.

18. Had Shell's victories been upheld, tenants would have been forced into the court system. However, the decisions were overturned and the 1984 charter amendment also plugged these loopholes.

19. Interview with Susan Packer Davis, July 27, 1984.

20. Shell's suit was filed on behalf of Donald T. Sterling, a millionaire apartment owner and owner of the Los Angeles Clippers of the National Basketball Association. The board had awarded rent cuts totaling $2,030 annually to tenants in Sterling's 32-unit building in Santa Monica.

21. Interview with Leslie Lambert, August 13, 1984.

22. From a "mobilization" perspective, its timing was excellent since all of the SMRR seats were up for reelection and rent control was a proven ballot issue. In fact, the impetus for an amendment began with some community activists, but the city council and the rent-control board altered the timing of the move and "took it off the streets," as one activist put it. The activist wanted to do tenant organizing. The city council wanted to do "electoral organizing."

23. A rent board attorney estimated in 1982 that as many as 2,500 of Santa Monica's 35,000 rental units had remained vacant since rent control was implemented in 1979 (*Evening Outlook,* February 19, 1982). One of Santa Monica's biggest landlords, Larry Kates (see Chapter 4) bragged about having 104 vacant units.

24. In 1982, officials of ACTION were sued by the Tenant Organizing Project (TOP) for allegedly maintaining a "blacklist" that would exclude CED members from renting. Although landlords denied the existence of a blacklist, they did ask their members to supply the organization with the names and phone numbers of tenants

so that those opposed to Tom Hayden could purportedly be mobilized on election day (*Evening Outlook,* October 15, 1982).

25. Interview with Donald Howland, March 13, 1985.

26. John Gilderbloom has suggested that the "professionalization" of landlords has caused landlords to behave this way in general, seeking higher income tenants because these, in turn, enable them to charge more rent (Gilderbloom, 1985a). As we noted before, his findings point to the fact that the current actions of landlords in Santa Monica are an extension of what occurs under "market" conditions. However, Santa Monica is also affected by an unusual degree of polarization. There is a great deal of anger in the community, which may raise the willingness of even small landlords to undertake politically symbolic acts. Economically, most of them cannot afford it, however, which raises the perception of the larger landlords as "heroes" who represent all "oppressed" landlords through symbolic acts. In 1985, James Baker referred to a Summit Conference of the Five Most Oppressed Communities (rent-controlled communities including Santa Monica) where landlords discussed united action (interview with James Baker, March 11, 1985).

27. Interview with Pete Sevino, June 29, 1984.

28. Discussions of a repair program with pass-throughs to tenants were widely perceived by tenants as a sellout. As one member of the Pico Neighborhood Association asked, incredulously, "The *rent board* is proposing this? What do we need a rent board for, then?" A February 17, 1985, letter to the deputy city attorney from a group of tenants states: "It is unfortunate that the Rent Control Board no longer represents the tenants but rather the landlords solely. Their constant efforts to undermine the rent control law and continuously find ways to take more money from the tenants and give it to the landlords is reprehensible. . . . It is our opinion that the Rent Control Board should be abolished due to its inaction on behalf of tenants. We sincerely hope that the City Attorney will rule the recently enacted Rent Control Board's "Interior Replacement Program" as illegal and that it should be struck down."

29. Interview with Michael Tarbet, June 24, 1990.

30. Dolores Press, who would be elected as a SMRR councilmember in 1981, first served on the rent board at this time. Landlords fielded oppositional candidates for the rent board each time, but only SMRR-endorsed candidates won.

31. A speaker at the rally, having read the "just cause" eviction clause protecting tenants, shouted, "Are we going to stand for this pure crap? Are we?" "NO!" roared the crowd (*Evening Outlook,* June 8, 1979).

32. Interview with Bill Allen, July 14, 1984. Allen also recalled that at his swearing in "a landlord said, 'May God help Santa Monica from this day on'" (*Evening Outlook,* February 17, 1982).

33. Interview with Susan Packer Davis, July 27, 1984.

34. Interview with Pete Sevino, June 29, 1984.

35. This was very different from what Ralph Turner (1983:178) defines as "transformative" social relationships, where "The dominating group must learn to view the depressed group with a new kind of respect, and depressed group members must learn appropriate self-assertion and motivation for new roles."

36. Interview with Barbara Jo Osborne, July 22, 1984.

37. Interview with Renee Gould, August 11, 1984.

38. This was the HOME initiative sponsored by the All Santa Monica Coalition (see Chapter 4). It was designed to separate SMRR from voters who were aspiring owners, relying on SMRR's aversion for private ownership. This was the only way that SMRR's opposition could take the "pocketbook issue" that had locked SMRR and rent control into power and attempt to turn it against them. The 1983 HOME initiative was denounced publicly by Ralph Nader in his role as consumer advocate.

39. Interview with Cary Lowe, November 23, 1985.

40. Interview with Ed Kirshner, March 14, 1985. The limited equity co-op removes property from the speculative market since tenants, having purchased a share in the co-op to buy their unit, receive, on the sale of their unit, only the original purchase price, interest, and the value of any improvements. While there was enthusiasm among some progressive activists for the option of developing co-ops in the city, it was not something that the city administration itself gave priority to (see Chapter 7). It thus remained an undeveloped option in the progressive housing package.

41. For example, the first building, in poor shape and inhabited by drug dealers, was purchased in December 1983. Federal money was disbursed by the city of Santa Monica as a loan to the developer, which in this case was Santa Monica Community Corporation, requiring no payment of interest. If the property is kept affordable for twenty-five years, the stipulation is that the loan will be forgiven.

42. Introductory quotes are from an interview with John Alshuler, July 11, 1984, and an interview with Ken Genser, July 17, 1984.

43. Interview with Paul Silvern, March 13, 1985. As the Land Use Element points out, the idea of developer agreements was, ironically, initiated by developers themselves in order to circumvent stalled court cases; California enabling legislation in 1979 cleared the way for their usage.

44. This was particularly true in California cities fronting on the ocean, such as San Francisco, Santa Barbara, and San Diego. A general concern with city revenues in the wake of Proposition 13 also led cities to experiment with such things as inclusionary zoning, requiring large developers to construct a percentage of affordable housing along with more luxury-oriented uses.

45. The Land Use Element had not been updated since 1956, a sign of the lack of questioning of any of the taken-for-granted relationships in the city. As then Assistant

City Manager John Jalili (interview, August 3, 1984) pointed out, there are always undetermined economic costs of a review process to developers. Due to Santa Monica's desirability, developers were more willing to risk the time and money in the first place.

46. CIPA's involvement, indeed, would be much deeper than that of community organizations, such as Mid-City Neighbors or OPCO. Many members of these groups were surprised to see height limits increased in the amended version. SMRR council-members argued that in principle they were bound to encourage participatory democracy. Over time, a number of them came to be perceived as selling out to developers. For example, Jim Conn got into trouble with his OPCO constituency in 1985 for approving the plans of one of his chief rivals, a Main St. developer, without consulting the community. His justification was that "We want to try to get away from surprising [developers] in the last minutes. We are trying to make the development process predictable and consistent" (*Evening Outlook,* January 7, 1985).

47. The hotel was always the least credible element in the project from the point of view both of planners (one of whom stated that the developers "had delusions of grandeur") and of financiers, who eventually refused to fund the hotel phase of the project.

48. The firm's bitterness was escalated by the fact that during a period of high interest rates the cost of having projects "sitting" is considerably higher than usual.

49. For 41 of the units completed in 1984, a $2.1 million state housing subsidy covered the construction costs, while land, architectural, engineering, and other costs not related to construction were paid for by Welton Becket. (*Santa Monica Seascape,* March 1984).

50. When Mid-City Neighbors presented their plan for the park, it was clear that the "community" they had in mind as users was a different one from that originally assumed by Welton Becket. The uses suggested were more diverse and accessible to varied income groups; Mid-City Neighbors asked for children's play equipment, including swings and a sandbox, a quiet area with chess and game tables, a picnic lunch site for employees, a walk path (as opposed to the jogging track suggested by Welton Becket), the work of local artists, volleyball courts, and broad access to the park and tennis courts.

51. Interview with Paul Silvern, March 13, 1985.

52. After being at a standstill for some time, this project was sold to a new developer who sought some amendments to the agreement.

53. Due to construction costs for the condominiums, some modifications of the agreement were sought.

54. There have been protests against the city council for encouraging such projects. The city council, including some SMRR candidates, have been seen as too willing to promote large-scale growth and development without opting for other land uses. Over time, a persistent slow- and no-growth movement has emerged in the city.

55. As then City Manager John Alshuler was to tell a planning group in 1983, "We don't have much choice without federal housing programs. We've gotten 250 new units of low- and moderate-income housing with no federal subsidy in the last year. I think that's a remarkable accomplishment for a city of 90,000 people." (Fulton, 1985:8).

56. Interview with Ken Genser, July 17, 1984.

57. Interview with Herb Katz, July 13, 1984.

58. Interview with Frank Hotchkiss, July 23, 1984.

59. Interview with Dennis Zane, June 30, 1984.

60. The special attention that progressives paid to traditionally neglected neighborhoods brought charges of unfairness from groups that were more accustomed to having power. As SMRR opponent on the city council David Epstein stated in a letter to the editor of the *Evening Outlook,* there were many groups from Ocean Park not represented by OPCO—homeowners, residents of the towers, condominium owners, and golfers. He accused OPCO of formulating with the developer a secret deal that would result in the construction of "ultra-chic condominia with subsidized housing for a few chosen 'poor' that will be living at the expense of the public— those of us who work for a living." The saga of the Ocean Park Redevelopment Project, which began when urban renewal wiped out the beachfront community populated by senior citizens (see Chapter 3) and which still posed problems for recent administrations, is not told here due to lack of space (for details, see Čapek, 1985). However, it proved to be a major bone of contention between and within different factions of the city, including progressive disagreements about what developer trade-offs should be.

61. A net decrease of 10 percent was noted in acres of industrial land use since 1975. Industrial space was projected to increase only by 7.4 percent. In the Olympic corridor, industrial uses declined by 13 percent while advanced technology space increased by 45 percent and office space increased by 33 percent. Population, on the other hand, was only expected to grow by 5 percent by the year 2000. (Land Use Element, Draft).

62. SDC was a chief stake in the Welton Becket negotiations since it had agreed to occupy office space in the development and claimed that it would otherwise be forced to relocate. It subsequently made a decision to relocate anyway.

63. This is a problem that exists in the city regardless of who is in office. The housing prices are among the highest in the nation, and a significant shortage exists. One solution would be to increase density and to build upward, but no city council under present circumstances would promote an idea opposed by such a broad cross-section of the community. Developer agreements were one solution. As Ken Edwards told disgruntled representatives of the business community, "You should ask the developers who have built 3,000 units of low- and moderate-income housing. Inclusionary zoning is not that radical an idea—developers in Orange County pushed for it because housing was needed for employees" (*Evening Outlook,* July 3, 1981).

64. Interview with Aubrey Austin, March 15, 1985.

65. Interview with Robert Gabriel, March 12, 1985.

66. Interview with Manny Hellerman, August 7, 1984.

67. Ken Edwards and others worried about a "politics of revenge" that would take place if SMRR lost its voting majority. He predicted that if the voting balance changed, "SMRR opponents will make Ruth Goldway look like Mother Teresa." In 1985, after SMRR had lost its majority, Edwards remarked, "The loss of the majority brought home the reality that we took a lot of things for granted. Now there are some very subtle changes between what SMRR stood for, what a progressive government is, and what a do-nothing government is." He, and others, noted that the first programs to lose funding were those overtly associated with SMRR. Many of the progressive reforms were quietly institutionalized, however (interview with Ken Edwards, March 13, 1985).

68. This is not to imply that the couple's "economic" view was amoral. A factor of great significance in the Santa Monica battle was precisely the fact that a set of beliefs centered around free enterprise embodied a moral sense of order to many people.

69. A candidate who ran against SMRR incumbents in the 1984 city council recognized this. Making an issue of the regulation of condominium owners by rent control, this individual recognized that, "Condos aren't a huge factor, there are only about seventeen hundred, and a quarter to a third of them are rented. But there is a very big issue of government tentacles, of ownership control. People want to know if CED believes in private property. That's an issue they want to cloud over. Their side, as our side, has a spectrum" (anonymous interview, August 14, 1984).

70. Minority populations have been shrinking in Santa Monica for a number of years. For example, the Pico neighborhood population stabilized at around fourteen thousand between 1970 and 1980, following a significant drop in the previous decade of about seven thousand persons. Between 1960 and 1980, the black population dropped from 3,625 to 2,375. The Latino population, on the other hand, doubled since 1960 and was recorded as 5,552 in 1980 (Hernandez, 1983). In Santa Monica city schools, the percentage of minority students has been growing, with minorities currently representing three-quarters of the school population. According to the *Evening Outlook* (December 29, 1984), six out of eight elementary schools had a minority population between 58 percent and 81 percent, while the other two, in the north-of-Wilshire area, had a white population of 70 percent or more. While most of the increase has been Latino, white children have been leaving the district in greater numbers. This makes the issue of school closings something that disproportionately affects the Latino population, as recent demonstrations by parents have shown. Research also indicated that there were 2.9 residents per household among Latinos in 1960, while the overall neighborhood rate was 2.3. In 1980, the figures were, respectively, 3.7 and 3.31 (Hernandez, 1983).

71. The Latino Task Force, an advisory body set up in February 1984 by the city council to study city services and Latino participation, concluded that a maximum of 35 percent of the Latino community was being serviced satisfactorily (*Evening Outlook,* September 21, 1984). They pointed to bilingual as well as bicultural differences that keep information from getting through to the Latino population. For example, concepts were often translated incorrectly on governmental literature, not using "communicational Spanish," so that they were misunderstood. A typical problem for PNA was how to reach these separate populations during a large community meeting—should they provide a translator or have two separate sessions divided by language?

72. Regrettably, Casson was not available to be interviewed because he was transferred out of his Santa Monica parish, a loss deeply felt by the community. Many people imputed this transfer to his activism. In a more affluent neighborhood, the Reverend Al Smith, pastor of the Presbyterian church, would also be censured by the church for his activism when he ran on a 1983 SMRR ticket for city council—the only "senior citizen" to do so (interview with Al Smith, July 28, 1984).

73. In a view that was more characteristically liberal than progressive, SMRR candidates expected support from the Pico community because it was viewed as being "oppressed." In actual fact, issues of race intersected with issues of class in a highly complex way, and this support did not materialize in any significant fashion. As a Pico resident put it, "We need people who want to see us make progress. We will *not* house another halfway house, etcetera. We have more than our share . . . . Proposition X was a disaster. SMRR worked with the landlords. If *this* is what they're doing, it's time for us to look at some more candidates" (interview with Sandra Sanderson, August 8, 1984). While SMRR's own relationship with minority communities was not particularly strong, other issues of race and turf surfaced in the neighborhood that were not directly related to SMRR.

74. Anonymous interview, March 14, 1985.

75. Interview with Sandra Sanderson, August 8, 1984.

76. These comments are consistent with the observations made regarding the behavior of planners and professionals in working-class communities (Clavel, Forester, and Goldsmith, 1980).

77. The Pico neighborhood traditionally opposed the proposals debated by the rent board that would offer landlords incentives to make repairs by permitting pass-throughs to tenants. They have seen this as rewarding landlords for their "deliberate planned neglect" (*Evening Outlook,* September 15, 1982).

78. Anonymous interview, March 14, 1985.

79. Anonymous interview, March 14, 1985.

80. A CCSM participant noted that the passage of Proposition X in 1984 contributed to the difficulty of purchasing buildings (interview with Doris Ganga, July 31, 1984).

81. The Latino population is seen by many as being disproportionately vulnerable in terms of housing. For example, when in 1982 a shorter petition form for landlord pass-throughs was being debated, which would be automatically approved if tenants did not oppose it within ten days, Doris Ganga expressed the concerns of many others when she said that "many tenants, especially Spanish-speaking and undocumented workers, would not object for fear of losing their homes through a retaliatory eviction," making approval for landlord increases automatic (interview with Doris Ganga, July 31, 1984).

82. Serious charges of "ageism" have been leveled at the city staff by senior activist Morrie Rosen, who has a long history of working for the rights of senior citizens (interview with Morrie Rosen, August 7, 1984).

83. Interview with John Gabree, August 4, 1984.

84. This should not be underestimated since it has to do with the public social construction of fairness. It also works to counteract the still existing negative images of the Pico neighborhood. As an individual involved in a failed developer negotiation with Martin Cadillac recalled, "Someone said, 'It's only down in that neighborhood' " (interview with Herb Katz, July 13, 1984).

85. There is important evidence that negotiating with community organizations can serve to "rationalize" the process for developers. When OPCO was temporarily de-funded under the progressive majority (councilmember Jim Conn was eliminated from the voting due to "conflict of interest," a judgment that was later rescinded), it found developer representatives to testify in its favor.

86. Interview with Doris Ganga, July 31, 1984.

87. Interview with Audrey Parker, September 7, 1988.

88. Some liberals disagree with this, saying that such efforts were under way before the progressives came in, but if one looks at legislation that the city council was able to pass, it becomes clear that these liberal voices were drowned out by conservative ones. Change required a group willing to break with the rhetoric of free enterprise sanctified by tradition.

## Chapter 6

1. Interview with Doug Samuel, June 17, 1988.

2. Personal communication with Joe Feagin, January 15, 1991.

3. This section has been taken from Joe R. Feagin, John Gilderbloom, and Nestor Rodriguez "Private-Public Partnerships: The Houston Experience" in Gregory Squires (editor) *Unequal Partnerships*. New Brunswick, NJ: Rutgers University Press. I have made several revisions from the original and updated certain parts. Our thanks to the publisher, Rutgers University Press, and my co-authors for permission to reprint a revised portion of the chapter.

4. Donald I. Hovde, Undersecretary at the Department of Housing and Urban Development, made these comments on the back cover of Johnson's (1982) book.

5. According to officials of the Houston Housing Authority, twelve thousand persons are currently on the waiting list for section 8 assistance and another ten thousand to get into public housing.

6. In terms of housing costs, one out of four disabled and elderly Houstonians were paying unaffordable housing payments, while close to one half of low- and moderate-income families had excessive housing costs. Despite this problem, only a tiny fraction of the persons surveyed received any government housing assistance. Given the federal government's drastic cutbacks in housing programs, Houston will have to look to local solutions to resolve inadequate housing design and unaffordable housing payments. The city, however, has provided little support for such programs as house sharing, congregate services, equity conversion, cooperative housing, and urban homesteading.

7. Michael Smith's (1979) *The City and Social Theory* provides the best overview of the sociology of planning and design. This book reviews and critiques the work of Louis Wirth, Georg Simmel, Theodore Roszak, Richard Sennett, and various progressive planners. Of special interest is Smith's (1979:26-44) account of Wirth's theory of urban planning, which called for centralized metropolitan planning by trained experts which could bring rationality and consensus to the city. He was opposed to neighborhood planning and argued for "highest and best use" concerning land.

## Chapter 7

1. Since social reality is interactive rather than linear (Gamson, 1988), there is a certain irreducible mystery, or "emergent" quality, to social movements. Movement activists know this, describing how sometimes events just "click." While we look in turn at a number of theories and explanatory variables, this analysis can only be applied to selected dimensions of our case study. The other dimensions serve a documentary function—the telling of a story and the capturing of an unfolding process of social change. We believe that this is useful in its own right and will, we hope, facilitate comparisons in the future.

2. As Dennis Zane once remarked, "I don't know what all the answers are except that politics is a serendipitous affair. If anybody analyzes this stuff and never gets into exhaustion, never gets into personal likes and dislikes, or conflict between individuals, or love between individuals, or changing sexual relationships and patterns. . . .hey, it's superficial" (interview with Dennis Zane, June 30, 1984).

3. When President Reagan assumed office, the amount of money spent by the federal government for defense was seven times greater than for low-income housing; by 1988, the difference increases to forty-four fold. Housing assistance has been slashed by 78 percent, while defense spending has increased by 31 percent. Today 27 cents

of every tax dollar is spent on defense, while only one half a penny is spent on housing programs. Money targeted for section 8 has been cut by 82 percent; the section 202 program (elderly/handicapped loans) has been slashed, and section 235 (homeowner-ship program) has been eliminated. President Bush's 1989 budget plan means a $5 billion increase in military spending and a virtual freeze on government housing.

4. To examine the full range of possibilities of a Weberian analysis of the city, the following books are useful: *Rethinking Rental Housing* by John Gilderbloom and Richard Appelbaum; *Whose City?* by R. E. Pahl; *Power and Crisis in the City* by Roger Friedland; and *Social Theory and the Urban Question* by Peter Saunders.

5. In addition, Tucker's regression analysis only controlled for two variables at a time and failed to control for such critical variables as a city's median rent level.

6. In this section, we have drawn from the work of Gilderbloom and Appelbaum, 1988:144–9) by both revising and expanding on their arguments on the politics of rent control.

7. Interview with Wayne Bauer, June 21, 1984.

8. Rachel Bratt's new book, *Rebuilding A Low-Income Housing Policy,* gives a detailed account of the recent emergence of community-based housing programs. Bratt's book integrates numerous studies that have been conducted by herself and several of her graduate students at Tufts and by others evaluating community-based housing programs. Bratt is perhaps the country's leading expert in this area. The book is especially timely given the numerous legislative bills in Congress to support community-based housing programs.

9. In this section, we have drawn from the work of Gilderbloom and Appelbaum, 1988:188) by both revising and expanding on their arguments for cooperative housing. We were also influenced by the work of Lauber and Hinojosa (1984), Clavel (1986), and the Institute for Policy Studies (1989) as well as discussions with Ed Kirschner, Hank Savitch, and Joel Rubenzahl. Savitch also pointed out that in Holland the rapid increase in ownership of housing has not dampened progressive grass-roots movements there (see also Weesep, 1986).

10. At the local level, several more direct programmatic responses can be made. Certain selective government actions and policies could produce some rather dramatic changes in the lives of the disadvantaged. First, local officials could endorse and fund house sharing, sale/lease-back programs, cooperatives, and homesteading programs. Community development block grant funds could be used to fund organizations that sponsor these important and vital programs. Second, a number of section 8 certificates should be made available for cooperative, house sharing, and sale/lease-back programs. This would further encourage the development of these programs—especially cooperatives, which need these kinds of incentives. Third, prohibitions against in-law apartments should be abolished, these units offer a significant number of housing opportunities for elderly and disabled persons in middle-class neighborhoods. In-law apartments, whether located in the attic, garage, or basement, integrate individuals

into good neighborhoods at a reasonable cost. One fourth of all community development block grants should be set aside to fund nonprofit housing corporations to build cooperative housing. CDBGs should also be used to finance fair housing laws.

CDBGs should fund an Independent Housing Service, which would provide technical advice to builders wishing to construct or convert housing for use by the elderly and disabled (Gilderbloom and Rosentraub, 1990). Such a service could provide technical assistance in the placement, design, and financing of housing for disadvantaged populations. An independent Housing Service would provide architectural consultation free of charge to landlords and developers interested in modifying a housing unit for a disabled person. In addition, this agency would also provide grants or loans to landlords and developers to cover the cost of constructing a barrier-free living environment. To make sure that these units remain affordable, certain stipulations must be made to regulate the rent or cost of the unit over a minimum of twenty years. Finally, an Independent Housing Service could also serve as an advocate for the disabled community. Efforts should also be made to encourage house sharing by those individuals who are house rich yet cash poor.

Numerous cities have funded technical services for disadvantaged residents to secure low-income housing and neighborhood development. San Francisco's Independent Housing Service, funded by the office of the mayor, provides loans and architectural services to modify housing for persons with disabilities. It also advises the mayor and board of supervisors on issues of concern to the elderly and disabled.

Planning should also be aimed at providing affordable and barrier-free housing environments. New multifamily housing units on the ground floor should be made accessible to wheelchair users. The cost of designing new housing units that are accessible is only a few hundred dollars, compared with the thousands of dollars it takes to modify a unit designed for an ablebodied user. All new housing developments should be required to provide sidewalks with curb cuts, timed lights, and bus shelters. Large housing developments should also be required to have a certain number of units that are accessible and affordable. Secondary units in traditional single-family houses should be encouraged as they offer a significant number of housing opportunities for low-income persons. All cooperative and urban homesteading programs should set aside at least 15 percent of the units for persons with disabling conditions. The need for action is great and is required to develop a strategy to attack the housing crisis.

# References

Achtenberg, Emily P. and Peter Marcuse 1983. "Towards the decommodification of housing: A political analysis and progressive program." In Chester Hartman (ed.), America's housing crisis: What is to be done? Boston: Routledge and Kegan Paul. Pp. 202–31.

Achtenberg, Emily P. and Michael Stone 1977. Tenants First! A Research and Organizing Guide to FHA Housing. Cambridge: Urban Planning Aid.

Adams, J. S. 1984. "The meaning of housing in America." Annals of the Association of American Geographers 74:515–27.

Adamson, Madeleine and Seth Borgos 1984. This Mighty Dream: Social Protest Movements in the United States. Boston: Routledge & Kegan Paul.

Agnew, J. W. 1978. "Market relations and locational conflict in cross-national perspective." In Kevin Cox (ed.), Urbanization and conflict in market societies. New York: Methuen. Pp. 128–43.

Agnew, John A. 1981. "Homeownership and the Capitalist Social Order." In Michael Dear and Allen J. Scott (eds.), Urbanization and urban planning in capitalist society. London and New York: Methuen. Pp. 457–80.

Alford, R. and H. Scoble 1968. "Sources of local political involvement." American Political Science Review 62:1192–1205.

Alinsky, Saul 1971. Rules for radicals. New York: Random House, Vintage Books.

Angotti, Thomas 1977. "The housing question." Monthly Review, October 1977 vol. 29, no. 5:39–51.

Apartment Age, 1984. "Facts on Proposition 13." Newsletter of Apartment Association of Greater Los Angeles. Los Angeles, CA: Apartment Association of Greater Los Angeles.

Appelbaum, Richard P. 1978. Size, growth, and U.S. cities. New York: Praeger.

Appelbaum, Richard P. 1986. "An analysis of rental housing in Los Angeles, Santa Monica, Berkeley, and West Hollywood under Current Rent Control and A.B 483." California State Senate: Senate Rules Committee, unpublished report.

Appelbaum, Richard P. 1990. "Down and out in America: The origins of homelessness by Peter Rossi, and Address Unknown: The homeless in America by James Wright." American Journal of Sociology, vol. 96, no. 1 (July) p. 255–58.

Appelbaum, Richard P. and J. I. Gilderbloom 1990. "The redistributional impact of modern rent control." Environment and Planning A, vol. 22:601–14.

Appelbaum, Richard P., Jennifer Bigelow, Henry Kramer, Harvey Molotch, and Paul Relis 1976. The effects of urban growth: A population impact analysis. New York: Praeger.

Appelbaum, Richard P., Michael Dolny, Peter Dreier, and John I. Gilderbloom 1990. "Scapegoating rent control: Masking the causes of homelessness." Briefing Paper. Washington, D.C.: Economic Policy Institute.

Atlas, John 1982. National tenants union platform: Rent control plank draft. East Orange, NJ: National Tenants Union.

Atlas, John and Peter Dreier 1980a. "Legislative strategy: Fighting for rent control." Shelterforce vol. 5, no. 4, October 1980.

Atlas, John and Peter Dreier 1980b "The housing crisis and the tenants' revolt." Social Policy 10, 4:13–24. January/February 1980.

Atlas, John and Peter Dreier 1981. "Making tenants' vote count in New Jersey." Social Policy May/June 1981.

Atlas, John and Peter Dreier 1988. "Ingredients for a housing action agenda in '88: Tenants rights and homelessness." Shelterforce 11,2 (August/September):8–11.

Baar, Kenneth 1977. "Rent control in the 1970's: The case of the New Jersey tenants' movement." Hastings Law Journal 28 (January 1977):631–83.

Baar, Kenneth and Dennis Keating, 1975. "The last stand of economic substantive due process—the housing emergency requirements for rent control." Urban Lawyer 7; 3:490–501.

Baar, Kenneth. 1983. "Guidelines for Drafting Rent Control Laws: Lessons of a Decade." Rutgers Law Review 35:4:721–885.

Baar, Kenneth and Dennis Keating 1981 "Fair return standards and hardship appeal procedures: A guide for New Jersey rent leveling boards." Berkeley, CA: National Housing Law Project.

Baar, Kenneth and Garry Squire, 1987, Perspectives on the Rental Housing Market in the Santa Monica Area. Santa Monica, CA: Squire and Associates

Babbie, Earl 1988. The practice of social research. Fifth Edition. Belmont, CA: Wadsworth.

Bach, Eve, Thomas Brom, Julia Estrella, Lenny Goldberg, and Ed Kirshner 1976. The Cities' Wealth. Washington, D.C.: National Conference on Alternative State and Local Public Policies.

Bach, Eve, Nicholas Carbone, and Pierre Clavel 1982. "Running the city for the people." Social Policy (Winter):5–23.

Ball, Michael 1976. Owner-occupation. In M. Edwards, F. Gray, S. Merrett, and J. Swann (eds.), Housing and class in Britain. London: Political Economy of Housing Workshop of the Conference of Socialist Economists, Pp. 24–29.

Barber, Benjamin R. 1984. "Political talk—and 'strong democracy.' " Dissent 31 (Spring):215–22.

Barnes, Peter 1981. "Lamenting the rent." In John I. Gilderbloom (ed.), Rent control: A source book. Santa Barbara, CA: Foundation for National Progress. Pp. 16–20.

Barnes, S. H. and M. Kaase 1979. Political action: Mass participation in five western democracies. London: Sage.

Bellah, Robert N., Richard Madsen, William M. Sullivan, Ann Swidler, and Steve M. Tipton 1985. Habits of the heart. Berkeley: University of California Press.

Benson, Andrew 1988. "Arts council gets $15,000 in CD funds." Houston Post (June 16), sec. A, p. 10.

Berger, Peter L. and Thomas Luckmann 1966. The Social Construction of Reality. Garden City, NY: Doubleday.

Bernstein, Alan 1988. "Recollections of King's visits to Houston conflict." Houston Chronicle (April 3), sec. 1. p. 8.

Berry, Brian J. L. and John Kasarda 1977. Contemporary urban ecology. New York: Macmillan.

Betz, J. 1981. "Rental housing crisis called calamity." Los Angeles Times, October 4, 1981, sec. VIII-23.

Birkenfeld v. City of Berkeley, CA., 550 P. 2d 1001 California Reporter.

Bivins, Ralph 1988. "Losing Money: Area landlords find it cheaper to demolish excess apartments." Houston Chronicle (March 27), sec. 5, p. 1.

Block, Walter and Edgar Olsen 1981. Rent control: Myths and realities. Vancouver, British Columbia: The Fraser Institute.

Bluestone, Barry and Bennett Harrison 1982. The deindustrialization of America. New York: Basic Books.

Blum, Terry C. and Paul William Kingston 1984. "Homeownership and social attachment." Sociological Perspectives 27, 2:159–80.

Blumer, Herbert 1939. "Collective behavior." In Robert Park (ed.), An outline of the principles of sociology. New York: Barnes and Noble, Inc. p. 219–80.

Blumer, Herbert 1951. "Collective Behavior." In A. M. Lee (ed.), Principles of sociology. New York: Barnes and Noble. Pp. 99–121.

Boggs, Carl 1983. "The new populism and the limits of structural reforms." Theory and Society 12, 3. Pp. 343–63.

Boggs, Carl 1986. Social movements and political power. Phildelphia: Temple University Press.

Boyer, Richard and David Savageau 1981. Places rated almanac. New York: Rand McNally & Company.

Boyte, Harry C. 1980. The backyard revolution. Philadelphia: Temple University Press.

Boyte, Harry C. 1984. "Communitarianism and the Left: A Discussion." Dissent (Fall):475-78.

Boyte, Harry C. and Frank Riessman 1986. The new populism: The politics of empowerment. Philadelphia: Temple University Press.

Boyte, Harry and Sara M. Evans 1984. "Strategies in search of America: Cultural radicalism, populism and democratic culture." Socialist Review 14,3:73-100.

Boyte, Harry C., Heather Booth and Steve Max 1986. Citizen action and the new American populism. Philadelphia: Temple University Press.

Bratt, Rachel G. 1989. Rebuilding low-income housing policy. Philadelphia: Temple University Press.

Braungart, Richard C. 1984. "Historical generations and youth movements: A theoretical perspective." Research in Social Movements Conflict and Change 6:95-142.

Brown, Peter 1988. "Houston badly needs planning, design." Houston Post (May 15), sec. E, p. 3.

Brubaker, Laurel 1986. "How Houston really landed Grumman." Houston Business Journal (October 13, 1986), p. 3.

Bullard, Robert 1985. Decent and affordable housing for low and moderate income families. Testimony of Public Housing Needs and Conditions in Houston, before Subcommittee on Housing and Community Affairs, House of Representatives, 99th Congress, 1st session, (October 14). Washington, D.C.

Bullard, Robert 1987. Invisible Houston: The black experience in boom and bust. College Station, TX: Texas A & M Press.

Byars, Carol 1988. "Tenant of Mercado del Sol to Appeal Eviction Ruling." Houston Chronicle (January 26, 1988), sec. 1, p. 18.

Cantril, Harvey 1941. The psychology of social movements. New York: Wiley.

Čapek, Stella M. 1989. "Missing Social Actors: Tenants and Collective Organizing in Arkansas." Paper presented at the annual Southwest Social Science Association, Little Rock, Arkansas, March 31, 1989.

Čapek, Stella M. 1985. "Urban progressive movements: The case of Santa Monica." Ph.D. Dissertation, University of Texas at Austin.

Čapek, Stella and John Gilderbloom 1990. "Tenants: second class citizens." Shelterforce, vol. 12, no. 4 (March/April):17.

Carden, M. L. 1978. "The proliferation of a social movement: Ideology and individual incentives in the contemporary feminist movement." Research in Social Movements, Conflict and Change 1:179–96.

Carnoy, Martin and Derek Shearer 1980. Economic democracy. New York: M. E. Sharpe.

Castells, Manuel 1977. The urban question. London: Edward Arnold.

Castells, Manuel 1983. The city and the grassroots. Berkeley: University of California Press.

Chadwick, Susan 1988. "Sunday in the parks." Houston Post (October 14), sec. D, p. 1.

Chafetz, Janet Saltzman and Anthony Gary Dworkin 1986. Female revolt: Women's movements in world and historical perspective. Totowa, NJ: Rowman and Allanheld.

Clark, Rosanne 1985. "Development council maps economic strategy." Houston (February):9–13

Clavel, Pierre 1982. "Planning under progressive majorities." Working Papers in Planning. Ithaca, NY: Cornell University.

Clavel, Pierre 1986. The progressive city: Planning and participation, 1969–1984. New Brunswick, NJ: Rutgers University Press.

Clavel, Pierre, John Forester, and William Goldsmith 1980. Urban and regional planning in an age of austerity. New York: Pergamon Press.

Cloward, Richard A. and Frances Fox Piven 1986. Foreword to Organizing the movement: The Roots and Growth of ACORN by Gary Delgado. Philadelphia: Temple University Press.

Cobb, Kim 1987. "Apartment group taking credit for inspector layoffs." Houston Chronicle (May 12), sec. 1, p. 12.

Cockburn, Alexander and James Ridgeway 1981. "Revolt in Reagan's backyard." Village Voice, April 22–28.

Cohen, Jean L. 1985. "Strategy or identity: New theoretical paradigms and contemporary social movements." Social Research 52,4:663–716.

Comptroller General 1979. Rental housing: A national problem that needs immediate attention. Washington D.C.: General Accounting Office.

Conlon, Michael 1988. "Jackson equates Houston, S. Africa." Houston Post (March 1), sec. 1, p. 1.

Coser, Louis 1969. "The visibility of evil." Journal of Social Issues 12:101–9.

Cox, Kevin 1981. "Capitalism and conflict around the communal living space." In Michael Dear and Allen Scott (eds.), Urbanization and urban planning in capitalist society. London: Methuen. Pp. 431–55.

Cox, Kevin 1982. "Housing tenure and neighborhood activism." Urban Affairs Quarterly 18, 1:107–29.

Crick, Bernard 1964. In Defense of Politics. London: Penguin Books.

Crown, Judith 1986. "HEDC sets goals for growth by year 2000." Houston Chronicle (April 2, 1986), p. 1.

Crump, Spencer 1962. Ride the big red cars: How trolleys helped build southern California. Los Angeles, CA: Crest.

Cuff, Dana 1985. "Allen Parkway Village and Houston's low-cost housing." In Public Hearing Needs and Conditions in Houston. Hearings before Subcommittee on Housing and Community Development, Committee on Banking, Finance, and Urban Affairs. House of Representatives, 99th Congress, 1st session. (October 14). Washington, D.C.: Government Printing Office.

Curtis, Russell and Louis Zurcher 1971. "Social movements: An analytical exploration of organizational forms." Social Problems 21, 3:356–70.

Curtis, Russell and Louis Zurcher 1973. "Stable resources of protest movements: The multi-organizational field." Social Forces 52, 1:53–60.

Dawson, Bill 1988. "Houston ranks 2nd among cities with worst ozone levels." Houston Chronicle (May 4) p. 24.

Daykin, David (1987). "The limits of neighborhood power: Progressive politics and local control in Santa Monica." In Business Elites and Urban Development. Albany: State University of New York Press. Scott Cummings (ed.), Pp. 357–87.

Delgado, Gary 1986. Organizing the movement: The roots and growth of ACORN. Philadelphia: Temple University Press.

Dennis, Mike 1990. Santa Monica Year-end Financial Report. Santa Monica, CA: City of Santa Monica.

Devine, Richard J. 1986. "Who benefits from rent control?" Oakland, CA: Center for Community Change.

Domhoff, G. William 1978. Who really rules? New Haven and community power re-examined. Santa Monica, CA: Goodyear Publishing Company, Inc.

Downing, Margaret 1988. "El Mercado Could Work, Analysts Say." Houston Post (February 14, 1988), p. 1D.

Downing, Margaret and Steve Friedman 1988. "Warning unheeded by city planners?" Houston Post (February 14, 1988), p. 1A.

Dreier, Peter 1979. "The Politics of Rent Control." Working Papers 6:55–63.

Dreier, Peter 1982. "The status of tenants in the United States." Social Problems 30, 2:179–98 (December).

Dreier, Peter 1984. "The tenants movement in the United States." International Journal of Urban and Regional Research, vol. 8, no. 2:256–79.

Dreier, Peter and John Atlas 1980. "The housing crisis and the tenants' revolt." Social Policy (January):13–24.

Dreier, Peter and John Atlas 1990. "Eliminate the mansion subsidy." Shelterforce (May/June), vol. XII:5, pp.10–11, 21.

Dreier, Peter and Rebecca Stevens 1990. "The affordability gap: employers must face housing squeeze." Shelterforce (May/June), vol. XII:5, pp. 6–7.

Dreier, Peter, John I. Gilderbloom, and Richard P. Appelbaum 1980. "Rising rents and rent control: Issues in urban reform."In Pierre Clavel, John Forester, and William Goldsmith (eds.), Urban and regional planning in an age of austerity. New York: Pergamon Press. Pp 154–76.

Duncan, S. S. 1981. "Housing policy, the methodology of levels, and urban research: The case of Castells." International Journal of Urban and Regional Research 5, 2:231–54.

Edelman, Murray 1967. The symbolic use of politics. Chicago: University of Illinois Press.

Eder, Klaus 1985. "The new social movements: Moral crusades, political pressure groups, or social movements?" Social Research 52, 4:869–90.

Engels, Fredrich 1955. The housing question. Moscow, Progress Publishers.

Esping-Anderson, Gosta, Roger Friedland, and Erik Olin Wright 1976. "Modes of class struggle and the capitalist state. In Kapitalistate, 4–5:186–220.

Evans, Sara 1979. Personal politics. New York: Knopf.

Evans, Sara M. and Harry C. Boyte 1982. "Schools for action: Radical uses of social space." Democracy 2, 4:55–65.

Evans, Sara M. and Harry C. Boyte 1986. Free spaces: The sources of democratic change in America. New York: Harper Row.

Fainstein, Norman 1985. "Class and Community in Urban Social Movements." Urban Affairs Quarterly 20, 4:557–64.

Fainstein, Norman I. and Susan S. Fainstein 1974. Urban political movements: the search for power by minority groups in American cities. Englewood Cliffs, NJ: Prentice-Hall Inc.

*References*

Feagin, Joe 1983. The urban real estate game. Englewood Cliffs, NJ: Prentice-Hall Inc.

Feagin, Joe R. 1988. The free enterprise city: Houston in political-economic perspective. New Brunswick, NJ: Rutgers University Press.

Feagin, Joe R. and Stella M. Čapek 1991. "Grassroots movements in a class perspective." Research in Political Sociology 5:27–53.

Feagin, Joe R., John I. Gilderbloom, and Nestor Rodriguez 1989. "Private-public partnerships: The Houston experience." In Gregory Squires (ed.) Unequal partnerships: The political economy of urban redevelopment in postwar America. New Brunswick, NJ: Rutgers University Press. p. 240–259.

Feagin, Joe and Robert Parker 1990. Building American Cites: The Urban Real Estate Game. Englewood Cliffs, NJ: Prentice Hall

Ferree, Myra Marx and Frederick Miller 1985. "Mobilization and meaning: Toward an integration of social psychology and resource perspectives on social movements." Sociological Inquiry 55, 1 (Winter):38–61.

Fireman, Bruce and William Gamson 1979. "Utilitarian logic in the resource mobilization perspective." In Mayer Zald and John McCarthy (eds.), The dynamics of social movements. Cambridge, MA: Winthrop. Pp. 8–44.

Fisher, Claude 1982. To dwell among friends: Personal networks in town & city. Chicago: University of Chicago Press.

Fisher, Robert 1984. Let the people decide: Neighborhood organizing in America. Boston: Twayne.

Fisher, Robert 1985. Public housing in houston: The issue is democracy in public housing needs and conditions. Hearings before Subcommittee on Housing and Community Development of Committee on Banking, Finance and Urban Affairs, House of Representatives, 99th Congress, 1st session (September 18) Washington D.C. Government Printing Office. p. 159–64.

Fisher, Robert 1987. "Expanding the tenants' movement: Building on ideology." Shelterforce 10, 4:16–17.

Fisher, Robert 1988. "Houston is moving to the left." Houston Chronicle (January 24), sec. 6, p. 1.

Fisher, Robert and Joseph Kling 1989. "Community Mobilization Prospects for the Future." Urban Affairs Quarterly 25, 2:200–11.

Flacks, Richard 1971. Youth and social change. Chicago: Methuen.

Flacks, Richard 1988. Making history: The radical tradition in American life. New York: Columbia University Press.

Flanigan, William H. and Nancy H. Zingale 1979. Political behavior of the American electorate. Boston: Allyn and Bacon.

Flournoy, Craig 1985. "Housing for elderly segregated." Dallas Morning News (February 11), sec. A, p. 16.

Foley, Donald L. 1980. "The sociology of housing." In Alex Inkeles (ed.), Annual Review of Sociology, vol. 6, pp. 457–78.

Forester, John 1980. "Critical Theory and Planning Practice." In Pierre Clavel, John Forester, and William Goldsmith (eds.), Urban and Regional Planning in an Age of Austerity. New York: Pergamon Press. Pp. 326–42.

Franklin, Scott B. 1981. "Housing cooperatives: A viable means of home ownership for low-income families." Journal of Housing (July):392–98.

Freeman, Jo 1983. Social movements of the sixties and seventies. New York: Longman, Inc.

Fried, Marc 1973. "Grieving for a lost home." In L. J. Duhl (ed.), The urban condition. New York: Basic Books. Pp. 151–71.

Friedland, Roger 1982. Power and crisis in the City. London: MacMillan Press.

Friedman, Steve 1988. "Houston trails other cities in slice of federal grant spent on housing: 10% here compared to Boston's 75%." Houston Post (November 6), sec. A, p. 20.

Friedman, Steve and Kate Thomas 1988. "City probing new troubles with HUD funds." Houston Post (July 24), sec. A, p. 1.

Friedmann, John 1981. "Life space and economic space: Contradictions in regional development." University of California, Los Angeles School of Urban Planning manuscript.

Fulton, William 1985. "On the beach with the progressives." Planning (January):4–9.

Gale, Richard P. 1986. "Social movements and the state: The environmental movement, countermovement, and government agencies." Sociological Perspectives 29, 2:202–40.

Gamson, William 1975. The strategy of social protest. Homewood, IL: Dorsey Press.

Gamson, William 1988. "Political discourse and collective action." In International Social Movement Research, vol. 1. Supplement to Research in Social Movements, Conflicts and Change. Greenwich, CT: JAI Press. Pp. 219–44.

Gamson, William, B. Fireman and S. Rytina 1982. Encounters with unjust authority. Homewood, IL: Dorsey Press.

Gans, Herbert 1982. The urban villagers. Revised edition. New York: Free Press.

Garner, Roberta and Mayer Zald 1986. "The political economy of social movement sectors." In Gerald Suttles and Mayer Zald (eds.), The challenge of social control: Citizenship and institution building in modern society; essays in honor of Morris Janowitz. Norwood, NJ: Ablex. Pp. 119–45.

Gaventa, J. 1980. "Power and powerlessness: Quiescence and rebellion in an Appalachian valley." Urbana, IL: University of Illinois Press.

General Adjustment Subcommittee, 1979, "Recommendation of Rent Increases." City of Santa Monica. unpublished paper.

Gilderbloom, John I. 1976. "Report to Donald E. Burns, Secretary of Business and Transportation Agency, on the validity of the legislative findings of A. B. 3788 and the economic impact of rent control." Sacramento, CA: California Department of Housing and Community Development.

Gilderbloom, John I. 1978. "The impact of moderate rent control in the United States: A review and critique of existing literature." Sacramento, CA: State of California, Department of Housing and Community Development.

Gilderbloom, John I. 1980. "Moderate rent control: The Experience of U.S. cities." Washington, D.C.: National Conference on Alternative State and Local Public Policies.

Gilderbloom, John I. 1981a. "Moderate rent control: Its impact on the quality and quantity of the housing stock." Urban Affairs Quarterly 17, 2:123–42.

Gilderbloom, John I. 1981b. Rent control: A source book. San Francisco: Foundation for National Progress.

Gilderbloom, John I. 1983. "Toward an understanding of inter-city rent differential: A sociological contribution." Ph.D. Dissertation, University of California, Santa Barbara, August 1982.

Gilderbloom, John I. 1984. "Redistributive impacts of rent control in New Jersey." Paper presented at the American Sociological Meetings, San Antonio, Texas, August 1984.

Gilderbloom, John I. 1985a. "Social forces affecting landlords in the determinatiom of rent." Urban Life 14, 2:155–79.

Gilderbloom, John I. 1985b. "Toward a sociology of rental housing markets." Paper presented at the American Sociological Association Meetings, Washington, D.C., August 28, 1985.

Gilderbloom, John I. 1985c. "Houston's rental housing conditions: Longitudinal and comparative analysis." In Public Housing Needs and Conditions. Hearings before Subcommittee on Housing and Community Development of Committee on Banking, Finance and Urban Affairs, House of Representatives, 99th Congress, 1st session (September 18). Washington, D.C.: Government Printing Office. Pp. 145–59, 164–66.

Gilderbloom, John I. 1986. "The impact of rent control on rent in New Jersey communities." Sociology and Social Research 71:1.

Gilderbloom, John I. 1988. "Tenants' movements in the United States." In Elizabeth Huttman and Willem van Vliet (ed.), Handbook of housing and the built environment in the United States. New York: Greenwood Press. Pp. 269–82.

Gilderbloom, John I. 1990a. "A progressive approach to the housing crisis." San Francisco, CA: Foundation for National Progress, Housing Information Center.

Gilderbloom, John I. 1990b. "The Impact of Housing Status on Political Beliefs." San Francisco, CA: Foundation for National Progress, Housing Information Center.

Gilderbloom, John, forthcoming, The Politics of the Rental Housing Crisis. San Franscisco, CA: Foundation for National Progress.

Gilderbloom, John I. and Dennis Keating 1982. "An evaluation of rent control in Orange." San Francisco: Foundation for National Progress, Housing Information Center.

Gilderbloom, John and Mike Jacob 1981. "Consumer price index rent increases." In Gilderbloom (ed.), Rent control: A source book. Pp. 35–40.

Gilderbloom, John I. and Richard Appelbaum 1984. "Rent control in the United States: A brief summary of recent studies." Paper presented at the American Association of Housing Educators conference, Washington, D.C., August 6, 1984.

Gilderbloom, John I. and Richard P. Appelbaum 1988. Rethinking rental housing. Philadelphia: Temple University Press.

Gilderbloom, John I. and Nestor Rodriguez 1988. "Hispanic housing conditions in the United States: Technical tables and methodology." Working Paper. Austin, TX: University of Texas, Center for Mexican American Studies.

Gilderbloom, John I. and Nestor Rodriguez 1990. "Hispanic rental housing needs in the United States: Problems and prospects." Working Paper. Austin, TX: University of Texas, Center for Mexican American Studies.

Gilderbloom, John I., Mark Rosentraub, and Robert Bullard 1987. "Financing, designing, and locating housing and transportation services for the disabled and elderly." Houston: University of Houston Center for Public Policy.

Gilderbloom, John I. and Mark Rosentraub 1990. Creating the Accessible City: Proposals for Providing Housing and Transportation for Low Income, Elderly and Disabled People. American Journal of Economics and Sociology. vol. 49, no. 3, Pp. 271–282.

Gitlin, Todd 1980. The whole world is watching: Mass media in the making and unmaking of the new left. Berkeley: University of California Press.

Gitlin, Todd 1989. The sixties. New York: Bantam.

Glen, Maxwell and Cody Shearer 1980. "Reagan and rent control." Sacramento Bee, December 11, 1980.

Goering, John and Coulibably Modibo 1988. Explorations in the sociology of public housing segregation. Washington, D.C.: U.S. Department of Housing and Urban Development, Office of Policy Development and Research. Draft.

Goffman, Erving 1974. Frame analysis. Cambridge: Harvard University Press.

Goodman, Paul 1956. Growing up absurd. New York: Random House.

Goodwyn, Lawrence 1978. The populist movements. New York: Oxford University Press.

Gottdiener, Mark 1985. The social production of urban space. Austin, TX: University of Texas Press.

Gottdiener, Mark 1987. The decline of urban politics. Newbury Park, CA: Sage.

Gramsci, Antonio 1971. Selections from the Prison Notebooks. New York: International Publishers.

Grandolfo, Jane A. 1988. "$14 million in tax credits for aiding homeless may be wasted." Houston Post (June 4), sec. A, p. 21.

Grandolfo, Jane A., 1988. "Lack of zoning complicates anti-porn fight." Houston Post (October 8) p. 1.

Gravois, John 1986. "HEDC weighs strings attached to tax dollars." Houston Post (April 14, 1986), sec. A, p. 1.

Griffiths, Bruce V. 1985. "Statement of Bruce V. Griffiths, staff counsel of American Civil Liberties Union." Public Housing: Needs and Conditions in Houston. Hearings before Subcommittee on Housing and Community Development, Committee on Banking, Finance, and Urban Affairs, House of Representatives, 99th Congress, 1st session (October 14) Washington, D.C.: Government Printing Office.

Gurr, Ted 1970. Why men rebel. Princeton: Princeton University Press.

Gusfield, Joseph R. 1981. "Social movements and social change: Perspectives of linearity and fluidity." Research in Social Movements, Conflict and Change 4:317–339.

Guterbock, T. 1980. Machine politics in transition: Party and community in Chicago. Chicago: University of Chicago Press.

Habermas, Jurgen 1971. Knowledge and human interests. Boston: Beacon Press.

Habermas, Jurgen 1975. Legitimation crisis. Boston: Beacon Press.

Hall, Peter 1981. "Squatters' movement solidifies." Rolling Stone (September 17).

Halle, D. 1984. America's working man: Work, home and politics among blue collar property owners. Chicago: University of Chicago Press.

Harloe, Michael 1977. Captive cities: Studies in the political economy of cities and regions. London: John Wiley and Sons.

Harrington, Michael 1962. The other America. New York: Macmillan.

Harrington, Michael 1968. Toward democratic left: A radical program for a new majority. New York: Macmillan.

Hartman, Chester 1984. The transformation of San Francisco. Totowa, NJ: Rowman and Allenheld.

Hartman, Chester and Michael Stone 1980. "A socialist housing program for the United States." In Pierre Clavel, John Forester, and Willam M. Goldsmith (eds.) Urban and Regional Planning in an Age of Austerity. New York: Pergamon. Pp. 219-250.

Hartman, Chester, Dennis Keating, and Richard LeGates 1981. Displacement: How to fight it. Berkeley: National Housing Law Project.

Harvey, Davis 1973. Social justice and the city. London: Edward Arnold.

Harvey, David 1975. "The political economy of urbanization in advanced capitalist societies: The case of the United States." In (eds.), Gary Gappert and Harold Rose "The social economy of cities: Urban affairs annual review." Beverly Hills: Sage Publications. Pp. 119-164.

Harvey, David 1976. "Labor, capital and class struggle around the built environment in advanced capitalist societies." In Kevin Cox (ed.), Urbanization and conflict in market societies, politics and society. Chicago: Maaroufa Press. Pp. 625-95.

Harvey, David 1978. "The urban process under capitalism: A framework for analysis." In Michael Dear and Allen Scott (eds.), Urbanization and urban planning in capitalist society. London: Methuen. Pp. 91-122.

Harvey, David 1979. "Rent control and a fair return." Baltimore Sun, September 20, 1979.

Harvey, David 1981. "Rent control and fair return." In John I. Gilderbloom (ed.), A source book. Santa Barbara, CA: Foundation for National Progress, Housing Information Center 1979. Pp. 80-82.

Harvey, David 1985. Consciousness and the urban experience: studies in the history and theory of capitalist urbanization. Baltimore, MD: Johns Hopkins Press.

Hayden, Tom 1970. Trial. New York: Holt, Rinehart, and Winston.

Hayden, Tom 1981. "The Future of Politics in Liberalism." Nation (February 21), p. 193, 208-12.

HEDC (Houston Economic Development Council), 1986, Strategic Priorities Agenda. unpublished paper.

Heffley, Dennis and Rex Santerre 1985. "Rent control as an expenditure constraint: Some empirical results." Paper presented at the annual meeting of the Eastern Economic Association. Pittsburgh, PA: March 23, 1985.

Hensel, Bill 1988. "Low prices a boon for subsidized housing conference says." Houston Post (May 14) p. A/21.

Hernandez, Nelson 1983. "Pico Neighborhood Association: A field site project." Research paper conducted for the Department of Chicano Studies, University of California, Los Angeles.

Heskin, Allan D. 1981a. "A history of tenants in the United States: Struggle and ideology." International Journal of Urban and Regional Research [Special Issue on Housing], 5, 2:178–204.

Heskin, Allan D. 1981b. "Is a tenant a second class citizen?" In John I. Gilderbloom (ed.), Rent Control: A source book. San Francisco: Foundation for National Progress, Housing Information Center. Pp. 95–106.

Heskin, Allan D. 1981c. Tenants and the American dream: The ideology of being a tenant, mimeograph. Los Angeles: University of California, School of Urban Planning and Architecture.

Heskin, Allan D. 1983. Tenants and the American dream: Ideology and the tenant movement. New York: Praeger.

Heskin, Allan 1984. "After the battle is won." Manuscript, UCLA Graduate School of Architecture and Planning.

Hohm, Charles F. 1984. "Housing aspirations and fertility." Sociology and Social Research (April) 68(3):350–363.

Homenuck, H. P. M. 1973. "A study of high rise: effects, preferences and perceptions." Toronto: Institute of Environmental Research, Inc.

Hoover, Herbert 1923. How to own your own home. Foreword. Washington, D.C.: U.S. Department of Commerce.

Houston Housing Authority 1987. Assisted Housing in Houston-Harris County, Texas. unpublished paper.

Huttman, Elizabeth 1987. "Homelessness as a housing problem in an inner city in the U.S." California State University at Hayward, Department of Sociology, mimeo.

Inglehart, R. 1977. The silent revolution: Changing values and political styles among western publics. Princeton, NJ: Princeton University Press.

Institute for Policy Studies, Working Group on Housing 1989. The right to housing. Washington, D.C.: Institute for Policy Studies.

Jackson, Kenneth T. 1985. Crabgrass frontier: The suburbanization of the United States. New York: Oxford University Press.

Jacob, Mike 1979. "How rent control passed in Santa Monica, California." Oakland, CA: California Housing Action and Information Network.

Jacobs, Jane 1961. The death and life of great American cities. New York: Random House.

Jaret, Charles 1983. "Recent neo-marxist urban analysis." Annual Review of Sociology 9:499–525.

Jenkins, J. Craig 1983. "Resource mobilization theory and the study of social movements." Annual Review of Sociology 9:527–53.

Jenkins, J. Craig and Craig M. Eckert 1986. "Channeling black insurgency: Elite patronage and professional social movement organizations in the development of the black movement." American Sociological Review 51, 6:812–29.

Johnson, M. Bruce 1982. Resolving the housing crisis. Cambridge, MA: Ballinger Books.

Judd, Dennis 1984. The politics of American cities. Boston: Little, Brown.

Kann, Mark 1982. The American Left. New York: Praeger.

Kann, Mark 1983. "Radicals in power: Lessons from Santa Monica." Socialist Review 69 (13, 3), May-June:81–101.

Kann, Mark 1986. Middle Class Radicalism in Santa Monica. Philadelphia: Temple University Press.

Kanter, Rosabeth Moss 1972. Commitment and community: Communes and utopias in sociological perspective. Cambridge: Harvard University Press.

Kasindorf, Martin 1982. "Santa Monica tilts left." Newsweek, January 4, 1982.

Katznelson, Ira 1981. City trenches: Urban politics and the patterning of class in the United States. Chicago: University of Chicago Press.

Kelley, Jonathan, Ian McAllister, and Anthony Mughan 1984. "The decline of class revisited: Class and party in England, 1964–1979." Presented to the annual meeting of the American Sociological Association, San Antonio, TX, August 31, 1984.

Kemeny, Jim 1977. "A political sociology of homeownership in Australia." The Australian and New Zealand Journal of Sociology 13:47–52.

Kemeny, Jim 1980. "Homeownership and privatization." International Journal of Urban and Regional Research 4, 3:372–87.

Kemp, Jack 1990. "Tackling poverty: Market-based policies to empower the poor." Policy Review (Winter) no. 51:2–5.

Kingston, Paul William, John L. P. Thompson, Douglas M. Eichar 1984. "The politics of homeownership." American Politics Quarterly (April) 12, 2:131–50.

Kirschman, Mary Jo 1980. "Winning rent control in working class city." Baltimore: Rent control campaign, July 1980, mimeo.

Klandermans, Bert 1984. "Social psychological expansions of resource mobilization theory." American Sociological Review 49, 5:583–600.

Klandermans, Bert 1986. "New social movements and resource mobilization: The European and the American approach." Journal of Mass Emergencies and Disasters.

Klandermans, Bert and Dirk Oegema 1987. "Potentials, networks, motivations, and barriers: Steps toward participation in social movements." American Sociological Review, vol. 52 (August):519–31.

Klandermans, Bert and Sidney Tarrow 1988. "Mobilization into social movements: Synthesizing European and American approaches." International Social Movements Research, vol. 1:1–38.

Krauss, Celene 1983. "The elusive process of citizen activism." Social Policy 14, 2:50–55.

Kriesi, Hanspeter 1988. "The interdependence of structure and action: Some reflections on the state of the art." International Social Movements Research, vol. 1:349–68.

Krumholz, Norman and John Forester, 1990. Making Equity Planning Work. Philadelphia, PA: Temple University Press.

Kuttner, Robert 1982. "Economic jeopardy." Mother Jones, vol. 7 no. 4:28–35, 52–54.

Kuttner, Robert 1990. "Bleeding-heart conservatism." The New Republic, vol. 8, no. 2:256–79.

Lauber, Daniel and Jesus Hinojosa 1984. "Viewpoint." Planning (April) p. 18.

Lawson, Ronald n.d. "Labor unions and tenant organizations: A comparison of resource mobilization, strategic leverage and impact." Flushing, NY: Queens College, Urban Studies Department, mimeo.

Lawson, Ronald 1983. "A decentralized but moving pyramid: The evolution and consequences of the structure of the tenant movement." In Jo Freeman (ed.), Social Movements of the sixties and seventies. New York: Longman. Pp. 119–132.

Lawson, Ronald 1984. "Owners of last resort: An assessment of the track record of New York City's early low income cooperative conversions." New York: New York City Department of Housing Preservation and Development, Office of Program and Management Analysis.

Lawson, Ronald 1986. The tenant movement in New York City, 1904–1984. New Brunswick, NJ: Rutgers University Press.

Leight, Claudia, Elliot Lieberman, Jerry Kurt and Dean Pappey 1980. "Rent control wins in Baltimore." Moving on. Chicago: New America Movement.

Leites, Nathan and Charles Wolf, Jr. 1970. Rebellion and authority. Chicago: Markham.

Levine, Ned and Gene Grigsby 1987. "The impacts of rent control on Santa Monica tenants." Los Angeles: The Planning Group.

Lipsky, Michael 1970. Protest in city politics: Rent strikes, housing and the power of the poor. Chicago: Rand McNally and Company.

Listokin, David with Lizabeth Allewelt and James J. Nemeth 1985. Housing receivership and self-help neighborhood revitalization. New Brunswick, NJ: Center for Urban Policy Research.

Logan, John and Harvey Molotch 1987. Urban fortunes: The political economy of place. Berkeley, CA: University of California Press.

Lowe, Cary and Richard Blumberg 1981. "Moderate regulations protect landlords, as well as tenants." In John I. Gilderbloom (ed.), Rent control: A source book. Santa Barbara: Foundation for National Progress. Pp. 72–75.

Lowry, D. and L. Sigelman 1981. "Understanding the tax revolt: Eight explanations." American Political Science Review 75:963–74.

Lyman, Stanford M. and Marvin B. Scott 1967. "Territoriality: A neglected sociological dimension." Social Problems 15:236–48.

MacIntyre, Alasdair 1984. After virtue. Notre Dame, IN: University of Notre Dame Press.

Mannheim, Karl [1928] 1972. "The problem of generations." In Philip G. Altbach and Robert S. Laufer (eds.), The New pilgrims: Youth protest in transition. New York: David McKay. Pp. 101–38.

Mankin, Eric 1981. "You can win city hall." Mother Jones, December.

Marcuse, Peter 1981a. "The strategic potential of rent control." In John Gilderbloom (ed.), Rent control: A source book. Santa Barbara, CA: Foundation for National Progress, Housing Information Center. Pp. 86–94.

Marcuse, Peter 1981b. Housing abandonment: Does rent control make a difference? Washington, D.C.: Conference on State and Local Policies.

Marcuse, Peter 1981c. "Private real estate interests and the details of rent control laws," In John Gilderbloom (ed.), Rent control: A source book. Santa Barbara, CA: Foundation for National Progress, Housing Information Center. Pp. 129–136.

Martin, Phillip 1976. "The Supreme Court's quest for voting equality on bond referenda." Baylor Law Review, vol. 28:25–37.

*References*

Marwell, Gerald and Pamela Oliver 1984. "Collective action theory and social movements research." Research in Social Movements, Conflict and Change 7:1-27.

Marx, Gary 1979. "External efforts to damage or facilitate social movements: Some patterns, explanations, outcomes, and complications." In Mayer Zald and John McCarthy (eds.), The dynamics of social movements. Cambridge, MA: Winthrop. Pp. 94-125.

Massey, Douglas S., and Nancy A. Denton 1987. "Trends in the residential segregation of blacks, Hispanics, and Asians: 1970-1980." American Sociological Review (December), vol. 52:802-25.

McAdam, Doug 1986. "Recruitment to high-risk activism: The case of Freedom Summer." American Journal of Sociology 92:64-90.

McAdam, Doug 1988. "Micromobilization contexts and recruitment to activism." International Social Movements Research, vol. 1:125-54. Supplement to Research in Social Movements, Conflicts and Change. Greenwich CT: JAI Press.

McAdam, Doug 1989. "The biographical consequences of activism." American Sociological Review 54 (October):744-60.

McCarthy, John D. 1983. "Social infrastructure deficits and new technologies: Mobilizing unstructured sentiment pools." Unpublished paper, Catholic University, Washington, D.C.

McCarthy, John and Mayer Zald 1977. "Resource mobilization and social movements: A partial theory." American Journal of Sociology 82, 6:1212-1241.

McCarthy, John D. and Mayer N. Zald 1973. "The trend of social movements in America: Professionalization and resource mobilization. Morristown, NJ: General Learning Press.

McComb, David G. 1969. Houston: A history. Austin TX: University of Texas Press.

McKee, Cindy 1981. "Tenants help elect progressive mayor." Shelterforce Spring, 6:2.

Melosi, Martin 1987. "Forms of community and the growth of Houston." Paper presented at University of Houston convocation: Houston: In search of a vision. October 30-31, 1987.

Melucci, Alberto 1980. "The new social movements: A theoretical approach." Social Science Information 19:199-226.

Melucci, Alberto 1981. "Ten hypotheses for the analysis of new movements." In Diana Pinto (ed.), Contemporary Italian Sociology: A Reader. Cambridge: Cambridge University Press. Pp. 173-194.

Melucci, Alberto 1985. "The symbolic challenge of contemporary movements." Social Research 52: 789-816.

Memmi, Albert 1967. The colonizer and the colonized. Boston: Beacon Press.

Merton, Robert 1948. "The social psychology of housing." In Wayne Dennis et al. (eds.), Current Trends in Social Psychology. Pittsburgh: University of Pittsburgh Press. Pp. 163–217.

Merton, Robert K. 1968. Social theory and social structure. New York: Free Press.

Mills, C. Wright 1940. "Situated actions and vocabularies of motive." American Sociological Review 5:904–13.

Moberg, David 1983a. "From rent control to municipal power." In These Times, January 12–18.

Moberg, David 1983b. "Local left leaders: Is reform enough?" In These Times, June 1–14: 2 and 13.

Mollenkopf, John and Jon Pynoos 1973. "Boardwalk and park place: Property ownership, political structure and housing policy at the local level." In Jon Pynoos, Robert Schaffer, and Chester Hartman (eds.), Housing urban America. Chicago: Aldine. Pp. 56–74.

Molotch, Harvey L. 1976. "The city as growth machine: Toward a political economy of place." American Journal of Sociology 82, 2:309–32.

Moore, Barrington 1978. Injustice: The social bases of obedience and revolt. White Plains, NY: Sharpe.

Morris, Aldon D. 1984. The origins of the civil rights movement. New York: Free Press.

Morris, Earl W., Mary Winter, and Mary Ann Sward 1984. Reporting error and single-family home ownership norms and preferences." Housing and Society 11, 2:82–97.

Morrissy, Patrick 1987. "Housing receivership: A step toward community control." Shelterforce 10, 1:8–10.

Mottl, Tahi 1980. "The analysis of countermovements." Social Problems 27, 5:620–35.

Mumford, Lewis 1961. The City in History. New York: Harcout Press.

Myerhoff, Barbara 1979. Number Our Days. New York: Dutton.

Nader, Ralph 1973. Politics of land. New York: Grossman Publishers.

Neighborhood Support Center 1989. "Fact sheet: Incentive housing program of the Santa Monica rent control board." Santa Monica, CA: Neighborhood Support Center.

Novak, Michael 1982. The Spirit of Democratic Capitalism. New York: Simon and Schuster.

Oberschall, Anthony 1973. Social conflict and social movements. Englewood Cliffs, NJ: Prentice Hall.

O'Connor, James 1973. The fiscal crisis of the state. New York: St. Martins.

O'Connor, James 1979. "Rent control is absolutely essential." City on Hill Press, University of California, Santa Cruz, March 1, 1979.

O'Connor, James 1981. "Rent control is absolutely essential." In John Gilderbloom (ed.), Rent control: A source book. Foundation for National Progress Housing Information Center. Pp 83–85.

Offe, Claus 1985. "New social movements: Challenging the boundaries of institutional politics." Social Research 52:817–68.

O'Grady, Eileen 1987. "HEDC surpasses goal, raises \$7.2 million." Houston Post (February 28), 1. sec. F, p. 1.

Oliver, Pamela 1984. "If you don't do it, nobody else will: Active and token contributors to local collective action." American Sociological Review 49:601–10.

Olson, Mancur 1968. The logic of collective action. New York: Shocken.

Opp, Karl Dieter 1985. "Soft incentives and collective action: Some results of a survey on the conditions of participating in the anti-nuclear movement. Hamburg: Institut fur Soziologie.

Opp, Karl Dieter 1988. "Community integration and incentives for political protest." International Social Movement Research, vol. 1, pp. 83–101. Supplement to Research in Social Movements, Conflicts and Change, Greenwich, CT: JAI Press.

Orbell, J. M. and T. Uno 1972. "A theory of neighborhood problem solving: Political action vs. residential mobility." American Political Science Review 61:471–89.

Orum, Anthony, 1990. "Getting down to cases." Community and Urban Sociology Newsletter. Washington D.C.: American Sociological Association, vol. XIX, no. 3 (Summer) p. 3.

Pahl, Ray E. 1975. Whose city? Middlesex, Eng.: Penguin Books, Ltd.

Park, Robert E. 1952. Human communities. Glencoe, IL: Free Press.

Parker, Robert and Joe Feagin, forthcoming. "Houston: Administration by an Economic Elite." In Hank Savitch and John Thomas (eds.), Big city politcs in transition. Beverly Hills, CA: Sage.

Perlman, Janice 1979. "Grassroots empowerment and government response." Social Policy 10:16–21.

Perrow, Charles 1979. "The sixties observed." In John McCarthy and Mayer Zald (eds.), The dynamics of social movements. Cambridge, MA: Winthrop. Pp. 192–211.

Pickvance, Christopher 1985. "Spatial policy as territorial politics." In G. Reese (ed.), Political action and social identity. London: MacMillan. Pp. 117–142.

Pindyck, Robert S. and Daniel L. Rubinfald 1976. Econometric Models and Economic Forecasts. New York: McGraw-Hill.

Piven, Frances Fox and Richard Cloward 1971. Regulating the poor. New York: Pantheon.

Piven, Frances Fox and Richard Cloward 1979. Poor people's movements. New York: Vintage Books.

Plant, Raymond 1974. Community and ideology. London, Boston: Routlege and Kegan Paul.

Plotke, David 1990. "What's so new about new social movements?" Socialist Review 90, 1:81–102.

Portes, Alejandro 1971. "On the logic of post-factum explanations: The hypothesis of lower-class frustration as the cause of leftist radicalism." Social Forces 50:26–44.

Poulantzas, Nicos 1968. Pouvoir politique et classes sociales. Paris: Maspero.

President's Commission on Housing 1981. Interim Report. Washington, D.C.: U.S. Government Printing Office.

President's Commission on Housing 1982. Report of the President's Commission on Housing. Washington, D.C.: U.S. Government Printing Office.

President's Commission on Housing 1983. Final Report. Washington, D.C.: U.S. Government Printing Office.

Priest, Donald E. 1980. "Regulatory reform, housing costs, and public understanding." Urban Land 39:4 (April):3–4.

Protash A. and M. Baldassare 1983. "Growth policies and community status." Urban Affairs Quarterly 18:397–412.

Quadeer, M. A. 1981. "The nature of urban land." American Journal of Economics and Sociology 40 (2): 165–182.

Recer, Paul 1978. "The Texas city that's bursting out all over." U.S. News and World Report. November 27, 1978, p. 47.

Reinken, Charles 1988. "The start of pollution solution?" Houston Post (Jul 20), sec. E, p. 1.

Rex, J. 1968. "The sociology of a zone of transition." In Ray Pahl (ed.), Readings in Urban Sociology. London: Pergamon. Pp. 211–231.

Rex, J. and R. Moore 1967. Race, community and conflict. Oxford: Oxford University Press.

Rogers, E. M. 1983. Diffusion of innovation. New York: Free Press.

Rollins, Judith M. 1985. Between women: Domestics and their employers. Philadelphia: Temple University Press.

Rollins, Judith M. 1986. "Part of a whole: The interdependence of the civil rights movement and other social movements. Phylon XLVII, 1:61–70.

Romo, Ricardo 1983. East Los Angeles: History of a barrio. Austin: University of Texas Press.

Rose, Hilary 1986. "Beyond masculinist realities: A feminist epistemology for the sciences." In Ruth Bleier (ed.), Feminist Approaches to Science. New York: Pergamon Press. Pp. 57–76.

Rosenberg, Morris and Ralph H. Turner 1981. Social Psychology: Sociological Perspectives. New York: Basic Books.

Rosentraub, Mark and Robert Warren 1986. "Tenants' associations and social movements: The case of the United States." Paper presented at the Urban Affairs Association meetings, Fort Worth, TX. March 8.

Ross, Robert J. 1983. "Generational change and primary groups in a social movement." In Jo Freeman (ed.), Social movement of the sixties and seventies. New York: Longman. Pp. 177–89.

Rothschild-Whitt, Joyce 1979. "Conditions for democracy: Making participatory organizations work." In John Case and Rosemary Taylor (eds.), Co-ops, communes & collectives. New York: Pantheon Books. Pp. 215–44.

Rudé, George 1980. Ideology and popular protest. New York: Knopf.

Santa Monica Housing Element. 1984. City of Santa Monica housing element. Santa Monica, CA: City of Santa Monica Department of Planning.

Saunders, Peter 1978. "Domestic property and social class." International Journal of Urban and Regional Research 2:233–51.

Saunders, Peter 1979. Urban politics: A sociological interpretation. London: Hutchinson.

Saunders, Peter 1981. Social theory and the urban question. New York: Holmes and Meier.

Saunders, Peter 1984. "Beyond housing classes: The sociological significance of private property rights in means of consumption." International Journal of Urban and Regional Research 8, 2:202–27.

Savitch, Hank 1979. Urban policy and the exterior city: Federal, state and corporate impacts upon major cities. New York: Pergamon Press.

Sawers, Larry and Howard M. Wachtel 1975. The distributional impact of federal government subsidies in the United States. In Kapitalistate, no. 3 (Spring):52–6

Schur, R. 1980. "Growing lemons in the Bronx." In Working Papers for a New Society 8 (July-August):42–51.

Schutz, Alfred 1962. "On multiple realities." In Collected Papers, vol. 1. The Hague: Martinus Nijhoff. Pp. 207–59.

Scotch, Richard 1984. From good will to civil rights: The transformation of federal disability policy. Philadelphia: Temple University Press.

Scott, Marvin B. and Stanford M. Lyman, 1968. "Accounts." Amercan Sociological Review 33:46–62.

Selznick, Phillip 1948. "Foundations of the theory of organizations." American Sociological Review, 13:23–35.

Shearer, Derek 1982a. "Planning and the new urban populism: The case of Santa Monica, California." Journal of Planning Education and Research 2:1 (Summer). Pp. 20–26.

Shearer, Derek 1982b. "Popular planning." New York Times, March 16, 1982.

Shearer, Derek 1982c. "How the progressives won in Santa Monica." Social Policy (Winter):7–14.

Shearer, Derek 1984a. "Planning with a political face." The Nation, December 31–January 7, 1984.

Shearer, Derek 1984b. Citizen participation in local government: The case of Santa Monica, California. International Journal of Urban and Regional Research (December) 8, 4:573–86.

Shearer, Derek 1984c. "Economics for the Grass Roots." The Progressive, June 1984, Pp. 25–27.

Shearer, Derek 1989. "In search of equal partnerships: Prospects for progressive urban policy in the 1990s." In Gregory D. Squires (ed.), Unequal partnerships: The political economy of urban redevelopment in postwar America. New Brunswick, NJ: Rutgers University Press.

Shelton, Beth Anne, Nestor Rodriguez, Joe Feagin, Robert Bullard, and Robert Thomas 1989. Houston: Growth and decline in a sunbelt boomtown. Philadelphia: Temple University Press.

Shipnuck, Leslie, Dennis Keating, and Mary Morgan 1974. "The people's guide to urban renewal." Berkeley, CA: A Community Defense Manual.

Shulman, David 1980. Real estate valuation under rent control: The case of Santa Monica. Los Angeles: University of California, Business Forecasting Project, 2 mimeo.

Siegan, Bernard 1972. Land use without zoning. Lexington, MA: D.C. Heath.

Smelser, Neil J. 1963. Theory of collective behavior. New York: Free Press of Glencoe.

Smith, David 1979. The public balance sheet: A new tool for evaluating economic choices. Washington, D.C.: Conference on Alternative State and Local Policies.

Smith, Michael P. 1979. The city and social theory. New York: St. Martins Press.

Snow, David A. and Robert D. Benford 1988. "Master frames and cycles of protest." Invited paper presented at the Workshop on Frontiers in Social Movement Theory, Ann Arbor, MI, June 8–11, 1988.

Snow, David A., Louis A. Zurcher, Jr. and Sheldon Ekland-Olson 1980. "Social networks and social movements: A microstructural approach to differential recruitment." American Sociological Review 45:787–801.

Snow, David A., E. Burke Rochford, Jr., Steven K. Worden, and Robert D. Benford 1986. "Frame alignment processes, micromobilization, and movement participation." American Sociological Review 51:464–81.

Staggenborg, Susan 1988. "Consequences of professionalization and formalization in the pro-choice movement." American Sociological Review 53:585–606.

Starr, Paul and Gosta Esping-Anderson 1979. "Passive intervention." Working Papers for a New Society, VII, 2 (July/August):14–25.

Steinberger, P. 1981. "Political participation and community: A cultural/interpersonal approach." Rural Sociology 46:7–19.

Stephens, John 1986. The transition from capitalism to socialism. Champaign, IL: University of Illinois Press.

Sternlieb, George 1966. The tenement landlord. New Brunswick, NJ: Rutgers University Press.

Stone, Michael 1983. "Housing and the economic crisis: An analysis and emergency program. In Chester Hartman (ed.), America's housing crisis: What is to be done? Boston: Routledge and Kegan Paul. Pp. 99–150.

Storrs, Les 1974. Santa Monica: Portrait of a city yesterday and today. Santa Monica: Santa Monica Bank.

Stuart, Lettice 1989. "Foreclosed homes for people with modest incomes." New York Times (March 12); Real Estate Section, p. 35.

Suttles, Gerald 1972. The social construction of communities. Chicago: University of Chicago Press.

Sykes, G. 1951. "The differential distribution of community knowledge." Social Forces 29:376–82.

Tabb, William K. and Larry Sawers 1978. "Marxism and the metropolis." In Marxism and the metropolis: New perspectives in urban political economy. New York: Oxford University Press. Pp. 4–19.

Tarrow, Sidney 1983. Struggling to reform: Social movements and policy change during cycles of protest. Western Societies Paper N. 15. Ithaca, NY: Cornell University.

Thomas, Kate, and Margaret Downing 1988. "HUD clears Whitmire associate: No benefit found from sister's transaction with city." Houston Post (August 6), sec. A, p. 3.

Thomas, W. I. and Dorothy Thomas 1928. The Child in America: Behavior Problems and Programs. New York: Knopf.

Thompson, E. P. 1966. The making of the English working class. New York: Vintage Books.

Tilly, Charles 1978. From mobilization to revolution. Reading, MA: Addison-Wesley.

Touraine, Alain 1971. The postindustrial society. New York: Random House.

Touraine, Alain 1985. "An introduction to the study of social movements." Social Research 52:749-87.

Traugott, Mark 1978. "Reconceiving social movements." Social Problems 26:38-49.

Tucker, William 1987. "Where do the homeless come from?" National Review, September 25, Pp. 32-43.

Tucker, William 1989. "America's homeless: Victims of rent control." The Heritage Foundation, Backgrounder, No. 685 (Janary 12).

Turkle, Sherry Roxanne 1975. "Symbol and festival in the French student uprising (May-June 1968). In Sally Moore and Barbara Myerhoff (eds.), Symbols and politics in communal ideology. Ithaca and London: Cornell University Press. Pp. 68-100.

Turner, Ralph 1969. "The public perception of protest." American Sociological Review 34:815-31.

Turner, Ralph 1983. "Figure and ground in the analysis of social movements." Symbolic Interaction 6, 2:175-86.

Turner, Ralph H. and Lewis M. Killian 1972. Collective behavior. Second Edition. Englewood Cliffs, NJ: Prentice-Hall.

U.S. Bureau of the Census 1979a. Current population reports, series P. 20, No. 344, "Voting and registration in the election of November 1978." Washington D.C., U.S. Government Printing Office.

University of Houston, Center for Public Policy 1988. Houston Metropolitan Area Survey. Houston, TX: University of Houston Center for Public Policy.

Urban, Jerry 1988. "El Mercado squabble is on hold pending appeal of eviction orders." Houston Cronicle (January28), sec. 1, p. 3.

Useem, Bert 1980. "Solidarity model, breakdown model, and the Boston anti-busing movement." American Sociological Review 45:357–69.

Walton, John 1984a. "Alternatives to failed urban policy: Austerity and the New Populism." Paper presented at the American Sociological Association, August 1984, San Antonio, TX.

Walton, John 1984b. "Culture and economy in the shaping of urban life: General issues and Latin American examples." In John Agnew, John Mercer, and David E. Sopher (eds.) The City in Cultural Context. Boston: Allen and Unwin. Pp. 76–93.

Weber, Max 1946. "Bureaucracy." In Hans Gerth and C. Wright Mills (eds.), Max Weber: Essays in sociology. New York: Oxford University Press. Pp. 196–244.

Weber, Max 1947. The theory of social and economic organization. New York: Macmillan.

Weesep, J. Van 1986. Dutch housing: Recent developments and policy issues." Housing Studies 1:61–66.

Whalen, Jack and Richard Flacks 1989. Beyond the barricades: The sixties generation grows up. Philadelphia: Temple University Press.

Whyte, William Holly 1988. City: Rediscovering the center. New York: Doubleday.

Williams, J. A. 1971. "The multifamily housing solution and housing type preference." Social Science Quarterly 52:543–59.

Williams, John 1988. Houston Faces Dim Future Experts Predict in Poll. Houston Chronicle (May 5), sec. 1, p. 26.

Wilson, David S. 1989. "Santa Monica, Calif.: A $300 million office complex designed to please pedestrians." New York Times (May 14), sec. 13, p. 19.

Wilson, Kenneth and Anthony Orum 1976. "Mobilizing people for collective political action." Journal of Political and Military Sociology 4, Fall 1976, pp. 187–202.

Wingo, L. 1973. "The quality of life: Toward microeconomic definition." Urban Studies 10:3–18.

Wirth, Louis 1947. "Housing as a field of sociological research." American Sociological Review 12, 2:137–42.

Wuthnow, Robert, and James Hunter, Albert Bergesen, and Edith Kurzweil 1984. Cultural analysis. London: Routledge and Kegan Paul.

Zald, Mayer N. and Robert Ash 1966. "Social movement organizations: Growth, decay and change." Social Forces 44:327–40.

Zald, Mayer N. and John D. McCarthy 1973. The trend of social movements in America: Professionalism and resource mobilization. Morristown, NJ: General Learning Press.

Zald, Mayer N. and John D. McCarthy 1977. "Resource mobilization and social movements: A partial theory." American Journal of Sociology 82, 6:1212–41.

Zald, Mayer N. and John D. McCarthy 1980. "Social movement industries: Competition and cooperation among movement organizations." Louis Kriesberg (ed.), Research in Social Movements, Conflict and Change 3:1–20.

Zald, Mayer N. and Bert Useem 1987. "Movement and countermovement interactions: Mobilization, tactics and state involvement." In Mayer N. Zald and John D. McCarthy (eds.), Social movements in an organizational society. New Brunswick, NJ: Transaction Books. Pp. 247–72.

Zeitlin, Maurice 1981. "Tenant power to political power." The Nation, July 4, Pp. 15–17.

Zurcher, Louis and David Snow 1981. "Collective behavior: Social movements." In Morriss Rosenberg and Ralph H. Turner (eds.), Social Psychology: Sociological Perspectives. New York: Basic Books. Pp. 447–82.

Zygmunt, J. 1972. "Movements and motives: Some unresolved issues in the psychology of social movements." Human Relations 25:449–67.

# Index